Abraham Hayward

Sketches of Eminent Statesmen and Writers

With Other Essays: Vol II.

Abraham Hayward

Sketches of Eminent Statesmen and Writers
With Other Essays: Vol II.

ISBN/EAN: 9783337096038

Printed in Europe, USA, Canada, Australia, Japan

Cover: Foto ©ninafisch / pixelio.de

More available books at **www.hansebooks.com**

SKETCHES

OF

EMINENT STATESMEN AND WRITERS,

WITH OTHER ESSAYS.

[*Reprinted from the " Quarterly Review," with Additions and Corrections.*]

BY A. HAYWARD, Q.C.

IN TWO VOLUMES.
VOL. II.

LONDON:
JOHN MURRAY, ALBEMARLE STREET.
1880.

CONTENTS OF VOL. II.

	PAGE
MADAME DE SÉVIGNÉ	1
SAINT-SIMON	67
MADAME DU DEFFAND AND HER CORRESPONDENTS ...	129
HOLLAND HOUSE	186
STRAWBERRY HILL	243
BYRON AND TENNYSON	305
THE REPUBLIC OF VENICE: ITS RISE, DECLINE, AND FALL ...	360

MADAME DE SÉVIGNÉ.[1]

(*From the Quarterly Review, January,* 1873.)

"MADAME DE SÉVIGNÉ, like La Fontaine, like Montaigne, is one of those subjects which are perpetually in the order of the day in France. She is not only a classic, she is an acquaintance, and, better still, a neighbour and a friend."[2] She will never be this, or anything like it, in England. Her name is equally familiar, almost as much a household word; and there are always amongst us a select few who find an inexhaustible source of refined enjoyment in her letters. The Horace Walpole set affected to know them by heart: George Selwyn meditated an edition of them, and preceded Lady Morgan in that pilgrimage to the *Rochers* which she describes so enthusiastically in her "Book of the Boudoir." Even in our time it would have been dangerous to present oneself often at Holland House or the Berrys', without being tolerably well up in them. Mackintosh rivalled Walpole in exalting her. But the taste is not on the increase: the worshippers decline apace: we hear of no recent English visitors to the Breton shrine: the famous flourish about the Grande Mademoiselle marriage, with the account of the death of Vattel, form the sum of what is

---

[1] *Madame de Sévigné: her Correspondence and Contemporaries.* By the Comtesse de Puliga. 2 vols. London, 1873.

[2] Sainte-Beuve, "Causeries de Lundi."

correctly known on this side of the Channel of her epistolary excellence: her personal history is not known at all, and maternal love is the only quality which nineteen cultivated people out of twenty could specify in illustration of her character. Yet no man or woman ever lived who was less national (in the exclusive sense) or more cosmopolitan in heart and mind, in feeling and in thought. It is not French nature, but human nature in its full breadth and variety, that she represents or typifies. Her sparkling fancy, her fine spirit of observation, her joyous confiding (and self-confiding) frankness, her utter absence of affectation, her generosity, her loyalty, her truth, are of no clime. Indeed we are by no means sure that her most sterling qualities will not just now be best understood, felt, and appreciated out of France.

Nor are the incidents with which they are mixed up, the topics which call them forth or give occasion for them, of so local and temporary a character as to repel the general reader. She is the chief chronicler of the three stirring and eventful epochs which constitute what is commonly called the age of Louis Quatorze: the choicest materials for its history are to be found in her Letters; and her private life cannot be told without connecting it, at many trying and interesting conjunctures, with the lives of her most illustrious and celebrated contemporaries. The pupil of Ménage and Chapelain, the pride of the Hôtel Rambouillet, the object of vain pursuit to such men as Bussy, Conti, Fouquet, and Turenne, the friend or associate of de Retz, Rochefoucauld, Corneille, Racine, Molière, La Fontaine, Pascal, Bossuet, La Grande Mademoiselle, the Scudérys, Madame la Fayette, Madame Maintenon—in short, of almost every Frenchman or Frenchwoman of note for more than half a century,—she might be made the central figure of a series of historic groups, had she never been known to fame as a letter-writer. Neither can we admit the argument that all who wish to become intimately acquainted with her, to make her (what Sainte-Beuve says she is in France) a neighbour and a friend, will always repair by preference to French writers: to the exhaustive "Mémoires" of Walckenaer, or the critical "Notice" of Mesnard.¹ Porson frankly admitted that, consummate Grecian as he was, he never read a Greek play as easily as an English newspaper; and there is a numerous class in this country who approach the French classics with more hesitation and diffidence than Porson felt towards the Greek. They come to them as to a task: they are often obliged to pause and construe as they proceed; and therefore is it that an English biography of a Frenchwoman so far famed, yet (as regards England) so really little known as Madame de Sévigné, may confidently reckon on a favourable reception; provided it fulfil the conditions which an English public is fairly entitled to exact.

The work before us fulfils many of them. Madame de Puliga has diligently studied her subject in all its bearings; she is thoroughly imbued

---

[1] M. Paul Mesnard is the author of the "Notice biographique" prefixed to the annotated edition of the Letters in fourteen volumes, royal octavo, forming the commencement of the collection entitled, "Les Grands Ecrivains de la France." Hachette, Paris, 1862. The fullest account of Madame de Sévigné and her times (to 1680) is to be found in the "Mémoires touchant la Vie et les Ecrits de Marie de Rabutin-Chantal, Dame de Bourbilly, Marquise de Sévigné," &c., &c. By Baron Walckenaer, six volumes with the Continuations. Amongst the abridged editions of the Letters, the best is the one of 1870, with a "Notice" by M. P. Jacquinet and a Treatise on her epistolary style by M. Suard. There is a useful English work, published in 1842, entitled "Madame de Sévigné and her Contemporaries," composed of a series of biographical notices, one of which, of about thirty pages, is devoted to *Mesdames de Sévigné et Grignan.*

with the spirit of the period of which she treats: she is at home with both correspondents and contemporaries: without aiming at research or originality (for which there was neither room nor occasion on so beaten a track), she has made a judicious selection from the embarrassing abundance of materials accumulated to her hands: treading frequently on very delicate ground, she is never wanting in feminine refinement or good taste; and although she occasionally provokes a feeling of opposition by dwelling too often and too ecstatically on the virtues of her heroine, she somehow manages to bring us very nearly round to her opinion in the end.

Unluckily there is one condition that is not fulfilled. When we were expecting Madame de Sévigné in a simple English dress, she is presented to us in a costume which has obviously been fashioned after French models and is rather showily adorned with French point. In other words, the language and phraseology lead to the impression that the accomplished authoress had been accustomed to think and write exclusively in French, and that this is her first serious or sustained effort in English composition. Her style is cramped and artificial, neither flowing nor idiomatic, till she warms. But by the time she has completed half her first volume, she has worked herself tolerably free of her Gallic tendencies; which are faintly discernible in the second, and will not be found to deduct materially from the sterling value of the book. Its range is wide, and the foreground is so crowded by "contemporaries" as to require no ordinary stretch of attention to keep Madame de Sévigné distinctly in view throughout. It strikes us, therefore, that a sketch of her and them on a more reduced scale may prove a useful introduction to the complete and rather diffuse biography.

Marie de Rabutin, or de Chantal, or de Chantal-Rabutin, as she was alternately called before she became Marquise de Sévigné, was paternally descended from an ancient and illustrious race. She was born at Paris on the 5th February, 1626, and within six years became an orphan. Her father was killed fighting against the English under Buckingham at the Isle of Rhé, on July 22, 1627, and her mother died some time in 1633, leaving Marie to the care of a maternal grandmother, who died within twelve months, when the child fell under the charge of her maternal grandfather, Philippe de Coulanges, and he also dying before she had attained her tenth year, a family council was held to name a guardian. The choice fell on her uncle, the Abbé de Coulanges, Prieur de Livry, a man of twenty-nine, who discharged his trust so kindly and efficiently, that she never ceased proclaiming the boundless debt of gratitude she owed to him, and gave him the name of *Bien Bon*, by which he is indelibly associated with her memory. It is worth noting in contrast with the depth of the maternal love which afterwards grew into an absorbing passion, that she manifests no filial tenderness. She never mentions or so much as alludes to her mother in her voluminous correspondence, and when two or three times she names her father, it is in reference to his faults. In a letter to her daughter, July 22, she adds, after the date, "*Jour de la Madeleine, où fut tué, il y a quelques années, un père que j'avais.*"

It would seem that *Bien Bon* made no attempt to replace the mother and grandmother by a female companion or governess. The only instructors of whom we hear are Ménage and Chapelain, and

Ménage did his best to turn the relation of master and pupil into a romance of the Cadenus and Vanessa kind. But in his case the position was reversed: Marie did not fall in love with him, as Esther Vanhomrigh fell in love with Swift, and he could not have exclaimed like the Dean,

> "That innocent delight he took
> To see the virgin mind her book,
> Was but the master's secret joy
> In school to hear the finest boy."

Madame de Puliga says: "We must not be surprised at this. In the seventeenth century, rank created such a separation, birth threw such a gulf between human beings, that tender sentiments from those in an inferior station of life were deemed of little consequence. A woman of quality would take a pride in inspiring such feelings, but she was never supposed to be disturbed by their existence. Ménage might then freely declare himself the slave of Mademoiselle de Chantal, and she consent to treat him as such." We notwithstanding take the liberty of being somewhat surprised at a man of Ménage's intellectual mark playing the fool in this fashion, and we have our misgivings whether it was more a matter of course in the seventeenth than the nineteenth century for young ladies of quality to treat their tutors as Lady Clara Vere de Vere treated her yeoman lover, when, after luring him on to a declaration—

> "She fixed him with a vacant stare,
> And slew him with her noble birth."

Clearly, Ménage did not think himself fairly used or treated according to the laws of the game. He was deeply hurt, and very angry. Remembering, probably, the adage that the quarrels of lovers are the renewal of love, he tried to create an interest by getting up a quarrel; and we find from the lady's letters that he resorted to the hackneyed commonplace expedient of a simulated sense of wrong:

"You wish to make me appear ridiculous by telling me that you have only quarrelled with me because you are sorry for my departure. If this were so, I should merit a lunatic asylum, and not your hatred; but there is all the difference in the world, and my only difficulty is in comprehending that, when one loves and regrets a person, it is necessary, on that account, to treat her with the extreme of coldness the last time one sees her. It is a most extraordinary mode of acting, and as I was not used to it, you must excuse my surprise."

She must have got well accustomed to it ere long, for we find admirers by the dozen brought one after the other, or three or four at once, to the same condition as Ménage; and she was actuated by the same spirit of refined coquetry through life: her guiding rule or principle—the counterpart of the one commended by Lord Chesterfield to his son—being to make every man in love with her and every woman her friend.

"It was the property of her quick and ready nature," says Cousin, "to put herself in unison with all who conversed with her. She is frivolous with Coulanges; she is rakish (*gaillarde*) enough with Ninon, austere with Pascal, sublime with Bossuet: with Bussy, her quickened malice spares nobody." Constantly playing with edged tools, she never cuts her fingers; her pitcher is never broken, although it goes often to the well, but it has frequently been made a question, to which we shall in due time recur, whether her impunity was owing to good fortune or good conduct, to the strength of her principles or the coldness of her heart.

It incidentally appears, from a colloquy at the Hôtel Rambouillet, in which both her instructors took part, that she was not taught the learned languages. "Is it possible," said Madame de Rambouillet, " that M. Ménage has not yet made verses for Madame de Sévigné?"—"He has made verses," replied Chapelain, "for Mademoiselle Marie de Rabutin, and also for Madame la Marquise, not only in French but in Italian, too."— "And I wager," broke in Saint-Pavin, " that he has also made verses to her in Latin and Greek."— " M. Ménage," remarked Madame de Sévigné, "is too much my friend to make me ashamed of my ignorance by addressing to me verses in languages which I do not understand."

Either the rule restricting the introduction of girls into society did not exist in Madame de Sévigné's time, or she was made a marked exception to it, for she was not married till she was in her nineteenth year. She was brought out at Paris (to use her own expression) *de bonne heure;* and the sensation she made in the highest circles was in accordance with her personal attractions, her fortune, and her birth. This Burgundian heiress was valued at little less than a million of livres, including expectations; and, if not a regular beauty, she had charms and fascinations which it would be difficult to match. She was a brilliant *blonde.* All contemporary accounts agree in the translucent fairness and freshness of her complexion, the rich profusion of her light glossy hair, the exquisite harmony and play of her features, the elegance of her figure, the grace of her movements, the speaking sparkling expression of her eyes; and even the satirical portrait of Bussy-Rabutin transmits the image of an undeniably pretty woman, who sang agreeably, danced admirably, and blended sense and sentiment with ready wit and unaffected gaiety when she talked.

The Comte de Bussy-Rabutin was her near relation, and played so influential a part, commonly that of an evil genius, in her life, that his character must be kept constantly in mind. He was emphatically what Mr. Carlyle calls the *roué* Duc de Richelieu, " famous blackguard man." Brave to rashness, very clever, very unscrupulous, high born, handsome, accomplished, dissipated to excess, equally ready with sword and pen, he has left his mark on his age, and he did his best to leave his mark, a black and indelible one, on the fair fame of his fair cousin. She figures in his " Histoire amoureuse des Gaules " under the name of Madame de Cheneville, and after throwing out every illnatured insinuation he can hit upon, he is obliged to admit that, in point of personal purity, she was irreproachable. He puts a good (and false) face on one of the disappointments which induced him to introduce her in the scandalous chronicle which he termed a history:

"Her fortune, which suited mine very well, made my father wish me to marry her; but although I did not know her then so well as I do now, I did not fall in with the desire of my father: a certain harebrained manner which I observed in her made me afraid of her, and I thought her the prettiest girl in the world to be the wife of another."

The fact is, whatever the designs of his father, he was never named as a pretender for her hand; and it is in the highest degree improbable that her uncle would have tolerated in that capacity an unprincipled spendthrift, who was accused of having raised money by false pretences on the strength of the procuration under which he attended the family council for the appointment of her guardian. A husband was chosen for her from considerations of fitness in respect of fortune and position, and it does not appear that, prior to her marriage, any sort of preference was betrayed by her. It was a marriage of reason, and promised well at starting. Henri, Marquis de Sévigné, was young, well born, highly connected, rich, and handsome; and when he carried off his bride to his château of *Les Rochers*, which she was destined to render famous, there was everything to betoken a long and happy union: nothing to prognosticate an unhappy one, to be suddenly cut short: unless, indeed, we accept as ominous an incident which delayed the marriage for some months. They were to be married in May, 1644; but the Marquis received so severe a wound in a duel wantonly provoked by him, that his life was in danger, and the ceremony was not performed till the 4th of August in that year. There is a copy of verses, the joint composition of Bussy and Lenet, addressed to the young couple in March, 1646, beginning:

> "Salut à vous, gens de campagne,
> A vous, immeubles de Bretagne,
> Attachés à votre maison
> Au-delà de toute raison."

It is not till the autumn of 1646 that we find them settled at Paris, where (October 10) Françoise Marguerite, the idolized daughter, afterwards Madame de Grignan, was born. Herself the centre of a distinguished circle, Madame de Sévigné is best remembered at this period as a prominent member of that which clustered round Catherine, Marquise de Rambouillet, the Arthénice of the "Grand Cyrus," who exercised the most marked, refining, and improving influence on her age. Her hotel, with its suite of rooms opening on one another, its garlands of flowers, its *ruelle*, and its blue chamber, was as much an original creation of her own designing as her society; and it is altogether a mistake to confound her and her friends with the *Précieuses Ridicules* of Molière.[1] An interval of many years, including the subversive and demoralising *Fronde*, separates the close of her reign, the rich setting of her sun, from the appearance of this comedy; and the term *Précieuse*, made ridiculous by an ensuing generation of imitators, was first conferred and accepted as a tribute and a eulogy:

"All who frequented the Hôtel de Rambouillet," says Walckenaer, "soon adopted nobler manners and purer language, devoid of provincialism. The women in particular, to whom more leisure and a more delicate organisation give a readier and finer social tact, were the first to profit by the advantage which was offered them by this constant community of cultivated minds and association of persons unceasingly occupied in emulating what was most agreeable and fitted to please in each. Consequently those who formed part of these assemblies speedily became easily distinguishable from those who were not admitted to them. To show the esteem in which they were held, they were named the *Précieuses*, the *Illustrious:* which was always given and received as an honourable distinction during the long space of time that the Hôtel de Rambouillet retained its influence."

Madame de Puliga, after speaking of the Hôtel as that earthly paradise of which Madame de Rambouillet's *ruelle* was the centre, adds:

"The *ruelle*, a word in daily use in the seventeenth century and having then a more extended signification than in the present day, it will perhaps be necessary to

[1] This comedy was acted for the first time on the 18th November, 1659. A spurious copy having got abroad, Molière printed it in 1660 with a Preface, in which he says : " Les véritables précieuses auraient tort de se piquer lorsqu'on joue les ridicules qui les imitent mal." The distinction is clearly drawn by Cousin in the first chapter of his "Madame de Sablé."

explain more clearly of what it consisted. The bed, at that time monumental and magnificently adorned, stood in the centre of one end of the room, and for princesses and ladies of high quality it was raised from the ground by a few steps, called the *estrade*. Near the foot of the bed, and dividing the apartment, stood a gilt balustrade, such as may still be seen in the room of Louis XIV. at Versailles. Each side of the bed within that reserved space was called the *ruelle*: it was often still more enclosed by a colonnade reaching from the ground to the ceiling, and it then formed an *alcôve*.

"Madame de Rambouillet was early afflicted with a singular malady which compelled her to shun both fire and sunshine: she could not encounter either without the blood boiling in her veins. In her *alcôve*, surrounded by flowers, by books, by the portraits of those she loved, she sat enthroned, and received from all that homage so justly her due."

Her assemblies, according to Walckenaer, dated from the conclusion of the reign of Henry IV. (1610), shone with all their lustre during the reign of Louis XIII., began to decline under the regency and the Fronde, and had lost all their social supremacy when Louis XIV. was of an age to hold his court in person. Or—to draw the line still more definitely between the intellectual or literary epochs popularly confounded—Malherbe, Corneille, Balzac, and Voiture, belong almost entirely to the first: Saint-Évremond, Ménage, Sarrasin, Chapelain, principally to the second: Pascal, Bossuet, Molière, La Fontaine, Racine, Boileau, Pellisson, to the third. The highest testimony in favour of this *salon* and its founder was given by one of the most celebrated French preachers from the pulpit. In his funeral sermon on the death of Madame de Rambouillet's daughter Julie, Fléchier thus introduced and apostrophised (as it were) the recollections of his youth:

"Do you remember those rooms which are still regarded with so much veneration, where the mind grew pure, where virtue was reverenced under the name of the incomparable Arthénice: where so many persons of quality and merit met, composing a select Court, numerous without confusion, modest without constraint, learned without pride, polished without affectation?"

To convey a vivid impression of the Rambouillet *salon* when Madame de Sévigné entered it, M. de Walckenaer peoples it anew by a fiction which he declares to be, down to the minutest details, in exact conformity with fact. He chooses an afternoon in 1644, when the company are assembled to hear Corneille read his tragedy of "Théodore;" and conspicuous amongst the gay group, besides the hostess and her daughters, are the Princess of Condé, Rochefoucauld, the Duchesse de Longueville, the Marquise de Sablé, the Duchesse de Chevreuse, the Marquis and Marquise de Sévigné, Balzac, Ménage, the Scudérys, Bensérade, Chapelain, Voiture, and (by a slight anachronism) Bossuet. After a fair allowance of lively repartee, they play blindman's-buff (*colin-maillard*) whilst waiting for the author of the "Cid," which might be thought an odd resource for such an eminently intellectual set, did we not recall Madame de Merlin's avowal of a liking for innocent games (*les jeux innocens*) "with people who are *not* innocent," and remember that, after Madame de Sévigné had been blinded in her turn on another occasion at Madame de Chevreuse's, this graceful impromptu was addressed to her by M. de Montreuil:

"De toutes les façons vous avez droit de plaire,
Mais surtout vous savez nous charmer en ce jour:
Voyant vos yeux bandés, on vous prend pour l'Amour:
Les voyant découverts, on vous prend pour sa mère."

Which may be paraphrased:

"You charm when you walk, talk, or move,
　Still more on this day than another;
When blinded, you're taken for Love,
　When the bandage is off—for his mother."

Blindman's-buff harmonises well enough with gallantry; and we learn from the best authority that a good deal of sentiment, or simulated passion, seldom penetrating below the surface or leading to scandal, gave piquancy to the commerce between the sexes in this society.

"Love," says Mademoiselle de Scudéry, "in the Court of Paphos (Paris) is not a simple passion, as in other countries, but a passion of necessity and good breeding. All men must be enamoured, and all women loved. None are indifferent; and coldness of heart, to those who are capable of it, is reproved as a crime. It is considered such a reproach to be free of all ties, that those who are not in love pretend to be so. . . . It is permitted to the ladies to employ a few innocent artifices to subdue the hearts of men. The desire to please is not a crime: complacency even is laudable, provided there is no meanness. To express all in a few words, everything that can render women amiable, and cause them to be admired, is allowable, if it offends neither purity nor modesty, which qualities, in spite of the prevailing gallantry of our island, are the principal virtues of all the ladies. Thus, having discovered the means to blend innocence and love, they spend a life at once agreeable and diverting."

Cousin gives much the same account of the manner in which they played at love-making. A gentleman might be *aux petits soins* as long as it suited him; he might even advance some way into the *pays du tendre*, but if he transgressed the conventional lines of demarcation, or made serious approaches towards the citadel, he would speedily find himself in the position of the adorer in

Suckling's ballad, when his advances were met with smiling indifference:

> "I sent to know from whence and where
>   These smiles, and this relief?
> A spy inform'd, Honour was there,
>   And did command in Chief.
> March, march (quoth I), the word straight give,
>   Let's lose no time, but leave her,
> That giant upon air will live,
>   And hold it out for ever."

The moral atmosphere of this seat of the Muses and Graces was of so bracing or preservative a quality that the heroines of the Fronde, who afterwards allowed themselves the most unrestrained licence, the Duchesses de Longueville and de Chevreuse, stood rebuked by the genius of the place; and the unmarried daughters of the house received their full share of high-flown flattery and euphuistic homage without the semblance or suspicion of a taint. Madame de Puliga speaks thus of one of them who did not marry till past thirty:

> "For twenty years Julie d'Angennes was a queen, the very soul of the circle over which her mother presided. It was she who inspired poets: men worshipped her, and women loved her: her amiability satisfied every claim upon her; and the lovers she discouraged she succeeded in not displeasing. Her manners were such as may be imagined from the school in which she had been brought up. Born for the world and its pleasures, she was its delight, and herself delighted in it. Julie d'Angennes shared the perilous maxims of her intimate friend the Marquise de Sablé, that women are created to be adored; that they alone inspire noble resolutions; and that a worthy recompense for every sacrifice is the bestowal of their esteem and friendship."

The Prince de Conti said of Voiture, "If he was one of us, we should not put up with such behaviour;" and the remark indicates both the position held by men of letters, not born in the purple, and the social licence they assumed in the Hôtel Rambouillet. Madame de Sévigné might have said the same of her former tutor and persevering admirer, Ménage, who employed the language of passion as freely as a marquis or a duke; whilst she trifled with him in the precise manner which, without driving him from her or depriving her of her daily dose of flattery, was most annoying to his vanity and fatal to his hopes. One of Liston's best parts was an old bachelor who boasted, without suspecting why the distinction was conferred upon him, of being universally pronounced a safe man, with whom a husband or father might trust the prettiest wife or daughter without risk. This is the very part which Ménage was unwilling to play. He felt like Rogers, who, when Lady Beresford offered to take him home from an evening party in her carriage, walked off in a huff, complaining that it was an unkind mode of reminding him of his age.

One day, Ménage happening to call just as Madame de Sévigné was going out shopping, she told him to get into her carriage and accompany her. The *savant*, vainly trying to hide his pique under raillery, told her that it was hard upon him for her, not content with the rigorous treatment he received, to appear to have so little fear of him or of scandal in connection with him. "Get into my carriage, I tell you," was her rejoinder. "If you make me angry, I will come and see you at your own house." She was as good as her word. Before leaving for the country, she went to bid him farewell. On her return she complained to him of his not having written to her. "I *have* written to you," he made answer, "but after reading my letter over again, I found it too passionate, and thought it had better not be sent."

If she bestowed a favour, it was always provokingly before the world. He relates in *Ménagiana*, that he had been holding one of her hands in his; and on her withdrawing it, M. Pelletier said to him, "Voilà le plus bel ouvrage qui soit sorti de vos mains." He made the most of these harmless freedoms. Finding himself alone in a carriage with the Marquise de Lavardin on their journey to the Rochers, he leant forwards to kiss her hands: "Monsieur Ménage," she remarked with a laugh, "you are conning your lesson (*vous vous recordez*) for Madame de Sévigné." She once (according to Bussy) kissed her old master before a circle of admirers, and answering to their looks of surprise, exclaimed, "It was thus that they kissed in the Primitive Church."

The worst of these things was that they were related without the accompanying circumstances, so that ill-natured conclusions might be based upon them. Thus Bussy:

"There is no woman who has more wit than she, and very few who have so much: her manner is diverting; there are some who say that, for a woman of quality, her character is a little too reckless. When first I was in the habit of seeing her, I thought this judgment ridiculous, and I excused her burlesque under the name of gaiety; now that I am no longer dazzled by her fire, I agree that she aims too much at jocularity. If one has wit, and particularly this sort of wit, which is gay, one has but to see her, one loses nothing with her: she listens to you, she enters justly into all you say, she divines you, and leads you ordinarily much further than you think of going. Sometimes also one opens a wide expanse of country to her: she is carried away by her heated fancy, and in this state she receives with joy anything one feels disposed to say to her, provided it is wrapped up: she even replies with usury, and conceives that she should lose ground if she did not go beyond what has been said to her. With so much fire, it is not strange that the discernment is moderate: these two things being commonly incompatible, nature cannot work a miracle in her favour. With her, a lively fool will always get the better of a serious man of sense."

This was written with studied malice, after more than one rebuff, owing to that very discernment which he denies. All her admiration for his brilliant qualities did not blind her to his defects. The worst that could be truly said of her was what Voltaire's Zadig says of Astarte: "Unhappily confident in her innocence, she neglects the necessary appearances. I shall tremble for her so long as she has no subject of self-reproach." This is the pith of Joseph Surface's sophistical argument with Lady Teazle: "What is it makes you so negligent of forms and careless of the world's opinion? Why, the consciousness of your innocence. What makes you thoughtless in your conduct, and apt to run into a thousand little imprudences? Why, the consciousness of your innocence.... Now, my dear Lady Teazle, if you would but once make a trifling *faux pas*, you can't conceive how cautious you would grow."

There are two other passages of arms between her and Ménage which throw light on their relations to each other. She was in the habit of making him the confidant of her most secret affairs. After an interview of this kind, he said to her, "I am now your confessor, and I have been your martyr."—"And I your Virgin," was her laughing retort.

On her inquiring after Ménage's health, he replied, "Madame, je suis enrhumé."—"Je *la* suis aussi." Assuming the tutor, he told her that, according to the rules of the language, she should say, "Je *le* suis." "You will speak as you please," she sharply replied; "but as for me, if I spoke so, I should believe I had a beard on my chin."

Small credit would redound to her for resisting temptation, had there been no more dangerous suitor; but, besides a long list of accomplished courtiers who laid siege in the received and permitted fashion to her heart, there was her cousin Bussy, in whom she retained an affectionate interest through life, always ready to take advantage of an unguarded moment, and utterly unscrupulous as to the means by which he attained any end, good or bad, in love or ambition, that he had proposed to himself. He was also the intimate friend of her husband, of whom he says, "Although he had *esprit*, all the attractions of Marie could not restrain him: he loved in all directions, and never loved anything so lovable as his wife." She did not hear of his irregularities, or turned a deaf ear to them, till he became attached to the celebrated Ninon de l'Enclos, born to be her evil genius; for, wonderful to relate, her husband, her son, and her grandson were successively enslaved by this French Aspasia—

"Age could not weary her, nor custom tire
Her infinite variety."

"The Marquis de Sévigné," says Conrart, in his Memoirs, "was in the habit of telling his wife that he believed she would have been very agreeable for another, but that, for his part, she could not please him. It was also said that there was this difference between her and her husband, that he esteemed and did not love her, while she loved and did not esteem *him*."

The Marquis was boasting to Bussy of an agreeable evening he had passed, adding, "You may well believe it was not with your cousin: it was with Ninon."—"So much the worse for you," replied Bussy; "my cousin is worth a thousand of her, and, if you were not her husband, you would think so too."—"Likely enough," rejoined the marquis. Bussy goes on to say that as soon as he could get away from the husband, he hurried to repeat what had passed to the wife, who reddened, as she well might, with vexation. A brief colloquy ensues: *Madame de S.*—"You must be mad to give me such advice, or you must think me mad." *Bussy.*—"You would be much more so, Madame, if you did not pay him off in his own coin, than if you repeated to him what I have told you. Revenge yourself, my fair cousin: I will go halves in your revenge; for, after all, your interests are as dear to me as my own." *Madame de S.*—"This is all very fine, Monsieur le Comte: I am not so exasperated as you think."

When he and the Marquis met the next day, the Marquis began: "I suspect you have let something drop to your cousin of what I told you yesterday about Ninon, because she has glanced at it to me."—"I," exclaimed this pattern of confidants; "I have not uttered a word about it to her. But, clever as she is, she has been so discursive on the chapter of jealousy that she sometimes hits upon the truth." The Marquis went away satisfied, and Bussy forthwith indited this epistle to the Marquise:

"I was not wrong yesterday, madame, in distrusting your imprudence. You have told your husband what I told you. You must be well aware that it is not on my own account that I make you this reproach, for all that can happen to me is to lose his friendship; and for you, madame, there is much more to fear. I have, however, been fortunate enough to disabuse him. Besides he is so persuaded that one cannot be 'honnête homme' without being always in love, that I despair of ever seeing you happy if you aspire to be loved by him alone. But let not this alarm you, madame; as I have begun to serve you, I shall not abandon you in the state in which you are. You are aware that jealousy has often more power to retain a heart than charms and merit. I advise you to give your husband a taste of it, my fair cousin, and I offer myself to you for that. If you bring him back by these means, I love you enough to resume my first part of your agent with him, and sacrifice myself again to make you happy. And if he must escape you, love me, my cousin, and I shall aid you to revenge yourself on him by loving you all your life."

The result is best told in the words of Bussy:— "The page to whom I gave this letter found her asleep, and whilst he was waiting till they awoke her, Sévigné arrived from the country. Having learnt from my page, whom I had not instructed about the matter, not foreseeing that the husband would arrive so soon; having learnt, I say, that he had a letter from me to his wife, Sévigné took it from him without suspecting anything, and having read it on the instant, told him not to wait, as there was no answer. You may judge how I received him: I was on the point of killing him, seeing the danger to which I had exposed my cousin, and I never closed my eyes during the following night. Sévigné, on his side, did not pass a better night than I; and the next day, after bitterly reproaching his wife, he forbade her to see me. She sent me word of it, assuring me that with a little patience all would come right some day or another."

It is stated in this same *Histoire* of his that Madame de Sévigné was devotedly attached to her husband, and that he had the fullest confidence in her. It is therefore Bussy's wounded vanity that speaks, when he tries to convey the impression that either one or the other thought him dangerous. It was the abuse of confidence, the treachery of gentleman to gentleman, that really exasperated Sévigné; and when, soon after this affair, he carried his wife into Brittany and left her there, it was not from any distrust or jealousy, but to enable him to lead a life of criminal and ruinous indulgence without restraint.

Ninon had a very simple method of keeping her numerous train of admirers from dropping off. They were one and all encouraged to hope. "*Attends mon caprice,*" was her constant reply to the more importunate, and they apparently had not long to wait; for early in her career she told a friend who questioned her about the number of her caprices, "*Pour le moment je suis à mon vingtième.*" Her sex was her misfortune; for it was said of her that she had every virtue which is esteemed in a man of chivalrous honour, in a gallant gentleman; and she never lost her hold on her most distinguished contemporaries. Scarron consulted her on his Romances; St. Évremond on his Poems; Molière on his Comedies; Fontenelle on his Dialogues; and La Rochefoucauld on his Maxims.[1] There is a story of a noble refugee entrusting half his fortune to an archbishop and half to Ninon. She faithfully fulfilled her part of the trust, whilst the archbishop utterly ignored *his*.

She soon flung over Sévigné for Rambouillet de la Sablière, to whom she wrote, "I shall love you for three months, which is three ages for me;" and Sévigné transferred his equally volatile affections to Madame de Gondran, for whom he incurred the most extravagant expenses and was guilty of all sorts of folly. Some strong remarks of a dis-

[1] "Biographie Universelle." The Baron de Walckenaer has devoted a chapter to her.

carded admirer, the Abbé de Romilly, having been repeated by Lacger, private secretary to the ex-Queen Christine, at a ball, Sévigné threatened to cane him, and Lacger, carefully avoiding any hostile message or encounter on his own account, told the Chevalier d'Albret, another angry rival, that Sévigné had joined with the object of their common pursuit in turning *him* into ridicule. The Chevalier sent a friend, the Marquis le Soyecour, to demand an explanation of Sévigné, who declared that he had used no such language, adding that he made this declaration for the sake of truth and by no means to justify himself, which he never did otherwise than sword in hand. In consequence of this answer a meeting was arranged for Friday, February 3, 1651, at midday.

Both were punctual to the minute. Sévigné, who brought the swords, began by repeating that he had never said of D'Albret what had been repeated to him, and that he was at his disposal. The two antagonists embraced. The Chevalier then said that they must fight all the same. The Marquis replied that this was his understanding, and that he had not come to the place to return without doing anything. Immediately they take their ground, and the combat begins. Sévigné makes three or four lunges at his adversary, who has his coat pierced without receiving a wound. In the act of resuming the offensive, he lays himself open; Albret takes his time and stands on his guard (*pare*); and Sévigné, rushing on his adversary, is run through the body and falls. He is carried back to Paris, where the surgeons immediately declare the wound mortal. He died the day after, regretting to die at twenty-seven. His friends, or rather the companions of his pleasures, had hurried to be present at his death. Amongst them was Gondran (the husband of the lady they were fighting about), the one amongst them who was the most sincerely affected by his loss.

Such is the detailed account of Conrart and other contemporary annalists; who add that he was little regretted, being, in fact, an ill-conditioned, as well as thoroughly worthless, fellow. But he is not the first ill-conditioned or worthless fellow who has inspired a woman of sense and principle with a durable affection, and he was deeply lamented by his widow. Her first care on arriving at Paris was to repair a want which she felt keenly. She had no likeness of him, nor a lock of his hair; and she took the extraordinary step of applying to Madame de Gondran, who satisfactorily responded to the application. By way of return, she caused to be remitted to this lady the whole of her letters to the dear defunct, which, according to Tallemant, were coarse in the extreme. Madame de Sévigné fainted away the first time she met the Chevalier d'Albret in company; and two years after the duel she was observed to turn pale and totter at a ball at the sight of Soyecour (the second). On seeing Lacger, the cause of the catastrophe, in an alley where she was walking at Saint-Cloud, she said, "There is the man in the world I hate the most, for the injury he has done me by his indiscretion." Two officers of the guards who happened to be with her offered to horsewhip him in her presence. "Do nothing of the kind," she said; "he is with several of my relations, whom you would be sorry to offend." And she turned with her escort into another alley.

She left Paris as soon as the necessary arrangements were completed, and did not return till the ninth or tenth month of the prescribed period of mourning; at the end of which she is again found mingling with constantly increasing *éclat* in the political, literary, and gay world of Paris. But that world had undergone material changes, mostly for the worse, since she first entered it. The Fronde was at fever heat, and Madame de Puliga, following the example of her French predecessors, devotes two chapters to the Fronde.[1] But we shall give our readers credit for knowing that it was a series of civil commotions, an intermittent civil war, lasting about four years (1648–1652), beginning with a cabal against Mazarin supported by the Queen Regent, Anne of Austria, and ending by the complete re-establishment of the royal authority. It abounded in striking episodes and romantic adventures; placing in broad relief the historic names of Condé, Turenne, de Retz, Mazarin, Rochefoucauld, the Duchesse de Longueville, Anne of Austria, the Grande Mademoiselle, etc., etc., who plotted against each other in such an entangled network of intrigues, that, about the time of Madame de Sévigné's return, they were split into five separate factions, engaged in a kind of quinquangular duel.

The society of the *Précieuses* was broken up, and the most select reunions were held at the little Luxembourg in the apartments of the Duchesse d'Aiguillon, the niece of the great cardinal. It was there that Pascal first attracted attention, not by logical or metaphysical subtlety, but by amusing and ingenious demonstrations in mathematical and physical science:

[1] She has merely abridged the ordinary accounts, and has obviously overlooked documents that have been recently brought to light. Thus, speaking of the father and mother of the great Condé, she says, "The husband and wife hated each other." The Duc d'Aumale ("Histoire des Princes de Condé," vol. ii. p. 284) merely says that they never manifested much tenderness for one another, and that the husband was jealous. There are grounds for believing that she was much attached to him, and that Henry IV. behaved to her much as he behaved to the fair Gabrielle.

> "Que l'on vit bien, en vérité
> Qu'un très-beau génie il possède;
> Et l'on traita d'Archimède."

Port Royal and the Jansenists were fast growing into importance, and already exercising a marked influence. They had formed an alliance, defensive and offensive, with Retz; with whom Madame de Sévigné sided fearlessly and consistently; and being thus constantly brought into contact with the best of them, she naturally fell in with their ways of thinking and their views. Although their tendency was to give a more serious tone to thought, to impose a beneficial restraint on manners, and to check frivolous occupations, there never was a time when amusement was more eagerly pursued, or intrigues of all sorts were more rife. The Grande Mademoiselle gave entertainments on the most magnificent scale twice a week, and it was at one of these that Charles II., then an exile, proposed for her. They were regularly attended by Madame de Sévigné, who also held receptions, which obtained notoriety by an adventure vividly illustrative of the times. We cannot find room for the details; but one admirer calls out another for not ceding the place of honour in her *ruelle*; and three or four duels, with three or four combatants on a side, are with difficulty prevented by the combined influence of the ladies and the police.

The Comte de Lude, who entered the list as one of her champions in this affair, was the suitor who, next to Bussy, was thought to have the best chances of success. In the course of the three following years we find the Prince de Conti, Turenne, and Fouquet (the magnificent Fouquet, who was deemed all-conquering), at her feet. In fact, her suitors were as numerous as the suitors of Penelope:

"Not more than twenty-five, already celebrated for her wit, her agreeability, her attractions: free to choose amongst a great number of competitors eager to dispute her hand, sufficiently conversant with the world to make a good choice. She might, by a new marriage, increase her fortune, and promise herself a happiness which her first husband seemed to have made her know only to render the privation of it more painful. But if she gave herself a master, she gave her children one. She impaired their fortunes if a new family compelled the division of her property. Could she flatter herself in that case with being able to preserve the same sentiments for the two dear creatures to whom she had given birth? Would a divided tenderness be always equally deep and lively? . . . If, then, a new marriage promised enjoyments and security for her future, it offered only losses and dangers for her children. After having made all these reflections, Madame de Sévigné did not hesitate, and took the resolution to condemn her whole life to widowhood, to consecrate her entire existence to her children."

So says M. de Walckenaer. But we hear of no proposals of marriage: her principal admirers were married men, and we suspect that the *preux chevaliers* of her time bore a marked resemblance in one respect to the knights of the Arthurian legend:

"And still those lovers' fame survives,
   For faith so constant shown,
There were two who loved their neighbours' wives,
   And one who loved his own."[1]

It could hardly be otherwise in a nation prone to gallantry, when marriages of inclination were the exception and marriages of reason the rule. Bussy was the husband of a second wife, and the father of two daughters, when he makes Madame De Sévigné the reluctant confidant of his intrigues with Mesdames de Gonville and de Montglat, in the mistaken hope of improving by jealousy his position with herself. He was a gambler, and had

---

[1] "The Bridal of Triermain," canto ii., and see the note.

just been boasting to her of such a run of luck that no one ventured to play with him; when fortune proved fickle, he was in want of money for his outfit in the coming campaign, and he wrote to her to beg the loan of ten thousand crowns on the security of a reversionary interest to that amount. She readily complied, being really glad of an opportunity of obliging him; but the management of her property had been left entirely to her uncle, the Abbé, and she never engaged in any pecuniary transaction without his advice, which was to delay the loan till some preliminary inquiries had been made. Her hesitation irritated Bussy, and, hard pressed as he was, he did not scruple to accept the loan of Madame de Montglat's diamonds. These he pawned for two thousand crowns, and then started for the army in the worst possible humour with his cousin, vowing never to speak or write to her again. It is from this epoch that the decline of his fortune is dated by his biographer—*Ex illo retro fluere et sublapsa referri:*

"If his rupture with her was not the sole cause of his subsequent mishaps, it certainly contributed largely to them. It is since he ceased to have her for a friend and confidant, since he had no longer the fear of her disapproval before his eyes, since he no longer stood in dread of her clever and useful raillery,—was no longer encouraged by her praises nor enlightened by her counsels, that he passed from prodigality to disorder, and from gallantry to debauch."[1]

On his return from the campaign, in which he highly distinguished himself, he joined a party of congenial spirits, who, with the view of escaping the restraints of the Holy Week, agreed to pass it at the château of Vivonne (first gentleman in

---

[1] Poitevin. Introduction to the "*Histoire amoureuse des Gaules.*"

waiting), four leagues from Paris. Here they indulged in orgies, little differing from those which the Hellfire Club celebrated at Medenham Abbey under the presidency of Wilkes. The rumour spread that they had made a mockery of the mysteries of religion and travestied the ceremonies of the Church. Coming to particulars, people accused them of having baptized frogs and sucking-pigs, and of having killed a man and supped upon him. These stories reached the King, and the perpetrators of the scandal were banished from Court and exiled to their country houses. This was one of the severest penalties that could be inflicted on a man of Bussy's ambitious views and lax habits; who would cordially have gone along with Buckingham in wishing (as the worst thing that could befall a sentient being) that the dog that bit him "might marry and live in the country with his wife." He amused his enforced leisure, gave vent to his irritation, and gratified his malice, by composing a series of lampoons and satirical portraits, which laid the foundation and at length took the form of his "Histoire Amoureuse des Gaules."

It was originally intended only for a small circle of friends; but, as almost always happens in such cases, he was betrayed by his vanity into showing it to persons who had no motive for secrecy. What was worse, he lent the manuscript to a new mistress, the Marquise de la Baume, for twenty-four hours: she employed them in copying it, and within a few weeks after her return to Paris, the worst passages had become the subject of comment in every *ruelle* about the Court. Exasperated out of all patience on discovering the treachery of the Marquise, he reproached her with such bitterness that, with true feminine spite, she sent a copy to Holland to be printed, with alterations and additions of the most mischievous and compromising sort. One of the spurious passages reflected on the King; and Bussy was sent to the Bastille, whence, after thirteen months' incarceration, he emerged without official or military rank, credit, or consideration; for he had been compelled to resign his dignities, and sell his company of light horse.

Then it was that Madame de Sévigné came forward with rare magnanimity to proffer a renewal of her friendship and a full pardon for her wrongs. They were of a nature that few women would have pardoned, unless the finest observers have been mistaken, and all history be false. Mrs. Western refused to prosecute the highwayman who declared with an oath, that such handsome b—s did not want jewels, but peremptorily insisted on the dismissal of Honor for saying that Sophia was the younger and handsomer of the two. Elizabeth was provoked into signing the death warrant of Mary by the letter in which her personal defects were spitefully recapitulated. Bussy's utmost malice was exerted to wound his cousin on this the most vulnerable side of her sex; as when he insinuates that she was not chary of her arms, probably from thinking that there could be no harm where there was no pleasure;[1] or when he describes her as unequal even to her eyes: "She has eyes of different colours, and, the eyes being the mirrors of the soul, these inequalities are like a warning given by nature to those who approach her, not to place great reliance on her friendship."

[1] " Je ne sais si c'est parce que ses bras ne sont pas beaux, qu'elle ne les tient pas trop chers, c'est qu'elle ne s'imagine pas faire une faveur, la chose étant si générale; mais enfin les prend et les baise qui veut : je pense que c'est assez pour lui persuader qu'il n'y a point de mal qu'elle croit qu'on n'y a point de plaisir."—*Histoire Amoureuse.*

A sweeping charge of illiberality is based on the delay of the loan : " There are people who place only sacred things as limits to their friendship, and who would do all for their friends except offend God. These people are called friends up to the altar. The friendship of Madame de Cheneville has other limits; this charmer is only a friend up to the purse. She is the only pretty woman in the world who has dishonoured herself by ingratitude." For what was she to be grateful to Bussy?

Although she spontaneously hurried to his support in his well-merited depression and disgrace, their intimacy could hardly be called cordial or unrestrained, till he found an opportunity of doing her an important service in his turn. Fouquet was one of the admirers who had given most umbrage to Bussy, and was apparently among the most persevering, for she wrote: " With him (Fouquet) I have always the same precautions and the same fears, which notably retard the progress he would willingly make. I believe he will be tired at last of always recommencing uselessly the same thing." When he was arrested in 1661, all his papers were seized, and amongst them were found several letters from Madame de Sévigné—Madame de Puliga says, "amongst his voluminous correspondence ; " but the whole mischief arose from their being found in his *cassette aux poulets*, the box ostentatiously devoted to his *billets doux* or love-letters. Her letters were certainly misplaced in this depository. Her own explicit explanation is contained in a letter to Ménage, which we copy *verbatim*, for the sake of the spelling, from the autograph in the possession of M. Feuillet de Conches :

. " Je vous remercie, mon cher monsieur, de toutes vos

nouuelles. Il y en a deux ou trois dans vostre lettre que ie ne sauois point. Pour celles de M. Fouquet, ie nentends parler dautre chose. Je pense que vous saues bien le deplesir que iay eü davoir esté trouuée dans le nombre de celles qui luy ont escrit. Il est vray que ce nestait ny la galanterie, ni linterest que mauoient obligee davoir vn commerce avec luy. Lon voit clairement que ce nestait que pour les affaires de M. de la Trousse; mais cela nempesche pas que ie naye esté fort touchée de voir quil les avoit mises dans la cassette de ses poulets, et de me voir nommée parmy celles qui nont pas eü des sentimens si purs que moy. Dans cette occasion iay besoin que mes amis instruisent ceux qui ne le sont pas. Je vous croy asses genereux pour vouloir en dire ce que Me de la Fayette vous en aprendra, et iay receu tant dautres marques de vostre amitié que je ne fais nulle facon de vous coniurer de me donner encore celle-cy."[1]

The contents of the *cassette* were seen by only three persons,—the King, the Queen, and the royal confessor, Tellier, who declared that Madame de Sévigné's letters were letters of business, interspersed with lively comments in her manner on the topics of the day; but the charity of the circle in which she mixed went no further than that of a female celebrity of our time, who made it a rule, she said, when she heard any scandal of a friend, to hope for the best and believe the worst. The calumny was a source of deep annoyance till it gradually died away from sheer emptiness; and there was something peculiarly aggravating in being given by common rumour to the financier who maintained, and had done much to prove, that every woman has her price. It was in this trying emergency that Bussy came to the rescue, and did excellent service by flinging down a bold defiance to her assailants and daring them to the proof. When Rouville, his brother-in-law, remarked that

[1] "Causeries d'un Curieux," vol. iii.

it ill became him, who had made so much noise about her, to rebuke others, he retorted, "I only tolerate noise of my own making."

It took three years to prepare for Fouquet's trial, years of wearing anxiety for his friends. When it began, it was watched with the keenest interest by Madame de Sévigné, whose letters to the Marquis de Pomponne contain the best account of the proceedings which we possess. They abound in dramatic scenes and incidents: they palpitate with emotion; and they glow with such tender sympathy as to have impressed Napoleon with the belief that a warmer feeling than friendship must have dictated them.[1] But when her feelings were touched, it was in her nature to run into extremes; her heart and mind are laid open for one who runs to read. She lets out all because she has nothing which she has reason to keep back. Thus, after going masked to see him pass from the court to the prison, she writes:

"I do not believe he recognized me; but I fairly own to you that I was strangely affected when I saw him enter that little door. If you knew how unhappy one is when one has a heart made like mine, you would pity me; but I think, from what I know of you, that you do not get off at a cheaper rate. I have been to see your dear neighbour (Madame Duplessis-Guénégaud). We have had a good talk about our dear friend (Fouquet). She has seen Sappho (Mademoiselle Scudéry), who has given her fresh courage. As for myself, I will go to her to-morrow to raise mine; for from time to time I feel that I have need of comfort. It is not that a thousand things are not afloat which ought to give hope; but, my God, I have so lively an imagination, that everything uncertain is death to me."

[1] "En lisant le procès de Fouquet (dans 'Les Lettres de Madame de Sévigné,') il remarquait que l'intérêt de Madame de Sévigné était bien chaud, bien vif, bien tendre, pour de la simple amitié."—*Mémorial de Sainte-Hélène.*

When people began to speculate on the sentence, when the accused was literally suspended between life and death, she writes again:

"Everybody is interested in this great affair. People speak of nothing else: they reason, they draw conclusions, they reckon on their fingers, they are moved to tenderness; they fear, wish, hate, admire, grow sad, are overcome: in a word, my poor friend, the condition in which we are for the moment is most extraordinary: it is a thing divine—the resignation and firmness of our dear unfortunate. He knows every day what passes, and volumes would have to be written in his praise."

When the sentence was passed, December 20th, she writes, "Praise God, Monsieur, and thank Him. Our poor friend is saved. Thirteen had sided with M. d'Ormesson and nine with Sainte-Hélène. I am beside myself with joy." She was thankful for small mercies. The sentence was confiscation of goods and perpetual exile; which the gracious monarch transmuted to perpetual imprisonment. Arraigned in the name of the public weal, at the bar of the French nation, or the bar of posterity, Fouquet would have merited his doom. But it was hard on him to be condemned by a monarch who had connived at his peculations, and only became awake to their enormity when his aspiring minister presumed to rival him in splendour and in love. Misplaced or not, Madame de Sévigné's sympathy does credit to her heart, and, in the teeth of the abounding proofs of sensibility in her letters, it is absurd to attribute her unfailing purity of conduct to coldness, or to deny her the merit of resisting temptations to which all around were yielding without reproach.[1]

[1] "Elle est d'un tempérament froid, au moins si on en croit feu son mari: aussi lui avait-il l'obligation de sa vertu, comme il disoit: toute sa chaleur est à l'esprit."—*Bussy.*

> "Let conquerors boast
> Their fields of fame: he who in virtue arms
> A young warm spirit against Beauty's charms,
> Who feels her brightness, yet defies her thrall,
> Is the best, bravest conqueror of them all."

And no less brave is she who in virtue arms a young, warm spirit against the seductive arts of a brilliant and dissolute society like that of which Madame de Sévigné formed part. Nor did conscious weakness compel her to fly from them. Madame de Puliga calls on us "to respect her when, a fond mother, she seeks retirement to devote herself to her two children." But she never did seek retirement to devote herself to them. On the contrary, she remained at Paris for the express purpose of giving them the best education; and it was during the most important stages of that education that she was the observed of all observers in the gayest circles of the capital.[1] Speaking of a visit to Paris in 1657, the Abbé Arnauld writes:

> "It was during this expedition that M. de Sévigné introduced me to the illustrous Marquise de Sévigné, his niece, whose name cannot be mentioned without praise by those who know how to value wit, agreeability, and virtue. A thing highly to her advantage and very singular may be told of her: that one of the most formidable pens of France (Bussy) having undertaken to calumniate her like many others, was constrained by the force of truth to attribute to

---

[1] "She remained in Paris all the winter (1655–1656) and did not even return, according to her custom, to the Rochers during the fine season. We may suppose that the animated pleasures of the capital contributed to retain her there. . . . It is possible that at the period of which we are now speaking (1657–1658), their education was the motive that retained her at Paris, and forced her to remain there." (*Walckenaer*). She was at most of the court entertainments, and was frequently the guest of Fouquet in 1658: her daughter being then fourteen and her son twelve. One of her reasons for preferring Paris was that the air of Brittany was bad for her complexion.

her purely imaginary defects, having been unable to discover any real. I fancy that I see her still as she appeared to me the first time I had the honour of seeing her,—arriving in her open carriage between her son and daughter; all three such as the poets represent Latona between the young Apollo and the little Diana; so much charm and beauty did the mother and children display. She did me the honour of promising me her friendship, and I am proud of having preserved to this hour so dear and so precious a gift. But I should add, to the praise of the sex, that I have found more fidelity in my female than in my male friends, having been more often deceived by the male *and never by the female.*"

The Abbé was a fortunate man, and probably a safe one. In a letter to her daughter, in 1667, Madame de Sévigné recalls a similar group:

"Monsieur de Pomponne remembers a day when you were a little girl at my uncle's. You were behind a window, with your brother, more beautiful, he says, than an angel; you said that you were a prisoner, that you were a princess banished from your father's house. Your brother was beautiful like you! you were nine. He reminded me of this day. He has never forgotten a moment when he has seen you."

The interest she took in them may have had a good deal to do with the exclusion of other interests; but we cannot agree with those who would fain convert her maternal love into a new virtue, or fling round it an additional halo, by supposing that she caught at it and clung to it as a plank of safety or a shield. If there be a passion or feeling inborn and instinctive, it is this. It cannot be adopted, or deepened for an emergency, at will. Her excess of fondness for her children was natural and spontaneous. It was not, and could not be, the result of a resolution to be good. She could no more have moderated than created it; and the result was that both boy and girl were spoiled. Flattery and indulgence planted or fostered in each the qualities that proved most injurious or unamiable in after life. They were well taught, so far as concerns acquirements and accomplishments, but the son grew up reckless and dissipated; the daughter haughty, vain, selfish, and cross-grained.

The advance of Mademoiselle Françoise Marguerite towards womanhood is marked by some verses of Saint-Pavin, from which it appears that *Manon*, as she was called in her thirteenth or fourteenth year, was annoyed at being so called: that she was beginning to form the charm of her mother's society, where the only name she went by was *la belle Madelonne*: that, giving up birds and dolls, she had acquired a taste for battledore and shuttlecock; a game which (as a well-known story[1] proves) may be turned to good account by coquetry. She was also said to be fond of *reversi*, a game of cards. It was when she was about a year older, in the winter of 1662-1663, that she was presented at court by her mother—*matre pulchrā filia pulchrior*—and she at once took rank with the received beauties:

"The sensation she created," says Madame de Puliga, "was great; her beauty being of a kind well calculated to excite admiration, though in some degree a tenderness of expression was wanting. To the dazzling complexion of a blonde she united perfect regularity of features; all her portraits, that painted by Mignard especially, represent her as singularly beautiful. There is in her countenance a remarkable harmony; it seems as if the most critical eye could not wish her in any single particular to be otherwise. Looking at this 'amiable countenance,' of which Madame de Sévigné speaks so often, the peculiarity of her daughter's

---

[1] Of the damsel, playing with the King, who, when the shuttlecock fell and was caught in her bosom, requested his Majesty to take it out.

beauty is readily understood. Yet there was something deficient in all this perfection: a lack of warmth, of geniality, an absence, too, of all those outward endearments which rendered her mother so fascinating, and which in the daughter silenced and repelled the admiration she called forth."

The Marquis de Tréville, a high authority, exclaimed, "This beauty will set the world on fire." Bussy pronounced her the prettiest girl in France;[1] and in La Fontaine's dedication of a fable to her are these lines:

> "Vous qui naquîtes toute belle,
> A votre indifférence près."
> "Beauty born, in every sense,
> Barring your indifference."

She herself was so lost in admiration of her own surpassing charms that, when her ex-master in philosophy, the Abbé de la Mousse, took the liberty of reminding her that, like all things human, they were subject to decay, "Yes," was her reply, "but they are not decayed yet." She was right enough here, and so was the English girl who, on being reminded by her spiritual guide that beauty was only skin deep, remarked that this was deep enough till people began going into society without their skins. It was probably the indifference or conceit which Mademoiselle betrayed in manner and expression that led many to award the palm to the mother, then thirty-seven. Thus Ménage:—

> "Je l'ai dit dans la famille,
> Et je le dirai toujours,
> Vous n'aimez point votre fille,
> Ce miracle de nos jours."

---

[1] "*La plus jolie fille de France.*" But the word *joli* meant then rather charming than pretty. Thus Madame de Sévigné writes in 1676 "Nos Français sont si aimables et si jolis."

> Par l'éclat incomparable
> De votre teint, de vos yeux,
> Par votre esprit adorable,
> Vous l'effacez en tous lieux."

Which may be paraphrased :—

> "Your love for her's a blind,
> Or you'd surely veil a while
> Those mirrors of your mind,—
> Your eyes, your lips, your smile.
> I say it in all places,
> I say it in all ways,
> Your brilliancy effaces
> This wonder of our days."

Confiding in her daughter's pride and coldness, or led away by the love of pleasure, Madame de Sévigné fearlessly carried her into the charmed circle where seductions were rife. The young lady was permitted to figure in ballets before the King in costumes peculiarly adapted to show off her attractions: as an Amazon, a sea-nymph, and Omphale, in succession. She was, of course, the object of frequent pursuit, but the most enterprising gallants, after a brief trial, gave up all hope of the prize; and when the perverted notions of the period marked or "spotted" her as an object of royal favour, this was deemed an exalted compliment, implying not the semblance of a slur.

In 1668, when the passion of the King for Mademoiselle de la Vallière began to cool, the Duc de Rohan was trying to secure the expected vacancy for his sister Madame de Soubise, and the Duc de Feuillade for Mademoiselle de Sévigné. On hearing this bit of news from Madame de Montmorency, Bussy, susceptible as he was on the point of family honour, replies, " I should be very glad if the King would attach himself to Mademoiselle de Sévigné, for the damsel is a great friend of mine, and he could not do better." Revolting as this sounds now, Bussy simply hoped his young relative would obtain a preferment which was coveted for their wives, daughters, sisters, and nieces by so-called honourable men. "Have you heard," writes Madame de Sévigné to Madame de Grignan, in 1671, " that Villarceaux, speaking to the King about a place for his son, adroitly took occasion to tell him that there were officious people who busied themselves in telling his niece that his Majesty had some designs on her: that, if this were so, he begged to be employed: that the affair would be better in his hands than in any other; and that he could bring it to a successful termination? The King burst out laughing, and told him, 'Villarceaux, you and I are too old to meddle with damsels of fifteen.'"

By common consent, the *belle Madelonne*, with all her beauty, cultivation and intelligence, was an uninteresting person, and year after year passed away without producing an acceptable suitor for her hand. She inspired no passion; and an alliance with her family—Frondeuse and Janséniste, with de Retz and Bussy for its illustrations—offered small prospect of rising in the only place in which young ambition then could rise, at court. The mother's impatience and irritation at the bad taste or want of spirit in the male sex, are betrayed in her correspondence. In reply to Bussy regretting that the young lady had not been so fortunate as her friend, Mademoiselle de Brancas, recently married to the Prince d'Harcourt, Madame de Sévigné writes, "The prettiest girl in France is your very humble servant: this name sounds agreeable enough: I am, however, tired of doing it the honours." Bussy replies: "The prettiest girl in France knows full well what I am to her. I long as much as you for another to aid you in doing the honours; it is in its bearings on her that I recognize the caprice of destiny, as well as in my own affairs." A month later, Madame de Sévigné resumes: "The prettiest girl in France is more worthy than ever of your esteem and friendship. Her destiny is so difficult to comprehend, that, as for me, I can make nothing of it." Emblems and devices were in vogue, and the device of this young lady (engraved on her seal) was a pomegranate, with the motto: *Il piv (piu) grato nasconde* (the pleasantest is concealed)—implying that her best qualities were unseen. The precise contrary was the fact.

A husband was found at last in the person of the Comte de Grignan, the head of an illustrious family, who had held high employments and buried two wives; aged thirty-seven, plain in person and distinguished in manners. The great event is thus announced to Bussy by Madame:

"I must tell you what no doubt will give you pleasure. It is, that at last the 'prettiest girl in France' marries not the prettiest young man, but one of the most 'honnêtes hommes' in the kingdom; whom you have long known. All his wives have died to make way for your cousin, and even his father and his son, out of extraordinary kindness; so, being richer than he has ever been, and being moreover by his birth, by his establishments, and by his good qualities such as we could wish, we do not haggle with him as it is customary to do, but put our trust in the two families that have gone before us. He appears much pleased at our alliance, and as soon as we hear from his uncle, the Archbishop of Arles—his other uncle, the Bishop of Uzés, being here—the affair will be completed before the end of the year. As I am a sufficiently precise lady, I would not fail to ask your advice and approbation. The public seem satisfied, that is much; for we are so foolish that we seem to regulate ourselves by *that*."

Bussy replies that she is right in supposing that the news would give him pleasure: "There is only one thing that alarms me for the prettiest girl in France: it is that Grignan, not yet an old man, is already at his third wife; he uses up almost as many wives as coats, or at least as coaches; with this drawback, I think my cousin fortunate; as for him, there is nothing wanting to his happiness." The bride elect was a little staggered by the same reflection, and although Bluebeard was the creation of a later age, she experienced, by anticipation, an ill-defined fear of such a character. Her scruples were got over, as well as the more reasonable objections of Retz to the uncertainty touching the Grignan estates, which Madame de Sévigné imprudently neglected to clear up. She paid over the dowry (60,000 francs) without inquiry, and the marriage took place on the 29th of January, 1669.

As marriages go, it may be called a happy marriage, in spite of the pecuniary embarrassments to which there are frequent allusions in the letters, and in spite of the husband's peculiar style of ugliness, which led to his being nicknamed *Matou* (Tom-cat). "It is certain," says M. de Walckenaer, "that Madame de Grignan was afraid of attracting the attention of the King. When she appeared at court with her husband, whose ugliness formed so strong a contrast to her own beauty, not only did she abstain from any refinement of dress, but she ventured to shock the despotic will of fashion, by hiding under a far from becoming garment the charms which the young women of her age were bound to display." In a letter of the following year, Madame de Sévigné asks: "Do you remember how sick we were of that horrid black cloak? This disregard of appearance was that of a virtuous woman; M. de Grignan may thank you for it; but it was very tiresome for the lookers-on." There was a Lady Edgeworth who, in consequence of the marked admiration of Charles II. at her presentation, refused to attend his court a second time. But one of the darkest catastrophes in English history was brought about by the opposite behaviour of a wife. When Athelwald, says Hume, entreated Elfrida to conceal her beauty from Edgar, "she promised compliance, though nothing was farther from her intention. She appeared before the King with all the advantages which the richest attire and the most engaging airs could bestow upon her, and excited at once in his bosom the highest love towards herself, and the most furious desire of revenge against her husband."

The Comte de Grignan was appointed Lieutenant-General of Provence (virtually Governor) in November, 1669, and immediately left Paris. Madame de Grignan, detained by her confinement and other causes, joined him in January, 1671. This, the first separation of mother and daughter, is the turning-point of their common history and, according to the biographers, the starting-point of the mother's epistolary fame. Expressing the popular notion, Madame de Puliga says, "The letters of Madame de Sévigné would not be the monument of genius they are, had Madame de Grignan remained in Paris; but not at such a price would Madame de Sévigné, we feel sure, have bought the eminent place posterity has awarded her." She was forty-five in 1671, and had been an assiduous correspondent since she was fifteen. She had already written most of the letters to Bussy which laid the foundation of her fame, the letters to Pomponne on the trial of Fouquet, and the letters to Coulanges describing the Grande Demoiselle and Lauzun romance. She would have gone on writing in the same fashion in any case, but she was evidently stimulated into restless, feverish activity by her passion for her daughter : her pen was consequently more prolific upon general topics, and we are exclusively indebted to the separation for the passages in which her maternal love is so exquisitely delineated and expressed.

But was that passion an improving or elevating one? Did it strengthen her mind? Was it creditable to her understanding? Was it not positively injurious both to the object and herself? M. de Walckenaer says that she had strong literary tendencies, but that maternal love was to her what the love of fame was to other gifted women who wrote books, and that her daughter was the sole public she cared about. If so, the world may have lost, instead of gaining, by her unrestrained tenderness. St. Simon terms it her sole defect; and, speaking of Arnauld d'Andilly, she tells her daughter:

"He scolded me very seriously, and told me I was mad not to think of converting myself; that I was a pretty pagan; that I made you my idol : that this sort of idolatry was as dangerous as any other, though appearing less criminal to me."

Far from thinking it criminal, she took pride in it. She writes from Livry :

"I make a little La Trappe of this place : I wish to pray to God and make a thousand reflections. I intend to fast a great deal for all sorts of reasons, and above all *m'ennuyer* for the love of God. But, my dear daughter, what I shall do much better than all this, is to think of you. I have done nothing else since I got here; and, unable to contain my emotions, I have seated myself to write to you at the end of the little dark walk you like so much, on the mossy bank on which I have seen you recline. But, my God! where have I not seen you here? And how all these thoughts pierce my heart! There is not a place, a spot, neither in the house, nor in the church, nor in the country, nor in the garden, where I have not seen you. In some way or other, I see you; you are present to me; I think and think again of all: my head and my mind are racked; but I turn in vain, I seek in vain: that darling child whom I love so passionately, is two hundred leagues away: I have her no longer; and then I weep without restraint."

This is genuine; yet the letters in which the same sentiment is produced and reproduced in touching forms of inexhaustible variety, bear a strong analogy to poetical compositions like Petrarch's Sonnets and Tennyson's *In Memoriam*. Except at the commencement, they spring quite as much from the imagination as the heart: the complaint, or sorrow, becomes by habit a luxury; and the writer finds a positive pleasure in exciting her fancy and then following its flow.

Conscious as she must have been of her daughter's defects of heart and temper, she writes in 1686:

"Is there any one in the world more enlightened, and more penetrated with reason and with your duties than you are? You know full well that you are above others; you have wisdom, judgment, discernment; uncertainty, because you are too enlightened; cleverness, insinuation, purpose, when you will; prudence, firmness, presence of mind, eloquence, and the gift of being loved when you desire it, and sometimes a great deal more than you desire. Paper is not wanting, nor the materials to fill it; but to say all in a word, you have in you all that is requisite to be whatever you aspire to. There are some people in whom the stuff is wanting. . . . My child, do not complain."

In the intercourse between these ladies, the maxim, "the absent are always in the wrong," was reversed. It was only when separated that they agreed; and their occasional meetings were invariably followed by heartburnings and regrets. As a married woman, wrapped up in her husband, her children and her establishments, Madame de Grignan felt the ridicule of being petted and fondled like a child, and sometimes allowed her temper to get the better of her vanity. In 1671, Madame de Sévigné writes:

"You tell me I have been unjust on the subject of your affection for me, but I have been so even more than you imagine; I hardly dare own to you to what extent I carried my folly. I have imagined you felt an aversion to me, and I have believed it because I fancied your behaviour towards me was that which I should adopt towards those I hate; and only consider, I believed this dreadful thing when most ardently wishing the contrary! In such moments—I must lay bare to you my entire weakness—if any one had thrust a poniard into my heart it would not have wounded me so mortally as that fancy."

In 1677: "Let us, my child, re-establish our reputation by another journey, when we will be reasonable, that is you; and when we shall not be told, You are killing one another."

Madame de Sévigné was an irreproachable administrator of her own property, never got into debt, and gave her son the best advice on that subject; but, on hearing that a *marchande* of Paris had been endeavouring to get some money due from the Grignans, she writes:

"Imagine making a journey of five hundred miles to ask for money from persons who send what they can, and are dying to send more! No person's arrival at Grignan could more have astonished me. When I heard it, I actually screamed. *You are reasonable, and did well not to ill-use her;* but how did you get out of her clutches and of her inundation of words in which one is drowned?"

For once, she hazarded a sensible remonstrance

against the high play in which the Grignans indulged:

"I hear on different sides that you both lose all you stake. Why, why, such ill-luck? why that perpetual little drain I have always found so inconvenient? . . .

"Continued ill-luck provokes and offends. We hate thus to be mocked by Fortune. The advantage others have over us is humiliating, though it be only a trifle. My love, Nicole expresses that so well. I hate Fortune, and am well convinced that she is blind to treat you in such a fashion. If she had but one eye, you would not be so unlucky."

And again, a month afterwards:

"You have wonderful ill-luck; you always lose. This swallows up a great deal of money. I cannot believe you have enough not to feel these continual losses. Take my advice, do not persist. I feel more than you do that perpetual ill-luck. Remember that you have spent all that money without diverting yourself. Quite the contrary; you have given five or six thousand francs to bore yourself. My child, I am getting too earnest; you must say, like Tartuffe, 'It is an excess of zeal.'"

A complete contrast to his sister, Charles, Marquis de Sévigné (born in 1648), was endowed with his mother's joyous temperament and much of her ready wit. When under the same roof with her, he fell in with her tastes and ways, walked, talked, and read with her, and was a most delightful companion, which may be one reason why she never idealises him when absent. He was brave and honourable, and had served with distinction; but he was dissipated and extravagant, a sort of Charles Surface in his way. The third Earl of Orford defined timber "an excrescence on the earth's surface, placed there for the payment of debts." Lord Alvanley having sent orders for the cutting down of more timber on his estate, the agent wrote that there was nothing left standing but the sign-posts.—"Then cut them down." The Marquis de Sévigné entertained the same view of the final cause of timber. His mother writes, in 1680:

"I was yesterday at the Buron, and returned at night. I thought I must have cried on seeing the degradation of this estate. It possessed the oldest trees in the world; and my son during his last journey had them felled. He also sold a little clump which was truly beautiful. All this is pitiable. He carried off four hundred pistoles, of which he had not a sou remaining a month after. It is impossible to understand what he does, nor what his stay in Brittany cost him, where he was like a beggar, for he had sent back his footman and his coachman to Paris, and he had no one but Larchemin with him in this town, where he remained two months. He has found out how to spend without keeping up an appearance, how to lose without gambling, and how to pay without getting out of debt; always a thirst for and a want of money in peace as in war. It is an abyss of I know not what, for he has not a single fancy, but his hand is a crucible in which gold melts. My child, you must endure all this. All those afflicted dryads I saw yesterday, all those venerable rural deities who no longer know where to find shelter, all those old crows established for two centuries in the horror of those woods, those owls, who in this obscurity announced by their mournful cries the miseries of all men—all these yesterday uttered plaints to me that sensibly touched my heart; and who knows that some of those old oaks have not spoken, like the one in which Clorinde was?[1] This place was a place of enchantment, if there ever was one."

His affair with Ninon made her tremble for his religious principles, to which, like other French mothers, she attached more importance than to his morals:

"But how dangerous she is, that Ninon! If you knew how she discourses on religion, you would be horrified. Her zeal to pervert young men is equal to that of a

[1] She refers to the 13th canto of Tasso's "Jerusalem Delivered."

Monsieur de St. Germains whom we saw once at Livry. She says your brother has the simplicity of a dove."

Soon afterwards:

"Ninon has thrown him over: he was unhappy when she was fond of him: he is in despair at her caring for him no longer, and so much the more that she does not speak of him with much respect. She says he has a soul of *bouilli*, a body of wet paper, a heart of pumpkin fricasseed in snow."

Besides lavishing the most fulsome praises on the daughter's beauty, which was real, the mother expatiates on her popularity, which was entirely fabulous:

"Madame du Gué has written to Monsieur de Coulanges that you are as beautiful as an angel. She is charmed with you, and well pleased with your politeness. . . . Do you know that to be remembered by you is considered a fortune? Those who are not, long for the distinction. The word you sent for my aunt is beyond price; you are very far from forgotten."

Bussy says, in a letter to Madame de Scudéry, in 1678:

"That woman [Madame de Grignan] has wit, but of so sour a kind, her pride is so insupportable, that she will make herself as many enemies as her mother has made friends and admirers."

In addition to the drain on her resources from the son's extravagances, Madame de Sévigné was frequently sending presents to her daughter: a pearl necklace, for which she paid twelve thousand livres, being one. She was therefore occasionally obliged to put the screw on her farmers and agents, who were always in arrear. Starting for Brittany in 1680, she writes: "I am going like a fury to be paid. I am determined not to listen to any excuses. It is a singular thing what a quantity of money is owing to me. I shall always be saying like the *Avare*: 'Money, money!'" She relents a little on arriving. "What annoys me is to be doing harm; but when I play at drowning, and ask myself which am I to drown, Monsieur de la Jarie (a farmer) or myself, without hesitation I say, Monsieur de la Jarie, and that gives me courage." Her courage rapidly melts away: "It is true that since I have arrived here, I have been giving away rather large sums: one morning 800 francs, another 1000, another 5000, etc. It seems I am joking, but it is a too positive fact. I find farmers and millers who owe me these sums, and who have not a sou to pay me; so I am compelled to give it to them." Fond as she was of town life, she has an unaffected fondness for rural enjoyments, and there is a natural ring in her burst of pleasure at being rid of some pretentious acquaintance at Vichy:

"At last I am going to be alone, and I am very delighted at it. . . . Provided they don't carry the country off with them, the river, the hundred of little woods and streams, the fields, and the peasants who dance in the fields, I consent to bid adieu to all the rest. The country alone will cure me."

Whether in town or country, she was never without objects of interest. She read a great deal: she fixed each Cynthia of the minute; and there was no phase of the national mind which she let pass unobserved, no fleeting passion in speculation or sentiment with which she did not fall in sufficiently to mark its tendency and appreciate its force. The attached friends with whom she lived in intimacy were so numerous that the puzzle is how she found time for all of them.

The Duchesse de Longueville was the dream of Rochefoucauld in his prime, Madame de la

Fayette his consolation in his decline. She said of him, "Il m'a donné de l'esprit, mais j'ai reformé son cœur." Madame de Sévigné was with them almost daily, and formed one of the circle at Rochefoucauld's house, to whom he read his "Maxims" for the express purpose of inviting comment. In reference to his sufferings from the gout, she writes: "His château en Espagne is to be well enough to be carried to his friends' houses or into his carriage to take the air. . . . He begged I would tell you that those racked on the wheel only suffer one moment what he undergoes half his life, and that he looks for death as his *coup de grâce*." When his son was killed and his grandson wounded at the passage of the Rhine: "I have seen his heart laid bare in this cruel affliction: he is in the first rank of all I know for courage, merit, tenderness, and reason. I say nothing of his wit and his agreeability."

The admirable character of him by De Retz was said to have been provoked by one of himself by Rochefoucauld, shown him by Madame de Sévigné. Speaking of Madame de la Fayette's grief at his death, she says: "Nothing could be compared to the confidence and charm of their friendship: my daughter, think of it; you will see that it is impossible to sustain a greater loss, and one which time can less easily compensate. *I have not quitted her during all those days.*" She writes to her daughter in 1671: "Did you not think the five or six fables (La Fontaine's) charming that are in the volume I sent you? We were all enchanted with them at M. de la Rochefoucauld's, and we learnt by heart 'Le Singe et le Chat.'" Several of the fables were submitted in manuscript or read to her prior to publication.

She was still more devoted to her distinguished

relative, De Retz, whom she called "the hero of the breviary," by way of contrast to Turenne, "the hero of the sword." In one letter she actually goes the length of telling her daughter: "The dear Cardinal has nearly put you out of my head." In another: "I must see our Cardinal to-night. I must pass an hour or two with him before he goes to bed." Again, "We strive to amuse our dear Cardinal;" and after mentioning that she had been of the party when Corneille, Boileau, and Molière read their newest works to him, she adds, "It is all they can do for his service, and it is not little." Not one of her numerous letters to him has been preserved.

Her literary taste and her prescience were long called in question on the supposition of her having said, "*Racine passera comme le café*"—neither Racine nor coffee having passed away or blown over. She said nothing of the sort. The phrase is La Harpe's, based on a pure fiction of Voltaire's. On the 16th March, 1672, she wrote: "Racine writes plays for La Champmesle:[1] this is not writing them for ages to come. If ever he ceases to be in love, it will be no longer the same thing. Our old friend Corneille for ever, then." Four years later, March 10th, 1676: "There you are, then, cured of coffee for good and all: Mademoiselle de Méri has also banished it. After such mishaps can we count upon fortune?" It is only by tearing these passages from the context, garbling them, and placing them in juxtaposition, that the semblance of authority can be produced by Voltaire when he states, "Madame de Sévigné is constant in the belief that Racine will not go far: she judged him like coffee, of which she said that people would soon leave it off." This having

---

[1] The actress with whom Charles de Sévigné fell in love.

passed without contradiction, he ventured a step further in the Preface to " Irene " :

" We are indignant with Madame de Sévigné, who wrote so well and judged so badly. . . . We are disgusted by this wretched party spirit, with this blind prejudice, which makes her say, The fashion of admiring Racine will pass away like the fashion of coffee."

When Racine was first set up as the rival of Corneille, the court and the playgoing public were divided into two factions, and Madame de Sévigné eagerly upheld her old friend and favourite Corneille.[1] As the warmth of controversy cooled, she became one of the most enthusiastic admirers of Racine. When coffee was first introduced, she complained of its heating properties, and recommended the dilution of it by milk; and one of her biographers, M. Aubenas, suggests that the merit of inventing *café au lait* is due to her.

" We sup every evening with Madame Scarron," writes Madame de Sévigné in 1671; " she has an amiable mind and marvellously straight. It is a pleasure to hear her reason on the horrible agitations of a country (the Court) she knows well: the despair felt by D—— when her place seemed so miraculous, the continual rages of Lauzun, the gloomy chagrin and melancholy ennui of the ladies of St. Germain,—and perhaps the most envied (Madame de Montespan) is not exempt: it is pleasant to hear her talk about all this. These discourses lead us sometimes very far

---

[1] In 1670, at the mischievous suggestion of Henrietta of England, Duchess of Orleans, the two great dramatists brought out each a tragedy on the same subject. Corneille, " Tite et Bérénice;" Racine, " Bérénice." The palm was awarded to Racine, who was then in the maturity of his genius. Corneille was in his decline. The history of the phrase in question is given in detail by M. Fournier in his " L'Esprit dans l'Histoire," chap. 1. He awards to Madame Cornuel the phrase attributed to Madame de Sévigné of *la monnaie de Monsieur de Turenne*, used to describe the generals who succeeded the great commander. It was Madame de Grignan who, when her daughter married a financier, said, " *Il faut quelquefois fumer ses terres.*"

from morality to mortality, one while Christian and one while political. We often speak of you: she likes your mind and your manners; so, when you find yourself here again, you will not have to fear being out of fashion."

The widow Scarron, who afterwards (1685) became the wife of the great monarch, had been selected by his mistress, Madame de Montespan, to take charge of her illegitimate children by his Majesty. This was her position when Madame de Sévigné passed every evening with her and attached so much importance to her good word. The fact is she was quietly working her way upwards in a way which inspired esteem, whilst it augured and justified success. *Rien n'est plus habile qu'une conduite irréprochable*, was her maxim; and Louis, satiated with pomps and vanities, tired of facile pleasures, fell, and fell irrevocably, under the yoke of a woman who told him unceasingly that all earthly enjoyment was as dust compared with the welfare of his soul. The serious turn he took about the middle of his reign, and the religious persecutions that ensued, were clearly owing to her influence; yet his religion was pure bigotry at best, whilst there was neither earnestness nor sincerity at any time in hers. She took it up, after a careful study of the King's character, as the instrument best adapted for her ends; and the selection does the highest credit to her perspicacity.

It was in reference to her diligent performance of her religious duties during the life of Scarron, who burlesqued everything, that she said, "I did not act thus to please God, but I wished to be looked up to: my passion was to make myself a name." On another occasion she declared there was nothing she would not do to get the reputation of a *femme forte*. She wrote to Ninon de l'Enclos in 1666, to tell Rochefoucauld that his book of "Maxims" and the book of Job were her only studies. In illustration of the King's religion it is authentically told that he objected to the appointment of a man to a foreign mission because he was a Jansenist, but withdrew the objection on being assured that the nominee was simply an Atheist. It was under the joint auspices of this well-assorted pair that the Edict of Nantes was revoked in 1685—the year of their marriage—and that an ascetic gloom settled down, during their joint lives, upon the Court.

It had already become the fashion to be devout, for frailty to take refuge in sanctity; and what was said of the chief heroine of the Fronde might have been said of many others: *Elle se sauve sur la même planche de l'ennui et de l'enfer.* Speaking of the example set by Madame de Sablé when she retired to Port Royal, M. Cousin says, "Elle donna à Port-Royal plusieurs belles pécheresses, entre autres, Madame de Longueville." Madame de Thianges is another striking instance; for she was ludicrously proud of her beauty and her birth, and a professed *gourmande* to boot. It was she who said that "one does not grow old at table"— *on ne vieillit point à table.* Madame de Sévigné's sketch of this lady is in her happiest manner:

"M. de Grignan is right in telling you that Madame de Thianges has given up her rouge, and wears high dresses. Under this disguise it is difficult to know her again. She is often now with Madame de Longueville *dans le bel air de la dévotion;* but she is still very good company and by no means an anchoret. I was sitting next her the other day at dinner, when a servant brought her a large glass of *vin de liqueur.* She turned to me and said, 'Madame, this fellow does not know that I am *dévote.*' This made us laugh. She speaks very naturally of her intentions and her change. She is on her guard in what she says of her neighbour; and when anything escapes her, she stops short, and utters a cry, detesting the bad habit. I find her more agreeable than before.

"There are bets that the Princesse d'Harcourt will not be *dévote* a year hence, at this hour that she is Dame du Palais, and will take again to rouge; for this rouge, it is the law and the prophets: all Christianity turns on rouge. As to the Duchesse d'Aumont, her taste is for burying the dead. They say that, on the frontier, the Duchesse de Charost killed the people with her quack medicines, and that the other Duchesse buried them offhand."

When the Marquis de la Fare abandoned Madame de la Sablière for the gaming-table, she took refuge in devotion; and Madame de Sévigné speculates on the many strange methods by which souls may be saved:

"You ask what has made this solution of continuity between La Fare and Madame de la Sablière. It is *bassette*. Would you have believed it? It is under this name that the infidelity stands confessed: it is for this prostitute, *bassette*, that he has given up this religious adoration. The moment was come when this passion was to cease, and even pass over to another object. Would one believe that *bassette* could be a way to salvation for any one? Ah, it has been truly said, there are five hundred thousand roads which lead to it."

It was not unusual for a fine lady of the Louis Quatorze period, who fell in with the fashion, to pass through three stages—to be by turns *galante*, *savante*, and *dévote*. Madame de Sévigné escaped being either, although, from the atmosphere in which she lived, a strong pressure was put upon her to be successively all three. But it required all her rectitude of understanding and genuine piety to keep her clear from the prevalent spirit of bigotry. When the Protestant divine, D'Abbadie, published a book on "The Truth of the Christian Religion"—which she calls "the most divine of all books"—the question was anxiously mooted whether the author, being a Huguenot, could be saved. Madame de Coligny "was ready to wager he would not die a Huguenot," deeming it "not possible that Jesus Christ would allow one who had so well served Him to perish." "And I," says Bussy, "who answer for nothing, I say that, if Abbadie dies in his religion, it would make me believe that we can be saved in both." Madame de Sévigné concurred with Bussy that, under such very peculiar circumstances, a Huguenot might be saved. The struggles she underwent are strikingly portrayed in her letters:

"One of my strongest desires would be to be devout; I plague La Mousse [the Abbé] every day on this subject. I belong neither to God nor the Devil. This state of mind annoys me, though, between ourselves, I think it the most natural in the world. One does not belong to the Devil, because one fears God, and that one has a principle of religion at bottom. One does not belong to God, either, because His law seems hard and one does not like to destroy oneself. This composes the lukewarm, whose great number does not surprise me at all. However, God hates them: we must, therefore, get away from them, and there's the difficulty."

This difficulty or dilemma must have been disagreeably present to her when she said, "Want of reason offends me: want of faith hurts me." The best and wisest have been frequently at a loss how to reconcile the two. When Madame de Maintenon thought she had solved the problem, Madame de Sévigné said to her, "*Vous êtes bienheureux d'être sûr de ces choses-là.*"

St. Simon reports that, in the hottest of the controversy about grace, she said, "Thicken me your religion a little: it is evaporating altogether by being subtilised."

There was a formulary condemning the Jansenist doctrines as heretical, which the nuns were required to sign, Pomponne's niece amongst the rest; and she writes to him:

"Our sisters of Sainte-Marie (Jesuits) said to me: 'At last, God be praised! God has touched the heart of this poor creature; she has put herself on the way of obedience and salvation.' From thence I go to Port Royal. There I find a great anchorite of your acquaintance (his father), who begins by saying to me, 'Well, this poor little goose has signed: God has abandoned her at last; she has taken the leap.' For my part, I was ready to die with laughter at thinking on what pre-occupation brings to pass. There is the world as it goes for you! I believe that the middle between these extremes is always the best."

Like Johnson, she dreaded advancing years and death:

"I find myself in a dilemma, which embarrasses me. I am embarked in life without my consent: I must leave it. This binds me to the earth, and how shall I leave it— where? by what gate? When will it be? In what disposition? Shall I suffer a thousand and a thousand pangs which will make me die despairing? Shall I have a brain fever? Shall I die of an accident? How shall I stand with God? What shall I have to offer Him? Fear, necessity—will these make my return to Him? Shall I have no other sentiment than that of fear? What can I hope? Am I worthy of Paradise? Am I worthy (*digne*) of Hell? What an alternative! What a dilemma! Nothing is so insane as to place one's salvation in uncertainty; but nothing is so natural, and the foolish life I lead is the thing in the world the most easy to understand."

Yet she met death with Christian resignation when it came suddenly upon her in a form and manner to realise her fears. She died at Grignan of the small-pox, on the 17th April, 1696, in the seventy-first year of her age, neither son nor daughter being present to receive her last wishes or close her eyes. Bussy, who long before her death had done her ample justice, wrote this inscription for her portrait:

"MARIE DE RABUTIN, FILLE DU BARON DE CHANTAL, MARQUISE DE SÉVIGNÉ, FEMME D'UN GÉNIE EXTRAORDINAIRE,
"ET D'UNE SOLIDE VERTU, COMPATIBLES AVEC BEAUCOUP D'AGRÉMENTS."

Madame de Puliga suggests that this inscription would form an appropriate epitaph, and concludes her book with it, translated thus:

"MARIE DE RABUTIN, MARQUISE DE SÉVIGNÉ, DAUGHTER OF THE BARON DE CHANTAL,
"A WOMAN of EXTRAORDINARY GENIUS AND SOLID VIRTUE,
"COEXISTENT WITH MANY CHARMS."[1]

The character of Madame de Sévigné lies on the surface. It presents so rare an assemblage of good qualities, so nicely balanced, so admirably adapted to her position and her sex, that it is a positive injustice to her to exaggerate them: and to introduce her to the English public with a flourish of trumpets, is a palpable mistake. Unduly raised expectation prepares the way for disappointment. Knowing how fond the ladies and gentlemen of the time were of drawing what they called portraits of one another, Madame de Puliga

[1] Walckenaer (vol. iii. p. 107) gives a different version of this inscription and we think an improved one, describing her as "Femme d'un Génie extraordinaire, et d'une Vertu compatible avec la Joie et les Agréments." "Solid Virtue" is clumsy; and "la Joie" was so characteristic of her, that it was said, "La joie de son esprit en fait la force." It will also be observed that "compatible" is singular, and not connected with "Génie." Madame de Puliga, without any apparent reason, converts it into "co-existent;" and in her translations from Madame de Sévigné she too frequently forgets that the best tribute to an admired author is to translate as literally as the genius of the language will admit.

might surely have spared us the three pages and a half of fulsome flattery by Madame de la Fayette with which the first chapter opens. Could it please or elevate a sensible woman of thirty-three, with a grown-up daughter, to be addressed in this fashion :

"It is not my wish to overwhelm you with praise, nor to trifle time away by saying that your figure is perfect, that your complexion has a bloom and freshness which assures us you are but twenty; that your mouth, your teeth, and your hair are unrivalled;—no, I will not tell you all this, your mirror alone is sufficient. But as you do not waste time by consulting it, it cannot tell you how charming you are when you speak; and this is what I must reveal to you.

. . . .

"Your mind is great, noble, fitted to dispense treasures, and incapable of stooping to the care of hoarding them; you are alive to *glory and ambition,* and no less so to pleasures: you appear born for them, and they appear to have been created for you; your presence augments diversions, and diversions augment your beauty when they environ you. In short, joy is the true state of your soul, and grief is more antipathical to you than any one else. You are naturally tender and passionate, but to the shame of our sex this tenderness has been useless to you, and you have confined it to your own, in bestowing it upon Madame de la Fayette."[1]

We are sorry to say that Madame de Puliga has been led away by her enthusiasm into much the same style of vague eulogy. She insists on calling her heroine "great"; and, in a spirited Preface, frankly recapitulating her claims as a biographer, she states that one of the chief aims in this "labour of love" has been "to shew

---

[1] This portrait or *éloge* was signed "*Un Inconnu.*" It was one of many composed at the suggestion of Madame de Sablé; who one evening proposed to the circle assembled in her salon that they should all write portraits or characters of one another or themselves. Madame de Sévigné fixes the date in 1659.

Madame de Sévigné, perhaps more than has yet been done, as a woman and as a philosopher." Madame de Sévigné was not "great"; and it is because she *was* every inch a woman that she was *not* a philosopher. Greatness, combined with goodness, implies lofty aspirations, comprehensive views, the subordination of purely personal to public ends, of the present to the future, of the family to the State. Philosophy is shown by self-control, by reducing things to their just value, by never suffering feeling or sentiment to get the mastery of reason. Madame de Sévigné was the child of impulse, tremulous as an Eolian harp to every passing breeze: she lived *au jour le jour* for the objects of her affection: she was wrapped up in her family and friends: she was never in advance of her age: she had no ambition: and if (which we doubt) she was ever attracted by glory, she gave up for her daughter what was meant for mankind.

In the first Arctic expedition under Ross, when the ships were icebound, private theatricals were got up by the officers for the amusement of the crew, one of whom, disgusted at what he thought the cold applause of a comrade, exclaimed, "I call it philosophy, by God." It must be from the same spirit of enthusiasm that the term "philosopher" has been applied as a term of praise to Madame de Sévigné.

The history of the famous Letters, including the times and manner of publication, is one of the most curious things relating to them. Epistolary excellence was not confined to Madame de Sévigné. Several of her female contemporaries rivalled her. Sainte-Beuve instances Madame de Coulanges, along with whom he might have named Madame de la Fayette; and Walpole says that, when he first fell in with Madame de Maintenon's letters, they made him jealous for his favourite. This may account, in some measure, for the little care taken of them by her correspondents; and she kept no copies. Bussy alone estimated them at their true value from the first: enlightened, doubtless, by their association with his own. The two cousins never came to a permanent breach, because they felt that they understood each other better than any one else understood either of them. When they clashed, it was like flint and steel, striking out sparks. Even when he persisted in writing to her in a manner which she disapproved, she could not make up her mind to forego the pleasure of the correspondence, but simply gave him warning that she would show all his letters to her aunt. She told him, "Vous êtes le *fagot* de mon esprit," *i.e.*, the fire-lighter or fire-reviver.

Portions of their correspondence were published in his "Mémoires" in 1694. Bayle, then at work on his Dictionary, was so struck by her share of it, that he wrote to a friend at Paris to inquire about her, saying, "I see nobody who doubts that the letters of Madame de Sévigné are better than Bussy-Rabutin's. This lady had a great deal of sense and wit. She deserves a place amongst the illustrious women of our age. . . . I should be very glad to know something of her history; I would willingly put her into my Dictionary." He did not carry out this resolution; and thirty-one years elapsed before any more of her letters were unearthed. Then they began to come out mysteriously and by driblets. First, "Lettres Choisies de la Marquise de Sévigné à Madame de Grignan sa Fille," published in 1725 by a printer of Troyes; no named editor; a volume of seventy-five pages, containing thirty-one letters or fragments of letters. Secondly, two volumes with the same title, in

1726, reprinted twice within the year, as well as an edition containing forty-three letters more, both by known, although not named, editors.[1] Eight years afterwards came the edition by the Abbé Perrin in six volumes, extended to eight volumes in 1754. The Abbé took strange liberties with his text, altering and suppressing at will; yet the learned and polite world were obliged to rest satisfied with the Letters in this unsatisfactory state, till the appearance of the first Monmerqué edition of 1843. That, so garbled and mutilated, they fascinated the most fastidious critics of the eighteenth century, is a decisive proof of their inherent excellence:

> "You may break, you may ruin the vase, if you will,
> But the scent of the roses will hang round it still."

"Then you have undone yourself with me," writes Walpole to Mann in 1749; "for you compare them (his own letters) to Madame de Sévigné's: absolute treason! Do you know there is scarce a book in the world I love so much as her Letters." They were adopted as the model of his own. "Her style," says Mackintosh, "is evidently copied, not only by her worshipper, Walpole, but even by Gray: notwithstanding the extraordinary merit of his matter, he has the double stiffness of an imitator and of a college recluse."

The main sources of their popularity may be the anecdotes, the historical sketches, the traits of character and manners, the witty sayings and fine reflections, that abound in them; but their distinctive charm to the amateur is their freshness, their vivacity, their high-bred ease and grace, the colloquial flow of the language—her art of pleasing

---

[1] Brunet, "Manuel du Libraire," 1864. But see Walckenaer, vol. iii. p. 344; and the *Notice* prefixed to the abridged edition of 1870. Perrin was the first editor who had the consent and co-operation of the family.

without ever once thinking about it—*son art de plaire, et de n'y penser pas*—of interspersing the simplest domestic details with sparkling turns and fancies, like the princess in the fairy tale who could not comb her hair without strewing the floor with pearls. They are conversation in writing, which (we agree with M. Suard) all letters from absent friends or relatives, with no definite end, should be. We almost fancy that we hear her talk as we are reading them, and we become attached to her as to a companion who brightens or lightens every topic that we touch upon. How well we can picture to ourselves her meeting her German friend the Princesse de Tarente (who was constantly in mourning for some scion of royalty) in colours, and saying to her with a curtsey, "*Madame, je me réjouis de la santé de l'Europe*": or orally concluding her account of the exiled Stuarts at St. Germain with the remark, "Pour le Roi d'Angleterre il y paroît content, *et c'est pour cela qu'il est là :*" or leaning her head upon her hand as she lets drop, "There may be so great a weight of obligation that there is no way of being delivered from it but by ingratitude." Her story of the Archbishop of Rheims (Tellier) might be told with good effect at a dinner-table:

"The archbishop was returning at a great pace from Saint-Germain—with a rush like a whirlwind. If he thinks himself a great lord, his people think him a still greater. He was rattling through Nanterre, *tra, tra, tra.* They met a man on horseback, *gare! gare! gare!* The poor man wishes to get out of the way: his horse does not, and so the coach and six horses knock the poor man and the horse head-over-heels, and pass over them, so completely over them, that the coach was overturned and turned upside down (*versé et renversé*); whilst the man and the horse, seeing no fun in having their bones broken, get up again as if by miracle, remount, the one upon the other, and take to their heels, and are running still, whilst the lackeys, and the coachman, and the archbishop himself are bawling after him : ' Stop the rascal ! stop him ! Give him a hundred lashes.' "

The Archbishop, in telling her the story, said :

"If I had caught that scoundrel, I would have broken his arms and cut off his ears ! "

Her reflections on the death of Louvois sound like spoken eloquence :

"He is no more then, this powerful and superb minister, whose *moi* occupied so much space—was the centre of so many things ! What interests to disentangle, what intrigues to follow, what negotiations to conclude ! . . . 'O my God ! a little time yet ! I want to humiliate the Duke of Savoy, to crush the Prince of Orange : one moment more.' No, you shall not have a moment, not one ! "

We do not doubt her when she says, *J'écrirais jusqu'à demain : mes pensées, ma plume, mon encre, tout vole.*" Yet whilst her thoughts, her pen, her ink are flying—whilst she is covering the ground at an archiepiscopal pace, she scatters maxims which Rochefoucauld or Vauvenargues would have meditated on for months without improving them:

" Les longues maladies, usent la douleur, et les longues espérances usent la joie !

" On n'a jamais pris longtemps l'ombre pour le corps : *il faut être, si l'on veut paraître.* Le monde n'a point de longues injustices ! "

Had Johnson read this when he laid down that, when the world thinks long about a matter, it generally thinks right ? She wrote of de Retz :

"Mon Dieu, qu'il est heureux ! que j'envierais quelquefois son épouvantable tranquillité sur tous les devoirs de la vie ! *On se ruine quand on veut s'acquitter !*"

Sir James Mackintosh, after finishing the perusal of her letters, sets down in his Journal:

"The great charm of her character seems to me a natural virtue. In what she does, as well as in what she says, she is unforced and unstudied: nobody, I think, had so much morality without restraint, or played so with amiable failings without falling into vice. Her ingenuous, lively, social disposition gave the direction to her mental power. She has so filled my heart with affectionate interest in her as a living friend that I can scarcely bring myself to think of her as being a writer, or as having a style; but she has become a celebrated, probably an immortal, writer, without expecting it: she is the only classical writer who never conceived the possibility of acquiring fame. Without a great power of style, she could not have communicated those feelings to others. In what does that talent consist?"

Want of space would prevent our speculating on this question were we ever so much inclined to it. But there is little use in analysing any talent or genius which is confessedly inimitable. "We expect," wrote Macaulay, "to see fresh Humes and fresh Burkes before we again fall in with that peculiar combination of moral and intellectual qualities to which the writings of Walpole owe their extraordinary popularity." We expect to see fresh Madame de Staëls, fresh Mrs. Somervilles, fresh George Sands, fresh George Eliots, before we again fall in with that rich and essentially feminine organisation to which the letters of Madame de Sévigné owe their extraordinary charm.

SAINT-SIMON.[1]

(*From the Quarterly Review, October,* 1875.)

We wonder why the ingenious gentleman who recently published a series of essays on "famous books" little read, did not include the Memoirs of Saint-Simon, one of the most striking specimens of the class. Considering their wide-spread renown and extraordinary merit, it is quite startling to find how few, at least in this country, of even the cultivated or literary class, have attempted a regular conscientious perusal, or indeed have done more than glance over a few chapters in an idle desultory way. The portentous length, the vast extent of ground to be got over, is one reason. Nineteen volumes, averaging from 450 to 500 closely-printed pages each, are enough to stagger the most eager amateur of bygone scandal or the most resolute searcher after the neglected truths of history.

But there have been other reasons for the tardy acceptance of these memoirs, for their long-delayed and still limited popularity, besides their length; and they present in this respect a curious contrast to the memoirs which have made most

---

[1] *Mémoires du Duc de Saint-Simon. Publiés par MM. Chéruel et Ad Regnier, fils, et collationnés de nouveau pour cette édition sur le manuscript autographe. Avec une notice de M. de Sainte-Beuve.* Paris, librairie Hachette et Cie. 1873–1875 (Nineteen volumes, without the Index).

noise in our time—memoirs written in obvious imitation of them, and falling as far short of the almost avowed model in knowledge of subject, insight into character, fine observation, and descriptive or analytic power, as in piquancy and originality. Mr. Charles Greville's Journals were published within ten years of his death, when the scandals they commemorated were fresh, at least fresh enough to injure or annoy: when the abundant depreciation and abuse could be keenly felt by the victims or their families, and as keenly relished by contemporaries always more alive to satire or censure than to praise. Now, the Memoirs of Saint-Simon do not come down further than 1723: he did not die till 1755; and immediately after his death, the Government laid an embargo on them on the plea that, he having filled a diplomatic mission, they must be partly of an official character. During many years it was only by special favour that friends of the minister for the time being obtained a sight of the manuscript, which consisted of eight large folio volumes of very close writing, all in the author's own hand. Partial access was permitted to Duclos and Marmontel, in their capacity of historiographers; and M. de Choiseul lent some of the volumes to Madame du Deffand.

According to the Marquis de Saint-Simon, "it was only in 1788, and on the eve of the revolution, that the Abbé Soulavie obtained leave to make some extracts and publish some fragments: a supplement, which he added in 1789, was followed by some other publication equally truncated."[1]

[1] Advertisement to the edition of 1842, edited by the Marquis de Saint-Simon, the representative of the family through a collateral branch, and the possessor of the original manuscript. All Saint-Simon's manuscripts were left by will to a cousin of the same name, the Bishop of Metz, without specifying the Memoirs. Soulavie's principal publication was

According to Sainte-Beuve, "it was starting from 1784 that the publicity of the memoirs began to make progress; but timidly, stealthily, by disconnected anecdotes and by bits. From 1788 to 1791, then later in 1818, there appeared successively extracts more or less voluminous, mutilated, and garbled." The Marquise de Créquy, apropos of one of these compilations, wrote, February 7, 1787, to Senac de Meilhan: "The 'Memoirs of Saint-Simon' are in the hands of the censor; of six volumes they will hardly make three, and it is enough." Again, September 28, 1788: "I apprise you that the 'Memoirs of Saint-Simon' are out, but much mutilated, if I am to judge from what I have seen in three great green bundles (*tapons*), and there were six. Madame de Turpin died: there I stuck fast: it is badly written, but our taste for the age of Louis XIV. renders the details precious to us."

In much the same tone Madame du Deffand had written to Walpole (December 2, 1770): "The Memoirs of Saint-Simon are always amusing; and as I prefer reading them in company, the perusal will last long. It would amuse you, though the style is abominable and the portraits ill drawn. The author was not a man of talent (*homme d'esprit*), but as he was *au fait* of everything, the things he relates are curious and interesting; I wish I could get you the reading of them."

Few writers suffer more than Saint-Simon from being read in fragments; his effects depend on the fulness and completeness of his narratives and

"Œuvres complètes du Duc de Saint-Simon contenant ses Mémoires sur le règne de Louis XIV., sur la régence du Duc d'Orléans et sur le règne de Louis XV.," etc. 13 vols., 8vo. Paris, 1790. In the "Biographie Universelle" it is termed "the most precious and the only authentic publication of this *littérateur*."

delineations; and we are therefore not surprised at the disadvantageous impression of the general public at the earlier periods of their acquaintance with him. But Madame du Deffand's estimate was formed from the original manuscript; and we know no plausible mode of accounting for it except that suggested by Sainte-Beuve, who remarks that "the style of Saint-Simon was too pointedly revolting to the habits of written style in the eighteenth century, and was spoken of pretty nearly as Fénélon spoke of the style of Molière and 'this multitude of metaphors not far removed from *galimatias*.' All the fine world of that time had done their rhetoric more or less in Voltaire."

In other letters, Madame du Deffand's admiration rises to enthusiasm: she tells Walpole that, if present at the readings, he would experience ineffable pleasure, that he would be fairly beside himself with delight; although she must have known that Walpole, the most fastidious of critics, was the least likely of her whole round of lettered correspondents to be amused by ill-drawn portraits in an abominable style. Voltaire, too, piqued by a contemptuous reference to himself, or foreseeing how much his superficial " Siècle de Louis XIV." must eventually suffer from collation, did his best to undermine the coming influence and authority of the memoirs, by announcing an intention to refute on their publication everything that had been inspired by prejudice or hate. Had he lived to execute this intention, he might certainly have hit many blots which the author has frankly told us would probably be discovered in his work. In a *Conclusion*, which might serve for a preface, Saint-Simon says:

"Next for impartiality: this point, so essential, and regarded as so difficult, I fear not to say impossible, for one who writes what he has seen and mixed in. We are charmed by straightforward and true people: we are irritated by the rogues who swarm in courts; we are still more so against those who have injured us. The Stoic is a fine and noble chimera. I do not then pique myself on impartiality, it would be vain. . . . At the same time I will do myself this justice, that I have been infinitely on my guard against my affections and my aversions, and most against the latter, so as not to speak of the objects of either without the balance in hand, to exaggerate nothing, to distrust myself as an enemy, to render an exact justice, and place the purest truth in broad relief. It is in this manner that I feel confident I have been entirely impartial, and I believe there is no other mode of being so."

Saint-Simon lived thirty-two years after the conclusion of the memoirs,[1] and was constantly employed in correcting and completing them. They contain no flying rumours: no transitory impressions: no hasty, ill considered, inconsistent views of men or events. He sets down nothing that he has not carefully verified or thoroughly thought out.

"As regards the exactitude of what I relate, it is made clear by the memoirs themselves that almost all is taken from what has passed through my hands, and the rest from what I have known through those who had managed the things I report. I name them; and their names as well as my intimate connection with them are beyond suspicion. That which I have learned from an inferior source, I mark: and that of which I am ignorant, I am not ashamed to own. In this fashion the memoirs are authentic at first hand. Their truth cannot be called in doubt; and I believe I may say that there have hitherto been none comprising a greater number of different matters, more weighed, more detailed, or forming a more instructive or more curious group. As I shall see nothing of it, this concerns me little; but if these memoirs see the light, I doubt not of their exciting a prodigious revolt."

[1] He died March 2nd, 1755.

If they had been published in full at any period prior to the revolution of 1789, the revolt, the outcry, with the resulting sale and circulation, would have been prodigious. But they were kept back till not only the personages who figure in his pages, but the society, the class interests, the entire state of things of which he treats, had died out or been swept away: till their attraction was purely historical or literary, without a wounded self-love or a gratified vanity to add to it. The publication of the first complete edition was not commenced till 1829.

"The sensation," says Sainte-Beuve, "produced by the first volume was very lively; it was the greatest success since that of Walter Scott's novels. A curtain was suddenly withdrawn from the finest monarchical epoch of France, and we were present like spectators at the representation. But this success, interrupted as it was by the revolution of 1830, was obtained more in the so-called world (of Paris) than in the public, which it reached at a later period and by degrees."

This edition satisfied the public demand till 1842, and one cause of its limited success was the erroneous principle on which it was based. In neglect or defiance of Buffon's maxim, "*Le style, c'est l'homme*," the editors had taken upon themselves to correct the style to the extent of destroying its individuality and materially impairing its force. There can be no stronger proof of the enormity of their error than the marked rise in the reputation of the writer in exact proportion as he was allowed to speak in his own pointed, coloured, incisive, picturesque, tangled, and irregular language. Observing this, the editors at length made up their minds to present him as they found him.

"This new edition (so runs the advertisement) is not a simple reproduction of that which was published in 1856—

1858. M. Ad. Regnier, *fils*, sub-librarian of the institute, has made, to establish the text, a scrupulous revision of the autograph manuscript of the author, which has been followed throughout with the greatest fidelity. Even where in this manuscript the errors were evident, he has only corrected them by warning the reader each time by a note; and he has placed between brackets the words which Saint-Simon had omitted through haste. The expressions, the turns, the inaccuracies, which might offer difficulty, are explained by notes. In a word, this new edition may be considered as the most exact reproduction that has hitherto been made of an author who, in spite of his grammatical irregularities, has deserved to be placed in the number of the great writers of France."

To convey an impression of his peculiarities we shall translate as literally as is consistent with a due regard to idiom; and it should be kept in mind that he was fully conscious of his defects. The last paragraph of the *Conclusion* runs thus:

"I was never of an academic turn, and I have been unable to get rid of the habit of writing rapidly. *To render my style more correct and more agreeable by correcting it, this would be to recast all the work, and this labour would be beyond my strength, it would run the risk of being ' ingrat.'* To correct well what one has written, one must know how to write well; it will easily be seen here that I have had no right to pique myself on it. I have thought only of the exactness and the truth. I venture to say that both are found strictly in my memoirs, that they are the law and the soul of them, and that the style merits a benign indulgence on their account. There is so much the more want of it that I cannot promise it better for the continuation which I propose to myself."

This paragraph will be found to have an important bearing on a question touching the plan, commencement and completion of the work, which was raised by the publication of Dangeau's Journal with the so-called Additions of Saint-Simon.[1]

[1] "Journal du Marquis de Dangeau, publié en entier pour la première

Beginning with 1684, and ending at the author's death in 1720, this journal comprises a brief barren record of the incidents of each day noted down each evening. "It is difficult" (remarks Saint-Simon) "to conceive how a man could have the patience and the perseverance to write such a work every day for more than fifty years, so meagre, so dry, so constrained, so cautious, so literal." He states that he did not see the journal till after Dangeau's death; and it did not come into the possession of the Duc de Luynes, who gave him his interleaved copy, till 1729, six years after the formal conclusion of Saint-Simon's Memoirs and thirty-eight years after their commencement.

Nothing is more common than for a man partially to resume a subject on which he has already written, or on taking up the life or diary of a contemporary, to dash off notes in amplification or correction of statements that excite or irritate him. Swift's marginal notes on Burnet are a familiar example. The perusal of Dangeau's Journal must have recalled many a half-forgotten episode, or occasionally opened a flood-tide of associations, which Saint-Simon hastened to fix without pausing to see whether this was not a superfluous labour. It would be, when so carried away, that he would be most liable to repetition or irregularity.[1] "When," says Sainte-Beuve, "he writes notes and commentaries on the Journal of Dangeau, he writes as one does for notes, flying (*à la volée*), heaping up and crowding the words, wishing to say everything at once and in the shortest space. I have elsewhere compared this petulance and this precipitation of

fois par MM. Soulié, Dussieux, de Chennevières, Mantz, de Montaiglon, avec les Additions inédites du Duc de Saint-Simon, publiées par M. Feuillet de Conches." Dix-neuf tomes. Paris, 1854–1860.

[1] He occasionally relates the same incidents twice over in the "Memoirs" —*e.g.* the quarrel between Louis and Louvois about the window.

things under his pen to an abundant spring struggling and bubbling through a narrow channel." Speaking of the effect of an abundance of ideas on style, Swift says: "So people come faster out of a church when it is almost empty than when a crowd is at the door."

It may readily be granted that, in the final revision of his memoirs, Saint-Simon turned these notes to account or borrowed some dates and facts from the journal; but that these notes or additions were the basis of his memoirs, or that he was indebted to any appreciable extent to Dangeau for their conception or mode of execution, strikes us to be an utterly untenable theory. Yet the editors of Dangeau (five in number) concur in stating that "the additions of Saint-Simon form incontestably *the first thought* of his magnificent memoirs;" and amongst other startling propositions in Mr. Reeve's elaborate essay, entitled "Saint-Simon," in his "Royal and Republican France," we find that "without Dangeau the Memoirs of Saint-Simon would perhaps never have existed in their complete form:" that "these notes (the additions) must be regarded as the basis of the memoirs;" and that "the fact that the memoirs *were written subsequently to the additions* is proved by innumerable circumstances to which we shall presently have occasion to refer."[1]

The utmost to which these innumerable circumstances amount is that, as was inevitable in contemporary memoirs or diaries, the same names, facts, dates and events constantly recur in both. "It would be tedious," remarks Mr. Reeve, after

[1] "Royal and Republican France: a series of Essays reprinted from the 'Edinburgh,' 'Quarterly,' and British and Foreign Reviews." By Henry Reeve, Corresponding Member of the French Institute. In two volumes. 1872. The essay on Saint-Simon is reprinted from the 'Edinburgh Review' for January, 1864.

quoting two or three instances, "to pursue this species of comparison any further, but every page of these vast collections might furnish similar examples. Dangeau supplies the simple fact, succinctly stated with chronological accuracy, and we believe that Saint-Simon seldom names a person or relates an occurrence (except those personal to himself) which do not occur in Dangeau's Diaries; but he immediately amplifies the event. He breathes life into those dead figures."

There is absolutely nothing in this coincidence, considering that the two men were dealing with the same period, the same society, and the same class of occurrences. After some depreciating remarks on Dangeau, Saint-Simon adds:

"With all this, his memoirs are full of facts not noticed in the gazettes; they will gain value as they grow old; *they will be of great use to any one who seeks to write with more solidity for an accurate chronology and to avoid confusion.*"

"It is impossible," says Mr. Reeve, commenting on this passage, "to acquit him of some want of candour in this reference to a work by which he himself largely benefited. Nobody would infer from this passage, and indeed the discovery has only been made very recently, that Saint-Simon alludes to himself in the sentence we have printed in italics. He it was who, undertaking to write the history of the period with greater solidity, condescended to borrow from Dangeau at least the chronological order of his narrative. But before we enter upon the proof of this curious species of plagiarism (if so it can be called) we must trace the history of the journal itself."

To assert that Saint-Simon largely benefited by the work is begging the whole question. In saying that it will be of great use for an accurate chronology, he merely means, of great use in verifying dates. How does this show that he borrowed the chronological order of his narrative? And what is that chronological order? Neither more nor less than the ordinary succession of days, months, and years. Can this be a subject of copyright? Is it not common property? As well accuse a writer who was verifying dates of plagiarising from the "Court Circular" or the "Annual Register."

Strange to say, Mr. Reeve, who lays so much stress on coincidence and chronological order, has fallen into a chronological error which materially affects his authority. "It may deserve to be noted that the Memoirs of Saint-Simon are not the memoirs of his life, nor did he ever intend that they should embrace the whole of that protracted period. They commence in 1695 with his entry into public life; they end in 1723 with the death of the Regent. The whole extent of them, therefore, is confined to twenty-eight years; although Saint-Simon lived thirty-two years after the event at which he brought them to a close."

They commence with his entry into public life (*i.e.* the army) early in 1691. The event at which he brought them to a close occurred on the 21st December, 1723. They therefore comprise thirty-three years, wanting two or three months. Mr. Reeve also states that "the first ten chapters of the memoirs are remarkably incoherent, as if the author had not yet settled the plan he was finally to adopt." These ten chapters include 1691, 1692, 1693, and part of 1694, years which Mr. Reeve ignores altogether. They include the portions which Saint-Simon submitted to the Abbé de la Trappe, with a tolerably clear indication of his plan. The Memoirs prior to 1695 comprise fourteen chapters, filling 220 pages.

There is extant a letter from Saint-Simon to the Abbé de la Trappe, dated the 29th March, 1699, in which, after referring to a former communication to the effect that, for some time past, he had been working on "a set of memoirs" of his life, he requests advice as to the best manner of speaking of himself, and incloses his narrative of the Luxembourg suit as a specimen—

"This, I think, is the sharpest and bitterest thing in my memoirs, yet I have endeavoured to adhere to the most exact truth. I have copied it from them where it is recorded here and there, according to the time at which we pleaded, and I have put it all together; and instead of speaking openly, *as in my memoirs themselves*, I name myself in this copy as I name others, so that I may hereafter keep it and use it without appearing to be the author. I have also added two of my portraits as specimens of the rest." [1]

This letter and the specimens prove incontestably that, as regards form, method, and substance, the memoirs for the first eight years were originally composed as they were definitively left, and there is no ground for supposing that a different method was adopted for the rest.

Rogers, during the later years of his life, devoted so much time and care to rewriting and correcting his verses with a view to the preservation of his fame, that he was compared to an old bear keeping itself alive by sucking its paws. Horace Walpole got back the originals of his letters to Sir Horace Mann, carefully collated them with the copies he

---

[1] In reference to this communication, Mr. Reeve says: "It is one of the strangest facts of this history that the tremendous revelations of the courts of kings and of the heart of man which lay buried for nearly a century from the world, should have been whispered for the first time in a cell of La Trappe." Saint-Simon's confidential communications with La Trappe ended with the life of his friend, the founder, who died October 26th, 1700; so that, if these tremendous revelations were first whispered at La Trappe, they could hardly have been first suggested by Dangeau.

had regularly kept, added a few touches, and left a fair transcript (mostly in his best handwriting) for posterity. Saint-Simon, judging from the condition of his manuscript, followed a similar course: he sometimes availed himself of subsequently acquired knowledge to complete a biographical notice or an historical summary; but to contend that because an occurrence posterior to 1730 is mentioned or introduced, the whole or the greater part of the memoirs must have been written subsequently to that date, is what Partridge would call a *non sequitur*: a logical device of which we have had abundant examples in this controversy. Saint-Simon mentions Voltaire as "devenu grand poëte et academicien." Voltaire did not become an Academician till April, 1746. Are we to conclude that the Memoirs were not in existence before then? Then, what becomes of the internal evidence—from fire, passion and vivacity—that the impressions were set down when they were fresh?

Mr. Reeve writes with confidence and authority: French critics of note have taken the same side; and Saint-Simon's place in literature, as well as his character for truth and honour, materially depends on the adoption or rejection of their theory. We had therefore no alternative but to state and examine the grounds on which it rests.

Although Saint-Simon, contrary to his avowed intention in 1723, left his memoirs incomplete, they comprise all the stirring and active passages of his life; and a brief recapitulation of these strikes us to be the best mode of conveying a correct impression of his character and position, an accurate understanding of which is indispensable to a just appreciation of his writings.

He was born, he tells us, on the night of the 15th January, 1675, the only son of Claude, Duc de Saint-Simon, peer of France, by a second wife, Charlotte de l'Aubespine. The title he bore from his birth was Vidame de Chartres, and he was brought up with the greatest care by his mother, a woman of sense and virtue. She made it (he says) her especial care to save him from the common fate of young men of assured rank and fortune, who, becoming their own masters at an early age, are thrown upon the world without natural protectors or advisers. Her anxiety on this score was enhanced by the advanced age of his father (nearly seventy at his birth), and the state of the family, which consisted of a paternal uncle eight years older that the Duc, and two maternal uncles, the one disreputable and the other ruined.

"She exerted herself to raise my courage, and excite me to become capable of repairing by my own energies voids so difficult to surmount. She succeeded in inspiring me with a great desire of it. She was not seconded by my taste for study and the sciences; but that which was innate in me for reading and history, and consequently to do and become something by emulation and the examples that I found in it (*i.e.* history), compensated this coldness for letters; and I have always thought that, if they had made me lose less time in the one (letters), and made me make a serious study of the other (history), I should have been able to become something in it."

This passage exhibits his exact state of mind and manner of writing at the commencement of the memoirs, before he had acquired the confidence in which he was by no means deficient in after life, or the vigour, fertility, and variety of expression which throw confused metaphors and harsh phraseology into the shade.

"This reading of history, and especially of particular memoirs of our own history of the later times since Francis the First, inspired me with the envy of writing those of what I might see, in the desire and hope of being something, and of knowing as well as I could the affairs of my time. The inconveniences did not fail to present themselves to my mind; but the firm resolution to keep them to myself appeared to me to provide for all. *I accordingly began in July*, 1694, being *mestre de camp* of a regiment of cavalry of my name, in the camp of Guenischeim (Germersheim), on the old Rhine, in the army commanded by the Marshal Duke of Lorges."

In a subsequent passage he states (what must also be false if the Dangeau theory be true) that the direct inspiration came from the Memoirs of Bassompierre. He entered the army in 1691, in his sixteenth year, more (he confesses) from a wish to get rid of his master in philosophy than from military ardour. The siege of Mons, formed by the King in person, had attracted all his young contemporaries for their first campaign; and what piqued him most was that, conspicuous amongst these was the Duc de Chartres, eight months younger than himself, with whom he had been partially bred up and had contracted as close an intimacy as the difference of rank allowed. After vainly trying his mother, he obtained the concurrence of his father, by representing that the King, having undertaken so great a siege this year, would repose the next, and that thus a brilliant opportunity would be lost or indefinitely postponed.

It was the rule for all young men of rank who entered the service, with the exception of the princes of the blood, to serve a year in one of the two companies of mousquetaires, and then as captain of a troop of cavalry or subaltern in the King's own regiment of infantry, before they were permitted to purchase a regiment. The first step, therefore, was for his father to take him to Versailles and present him as a candidate for a nomination in the mousquetaires. The King, remarking his slight stature and delicate appearance, objected that he was too young; to which it was adroitly replied that he would serve his Majesty the longer: thereupon his father was requested to name which regiment he preferred, and the nomination followed in due course.

We do not see how the siege of Mons could have been employed as an argument with his father, for it took place in the spring of 1691; and he complacently records that, when he was a mousquetaire of three months' standing in March of the following year, he mounted guard at Compiégne and was apprised of the royal intention to take the field again.

"My joy was extreme, but my father, who had not counted on this, repented having been overpersuaded by me, and made me feel it! My mother, after a little temper and pouting at my having been enrolled against her wish, was unwearied in bringing him to reason, and in having me supplied with an equipage of thirty-five horses or mules, and with wherewithal to live honourably on my means morning and evening. It was not without a provoking *contretemps* which fell out precisely twenty days before my departure."

The family steward had levanted with fifty thousand francs due to tradespeople whom he had returned in his accounts as paid.

Saint-Simon's equipment is prominently introduced by Macaulay in his animated and ornate description of the siege of Namur. "A single circumstance may suffice to give a notion of the pomp and luxury of his (the French king's) camp. Among the musketeers of his household rode, for the first time, a stripling of seventeen, who soon afterwards succeeded to the title of Duke of Saint-Simon, and to whom we owe those inestimable memoirs which have preserved, for the instruction and delight of many lands and of many generations, the vivid pictures of a France which has long passed away. Though the boy's family was then pressed for money, he travelled with thirty-five horses and sumpter-mules."[1] All the particulars of his first campaign are interesting :

"The King started on the 10th May, 1692, with the ladies, and I made the journey on horseback with the troops and all the service, like the other mousquetaires. I was accompanied by two gentlemen; the one, of long standing in the family, had been my governor, the other was my mother's equerry. The King's army was encamped at Gevries; that of M. de Luxembourg almost joined it. The ladies were at Mons, two leagues off. The King brought them to his camp, where he feasted them, and then treated them to the sight of the most superb review that probably has ever been seen of these two armies drawn up in two lines."

The tents of the Court, pitched in a meadow, were well-nigh inundated by the rain, which, he says, descended in torrents during the whole of the siege, greatly enhancing the reputation of St. Médard (the French St. Swithin) whose feast-day is the 8th of June. The soldiers uttered imprecations against the saint, and made a search for his images, of which they broke or burnt as many as they could find. The roads became impassable for carts or carriages, and Luxembourg's army was reduced to the same extremity for want of corn and forage as the English before Sebastopol. To lessen their privations, orders

[1] "History," vol. iv. p. 268. It appears from p. 65 that William's headquarters also were enlivened by a crowd of splendid equipages, and by a rapid succession of sumptuous banquets. In Shadwell's "Volunteers," the representative character has a train of cooks and confectioners, a waggon-load of plate, a rich wardrobe, and tent furniture chosen by a committee of fine ladies.

were given to the cavalry of the household to carry them sacks of grain, a duty which they deemed degrading to their dignity as a privileged corps. The first party told off for it positively refused; and the second were on the verge of mutiny, when the young Vidame sprang from his saddle, shouldered a sack, and laid it across the crupper of his horse. Clapping him on the shoulder and naming him, the commandant loudly demanded which of them could feel hurt or dishonoured by doing what was not disdained by the eldest son of a Duke, and his example was emulously followed by the troop. When this affair was reported at head-quarters it attracted the favourable notice of the King, who during the rest of the siege made a point of saying something civil to the young mousquetaire whenever an occasion offered. The citadel, which held out three weeks longer than the town, surrendered July 1st, 1692, and the Court returned to Versailles.

"On the 3rd of May, 1693, the King announced that he was going to Flanders to take the command of one of his armies as before; and that same day," says Saint-Simon, "about ten in the evening, I had the misfortune to lose my father, who was eighty-seven, and was dead almost as soon as he was taken ill: there was no more oil in the lamp." His feelings and proceedings on this event are thus related:

"I heard the sad news on returning from the *coucher* of the King, who was to purge the next day. *The night was given to the just sentiments of nature.* The next day I went betimes to find Bontemps (first valet-de-chambre), then the Duc de Beauvillier, who was in waiting and whose father had been the friend of mine. M. de Beauvillier showed me a thousand kindnesses with the princes whose governor he was, and promised to ask the King for my father's governments for me on opening the King's curtain. He obtained them at once. Bontemps, much attached to my father, hastened to tell me in the tribune where I was waiting; then M. de Beauvillier himself, who told me to be in the gallery at three, where he would send for me and have me introduced through the Cabinets, when the King had done dinner.

"I found the crowd had left the chamber. As soon as Monsieur (the Dauphin), who was standing at the foot of the King's bed, perceived me, 'Ah!' he exclaimed aloud; 'M. le Duc de Saint-Simon.' I approached the bed and made my acknowledgment by a low bow. The King inquired how this misfortune had happened, with much goodness for my father and myself; he knew how to season his favours. He spoke to me of the sacrament, which my father had been unable to take. I replied that only a short time since he had made a retreat of some days to Saint-Lazare, where he had his confessor and fulfilled his devotions; and I spoke of the piety of his life. The colloquy lasted some time, and ended by exhortations to continue to act wisely and well, and that he would take care of me."

It would seem that there was little time to lose or devote to the just sentiments of nature, for during a preceding illness of the father many had asked the King for his governments; d'Aubigné, Madame de Maintenon's brother, amongst others, to whom the King replied with unwonted sharpness, "Has he not a son?"

Starting with the reflection that birth and property do not always go together, Saint-Simon proceeds to explain how his father, having begun as a page to Louis XIII., rose to high favour, obtained valuable employments, and was created duke and peer. The stepping-stone of his fortunes was his adroitness in enabling the King, who was passionately fond of hunting, to change horses without putting foot to ground. This was effected by placing the tail of one parallel to the head of the other. Saint-Simon mentions this service with no apparent consciousness that it might have been performed equally well by a groom; and he relates an instance of his father's undue eagerness to curry favour, which a son bred in a purer atmosphere, or more sensitive to the family honour, would have been glad to suppress. The King was enamoured of one of the maids of honour, Mdlle. d'Hautefort, and was constantly talking about her to Saint-Simon *père*, who (says the son) could not understand how a king could be so pre-occupied by a passion and make no attempt to gratify it.

"He attributed it to timidity; and on this principle, one day when the King was speaking passionately of this young lady, my father proposed to be his ambassador, and bring the affair to a speedy conclusion. The King let him say on; then assuming a severe air: 'It is true,' he said, 'that I am in love with her; that I feel it; that I seek her; that I take pleasure in talking about her, and that I think of her still more. It is true, also, that all this comes to pass in me in my own despite, because I am a man and have this weakness; but the more my quality of king gives me extraordinary facilities for gratifying my passion, so much the more ought I to be on my guard against the scandal and the sin. I pardon you this time on account of your youth; but let me never hear you address similar language to me again if you value my affection.'

"It was a thunderclap to my father; the scales fell from his eyes; the idea of the King's timidity in his love disappeared in the brightness of a virtue so pure and so triumphant."

Although Saint-Simon labours hard to make it appear that his father, on being made duke and peer, was rather *arrivé* than *parvenu*, this was not the opinion of contemporaries. Malherbe thus mentions his first promotion in a letter to Peirex,

19th December, 1626: "You have heard of the dismissal of Barradas (first equerry to Louis XIII.). We have a Sieur Simon, page of the same stable, who has taken his place. It is a young lad of eighteen or thereabouts. The bad conduct of the other will be a lesson to him, and his fall an example to do better."

His father's death proved no interruption to his military duties. Immediately after the fulfilment of the last offices, he started for Mons where the army was to muster, being now a captain in the Royal Roussillon regiment of cavalry.

"The King set out on the 18th May (1693) with the ladies, made a halt of eight or ten days with them at Quesnoy, then sent them to Namur, and went on the 2nd June to place himself at the head of Marshal Bouffler's army, with which, on the 7th, he occupied the camp of Gemblours, so that his left was close to M. de Luxembourg's right, and people could pass from one to the other in safety. The Prince of Orange was encamped at the Abbey of Parc in such a manner that he could not receive supplies, and could not move out without having the two armies of the King upon his hands. He hastily entrenched himself, and thoroughly repented of having suffered himself to be so promptly driven to the wall. It has been ascertained since that he wrote several times to the Prince de Vaudemont, his intimate friend, that he was lost, and that he could only escape by a miracle. His army was inferior to the least of the King's, both of which were abundantly supplied with equipages, provisions, and artillery, and, as may be believed, were masters of the campaign."

Such being the position with the whole season for active operations before him, on the 8th June, the day after his arrival in camp, Louis suddenly announced to Luxembourg that he should return in person to Versailles, and that the bulk of the force under Boufflers would be sent to Germany under Monseigneur.

"The surprise of Luxembourg was unparalleled. He represented the facility of forcing the entrenchments of the Prince of Orange; of completely defeating him with one of the two armies, and following up the victory with the other. . . . But the resolution was taken. Luxembourg, in despair at seeing so glorious and easy a campaign, went down on both knees before the King, but could obtain nothing. Madame de Maintenon had vainly endeavoured to hinder the King's journey: she feared the absences; and so happy an opening of the campaign would have detained him long to gather the laurels himself: her tears at their separation, her letters after his departure, were the most potent, and carried the day against the most pressing reasons of State policy, of war, of glory. . . .

"The effect of this retreat was incredible, even amongst the common soldiers and the people. The general officers could not be altogether silent, and the rest spoke loudly of it with a licence which could not be restrained. The enemy neither could nor would restrain their surprise and their joy."

Macaulay, citing Saint-Simon—who is indeed the sole well-informed and trustworthy authority for the facts—contrives to give them a turn so as to palliate the bad strategy of William and put the worst possible interpretation on the weakness of Louis. "William (he says) had this year been able to assemble in good time a force, inferior indeed to that which was opposed to him, but still formidable. With this force he took his post near Louvain, on the road between the two threatened cities (Liége and Brussels) and watched every movement of the enemy." This gives no notion of the dangerous position he really occupied. As regards the motive of Louis' retreat: "The ignominious truth was too evident to be concealed. He had gone to the Netherlands in the hope that he might again be able to snatch some military glory without any hazard to his person, and had hastened back rather than expose himself to the chances of a pitched field." [1]

Nor was this, Macaulay adds, the first time that His Most Christian Majesty had shown the same kind of prudence. Seventeen years before, when opposed to the same antagonist under the walls of Bouchain, a similar opportunity offered of ending the war in a day. "The King called his lieutenants round him, and collected their opinions. Some cowardly officers, to whom a hint of his wishes had been dexterously conveyed, had, *blushing and stammering with shame*, voted against fighting. It was to no purpose that bold and honest men, who prized his honour more than his life, had proved to him that on all the pinciples of the military art he ought to accept the challenge rashly given." This, again, is a passage from Saint-Simon, coloured and exaggerated. He states that "Louvois, to intimidate the council, spoke first, like a reporter, to dissuade the battle." Three out of the four marshals present agreed with him; and in recommending the bolder course, the Marshal de Lorges, Saint-Simon's father-in-law, stood alone. The retreat on this occasion was generally attributed to Louvois, of whom Madame de Sévigné writes in the same year (1676), "Aire is taken; it is M. de Louvois who has all the honour. He has full power, and orders the advance and retreat of armies as he thinks fit."

After describing the manner in which Louvois was wont to dictate to commanders like Condé

[1] Vol. iv. pp. 401-403. Burnet says that "the French king, seeing that the practices of treachery on which he chiefly relied (for taking Liége) succeeded so ill, resolved not to venture himself in any dangerous enterprise, so he and the ladies went back to Versailles."—"History of his own Time," vol. iii. p. 153.

and Luxembourg, Macaulay says that he had become odious to Louis, and to her (Madame de Maintenon) who governed Louis. "On *the last occasion* on which the King and the minister transacted business together, the ill-humour on both sides broke violently forth. The servant in his vexation dashed his portfolio on the ground. The master forgetting (what he seldom forgot) that a king should be a gentleman, lifted his cane. Fortunately his wife was present. She, with her usual prudence, caught his arm. She then got Louvois out of the room, and exhorted him to come back the next day as if nothing had happened. The next day he came, but with death in his face. The King, though full of resentment, was touched with pity, and advised Louvois to go home and take care of himself. *That evening* the great minister died." The authorities cited are Burnet, Dangeau, and Saint-Simon, and not a hint is given of the slightest doubt as to the facts. But Saint-Simon tells a totally different story, and places the scene of violence in 1689 (two years before the death of Louvois), after the proposal of Louvois to burn Trèves had been set aside by the King.

"Some days afterwards, Louvois, who had the fault of obstinacy, and who had been led by experience not to doubt of carrying his point, came as usual to work with the King at Madame de Maintenon's. Towards the end of their business he said, that feeling scruples to be his Majesty's sole reason for not consenting to so necessary a measure, he had taken the responsibility on himself, and had already dispatched a courier with an order to burn Trèves immediately.

"The King was at the moment, and contrary to his disposition, so transported with anger, that he caught up the *pincettes* (tongs) from off the fireplace, and was about to throw himself on Louvois but for Madame de Maintenon, who threw herself between them, exclaiming: 'Ah, Sire, what are you about to do?' and took the *pincettes* from his hands. Louvois, however, made his way to the door. The King shouted after him to come back; and called out, with flashing eyes: 'Dispatch a courier instantly with a counter-order, and let him arrive in time, and understand that you shall answer for it with your head if a single house is burned.'"

There was no need of a counter-order, for the courier had been told to wait till after the interview; and the statement that the order had been actually sent was a trick of Louvois to secure the King's acquiescence in a foregone conclusion. He made his position worse with Madame de Maintenon by inducing Louis to leave her and the rest of the ladies at Versailles, when he undertook the siege of Mons in 1691; "and," adds Saint-Simon, "as it is the last drop which makes the cup overflow, a trifling occurrence at this siege completed the ruin of Louvois." The King, who piqued himself on his knowledge of military details, found a cavalry guard badly placed, and placed it differently. In going the rounds the same day after dinner, he chanced to pass before this same guard, which he found badly placed as before. Surprised and annoyed, he asked the captain who had placed him where he was, and was told Louvois. "But," rejoined the King, "did you not tell him that it was I who placed you?" "Yes, sire." The King, piqued, and addressing his suite, exclaimed: "Is not that Louvois all over? He thinks he understands war better than I do."

Saint-Simon was strongly prejudiced against Louvois, and says he was the author and soul of all the ruinous wars; one motive being to discredit Colbert (who was obliged to find the money) by their expense, and another to make himself necessary to the King. Thus, Saint-Simon attributes the war of 1688 to a quarrel about a window at the Petit Trianon, which the King declared to be out of proportion with the rest, whilst Louvois maintained the contrary. The King referred the point to Le Notre, who decided in his Majesty's favour; but Louvois still held out, and provoked the King into the use of angry and peremptory language in the presence of the workpeople and the suite.

"Louvois, who was not used to be treated in this fashion, returned home in a fury, and like a man in despair. Saint-Pouange, the Telladets, and the few familiars of all his hours, were alarmed, and eagerly wished to know what had happened. He at last told them; said he was a lost man, and that for some inches in a window the King forgot all his services, which had been worth him so many conquests; but that he would see to it, and get up such a war as would make the King have need of him, and let alone the trowel. He then gave way to a torrent of reproaches and rage. He was as good as his word: he kindled the war by the double election of Cologne; he confirmed it by carrying fire and sword into the Palatinate, and by giving free scope to the project against England," etc., etc.

Louvois died at Versailles on the 16th July, 1691.

"'I met him the same day,' says Saint-Simon, 'as I was coming away from the King's dinner. M. de Marsac was talking to him, and he was on his way to Madame de Maintenon's to transact business with the King, who was afterwards to walk in the gardens, where the people of the Court were permitted to follow him. About four o'clock in the afternoon, I went to Madame de Chateauneuf's, where I learnt that Louvois had been taken slightly ill at Madame de Maintenon's; that the King had insisted on his going home; that he returned on foot, when the illness suddenly got worse; that they hastily gave him some medicine, which he threw up, and died in the act of calling for his son, Barbezieux, who had not time to reach him, although under the roof at the time.'"

Dangeau's entry for July 16th, 1691, begins:

"The King worked in the afternoon with M. de Louvois, and about four o'clock perceived that M. de Louvois was ill. He sent him home."

Saint-Simon, who watched the King closely at the promenade after this event, thought he perceived symptoms of relief and elation in his Majesty's manner, and states that Louvois was to have been arrested and conducted to the Bastille within twenty-four hours had he lived; yet his immediate successor was his third son, the Marquis de Barbezieux, a young man of twenty-four, with marked disqualifications for the post. When these were pointed out to the King, he replied: "I formed the father, and I will form the son."

Louvois evidently understood his royal master, and risked little by contradicting him: the particular scene of violence mentioned by Macaulay occurred more than two years before his death; and there is no more ground for believing that he died from mortification at ill-treatment by Louis than that Dr. Johnson was driven saddened and broken-hearted from Streatham by Mrs. Piozzi. It was in a scene with Lauzun that Louis lifted and then threw away his cane.

When the King and the ladies returned to Versailles, Saint-Simon remained with the army, and was present at the battle of Neerwinden (Landen), of which he has left an animated and detailed account. Although he was in five charges and behaved with gallantry, he was passed over in the distribution of regiments vacated by the battle, and soon afterwards bought one for 26,000 livres; the purchase system being then in full force, not only for commissions in the army, but for all sorts of offices and places, civil and military.

In the course of the following year he engaged in an affair which, as he says, made a great noise, and was followed by (as regards him) most momentous results. Indeed, it influenced the whole of his life, and places in the strongest light the inherent weakness of his character. The Marshal Duc de Luxembourg, who had hitherto been content to take precedence as eighteenth amongst the dukes and peers, suddenly laid claim to stand second, on the strength of the Dukedom of Piney, which had come to him by a doubtful descent through females. Saint-Simon stood twelfth amongst those affected by this claim; and, considering the recent date of his creation and his youth, there was no intelligible motive, beyond restlessness and vanity, for his coming forward as the champion of his order. But he took the lead of the opposition from the first, threw his whole soul into the cause, and attached a degree of importance to his own personal share of it which went far to justify the sarcasm of Marmontel, that he (Saint-Simon) saw nothing in the nation but the nobility: nothing in the nobility but the peerage; and nothing in the peerage but himself.

The principal persons concerned or interested, the comparative eagerness and lukewarmness of the dukes, the quality of the tribunal, the various kinds of influence brought to bear, the Court intrigues, the plots, the under-plots, the chicanery of the judicial proceedings—all these, as handled by him, present a succession of dramatic groups and incidents which must be read in full to be appreciated. In selecting specimens we feel as if we were cutting out heads from an historic picture, yet portraits like those of Harlay (the first President) and Luxembourg strike by their force and individuality when they stand alone.

"He (Harlay) was learned in public law. He was well versed in the principles of many systems of jurisprudence;

he was on a par with those most versed in the belles-lettres; he was well acquainted with history; and above all, knew how to govern his Company with an authority which admitted of no reply, and which no First President had obtained. A pharisaical austerity, by the scope he gave to his public censures, made him an object of dread to parties, advocates, and magistrates, so that there was no one who did not tremble to have to deal with him. Supported in everything by the Court of which he was the slave, and the very humblest slave of all in real favour, a most finished courtier, and singularly astute politician—all these talents he turned exclusively to his ambition of ruling and rising, and founding the reputation of a great man: without genuine honour; without morals in private; with none but outward probity; without even humanity; in a word, a perfect hypocrite, *sans foi, sans loi*, without God and without soul, cruel husband, barbarous father, tyrannical brother, friend of himself alone, wicked by nature—taking pleasure in insulting, in outraging, in crushing, and never in his life omitting an opportunity of so doing. A volume might be filled with traits of him, and all the more striking because he had an infinity of wit, the mind naturally turned towards it, and always sufficiently master of himself to risk nothing of which he might have to repent."

The part taken by Harlay against the dukes was eminently displeasing to Saint-Simon, and the features of this portrait are evidently overcharged; but what he says of Harlay's wit, cutting sarcasm and subserviency, is substantially confirmed. An elderly lady of quality had christened him the old monkey. She had a cause which she gained; and on her calling to thank the President, he said: "You see, Madame, that the old *he*-monkeys (*singes*) like to oblige the old she-monkeys (*guenons*)." During the reading of a report, a third of the members of his court were talking and another third asleep, when he said: "If the gentlemen who are talking would do like the gentlemen who are sleeping, the gentlemen who are listening might hear."

A wealthy financier in a famine was threatened by the First President with the gallows if he did not sell all his corn within a month. The financier complained to the King, who advised him to comply with the order, adding: "If the First President has threatened to hang you, depend upon it he will be as good as his word." A similar story is told of the Duke of Wellington, when a commissary complained that Picton had threatened to hang him unless a certain number of bullocks were supplied within twenty-four hours.

In his finished portrait of Luxembourg, Saint-Simon struggled hard to overcome an avowed prejudice, and do justice to the illustrious commander under whom he had been proud to serve.

"A great name, great bravery, unrestrained ambition, *de l'esprit*—but an *esprit* of intrigue, of debauch, and of the great world—enabled him to surmount the disadvantage of a face and figure very repulsive at first, but (what no one who had not seen him can comprehend) a face and figure to which one got accustomed, and which—notwithstanding a hump, moderate in front, but very large and very pointed behind, with all the rest of the ordinary accompaniment of hunchbacks—*had a fire, a nobility, and a natural grace* that shone in his simplest actions. . . . Nothing more just than his *coup d'œil;* nobody more brilliant, more self-possessed, more full of resource than he in presence of the enemy or on a day of battle—with an audacity, a *flatterie*, and at the same time a *sangfroid*, which enabled him to see and foresee everything in the middle of the hottest fire and the most imminent risk of failure; there it was that he was great. For the rest, indolence itself. Little exercise without great necessity; play; conversation with his familiars; and every evening a supper with very few, almost always the same, and if there chanced to be any town in the vicinity, care was taken that there should be an agreeable mixture of the fair sex. Then he was inaccessible to all, and if anything urgent occurred, it was for Puysegur to look to it. Such with the army was the life of this great general; and such also at Paris, where the Court and the fine world occupied his days, and his pleasures his evenings."

It may prove neither uninteresting nor uninstructive to mark how far the brilliant historian, the studied and practised master of style, has improved upon this portrait from the pen of the grand seigneur, who disclaimed all the arts of authorship and was accused of writing like a barbarian by two or three generations of critics.[1]

"In valour and abilities Luxembourg was not inferior to any of his illustrious race. But, highly descended and highly gifted as he was, he had with difficulty surmounted the obstacles which impeded him in the road to fame. If he owed much to the bounty of nature and fortune, he had suffered still more from their spite. *His features were frightfully harsh; his stature was diminutive;* a huge and pointed hump rose on his back. His constitution was feeble and sickly. Cruel imputations had been thrown on his morals. . . . In vigilance, diligence, and perseverance he was deficient. He seemed to reserve his great qualities for great emergencies. It was on a pitched field of battle that he was all himself. His glance was rapid and unerring. His judgment was clearest and surest when responsibility pressed heaviest on him, and when difficulties gathered thickest round him. . . . . He was at once a valetudinarian, and a voluptuary; and in both characters he loved ease. He scarcely ever mounted his horse. Light conversation and cards occupied most of his hours. His table was luxurious; and when he had sat down to supper it was a service of danger to disturb him. . . . If there were any agreeable women in the neighbourhood of his camp, they were generally to be found at his banquets."[2]

From the terms on which Saint-Simon stood

[1] Chateaubriand said of Saint-Simon: "Il écrit à la barbare pour immortalité."
[2] Macaulay, Hist., vol. iv.

with Luxembourg, we may be sure that he softened nothing; and Voltaire describes Luxembourg as "always in love, and even often loved, although deformed (*contrefait*), and with a face little formed to please, having more of the qualities of the hero than the sage." The only authorities quoted by Macaulay, besides lampoons and caricatures, are Saint-Simon and Voltaire. Then why does he say that Luxembourg's features were frightfully harsh and his stature diminutive?

In the "Biographie Universelle," the description of Luxembourg is that "although *un peu contrefait*, he pleased by a physiognomy which revealed his soul." William was reputed to have said: *Je ne pourrai donc jamais battre ce bossu-là!* "*Bossu!*" exclaimed Luxembourg on hearing this, "what does *he* know of it? He has never seen my back." His death (of a pulmonary complaint) in 1695 was mourned as a national loss; but Saint-Simon regarded it from an exclusively personal point of view.

> "M. de Luxembourg did not see, during his last illness, a single one of the dukes he had attacked, nor did any one of them press to be received. I neither went nor sent once, although I was at Versailles, and I must own that I appreciated my deliverance from such an enemy."

The titles and rights of the Marshal Duke devolved upon his son, by whom the claim of precedence was revived and eventually established to the extreme surprise and lasting mortification of Saint-Simon, who, at the final hearing, lost all semblance of temper and self-command. He says that when Du Mont (the Luxembourg advocate) contended that resistance to the claim was disrespectful to the King—

"I started up to rush out, exclaiming against the imposture, and calling for justice on this scoundrel. M. de la Rochefoucauld held me back, and kept me silent. I was bursting with rage, still more against him than against the advocate."

The celebrated D'Aguesseau, the Advocate-general, spoke last, and occupied a day in summing up the arguments on both sides.

"He rested the next day, and on Friday, April 13th, 1696, reappeared to conclude. After keeping the audience a long time in suspense, he began to show himself; it was with an erudition, a force, a precision, and an eloquence beyond compare, *and concluded entirely for us.*"

The Judges unluckily concluded the other way, and Saint-Simon, after vainly endeavouring to stir up the other dukes to join in an appeal, drew up a memoir to the King, which was not presented because no other duke could be induced to join in it.

We are obviously indebted to the mortification inflicted by M. de Luxembourg's success for a malicious story of him, which illustrates the manners of the Court. The scene is a ball at Marly, to which he and his wife had been invited in consequence of the scarcity of dancers, she being a woman of irregular conduct who was commonly shunned by the respectable of her sex. "Her husband was probably the only person in France who knew nothing of her goings on, and had not the slightest distrust of her." He was suddenly required to take part in a masked ballet; and having come unprovided with a mask, requested his friend, the Prince de Conti, to supply him with one.

"Some time after the commencement of the ball, some of the dancers left the room and returned masked. I had just arrived, and I was already seated, when I saw, from behind, a quantity of muslin, surmounted by a stag's horns *au naturel*,—a whimsical headdress, so high that it caught in a lustre. Surprised at so strange a disguise we began asking each other who it could be? and were remarking that this mask must be tolerably sure of his brows to venture to deck them in this fashion, when the mask turned, and M. de Luxembourg stood confessed. The sudden burst of laughter was scandalous. He took it in good part, and told us with admirable simplicity that it was M. le Prince who had fitted him out in this fashion. A moment after arrived the ladies, and a little later the King. This was a signal for the laughter to recommence, and for M. de Luxembourg to show off before the company with a delightful confidence. His wife, notorious as she was and knowing nothing of this masquerade, lost countenance, and everybody, dying with laughter, was looking at the pair. This amusement lasted all the ball; and the King, in excellent humour as he always was, laughed with the rest; and people were never tired of admiring a trick so cruelly ridiculous, nor of talking of it for many days in succession."

Speaking of the mode of life at Marly, he says that there were balls every evening, which were kept up till eight in the morning; and that he and Madame de Saint-Simon never saw the light of day for three weeks. Practical jokes were a favourite amusement, with slight regard to consequences.

"Monsieur le Duc held the States of Burgundy this year in the place of Monsieur le Prince (de Condé), his father, who did not choose to go there. He here gave a great example of the friendship of princes, and a fine lesson to those who seek it. . . .

"One evening when he supped at home, he amused himself by plying Santeuil (famous for his Latin verses) with champagne; and from pleasantry to pleasantry he thought it a good joke to empty his snuff-box full of Spanish snuff into a large glass of wine, and make Santeuil drink it to see what would come of it. He was not long in learning: vomiting and fever set in, and in twice twenty-four hours the unhappy man died suffering the pains of the damned; but in sentiments of a sincere penitence with which he received the sacraments, and edified as much as he was regretted by a society little given to edification, but detesting so cruel an experiment."

One of the regular butts of the royal family was the Princesse d'Harcourt, whom Saint-Simon describes as untidy and unwashed; a kind of white fury, and a harpy to boot, with the effrontery, the malice, the thievishness, the violence; *elle en avait encore la gourmandise et la promptitude à s'en soulager, etc.* The Duke and Duchess of Burgundy were constantly playing tricks with this fair creature. One day they placed petards the whole length of the alley which led from the Château of Marly to the house where she lodged—

"She was horribly afraid of everything. Two chairmen were in attendance to carry her when she took her leave. When she was about the middle of the alley, and the whole party near enough to enjoy the spectacle, the petards began to explode, and she to cry for mercy, and the chairmen to make off. She struggled convulsively in the chair to the point of upsetting it, and shrieked like a demon. The company ran up to enjoy the scene, and hear her rail at all who approached her, beginning with the Duke and Duchess.

"Another time he fixed a petard under her seat in the saloon where she was playing at piquet; but, as he was going to set fire to it some charitable soul warned him that this petard would maim her, and prevented him. Sometimes they sent a score of Swiss with drums into her bedroom, who awoke her in her first sleep with this *tintamarre*."

"All these different affairs," says Saint-Simon, in reference to the proceedings in the Luxembourg suit, "were nothing in comparison of another to which they gave rise, which inflicted the greatest wound the peerage could receive, and became its leprosy and its cancer." This was the decisive measure suddenly taken by the King, by the advice of Harlay, giving the bastards (as they are plainly designated) precedence immediately next to princes of the blood. He ended, as is well known, by endowing them with all the incidents of legitimacy, including the right of succession to the throne. The Duc du Maine, the eldest of the King's natural children by Madame de Montespan, was the prompter of the grant of precedence, and the first to claim the privilege. This alone was enough to mark him out as an object of peculiar dislike to Saint-Simon, who has a malicious pleasure in relating how, shortly after his elevation, the bastard *par eminence* came to grief.

In the campaign of 1695 Marshal de Villeroy had manœuvred so successfully, that it appeared impossible for Vaudemont and his army to escape; and on the 13th August a courier was despatched to Versailles by Villeroy to announce an assured victory. M. du Maine, who commanded the left, was ordered to begin the action; but he hesitated till the opportunity was lost; shed tears, sent for his confessor, and exhibited other signs of the most pitiable pusillanimity on the field. Knowing the excessive affection of the King for his craven son, Villeroy did his best to conceal or gloss over the cause of failure in his report, and the courtiers were equally cautious not to wound his Majesty's feelings; but suspecting that something was kept back, he at length, during a visit to Marly, contrived to exact the truth from a favourite valet-de-chambre.

"This prince, outwardly so calm, and so master of his slightest movements in the most moving circumstances, on this unique occasion succumbed. On leaving the dinner-table at Marly with all the ladies, and in the presence of all the courtiers, he saw a valet, in the act of removing the dessert, put a biscuit in his pocket. On the instant he forgets all his dignity, and lifting the cane, which had just been presented to him with his hat, rushes on the valet, strikes him, abuses him, and breaks the cane upon his back. To say the truth, it was slight and easily broken. Then still holding it, and with the air of a man who had lost all self-control, and continuing to rate the valet who was already far off, he traversed the small saloon and entered the apartment of Madame de Maintenon, as he often did at Marly after dinner. On coming out he met his confessor, and loudly exclaimed, as soon as he caught sight of the holy father, ' *Mon Père*, I have given a rascal a sound beating, and broken my cane upon his back; but I do not believe I have offended God;' and then told him the pretended crime. All present were trembling still at what they had seen or heard from those present. Their fright redoubled at this revival; and the poor priest made appear that he approved, to avoid adding to the King's irritation before the world."

Some days elapsed before the real cause of this unbecoming burst of anger became known. Courtier as he was, the Duc d'Elbœuf could not refrain from having a sly hit at the "bastard" on this occasion. Towards the end of the campaign, he asked M. du Maine, before a large company, where he intended to serve during the following campaign, since, wherever it was, he should wish to serve there too; and, on being pressed for further explanation, he added, that with M. du Maine one was always sure of one's life. A similar sarcasm was levelled against an eminent member of the Bonaparte family at the commencement of the Italian campaign of 1859.

During all the winter of 1695 Saint-Simon's mother was trying to find him a good marriage; no very difficult matter, he insinuates, as he was regarded as a highly desirable match. "I was an only son, and I had a dignity and establishments which also made people think much of me." There was some talk of Mdlle. d'Armagnac, and Mdlle. de la Trémouille, and many others. At length the choice was considered to lie between two daughters of the Marshal de Lorges.

"The one (the eldest, aged seventeen) was a brunette with fine eyes; the other (aged fifteen), fair, with a perfect complexion and figure, a very pleasing face, extremely noble and modest air, and I know not what of the majestic by an air of virtue and natural sweetness. It was she, moreover, whom I loved the best, beyond all comparison, from the time I saw them both, and with whom I linked the happiness of my life, which she has solely and wholly constituted."

The King approved the match on its being formally notified to him by the Marshal: the articles were signed, and the bridegroom-expectant was passing all his evenings at the Hôtel de Lorges, when all of a sudden the marriage was entirely broken off on some pecuniary misunderstanding which "each interpreted in his or her own manner." Happily, an uncle of the bride, an old master of requests, arrived from the country and removed the difficulty by paying the difference.

"It is an honour which I am bound to render him, and I have never ceased to feel deeply grateful. *It is thus that God brings to pass what pleases Him by the least expected means.*"

The marriage was solemnised at midnight on the 8th April in the Chapel of the Hôtel de Lorges.

"We slept in the grand apartment. The next day M. d'Anneuil, who lodged opposite, gave us a grand dinner; after which the bride received all France on her bed at the Hôtel de Lorges, to which the forms of domestic life attracted the crowd, and the first who came was the Duchesse de Bracciano with her two nieces."

The Duchess had tried hard to secure him for one of the nieces, and came first to show that she was not piqued at the disappointment.

"My mother was still in her second mourning, and her apartments black and grey, which made us prefer the Hôtel de Lorges to receive the world. The day after these visits, to which only one day was devoted, we went to Versailles. In the evening it was the King's pleasure to receive the bride at Madame de Maintenon's, where my mother and hers presented her. On his way, the King spoke to me of her in a bantering tone, and he had the goodness to receive them with much distinction and praise.

"They were afterwards at the supper, where the new Duchess assumed her tabouret. On taking his place at table, the King said to her: 'Madame, if you please to be seated.' When his napkin was spread, seeing all the duchesses and princesses still standing, he rose from his chair and said to Madame de Saint-Simon: 'Madame, I have already begged you to be seated;' and all who ought to be seated took their seats, Madame de Saint-Simon between my mother and her own, *who was after her*."

In 1702 Saint-Simon quitted the service in disgust at seeing five of his juniors made brigadiers of cavalry over his head. It was not till after two months of wearing anxiety and frequent consultations with his friends that he resolved upon this step; and after sending in his letter of resignation, he waits at Paris to hear how it had been received by the King. Hearing nothing for eight days, he returns to Versailles on Shrove Tuesday, when he learns that the King, on reading his letter, had called up Chamillart (one of the Secretaries of State) to whom, after a short private conference, he exclaimed with emotion, "Hé bien! Monsieur, here is another man leaving us."

"I did not hear of anything else that fell from him. This Shrove Tuesday I re-appeared before him for the first time since my letter on his retiring after his supper. I should be ashamed to tell the trifle that I am about to narrate if it did not help to characterise him under the circumstances. Although the place where he undressed was well lighted, the almoner of the day, who held a lighted candle at his evening prayer, gave it back afterwards to the first valet-de-chambre, who carried it before the King as he resumed his seat. He glanced round, and named aloud one of those present, to whom the valet gave the candle. It was a distinction and a favour which had its value; so adroit was the King in making something out of nothings. He only gave it to those who were most distinguished by dignity and birth, very rarely to inferiors in whom age and services sufficed. *He often gave it to me*, rarely to ambassadors, except to the Nuncio, and in later times to the Spanish ambassador.

"You took off your glove: you came forward: you held the candle during the *coucher*, which was very short; you then gave it back to the first valet-de-chambre, who, if he chose, gave it to some one of the *petit coucher*.

"I had purposely kept back; and I was much surprised, as were the bystanders, to hear myself named; and on future occasions *I had it almost as often as before*. It was not that there were not in attendance many persons of mark to whom it might have been given, but the King was sufficiently piqued to wish that his being so should not be perceived. .

"This was also all I had of him for three years; during which he forgot no trifle, in default of more important occasions, to make me feel how offended he was."

One of these trifles—no trifles in his eyes—was that his wife was once invited to Trianon, where she could go without him, and not invited to Marly, where etiquette required that the husband should accompany the wife. Over-eagerness to magnify his own importance seems to have blinded Saint-Simon to the inconsistency of his statement. If the King continued giving the candle to conceal his pique, why did he make a point of showing that he was offended? As for the three years, he states that he came to a full explanation with his Majesty, ending in a reconciliation, in the course of the year following, 1703.

There were certain feast days on which, after mass and vespers, a lady of the Court *quêtait* (made a collection for the poor), being named for that duty by the Queen or Dauphiness. The ladies of the House of Lorraine, who claimed to be on a level with princesses of the blood, evaded it as beneath them: Saint-Simon, conceiving that the duchesses were entitled to hold their heads equally high, got up a cabal to bring about a general refusal on their part; and the result was that the collection became irregular and bade fair to be discontinued altogether. On hearing this, the King vowed that rather than the custom should be given up, the purse should be carried round by the Duchess of Burgundy; and that as for Saint-Simon, " he had done nothing since he quitted the service but study degrees of rank and get into squabbles with everybody; that he was the originator of all this; and that if he had his deserts, he would be sent so far off as to give no more trouble for a long time to come."

When his majesty's words were reported to him, he requested an audience, in which he expatiated on the propriety of placing the duchesses on the same footing as the princesses, and of compelling all to carry round the purse when their turn came; professing at the same time his entire readiness to carry it himself or turn churchwarden for the nonce. The freedom of his language, he boasts, conciliated instead of offending the King; and the audience, prolonged as a mark of special favour to the unusual length of half an hour, was so successful that, after reporting what had passed to the older courtiers, he twitted them with not being equally free when their interests and privileges were at stake.

It was customary for the King at the communion to be attended by two dukes, or a prince of the blood and a duke; but if a *fils de France* was present, he alone performed the duty (holding up a corner of the cloth) which otherwise devolved upon a duke. The Duke of Orleans having acted without a duke, Monsieur le Duc (de Condé) assumed the same privilege, whereupon the ever-watchful Saint-Simon takes alarm. He first tries some other dukes, but their tameness and meanness of spirit, their *mollesse et misère*, baffled him.

"I guessed as much, and had at the same time written to the Duke of Orleans in Spain all I thought best adapted to pique him; and with reference to the preservation of his rank above princes of the blood, not to suffer them to place themselves on a level with him by this usurpation on the dukes. On his return, I got him to speak to the King. The King begged to be excused. . . . In a word, nothing was done, and so the matter remained. . . . Although often subsequently pressed to be present at the King's communions, and at times when there were no princes of the blood at the Court—for the bastards had not yet appeared there—I could never bring my mind to it, and I have never since attended them."

In spite of repeated warnings, Saint-Simon persevered in raising questions of this kind; and his dislike to Vendôme, who was highly favoured by the King, led him into the extraordinary imprudence of offering and making a wager that Lille, which Vendôme was sent to relieve, would be taken without a battle. That he won the wager was no excuse for making it, indeed, made matters worse; and he naturally fell under the imputation that the wish was father to the thought. The king's looks had again become cold, or rumours had reached him of a cloud gathering at Versailles, when, in 1709, he took counsel with his wife and the chancellor as to the prudence of withdrawing altogether from the Court, and residing permanently, or the greater part of the year, at his country seat. They strongly disapproved the project, which we suspect he never seriously entertained; and emboldened by the success of his former audience, he applied to his friend Maréchal (surgeon-in-chief) to get him another.

"Maréchal thought a moment, then, looking me full in the face, 'I will do it,' he said with animation, 'and in fact there is no other course open to you. *You have already spoken to him several times;* he has always been satisfied at these; he will not fear what you will have to say to him, from the experience he has had already. I do not answer for it that he will consent, if he is well determined against you; but let me alone to choose my time well.'"

Maréchal was as good as his word, and chose his time well for making the request. "But," replied the King, "what can he have to say to me? there is nothing. It is true some trifles about him have come to my ears, but nothing of consequence; tell him to make himself easy, and that I have nothing against him." On Maréchal's still pressing for the audience, the King resumed, with an air of indifference, "Well then, agreed, when he will." Some days having elapsed, Saint-Simon walked up to the King's table as he was finishing his dinner, and reminded him of his gracious promise.

"He turned to me, and with a polite air, replied: 'When you will; I could very well at once, but I have business, and it would be too short,' and a moment after turned to me again, and said: 'But to-morrow morning if you choose.'"

The audience took place on the morrow, January, 1710; and after putting the best colour on the wager as implying no want of loyalty and patriotism, he began answering things which he supposed to have been repeated against him; to which the King, evidently attaching no importance to them, remarked that he had only himself to thank if evil tongues had been busy at his expense.

"'This shows you,' replied the King, assuming a truly paternal air, 'on what footing you are in the world, and you must own that this reputation, you in some measure merit it.' If you had never been engaged in affairs of ranks, if at least you had not appeared so excited about those that have arisen, and about the ranks themselves, people would not have that to say of you.'"

When the audience ended, Saint-Simon felt so confident of the impression he had made, that he begged the King to think of him for an apartment to enable him to pay more assiduous court.

"The King replied that there was none vacant, and with a half-bow, laughing and gracious, walked towards his other cabinets; and I, after a low bow, went out where I came in, after more than half an hour of the most favourable audience, and far above what I had ventured to hope."

The Court went to Marly on the 28th April, 1710.

"I had gone to La Ferté. Madame de Saint-Simon offered herself for this expedition. It was the first the King had made to Marly since the audience he had given me. We were of the party. I arrived there from La Ferté, *and I have since missed but one till the King's death*, even those which Madame de Saint-Simon could not join; and I remarked from this first that the King spoke to me and distinguished me more than people of my age without official position or familiarity with him."

On Sunday, the 5th June, 1710, the King, on returning from mass through the gallery, called to Saint-Simon to follow to the cabinet; where he was informed that Madame de Saint-Simon had been chosen, as a mark of esteem for her virtue and merit, to be lady of honour to the future Duchess of Berry. Then, after saying all sorts of obliging things of Saint-Simon and his wife, the King, "fixing him with a look and a smile meant to be winning," added: "But you must hold your tongue." The salary and appointments were fixed on the most liberal scale.

"He (the King) took marked care to form for us the most agreeable apartment at Versailles. He turned out d'Antin and the Duchesse Sforza to make out of the two a complete one for each of us. He added kitchens in the court below, a very rare thing at the château, because we always gave dinners, and often suppers, the whole time we were at Court."

He had clearly no reason to complain of the King, by whom he was almost invariably treated with considerate kindness and affability. We therefore read with surprise, in Mr. Reeve's carefully considered Essay, that "he was honoured with no distinction which could be withheld from him:" that "it is not clear that he ever had more than three conversations with Louis," and that the two-and-twenty years which he spent at that monarch's court "were spent in what, in the language of princes, is called disgrace."

Having got as much as he had any reason to expect from the old King, Saint-Simon began to turn his attention from the setting to the rising sun and fixed his hopes on the young Duke of Burgundy, the coming Marcellus of France, the son of the Dauphin (commonly called Monseigneur), on whom from early youth the proverb ran: "Son of king, father of king, never king." The event, remarks Voltaire, seems to favour the credulity of those who have faith in predictions, for he died on the 14th April, 1711.

Saint-Simon's description of the Court with its conflicting emotions when the heir-apparent was known to be at the last gasp, may be cited as one of the most favourable specimens of his style; and his own state of mind, which he frankly exposes, is well worth studying.

"My first movement was to inform myself more than once, to withhold full belief in what I saw and heard; then to fear too little cause for so much alarm; finally to fall back on myself by the consideration of the suffering common to all men, and that I should some day or other find myself at the gates of death. Joy, however, pierced through the momentary reflections of religion and humanity by which I tried to check myself: my particular deliverance seemed to me so great and so unhoped-for, that it seemed to me, with an evidence still more perfect than the truth, that the State gained all by such a loss. Amongst these thoughts, I felt in my own despite a shade of fear that the dying man might recover, and I was extremely ashamed of it."

The new Dauphin did not live long enough to realise Saint-Simon's expectations, or place him in a condition to show what an amount of political sagacity had been rendered useless (as he plainly intimates) by misplaced jealousy and unmerited distrust. The young prince died on February 12th, 1712, and Saint-Simon lost not an hour in flinging in his fortunes with the Duke of Orleans, the future Regent. If the contemplation of virtue exercised a centripetal force in the one case, the contemplation of vice did not exert a centrifugal influence in the other, for Saint-Simon's adherence to the pupil of Dubois continued unshaken to his death.

"He (the Regent) lived publicly with Madame de

Parabère: he lived with others at the same time: he amused himself with the jealousy and spite of these women: he was not the less on good terms with-all; and the scandal of this public seraglio, and that of the daily ribaldry and impieties of his suppers, was extreme and universally diffused."

Saint-Simon's solitary attempt to reform this mode of life was remarkable for the same spirit of indulgence that softened the reproof administered by the Scotch minister to Charles II. "The King's passion for the fair could not be altogether restrained. He had once been observed using some familiarities with a young woman, and a committee of ministers was appointed to reprove him for a behaviour so unbecoming a covenanted monarch. The spokesman of the committee, one Douglass, began with a severe aspect; informed the King that great scandal had been given to the godly; enlarged on the heinous nature of sin; and concluded with exhorting his Majesty, whenever he was disposed to amuse himself, to be more careful for the future in shutting the windows."[1]

"Lent," says Saint-Simon, "had commenced, and I foresaw a frightful scandal, or a horrible sacrilege for Easter, which could not but augment this terrible scandal." He, therefore, took the bold step of pointing out to the Regent the worldly consequences of profaning the Holy Week, feeling (he states) the hopelessness of producing an impression by dwelling on the outrage against religion and the offence in the eyes of God. On being asked what he had to propose, he replied that nothing was more simple. His Royal Highness had only to make a partial sacrifice of seven days, beginning with Easter Tuesday, which he was to pass at Villers-Cotterets in company with

[1] Hume, "History of England," ch. lxi.

five or six agreeable persons of his choice. "Walk, ride, drive, play, in short, amuse yourself; fast like the monks who made good cheer on Fridays when they fasted; don't remain too long at table, and restrain the conversation within the moderate bounds of decency; attend divine service on Good Friday and grand mass on Easter Sunday. This is all I require. Do this, and I will answer for it that all goes well."

This was the substance of his advice, with which the Regent eagerly closed; but his *roués*[1] and mistresses took the alarm: the slightest self-restraint might end in a thorough reform: he was over-persuaded to remain in Paris, leading much the same kind of life; and his sole concession to prudence or propriety was a public attendance at High Mass.

There was another act of independence on which Saint-Simon prided himself, the refusal to address the Regent as *Monseigneur*. He stood out, and stood alone, for *Monsieur*; and he explains at length his reasons for this preposterous singularity, of which the Regent took no notice. At a moderate estimate, more than a thousand pages of this publication are occupied by similar topics; by memoirs, protests, disquisitions, discussions and disputes about rank, title, seats, caps, modes of address and privileges. He had precedence on the brain: nature meant him for a master of ceremonies; and the gold stick or the white wand of a High Steward or Lord Chamberlain would have gratified the dearest wish of his heart.

He was named a member of the Council of Regency, but declined any office of individual responsibility, and his exact position is hit off

---

[1] This term was first used by the Regent to describe the companions of his convivial hours.

by M. Martin: "Il s'y trouva, de fait, dans son vrai milieu, critiquant beaucoup et ne faisant guère.[1] In his eyes all other measures were as naught compared with those for the humiliation of the Parliament, the degradation of the *legitimés*, and the elevation of the dukes. After giving an instance, far from convincing, of his constant postponement of all other considerations to the good of the State, he says:

"This is also seen in all I did to save the Duc du Maine against my two dearest and most lively interests, *because I believed it dangerous to attack him and the Parliament at once*, and because the Parliament was then the most pressing affair, which could not be deferred.

To postpone an act of personal vengeance with the view of making it more sure—this, then, was his highest conception of public duty or self-sacrifice. We presume it was from a similar devotion to the good of the State that, at the commencement of the Regency, he insisted that the demands of his order should be considered prior to the discussion of any other business. In reference to an interview which he and some other dukes had with the Regent, he says:

"M. le Duc d'Orleans made us a discourse, well gilded, to persuade us to make no innovation on the morrow; representing the trouble which this might introduce in the greatest affairs of the State which ought to be settled, such as the Regency and the administration of the kingdom, and the impropriety which would fall upon all of us of stopping them, and at least retarding them—all for our particular interests."

The most pressing affair for the Regent, the setting aside of the late King's will by a registered order or edict, raised instead of lowering the Par-

---

[1] "Hist. de France," vol. xv. p. 8.

liament, and left the rank and precedence of the Duc du Maine and the other *legitimés* unimpaired. It gratified neither of what Saint-Simon terms his two dearest and most lively interests. The day on which his vengeance was complete, when his exultation rose to extravagance, was the 26th of August, 1718, the day of the famous *lit de justice*, in which the powers of the Parliament were restricted, and the "bastards" (with the exception of the Comte de Toulouse) reduced to the rank of ordinary peers. Saint-Simon's description of the scene is his masterpiece; and the effect is heightened by his account of the preceding deliberations in the Council, and the manner in which the train was quietly laid for the grand explosion, so that it should burst upon the surprised legists and bastards like a thunderclap. Speaking of the First President (de Mesmes), who rose to deliver a remonstrance, he says:

"The scoundrel trembled, however, in pronouncing it. His broken voice, the constraint in his eyes, the sinking and trouble visible in all his person, gave the lie to the rest of the venom the libation of which he could not refuse to his company and himself. It was then that I tasted with inexpressible delight the spectacle of these haughty lawyers, who dare refuse us the salute, prostrate on their knees and rendering at our feet a homage to the throne, whilst seated and covered on the elevated seats at the sides of this same throne, these situations and these postures, so greatly disproportioned, alone plead with all the force of evidence the cause of those who, veritably and in effect, are *laterales Regis*, against this *vas electum* of the *tiers état!*"

The reading of the third declaration or order was almost too much for him.

"Each word was legislative, and carried a fresh fall. The attention was general, and held every one immovable so as not to lose a word, with eyes fixed on the clerk who was reading. Towards the third of this reading, the First

President, *grinding the few teeth he had left,* sank down with his forehead on his *baton,* which he held with both hands, and in this singular posture heard to the end this reading, so crushing for him, so resurrectionary for us.

"As for me, I was dying of joy. I was afraid that I should faint: my heart, dilated to excess, no longer found room enough to expand. The violence I put upon myself so as to let nothing escape, was infinite. Yet this torment was delicious. I compared the years of servitude—the sad days, when, dragged to Parliament as a victim, I had so many times served as a triumph to the bastards—the different degrees by which they had mounted to this height above our heads—I compared these, I say, to this day of justice and of rule, to this appalling fall, which with the same blow raised us by the force of the rebound. I recalled, with the most potent charm, what I had dared announce to the Duc du Maine the day of the scandal of the cap (*bonnet*) under the despotism of his father. My eyes witnessed at last the effect and the accomplishment of this measure. I felt indebted to myself; I thanked myself that it was by me it was brought about. I considered the radiant splendour in the presence of the King and so august an assembly. I triumphed; I was avenged; I swam in my vengeance. I enjoyed the full accomplishment of the most vehement and the most sustained desires of my life. I was tempted never to care for anything again."

* * * * *

"During the registration I cast my eyes round, and if I put some restraint on them, I could not resist the temptation of indemnifying myself on the First President. Insult, contempt, disdain, triumph, were darted at him to his very marrow from my eyes. He frequently looked down when he encountered my gaze; once or twice he fixed his on me, and I took pleasure in outraging him by stolen but black smiles which completed his confusion. I revelled in his rage, and found pleasure in making him feel that I did!"

There is a great deal more of the same sort; and all about matters which in no respect affected his real interest or honour, matters which a man of true dignity, even of his own frivolous generation, would have despised.

The last eventful episode in his public career was his Spanish embassy in 1721, which he undertook, he says, to obtain the rank of Grandee for his second son, and haply the Golden Fleece for the eldest. "I so thought to do a good stroke of business for my family and to return home in great content." He describes the scenes and ceremonies in which he took part with his wonted piquancy, or when, by royal command, he danced at a State ball, acquitted himself to admiration, and restored his wasted energies by a glass of excellent wine; as when, at a grand battue, he shot a fox, "a little before the proper time," *i.e.* without giving a royal sportsman a chance.

This embassy also gave occasion for a disquisition on the institutions and manners of Spain to which he had already devoted a large part of a volume. It is replete with information, tediously spun out, as are the rest of his digressive lucubrations and summaries of events. These, although he took great pains with them, will not enhance his reputation, which must rest on his narratives, his descriptions, his historic groups, and, above all, on his analysis and delineation of character.

Wonder is blended with admiration at the abundance and variety of his biographical sketches and portraits. They may be counted by hundreds, yet no two of them are alike: each has a physiognomy of its own, and is distinguished by the most unerring marks of individuality. This alone is a decided proof that they were drawn from the life. Invention and fancy are limited: nature is inexhaustible. He has been compared to Rubens for boldness of outline and richness of colouring; and he resembles Rembrandt in the artistic effects which he produces by strong contrasts of light and shade. The shade, however, is too frequently deepened by hatred, malice and uncharitableness: the moral tone is low: we are disposed to agree with Sainte-Beuve that "it is an immense and prodigious talent rather than a high and complete intellect;" and, taken all in all, we can hardly understand how any reader, learned or unlearned, can warm or puff himself into enthusiasm for the author or the man. Here, however, we are again at variance with Mr. Reeve; and coupling the wide circulation of his views with the decided manner in which they are advanced, it would be a dereliction of critical duty, indeed hardly complimentary to him, to pass them over as of no account.

"The French of the present day," he says, "look on Saint-Simon with mingled and inconsistent feelings. They are compelled to admit that the prodigious force and variety of his style raise him to the very highest rank in literature—as keen a wit as Molière; as fervent a Christian as Bossuet; as stern in his judgments as Tacitus; as fierce in his invectives as Juvenal."[1]

Nor is this all. His writings are "illuminated by the power of genius and the love of truth." One of his portraits (the Duke of Burgundy) is termed "magnificent," and another (Fénélon) "of transcendent beauty." We are told that "no one can read these memoirs without being struck with the unaffected piety of their author:" that "his nature was cast in a larger mould, and something of an heroic character mingled in all his thoughts;" whilst our commiseration is invoked for his unhappy fate in finding himself "one of a flock of courtiers, whose highest ambition was to light the king to his bedroom, or to hold his shirt when he was dressing."

[1] "Royal and Republican France," vol. i. p. 155.

But was not this Saint-Simon's highest ambition too? Was he not constantly fidgeting, fussifying, intriguing, quarrelling about forms and ceremonies? He would not attend the King's communion except in what he thought his proper place as duke. He would not allow his wife to join in the work of charity because it might compromise her dignity as a duchess; although he permitted her to retain her place as lady of honour in constant attendance on the Duchess of Berry, when that princess was leading a life of open and avowed licentiousness. In his "Discours sur le Duc de Bourgogne" he intimates pretty clearly that religion and Christian charity are very good things in their way, but may be carried too far in a prince.

"Therefore a less assiduous attendance at divine service all the Sundays and Feast days of the year would take nothing before God from Monseigneur of the chaste delight he finds in hearing His praises chanted."

This savours more of Lord Chesterfield or Polonius than of Bossuet. Saint-Simon's visits to La Trappe were like those of a fine lady to her confessor, after which she feels eager and qualified to start fresh. Improving on Clermont Tonnerre, he believed in his inmost soul that *Le bon Dieu n'aura jamais le cœur de damner un duc et pair*. His want of self-knowledge, and his inordinate self-esteem, saved him from self-reproach. With the examples of Lionne, Colbert, and Louvois before his eyes, he accounts for his not occupying a higher place in the royal favour by laying down that Louis had an intuitive aversion for men of capacity and integrity, who spoke their minds. His shortlived resolves to quit the Court were as unreal, and as barren of results, as Mr. Charles Greville's renunciations of the Turf. His actual retirement into private life (in 1723) was reluctant and enforced. Although he refused to accept shares in the Mississippi scheme from a shrewd anticipation of a crash, he received a large sum through Law as compensation for a paternal claim on the State that had lain dormant for nearly half a century.

The distinctive qualities of Tacitus and Juvenal are altogether wanting in Saint-Simon. He was not a deep thinker: he did not write to expose corruption or reform vice. He wrote to indulge his feelings; and he never meant what he wrote to see the light till the time at which it could be useful as a satire had long passed away. The persons he spared least were those who had wounded his vanity or offended his prejudices. The persons he praised most were those who had aided, obliged, or flattered him. This does not look as if he was uniformly actuated by the strong sense of justice or the pure love of truth. Piquancy of expression is his nearest approach to wit; and he had fortunately no humour, or he would have perceived the absurdity of much that he has usefully recorded from a conviction of its gravity. In delicacy (or indelicacy) he is about on a par with Swift, whose description of the Yahoos is the nearest literary parallel to Saint-Simon's account of the habits of some of the most distinguished personages who figure in his pages. We allude particularly to such passages as the sketch of the Duc de Vendôme's first acquaintance with Alberoni: the scene with the King and Madame de Maintenon in which the young and charming Duchess of Burgundy adopts a singular expedient for keeping herself cool at the theatre: the position in which she is portrayed chatting with her ladies of honour before retiring to rest with the Duke, who is in bed waiting for her; and the hurried visit of the Duchesse de Chevreux to a chapel on the road from Paris to Versailles. Yet, if such things had been suppressed, the picture of manners would have been incomplete.

With rare exception,[1] his general reflections are commonplace. He tells us absolutely nothing of the state or progress of art, science, literature, or philosophy. He seldom mentions a book, and only pays the tribute of passing praise to authors like Corneille, Racine, and La Bruyére, whose fame was established beyond dispute. He thus mentions Voltaire:

"Arouet, son of a notary, who was my father's and mine till his death, was exiled and sent to Tulle for very satirical and very impudent verses. I should not amuse myself by remarking so small a trifle, if this same Arouet, become great poet and academician under the name of Voltaire, had not ended by being a kind of personage in the republic of letters, and *even* a kind of 'important' amongst a certain world."

In 1710, when the Duke of Burgundy, the grandson of Louis, was twenty-eight, Saint-Simon, at the request of the Duc de Beauvilliers, reduced to writing the heads of a conversation regarding the conduct and demeanour most appropriate for the prince. This " Discours sur le Duc de Bourgogne," as it is entitled, contains not a syllable about political principles or measures; and was cautiously kept back from prudential reasons, which were equally strong against any oral or written communications to the same effect. He never specifies

---

[1] "So true is it that we forget still less the injuries we inflict, than those even which we receive" (vol. i. p. 78). He has here hit upon the same thought as Dryden:

"Forgiveness to the injured doth belong,
But they ne'er pardon who have done the wrong."

the subject of his conversations with the prince; but in proof of his liberality and comprehensiveness of view, Mr. Reeve says:

"Viewing with horror and aversion the ruinous decline of the monarchy, and anticipating from afar its dissolution if the course of events was not turned aside, he applied himself, in conjunction with the most illustrious of his friends, to form the political principles of the heir to the crown, the young Duc de Bourgogne, whose natural ferocity and pride had been effectually subdued by the benign authorities of Fénélon. Was there another at the Court of Versailles who would have inculcated on the future Sovereign of France, that kings are made for their subjects and not subjects for kings; who would, in 1710, have pointed to the States-General as the sole hope of the nation, and have contended that the strength and security of the ruler lay in the constitutional limitation of his power?"

The author of "Royal and Republican France," is here on his own ground, on which he may be supposed to see his way clearly; but, with all due deference, we submit that Saint-Simon did none of these things, and that one, at least, was already done to his hands. It was rather late in the day, considering the duke's age, to inculcate the doctrine that kings are made for their subjects and not subjects for kings, which had been familiar to him from boyhood, which (in Saint-Simon's words) "this Dauphin fully appreciated, and did not fear to assert openly and loudly." It is the moral of "Telemachus;"[1] and on hearing of the event which had so rapidly accelerated the approach of

[1] Telemachus says of Sesostris: "Il ne croyait être Roi que pour faire du bien à ses sujets." The wicked kings in Tartarus are punished amongst other things for "leur dureté pour les hommes dont ils auraient dû faire la félicité." "Telemachus," we need hardly add, was written for the instruction of this prince. It was first published, without the consent of the author, in 1699, and immediately suppressed by Louis, who took offence at the liberality of the opinions, and imagined Sesostris to be meant for himself.

his pupil to the throne, Fénélon wrote to him: "Il ne faut pas que tous soient à un seul; mais un seul doit être à tous pour faire leur bonheur."

We know of no recommendation of the States-General by Saint-Simon in 1710; but in 1715, after the death of the Dauphin, and shortly before the death of Louis, he laid some schemes before the Regent-expectant which show the spirit in which he would have proceeded to reform the most crying abuses. The primary cause, the *fons et origo*, of them all, in his eyes, was the exclusion of the nobles from the principal departments of the State. Speaking of the Controller-General and the four secretaries, he says:

"He (the Duke of Orleans) was not less wounded than I at the tyranny which those five kings of France exercised at their will and pleasure in the King's name, and in almost all without his knowledge, and the insupportable height to which they had climbed. . . .

"My design, then, was to begin by placing the nobility in the ministry, with the dignity and authority that became them, at the expense of the gown and pen, and to conduct affairs wisely by degrees, and according to the opportunities; so that, little by little, this *roture* should lose all the administrations which are not purely judicial, and that great lords and all nobility should, little by little, be substituted in all their employments, and always by preference in those which by their nature should be exercised by other hands, *in order to subject all to the nobility in every species of administration*, but with the precautions necessary against abuses."

He proposed to begin by Councils formed of nobles, with an eminent noble for president.

The state of the finances was so desperate, that Saint-Simon, after giving the fullest consideration to the subject, comes to the conclusion that the most advisable course would be a national bankruptcy, to be declared by edict; and it was to shelter the Regent from the responsibility that he proposed to convoke the States-General, throw all the odium upon them by getting them to pass the edict, and then send them about their business:

"Then I made him feel the address and the delicacy with which, above all things, it was necessary to make sure that the States should pronounce nothing; should decree nothing; should confirm nothing; that their acclamation should never be anything more than what is called *verba et voces*. . . . Thus the decoy (*leurre*) is complete; it is hollow throughout; the States-General acquire no rights from it; whilst the Duke of Orleans has all the essential through this specious and (to the nation) so interesting error. . . . The means of restraining the States, after having so powerfully excited them, appeared to me very easy. Protest, with confidence and modesty, that nothing is desired but their hearts, etc."

He then proceeds to recommend tactics which might be called Machiavellian, but for their transparent simplicity and absurdity. In short, the enlightened high-minded statesman, as he has been termed, saw "the sole hope of the nation" in a national bankruptcy and a shallow artifice. He expresses great disappointment when the Duke of Orleans, on becoming Regent, refuses to adopt this scheme. But in 1717, when the Duke, pressed by fresh difficulties, was disposed to have recourse to the States-General, Saint-Simon drew up a memoir (filling fifty pages) to prove that the golden opportunity had been let slip, and that the States might turn out dangerous and unmanageable:

"But besides the capital point of the relief of the people, which will put the whole kingdom on the side of the States, without weighing what is or what is not possible,—who can be sure of the number or the nature of the propositions which they may bring upon the *tapis*? The more violent the present situation, the more difficult the remedies, the more the blame of them is thrown on the past Government, so much the more will the States feel it incumbent on them to search for solid means of preventing their return; and through this desire so natural, even so just *if it were within their province*, so much the more will they try to give themselves authority for it. Now who can imagine, with any approach to precision, what means may be proposed? All that can be foreseen is that there are no possible means which would not weigh heavily on the royal authority, or which may not be put forward to bridle it.

* * * * *

" We are not in England; and God preserve a guardian and conservator of the royal authority, so enlightened as your Royal Highness, from giving occasion for the usages of this neighbouring kingdom; from which our kings have emancipated themselves for centuries, and of which ours would require a great account from you. No need of States-General to obtain aid from the peoples of France; the King, by himself alone, provides for it by his registered edicts and declarations."

Surely this is plain enough. The bare notion of a limited monarchy or a constitutional government never crossed Saint-Simon's mind, except to be discredited and repudiated. The longing desire of his life was to suppress the Parliament, the only semblance of a constitutional check: the *lit de justice*, which called forth so much unseemly and ungenerous exultation, was a downright act of despotism; and the words which brought his heart to his mouth were "*Le Roi* (a boy of eight) *veut être obéi, et obéi sur le champ!*" He despised the people, and did not know what civil or religious liberty meant. When the Regent, vividly impressed by the vast amount of injury, the depopulation and impoverishment, inflicted on the kingdom by the expulsion of the Huguenots, proposed recalling and emancipating them, Saint-Simon vehemently objected, on the ground that they would never be satisfied without equality, and that all the troubles resulting from their obstinate adherence to their peculiar opinions under successive sovereigns would be renewed.

Far from wishing for the re-establishment of the old aristocracy, Saint-Simon highly commends Richelieu for reducing them to what he terms their "just measure of honour, distinction, consideration, and authority"—to a condition which no longer admits of their "agitating" or "speaking loud to the King." When, therefore, Mr. Reeve compares the political principles of Saint-Simon to those of the Whig peers of 1688, the comparison is about as true as Mr. Disraeli's comparison of those same Whig peers to the Venetian oligarchy. When, again, Mr. Reeve appeals to Saint-Simon's proposal for convoking the States-General as a recognition of popular rights, he falls into an error analogous to that of the orator who called on the lieges to rally round their sovereign like the barons at Runnymede.

The terms "magnificent" and "transcendent beauty" are about as applicable to Saint-Simon's portraits as "heroic" to his cast of mind. His portrait of Fénélon is principally remarkable for the artistic skill with which the praise is qualified and the attractive features are shaded off, so as to produce the impression of a courtier-prelate who blended the grand seigneur with the priest, was all things to all men, and had his thoughts fixed more on this world than the next.[1] It is an ironical portrait, not a captivating one; it conveys no

---

[1] To cite a paragraph: "Plus coquet que toutes les femmes, mais en solides et non en misères, sa passion était de plaire, et il avait autant de soin de captiver les valets que les maîtres, et les plus petites gens que les personnages. Il avait pour cela des talents faits exprès, une douceur, une insinuation, des grâces naturelles et qui coulaient de source, un esprit facile, ingénieux, fleuri, agréable, *dont il tenait pour ainsi dire le robinet*, pour en verser la qualité et la quantité exactement convenable à chaque chose et à chaque personne."

sense of beauty to our minds: and we much prefer the portrait of the author of "Telemachus" by La Bruyère, as both more pleasing and more true.

There is one consideration, however, which may help to console the most ardent admirers of Saint-Simon when they cannot get colder or calmer critics to keep pace with them in their enthusiasm. If he had been in advance of his age instead of being on an exact level with it, the representative of his order, the type of his class—if he had been a stern moralist, a philosopher who despised forms and ceremonies, or a far-sighted high-principled statesman, he would not have been the Saint-Simon who has descended to us: he would not, and could not, have composed the most curious and valuable passages of his "Memoirs."

This is as clear as that we should not have had Boswell's Johnson, or Pepys' Diary, or Walpole's Letters, without the foibles, vanity, egotism, affectation, and love of gossip, to which the rare flavour of their writings is as certainly owing as that of the *foie gras* to the diseased liver of the goose. We cannot have it both ways. Men of an heroic cast of mind, of commanding genius, of lofty ambition, of elevated views, will not make it the chief business of their lives to struggle for straws and feathers and complacently record the struggle: to chronicle the current scandals or fix the fleeting follies of a Court; and it is precisely because Saint-Simon was not a Molière, a Bossuet, a Tacitus, a Juvenal, or a felicitous compound of all four, that he occupies his peculiar place in French literature: that he is hailed at last, by almost universal consent, as the author of the richest, most suggestive, illustrative, entertaining collection of contemporary anecdotes, scenes and characters which any age or country has produced.

MADAME DU DEFFAND
AND HER CORRESPONDENTS.[1]

(*From the Quarterly Review, July,* 1878.)

WE recently named Saint-Simon as a striking instance of a celebrity of whom little was popularly known in this country beyond the name. Madame du Deffand is another and still more striking instance. The reading public of England know next to nothing of her besides her connection and correspondence with Horace Walpole, forming a mere (if important) episode in the concluding years of her life. Yet that life is mixed up and blended with one of the most brilliant periods of the social and literary history of France. "Born," says M. de Lescure, "in the reign (en plein règne) of Louis XIV., and, by virtue of a privilege of longevity, which she shares with Voltaire and the Marshal de

---

[1] 1. *Lettres de la Marquise du Deffand à Horace Walpole. Auxquelles sont jointes des Lettres de Madame du Deffand à Voltaire, etc.* Nouvelle Edition, augmentée des *Extraits des Lettres d'Horace Walpole, etc.*, et précédée d'une Notice sur *Madame du Deffand* par M. Thiers. Deux volumes. Paris, 1864.

2. *Correspondance complète de la Marquise du Deffand, avec ses Amis, etc.*, classée dans l'*Ordre chronologique et précédée d'une Histoire de sa Vie, etc., etc.* Par M. de Lescure. Deux volumes. Paris, 1865.

3. *Correspondance complète de Mme. du Deffand avec la Duchesse de Choiseul, l'Abbé Barthélemy et M. Craufurt.* Publiée avec une Introduction par M. le Marquis de Sainte-Aulaire. Troisième édition, revue et considérablement augmentée. Trois volumes. Paris, 1877.

Richelieu, dying under Louis XVI. at the moment when the curtain is beginning to rise on the scene of the Revolution, Madame du Deffand is—along with Voltaire for ideas, with Richelieu for manners—one of the most complete representatives of the eighteenth century, one of the most perfect moral and literary types, one of the most indispensable and agreeable witnesses to be heard."

She lived on terms of intimacy with the most remarkable men and women of her time; and M. Thiers calls especial attention to the fact, that in her *salon* the men of rank were first brought in contact with the men of letters and lived with them on a perfect footing of equality. " What (he says) distinguished the suppers of Madame du Deffand from the dinners of Madame Geoffrin, was the high rank of the majority of the guests. The 'grands seigneurs philosophes' came to her to learn to depreciate the titles, the degrees, the prejudices—in a word, the classes on which their existence depended. In the houses of Madame Geoffrin, of Baron d'Holbach, of Helvetius, the philosophers were at home; at Madame du Deffand's they found themselves in the presence of those whose minds they led astray whilst preparing their ruin." Add, that all foreigners of distinction eagerly sought admission to her circle, and we see at once why it is still traditionally regarded as the most brilliant that ever existed in Paris: which is tantamount to saying, in any European capital.

Her correspondence is proportionally rich in famous names: famous in courts, camps, academies, and drawing-rooms,—in or for art, science, philosophy, history, wit, beauty, accomplishment, and gallantry. And those were days when people thought it right to maintain such reputation as they might possess for talent or ability by their letters; indeed, to make their letters a help or stepping-stone to celebrity. We have been made only too familiar with the tricks by which Pope first contrived to bring *his* before the world; and Horace Walpole's most cherished hopes of immortality were obviously built upon the studiously polished and carefully-copied epistolary compositions, the manuscripts (mostly autograph) of which may be seen as he left them at Strawberry Hill. His French contemporaries, with independent and recognised claims to distinction, were equally anxious to shine in this incidental and professedly unconscious way. D'Alembert took as much pains with his letters to Madame du Deffand as with his articles for the "Encyclopédie;" and Voltaire lavishes on her sheet after sheet of wit, thought, fine observation and profanity worthy of "Zadig" or "Candide."

Bearing in mind probably the Horatian maxim, "difficile est proprie communia dicere," hardly one of her friends, learned or illustrious, condescends to common things or the common mode of expression: *coûte que coûte*, they must shine; and we are constantly reminded by the eternal struggle after point that they are denizens of a country where fame has been won by an epigram or placed on a firm footing by a *bon-mot*. This adds materially to the piquancy of the collection and its value as an illustration of nationality. Madame de Genlis, who has left a vivid sketch of Madame du Deffand's *salon*, was struck by the light glancing tone of the conversation, and the rare introduction of grave topics: clearly not for lack of knowledge or ability. "I remember," writes Lord Bath (Pulteney), "that one day the conversation fell upon our history of England. How confused and surprised at the same time was I to see that the persons composing the company knew all that history better than we knew it ourselves."

A similar reflection on the want of grasp or depth will occur to the reader of the correspondence: who will look in vain for any glimpses of the historical future, any attempt to read the threatening signs of the political horizon, or any token that the highest and most cultivated section of French society were seriously impressed by the proximity or lurid pretokens of the revolutionary tempest, till it broke upon them. They never looked below the surface whilst the ground was trembling beneath their feet; and we shall find them discussing questions of sentiment, or speculating on the best method of getting rid of *ennui*, as if graceful frivolity were the best of virtues, to be amused the most imperative of duties, and the grand problem to be solved how to get through the day without a yawn.

Madame du Deffand has been fortunate in her editors and biographers. Between them they have left nothing to be desired or done in the way of information or research; and in our epitome of the known facts of her life, we need aim at little more than making a discriminating selection from the materials collected by them, especially by M. de Lescure and M. le Marquis de Sainte-Aulaire.

Marie de Vichy-Chamroud was born in 1697, a year after the death of Madame de Sévigné. In a letter to Walpole, dated December 25th, 1777, she writes: "To-day is my birthday. I should never have believed that I should see the year 1777. What use have I made of so many years? It is pitiable. What have I acquired? what have I preserved?" She was then eighty. Her birthplace, like that of Homer, is unknown; or, like that of the Iron Duke, doubted and disputed:

according to one authority, Auxerre; according to another, the Chateau of Chamroud, in the parish of Saint-Julien de Cray, now forming part of the arrondissement de Charolles (Saône-et-Loire). Her father, of an old Burgundian family, was Gaspar, Comte de Vichy-Chamroud, of whom nothing is recorded; her mother, Ann Brulard, daughter of the principal President of the Parliament of Burgundy. She had for godmother her maternal grandmother, Marie de Bouthillier de Chavigny, widow of the President Brulard and wife by a second marriage of César-Auguste, father of Etienne-François, Duc de Choiseul: hence the pleasantry which is constantly recurring in her letters of giving the name of "grand'maman" to the Duchesse de Choiseul, who was young enough to have been her granddaughter.

Left an orphan at an early age (the precise date is wanting), she was brought up at the convent of Madeleine de Traisnel, at Paris. M. de Lescure digresses to give an account of some of the convents of the same class, at which, the abbesses setting the example, the novices were quite as likely to learn the way to make love as the way to heaven. Hence probably the whim of the Duc de Richelieu, who had a portrait gallery of contemporary beauties, each attired in the costume of a *religieuse*. Certain it is, either that small pains were taken to initiate Marie de Vichy-Chamroud in sound principles of religion and morality, or that they lamentably failed. "One sometimes asks oneself," was her reflection at sixty-three, "if one would wish to return to such or such an age? Ah, I should not wish to become young again on condition of being brought up as I was brought up, to live only with the people with whom I have lived, and to have the sort of mind (*esprit*) and character that I have." While still a mere child she was a matured sceptic, and the spiritual directors who essayed to bring her back to the orthodox path ran no slight risk of being perverted by (instead of converting) her. One of these attempts is thus related by Chamfort:

"Madame du Deffand, when a young girl and in a convent, was preaching irreligion to her little comrades. The abbess sent for Massillon, to whom the young girl stated her reasons. Massillon went away saying: 'She is charming.' The abbess, who took the matter seriously, asked the bishop what book she should be made to read. He reflected a moment, and replied: 'A five-sous Catechism.' Nothing more could be got from him."

She herself tells the story with a variation:

"I remember that, in my youth, being at the convent, Madame de Luynes (her aunt) sent me the Father Massillon. My astonished genius trembled before his: it was not to the force of his reasons that I submitted, but to the importance of the reasoner."

"Excellent advice," exclaims M. de Sainte-Aulaire, "which unluckily recalls the famous recipe for catching little birds by putting salt upon their tails." We suspect that the prelate gave up her case as hopeless, which it proved; although, instead of taking the bold plunge to which her philosophic friends encouraged and invited her, she stood trembling and hesitating on the brink of disbelief to the last. As to the Catechism, she says: "I was like Fontenelle; I was hardly ten years old when I began to understand nothing in it." Once, after she had become blind, she desired the Epistles of St. Paul to be read aloud to her, and, impatient at the want of continuity in the narrative or reasoning, she interrupted the reader, exclaiming, "Well, but do *you* understand anything in all that?"

It is told of her, what has also been told of another celebrated Frenchwoman — *en ne prête qu'aux riches*—that she objected to praying (in the words of the Lord's Prayer) not to be led into temptation, on the ground that she had found temptation very pleasant. Another story is that she said she disliked praying to be made good, for fear she should be taken at her word.

Considering the freedom of her opinions, it is perhaps fortunate that nothing is recorded of her prior to her marriage, although this did not take place till she was twenty-one. It was arranged, as customary in her class, by her relatives or friends without consulting her inclinations, the essential point being that the connection should be suitable as regarded fortune and birth; and on the 2nd of August, 1718, she gave her hand to the Marquis du Deffand de la Lande, colonel of a regiment of Dragoons, and lieutenant-general of a district, &c. He was only eight years older, so that she had no reason to complain of disparity of years; but a graver disparity, that of character, tastes and modes of thought, was not long in manifesting itself. She is reported to have said of him "Il était aux petits soins pour déplaire." "*Ennui,*" was her frank confession, "has been, and always will be, the cause of all my faults." No wonder, therefore, that she soon got tired of a husband who was simply remarkable for dulness and respectability, and that she availed herself to the full of her privileges as a married woman to taste the long-coveted pleasures of the world.

The Parisian world was at its worst when she entered it. Depravation of morals, contempt of principle, unrestrained license of conduct, could not well be carried farther than they were carried under the Regency. The marriage tie was treated with undisguised ridicule; and the most flattering definition of a husband was, "une espèce de parapluie social." The intimate society of the Regent was almost entirely composed of profligates, male and female, and it is in this society that we find Madame du Deffand playing a prominent part within a year or two after her first appearance as a wife. The ladies who, one after the other, stood highest in their royal admirer's favour, Mesdames de Parabère, d'Averne, de Prie, were successively her friends. An entry in a contemporary journal (of Mathieu Marais), describing a *fête* at St. Cloud, runs: "Madame d'Averne was there resplendent, with Madame du Deffand and another lady. Many others had refused to be seen at it." A "joyous orgy" given by Madame du Chatelet to five friends at a cabaret, is described by the valet-de-chambre who ordered it and brought in the dishes:

"The supper began very late, and bore some resemblance to those of Tiberius in the island of Capri. The guests were Mesdames de Meuse, De Boufflers, Du Deffand, De Grafigny, and De la Popelinière. These ladies sent their servants to supper, and remained at table till five in the morning, after which they got into their carriages, which were in waiting, and returned home."[1]

Amongst other modes of dissipation by which she sought to baffle her constant persecutor, *ennui*, she tried play. "The odious passion, that of play!" she wrote to Craufurd, who was the slave of it. "I had it for three months: it detached me from everything; I thought of nothing else. It was *biribi* I was so fond of. I was shocked at myself, and cured myself of my madness." It

---

[1] "Voltaire et Madame du Chatelet: Révélations d'un Serviteur attaché à leur Personne, &c." Paris, 1863.

would seem from her manner of turning her dissipated acquaintances to account, that she was not solely actuated by the love of pleasure in seeking them. Marais sets down in his journal, under the date of Sept. 7, 1722, that she obtained from the Regent "by her intrigues, an annuity of six thousand livres, charged on the city, which are worth more than all the rest of her paper;" meaning, probably, her share in some of the bubble schemes then recently afloat, which were freely distributed amongst the Court ladies by the speculators." In a later entry of the same year he says: "Her husband has thrown her off; he could no longer endure her gallantries with Fargis, *alias* Delrieu, son of the partisan Delrieu, of whom it was said that he had 'tant *volé*' that he had thereby lost a wing. These are the people who have the favour of the Court, and our rents."

When, after the death of her royal protector, Madame de Prie was exiled to Courbepine, in Normandy, "she was accompanied," remarks an historian of the Regency, "by Madame du Deffand, her rival in beauty, in gallantry, and in malice. These two friends interchanged every morning couplets which they composed against each other. They had imagined nothing better to conjure away *ennui* than this amusement of vipers." This is confirmed by Madame du Deffand, who in a letter to Walpole gives a specimen of her own share in these epigrammatic duels, which does not leave a high impression of its piquancy.

When Mrs. Warren, the widow of the blacking manufacturer of once famous memory, was questioned about the authorship of the verses in praise of her merchandise, she proudly drew herself up and replied, "We keeps a poet." If a "Notice Historique" prefixed to any early edition of the

"Correspondance" may be trusted, Madame du Deffand had more than one poet in her suite. "Pieces in verse have often been attributed to her. I know none of which she is really the author. She addressed herself, as has been seen, to the muse of M. de Trémont; she had subsequently recourse to the complaisance of MM. Marmontel, Saint-Lambert, La Harpe, etc. It is they who made the verses that she sent in her name. They ordinarily accompanied those new year's gifts (*étrennes*) which she was in the habit of sending to some of her female friends." This may be partially true at the times of which he speaks; but she possessed the gift or knack of rhyming with facility, and there is no reason to doubt that she was the author of the parody on the "Inès de Castro" of Lamotte, which checked the popularity of that production in full career. M. de Lescure intimates that her parody was written to gratify Voltaire, with whom she appears to have struck up a friendship or alliance as early as 1722 or 1723; for in a letter of 1768, he writes, "I have been attached to you for more than five-and-forty years." In a letter (1725) to Madame de Bernière, at whose chateau, near Rouen, Madame du Deffand was staying, he writes, "I fancy that you are having charming suppers;" and he parodies, applying to these ladies, who passed for *gourmandes*, the verses of Voiture to Anne of Austria:

> "Que vous étiez bien plus heureuse
> Lorsque vous étiez autrefois
> Je ne veux pas dire *amoureuse*;
> La rime le veut toutefois."

About the same time he addressed to the same lady (Madame de Bernière) the impromptu subscribed "*Fait chez vous*, January 8, after dinner:"

> "Qui vous perd et qui vous attend
> Perd bientôt sa philosophie ;
> Et tout sage avec du Deffand,
> Voudrait en fou passer sa vie."

It would seem from this that Madame du Deffand's charm was of the more intellectual order; and if, at twenty-eight, she had given up intrigue for *gourmandise*, it may fairly be inferred that her imputed gallantries were more matters of custom and bad example, than of passion, sensibility, or heart. She fell in with the fashion: she was carried away in the vortex. It was computed, when her career began, that there were only three women of her condition belonging to the Court circle who lived respectably with their husbands. It is no very severe reflection on her that she did not constitute a fourth. The attempt she made to re-establish conjugal relations, with its results, is related by Mademoiselle Aïsse, who, proof herself (in one remarkable instance) against strong temptation, was by no means disposed to impose the same self-denial on her friends. "I have managed," she writes, "to bring Bertin acquainted with Madame du Deffand. She is handsome; she is full of grace: he finds her lovable. I hope he will begin with her a romance that will last him all his life." Shortly afterwards she continues:

"I wish to speak to you of Madame du Deffand. She had a violent desire to be reconciled to her husband. As she is clever, she justified this desire by very good reasons; she consequently acted on several occasions in a manner to render their reconciliation durable and becoming. Her grandmother dies, and leaves her four thousand livres a year. This improvement of her fortune afforded the means of offering her husband a more favourable condition than if she had been poor. She succeeded, as we foresaw.

She was complimented on all sides. I could have wished that she had not been in such a hurry: a noviciate of six months was still necessary, to be naturally passed by her husband with his father. I had my reasons for giving her this advice; but as this good lady mingles *esprit*, or, more properly speaking, imagination, with everything, she so managed matters that the amorous husband broke off his journey and came to set up house with her, that is, to the extent of dining and supping; for as to living together, she would not hear of it for three months, to avoid all suspicion injurious to her or her husband. It was the finest friendship in the world during six weeks. At the end of this time she got tired of this mode of life, and resumed an extravagant aversion for her husband. Without abruptly breaking with him, she put on so despairing desponding an air that he adopted the step of returning to his father's. She took all imaginable measures to prevent his return. I plainly put before her all the infamy of the proceeding. She has done her best to move me, and bring me over to her reasons. I stood firm. I remained six weeks without seeing her. There is no sort of baseness that she has not resorted to to prevent me from abandoning her."

This is preposterous. Mademoiselle Aïsse's position, little above that of a humble companion, renders the adoption of such a tone on her part improbable in the extreme; and the care Madame du Deffand took to guard her reputation shows that she had some worth caring for, instead of being, as her alleged friend goes on to represent her, entirely reckless of consequences:

" The end of this miserable conduct is, that she cannot live with anybody. The good lady has thought of nothing but her inclinations, and, without reflection, has judged a lover better than a husband. She remains the fable of the public, blamed by all the world, despised by her lover, shunned. She does not know how to set all this right, She throws herself at people's heads to make believe that she is not abandoned: this does not answer. She wears by turns a calm and an embarrassed air. This is her position, and the state of things between her and me."

This account is obviously overcharged. The lover is thrown in as a make-weight; and a sufficient explanation of her conduct will be found in her inevitable tendency to *ennui*. We know as a fact that she never forfeited her place in society or lost caste. That soon afterwards she was the most welcome and petted guest at Sceaux is a complete answer to the calumny. The presiding genius, the queen of this miniature Court, was the Duchesse du Maine, the granddaughter of the great Condé, Louise-Bénédicte de Bourbon, " the divine Ludovise," the woman in the world (goddess and shepherdess by turns) in whose honour there had been the greatest expenditure of impromptus and madrigals. She was so exacting in this sort of homage that Malézieux speaks of her courtiers as condemned to the "galères du bel esprit." She liked to be surrounded by as numerous and brilliant a circle as she could get together, less to enjoy the wit of others than to display her own. "I am very fond of society," was her naïve avowal; "all the world listens to me, and I listen to nobody."

She founded the order of "La Moucho à Miel," of which she was grand-mistress, with the device, taken from the "Aminta" of Tasso, of "*Picciola, sì, ma fa pure grave le ferite*" (Little, yes; but it wounds deep), in allusion to her diminutive figure. This order was solemnly conferred on Madame du Deffand, and the President Hénault wrote verses to commemorate the event. Mademoiselle de Launay (afterwards Madame de Staal), lady of honour and private secretary to the Duchess, referring to one of the first visits, writes:

"We had Madame du Deffand at Sceaux. No one has more wit, or has it more natural. The sparkling fire which animates her pierces to the bottom of every object, makes it come out of its own accord, and gives relief to the simplest lineaments. She possesses in the highest degree the talent of painting character, and her portraits, more vivid than the originals, render these better known than the most intimate commerce with them. She gave me quite a new idea of this kind of writing by showing me a portrait she had made of myself; but a little too much precaution and too much politeness had, contrary to her custom, kept her from the truth. I tried to draw it myself, to show where she was wrong, and gave it her."

This is the portrait of Madame de Staal, given in her "Memoirs," of which she naïvely said, "Je ne me suis peinte qu'en buste."

It would seem that it was not without a good deal of coaxing, and after stipulating for the apartment of her choice, that Madame du Deffand was induced from interval to interval to form one of the established circle at Sceaux:

"If the bad weather (writes Madame de Staal) makes your lodging at the little chateau inconvenient, you shall have in preference to all the world that which you wish. . . . But you must show yourself a little more in the day. If your trips to Paris were to become long and frequent, I believe there would be some difficulty in keeping an apartment in the great chateau often empty. . . . If you only appear in the evening and are much in Paris, her Royal Highness will take it very ill of you, if only for the bad example set of disobedience to her will in this place."

Although she avoided breaking with the Duchess, Madame du Deffand was already far advanced in the formation of a *salon*, which required her to make Paris her set place of residence. In 1742 we find her at a small house in the Rue de Beaune, the house in which Voltaire died, and by an odd coincidence it is he who was foremost in celebrating her suppers in this locality:

> "Formont, vous, et les du Deffand,
> C'est-à-dire les agréments,

> L'esprit, le bon goût, l'éloquence
> Et vous, plaisirs, qui valez tant!
> Plaisirs, je vous suivis par goût
> Et les Newton par complaisance."

The last line is an unkind hit at Madame du Chatelet, who was absorbed in the study of Newton. The death of Madame de Staal, in 1750, made Madame du Deffand's presence more than ever desirable at Sceaux; and from a sense of gratitude for the constant affection shown her by the Duchess, or real sympathy, she was induced to devote several weeks to a kind of existence which Voltaire hardly misdescribed when he wrote, "Do you know that you were slaves at Sceaux and Anet? yes, slaves in comparison with the true liberty one tastes at Potsdam with a king who has gained five battles."

We are met by a strange contradiction and confusion of dates when we try to fix the period and circumstances at and under which she removed to the apartment in the convent of Saint-Joseph with which the best days of her *salon* are associated. The author of the "Notice" already quoted says, that "disgusted by the death of M. de Tremont and that of her husband with the noise and slavery of society, and straitened in her means, she quitted her hotel and her habits of representation for a modest lodging, where she passed the last thirty years of her life." Her husband died in 1753, M. de Tremont in 1759, and, as she died in 1780, her thirty years' occupation must have commenced in 1750. After quoting a letter to her from Madame de Staal, July 1747, expressing doubt at her being reconciled to her apartment of St. Joseph, M. de Lescure continues:

> "This is the first time that there is any question of this installation. It is then in 1747 that, faithful to the usages

of the time, which opened to widows of quality (sometimes widows in the lifetime of the husbands) the asylum of the profane part of certain convents, where a woman of tact and position could enjoy at small expense the pleasures of retreat or those of society, Madame du Deffand established herself at the convent of Saint-Joseph."

This seems tolerably clear, yet unless she put off the furnishing for two years, it would appear, from another source equally well authenticated, that the installation did not take place till two years later. In a letter dated Constantinople, April 17th, 1749, the Comte des Alleurs, French Ambassador to the Porte, writes : "I am charmed that you are content with your Saint-Joseph lodging : I see you hence in this apartment, admiring the yellow-watered silk, and the flame-coloured bows. I forgive your love of ownership; it is the only mode of liking anything."

Her income after her husband's death, as she subsequently told Walpole, was 33,000 livres, little more than £1200 a year of our money; but quite sufficient, in her time at Paris, for the establishment she set up—that is, with good management, and by all accounts she was an excellent manager. An important change in her habits is indicated by a letter from Baron Scheffer, dated November 2nd, 1753:

"It is very true that the plan you have adopted of dining may prove as advantageous for society as for health. One meets at an earlier hour, and naturally enough the people who dine have acquired a tranquillity very agreeable to those with whom they live."

Rousseau (quoted with full assent by Rogers) justifies his " goût-vif-pour les déjeuners," by the remark, " C'est le temps de la journée où nous sommes les plus tranquilles, où nous causons le plus à notre aise." Sydney Smith gave the preference to breakfasts on the ground (open to grave doubt) that no one is conceited before one. It will be remembered that the Parisian dinner rather resembled our luncheon in its hour, absence of formality, and brevity.

During the ten years that Mademoiselle de Lespinasse remained with her, Madame du Deffand commanded the best society of Paris, including all the literary and scientific men of note, with the exception of Marmontel and Thomas—the constant *habitués* of Madame Geoffrin—and of Diderot and Grimm, who remained faithful to Baron d'Holbach. These ten years began in 1754, and, considering the relative position and personal qualities of the two ladies, the wonder is that the connection lasted beyond the first.

Mademoiselle de Lespinasse was the illegitimate daughter of the Comtesse d'Albon. Although she was entered in the parish registers as the legitimate child of a tradesman of Lyons, whose name was given her, the fact and all the circumstances of her birth were well-known in the province; and as she was born after the marriage of her mother, she might have put in a claim to inherit with the legitimate children according to the doctrine "pater est quem nuptiæ demonstrant." The fear of her taking this step, which she never so much as meditated at any time, seems to have been the primary motive with the Comte and Comtesse de Vichy for taking her under their protection and giving her a home; the Comte, Madame du Deffand's brother, having married a legitimate daughter of the Comtesse d'Albon. It would seem that they were content to keep her domesticated with their family, so as to be able to watch over her, and never thought of conciliating her by kindness.

She had been four years under their roof, charged with the education of their children, when she attracted the notice of Madame du Deffand, to whom she eagerly unbosomed herself:

"She told me that it was impossible for her to remain with M. and Madame de Vichy; that for a long time she had received from them the hardest and most humiliating treatment: that her patience was exhausted: that it was more than a year since she had declared to Madame de Vichy that she wished to leave them; that she could no longer endure the scenes they daily imposed upon her."

Writing to her friend, M. de Guibert, at a subsequent period, Mademoiselle de Lespinasse says:

"There is no misery I have not endured. Some day, my friend, I will narrate to you things that are not found in the romances of Prévost or Richardson."

To Madame du Deffand, with failing eyes and total blindness impending, the notion naturally occurred that her young friend was the person of all others best fitted for a companion. But on sounding her brother and sister-in-law she found them strongly opposed to her scheme, and resolute not to part with their *protégée* at the risk of her being encouraged to form hopes or plans inimical to their interests. The Duchesse de Luynes, on being consulted, gave it as her opinion that their opposition was unreasonable; and whilst the negotiation was proceeding, Mademoiselle de Lespinasse settled the matter, so far as living any longer with her so-called protectors was concerned, by taking up her abode in a convent at Lyons. This she quitted in the spring of 1754 for Madame du Deffand's apartment of Saint-Joseph, after a correspondence in which she received ample warning touching particular points of conduct;

although she could hardly have foreseen the hardships and trials that were in store for her. In April, 1754, Madame du Deffand writes:

"I hope, my queen, that I shall never have to repent of what I do for you, and that you would not take the step of coming to me if you had not thoroughly made up your mind, and if you had not decided not to make any attempt. . . . Having said this, it only remains for me to speak to you of the joy I should have to see and live with you. Adieu, my queen; pack up your things, and come to make the happiness and consolation of my life: it will not be my fault if it is not reciprocal.

* * * * *

"There is one article on which I must come to an understanding with you: it is, that the least artifice, and even the smallest art that you might put into your conduct with me, would be to me insupportable. I am naturally distrustful, and all those in whom I suspect *finesse*, become suspected by me to the point of my no longer placing any confidence in them. I have two intimate friends, Formont and D'Alembert: I am passionately attached to them, less by their agreeability and their friendship than by their extreme truthfulness. . . .

"You must then make up your mind to live with me in the greatest truth and sincerity: never resort to insinuation or exaggeration: in a word, never lose one of the greatest attractions of youth, which is *naïveté*. You have a great deal of *esprit*; you have gaiety; you are capable of sentiments; with all these qualities you will be charming so long as you give your *naturel* fair play, so long as you are without pretension and without equivocation."

When all had been arranged at Lyons, Madame du Deffand started for Paris, after announcing her speedy arrival and future mode of life to D'Alembert:

"The life I shall lead will suit you, I hope. We shall often dine together *tête-à-tête*, and we shall confirm each other in the resolution not to make our happiness depend on anybody but ourselves. I shall possibly teach you to endure men, and you will teach me to do without them."

Her mode of doing without them was to collect round her as many of the most distinguished as she could; and the mode of life she actually pursued for a period is correctly described by the author of the "Notice," who says that, instead of giving dinners on fixed days, like Madame Geoffrin, she gave *soirées*, beginning at six, occasionally followed by a supper. One of the aphoristic sayings attributed to her was, that "Suppers were one of the four ends (*fins*) of man." What are the other three?

Her blindness made day or night indifferent to her. She had formerly been in the habit of sitting up late, but the dawn at least warned her of the necessity of sleep. During the concluding twenty-six years of her life when night was never ending for her, it was only caprice, whim, or exhaustion that induced her to take to her bed, not to leave it till six in the evening, when she received her visitors. Mademoiselle de Lespinasse was compelled to keep nearly the same hours, it being a part of her regular duty to remain by the bedside of her patroness, reading aloud or conversing, not unfrequently till morning broke. She rose at five in the afternoon, an hour before Madame du Deffand, to prepare for the receptions; and it was her employment of this hour, rather than any impatience at the painful sacrifice of health and comfort imposed upon her, that caused the final and definitive rupture in 1764.

She had powers of conversation little, if at all, inferior to those of the Marquise. She was young, interesting, with a distinguished air and presence, and claims to what many called beauty, till it was impaired by the small-pox. She occupied a little room looking on the court where (suggests M. de Sainte-Aulaire) "some clerk of the War Office may be now at work, little thinking that during many years the highest notabilities of the last century were in the habit of meeting by appointment every day, between five and six, in his bureau." We doubt the many years, but it had for some time become the habit of Madame du Deffand's most distinguished friends to pass the hour prior to the opening of her *salon* with Mademoiselle de Lespinasse. "These," continued Marmontel, the chief authority for the incident, "were moments stolen from Madame du Deffand. This special rendezvous was consequently a mystery to her, for it was well foreseen that she would be jealous of it. To listen to her, it was nothing less than a treason. She cried out against it in the loudest terms, accusing this poor girl of seducing away her friends, and vowing that she would no longer nourish this serpent in her bosom."

But had she not good reason to complain? Was it not something very like a treason?—at all events a flagrant breach of the original compact she had insisted upon, an undeniable departure from the line of conduct she had pronounced essential to confidence? Was not this hour a serious encroachment on her rights? Were the friends who came to her after this preliminary interchange of mind the same as if they had come fresh, with the gloss of novelty on their gossip, their anecdotes, or their wit? Were they equally able to begin and carry on the conversation without any sense of restraint? Madame du Deffand had clearly right upon her side so long as she merely protested against the deceit practised on her; but when she would listen to no excuse, contrition, or promise of amendment, and as good as turned her young friend, now become her rival, into the streets, she placed herself completely in the wrong. More than one violent scene of crimination and recrimination took place between the ladies! and at the end of one of them, if we may believe La Harpe, Mademoiselle de Lespinasse, driven to despair, took sixty grains of opium, which, failing to produce death, threw her into terrible convulsions, which had a lasting effect on her nerves. Under the belief that she was dying, she said to Madame du Deffand, who was weeping at the foot of her bed, "It is too late, madame." Madame remained inexorable, and declined even a parting interview. In a final letter she says:

"I cannot consent to see you again so soon; and I cannot believe that it is a sentiment of friendship that makes you wish it. It is impossible to love those by whom one knows oneself to be 'detested,' 'abhorred,' etc., etc.; by whom 'one's self-love is unceasingly humiliated, crushed,' etc., etc. These are your very expressions, and the result of the impressions that you have long been receiving from those whom you call your true friends. They may be so in effect; and I wish with all my heart that they may procure you all the advantages you expect from them—pleasure, fortune, consideration," etc.

This was meant satirically, but the wish was amply fulfilled. The apartment in the Rue de Belle-Chase, to which Mademoiselle de Lespinasse removed, was furnished for her by the Duchesse de Luxembourg, and could boast a circle of *habitués* only second to that which met at the Convent; in fact, with rare exception, the same persons fluctuated between both. If there was one to whom Madame du Deffand thought she could dictate, it was D'Alembert; but when she imperiously gave him the alternative of breaking with her or Mademoiselle de Lespinasse, he decided without a moment's hesitation for the younger, to whom he afterwards became passionately attached.

This embittered the rupture; and on hearing of her death, in 1776, Madame du Deffand's first expression was, "She should have died fifteen years sooner; I should not then have lost D'Alembert." The *salon* of Mademoiselle de Lespinasse was the only one that came into momentary competition with that of Madame du Deffand, who, when what she thought undue importance was attached to Madame Geoffrin's in her presence, exclaimed: "*Combien de bruit pour une omelette au lard*" (What a fuss about a bacon omelette!)

According to Rochefoucauld the reason why the majority of women are little moved by friendship is, that it is insipid when they have felt love. It may be because Madame du Deffand was comparatively insensible to the tender passion, and only gave in to it as the fashion or habit of her youth, that she took so ardently to friendship. But eloquently as she expatiates on its charms, she failed to acquire credit for the excess of sensibility to which she lays claim. La Harpe lays down broadly that "it was difficult to have less sensibility and more egotism."

Under the title of "Idée des Liaisons de Paris," Grimm reports a pretended dialogue between her and the Count Pont-de-Veyle. She begins:

"'Pont-de-Veyle!' 'Madame!' 'Where are you?' 'At your chimney corner.' 'With your feet on the hearth, as one is among friends?' 'Yes, madame.' 'It must be owned that there are few *liaisons* of longer standing than ours.' 'That is true!' 'Yes, fifty years good; and in this long interval not a cloud, not even the semblance of a difference.' 'That is what I have always admired.' 'But, Pont-de-Veyle, may not that be because at bottom we have been always perfectly indifferent to one another?' 'That may well be, madame.'"

When Pont-de-Veyle died, says La Harpe, "she came to a large supper party at Madame de Marchais', where I was, and she was condoled with on her loss. *'Helas! he died this evening at six, otherwise you would not see me here.'* These were her very words, and she supped as usual, that is to say, very well; for she was very *gourmande.*"

M. de Sainte-Aulaire objects that Grimm was not personally acquainted with her, and appeals to the warm, exacting tone of her letters. Yet even these are not wanting in indications that she was deficient in tenderness, and commonly made head do duty for heart. Thus, in the correspondence with the President Hénault, when she labours hardest to persuade both him and herself that they are wrapt up in each other, she unconsciously betrays her incapacity for genuine affection; and although their contemporaries were less charitable on this point, we see no reason to doubt the entire innocence of their *liaison.*

He was forty-five when it commenced. "The poor President!" exclaims Grimm; "he may have been an agreeable adorer, never a passionate one; no one would do him this injustice." He said, pleasantly, of his own want of ardour in middle age that he began to be very glad when he mistook the hour, and arrived too late at a rendezvous. Yet he was too sentimental for Madame du Deffand, who finds fault with him for the one flight of gallantry in his letters with which a woman of fancy and feeling would have been charmed. She is at Forges taking the waters, and he at Paris, when, July 12, 1742, he writes:

"I went yesterday to *Brutus:* it was well attended. I was confirmed in what I have always thought, that it is the finest piece of Voltaire. Lanoue acted with that intelligence which you do not like, because it does not suppose fire; it is as if when one says that a girl on her preferment plays well on the harpsichord, this is as good as saying that she is not pretty. However, I found no want of fire. I returned to receive my company, which was not numerous, for we were only seven; the Maréchale, her daughter, Madame de Maurepas, Ceresti, Pont-de-Veyle, and myself. Our supper was excellent, and (what will surprise you) we amused ourselves. I own to you, that if, when it was over, I had known where to find you, I should have gone to look for you. *The weather was the finest imaginable, the moon was beautiful, and my garden seemed to long for you.* But, as Polyeucte observes, what is the use of talking of these things to hearts that God has not touched?"

She replies to this pretty burst in a letter, or rather postscript, in which, after some medical details of the effect of the waters, she says:

"I find I am growing thinner, and I see everybody else getting fatter. I should like to hear the answer to the consultations which I begged you to hold with Silva (the Paris doctor). I do not know whether it is one ounce or two of peeled cassia that I am to take, and as I do not sup, at what time I should take it. It is the moonlight, it is certain circumstances, that make you long for me. I am regretted and wished for according to the dispositions to which the beauty of the weather brings your soul; as for me, I long for you everywhere, and I know of no circumstance which could render your presence less agreeable. *The fact is, I have neither temperament nor romance.*"

She had only to go one step further, and say that she had neither body nor soul. According to her doctrine, it is lack of affection to wish to share a pleasure with a beloved object; and the poet of love was untrue to his vocation when he sang :

"Oh! best of delights, as it everywhere is,
  To be near the loved one! What a rapture is his,
  Who in moonlight and music thus sweetly may glide
  O'er the lake of Cashmere, with that One by his side!

If woman can make the worst wilderness dear,
Think, think what a heaven she must make of Cashmere!"

The President was not slow to see his advantage, and replied:

"You have neither temperament nor romance! I pity you from my soul; and you know as well as another the value of this loss, for I believe I have heard you speak of it. What you call romance in your letter—the memories, the moonlight, the idea of the places where we have seen any one we love, a phase of soul which makes us think more tenderly of them, a *fête*, a fine day, etc.—in a word, all that the poets have said upon this subject—it seemed to me that this was by no means ridiculous. But haply it is for my good that you do not like me to have all these follies in my head. Well, be it so. I beg pardon for all the rivulets, past, present, and to come; for their brothers, the birds; for their cousins, the elms; and for their great-grandfathers, the sentiments. There! I stand corrected, and my letters will henceforth be only agreeable to you by all the news I can pick up in the town, and imagine, to amuse you. I resume, then, the historic style, and I will speak no more of myself except in connection with facts."

He might have added, anticipating the fine remark of Johnson at Iona:—"Whatever withdraws us from the power of our senses—whatever makes the past, the distant, or the future predominate over the present, advances us in the scale of thinking beings"—

"And hence the charm historic scenes impart;
Hence Tiber awes, and Avon melts the heart.
Aërial forms, in Tempe's classic vale,
Glance through the gloom, and whisper in the gale,
In wild Vaucluse with love and Laura dwell,
And watch and weep in Eloïsa's cell."

It was for want of this faculty of association that she suffered so much from *ennui*, especially after the supply of external impressions was curtailed by blindness. From what an infinity of weariness and querulousness might she not have been saved by a spark of that inward light which irradiated and cheered the solitary and dark but wakeful hours of Milton!

> "Ah! who can tell the triumphs of the mind
> By truth illumined, and by taste refined?
> *When age has quenched the eye and closed the ear,*
> Still nerved for action in her native sphere."

She seems to have become aware of her mistake in trying to pass off the defect of her character as a merit, for directly afterwards she writes:

"You know, moreover, what I think, what I am, and what are my subjects of quarrel. For example, is it in good faith that you tell me I wish to emancipate myself from gratitude when I appear to doubt of your sentiments? Once for all, do you believe me actuated by such a motive? Oh, no; you see clear as day that when I remark in you a grain of true sentiment, it performs the miracle of the grain of mustard in Scripture: it transports mountains. Rarely do you let me enjoy this illusion, or this truth: but let us drop this, and not trouble my waters. They will really do me good."

Referring to the pleasure she received from his letters, she tells him that he has "l'absence délicieuse;" and he replies:

"You have never said a better thing than that I have 'l'absence délicieuse.' But all truths are not good to be told. I believe in effect that, if you had to arrange your life, you would divide it into two parts, and that I should have one. Absence is like the Elysian fields, in which all men are equal; or, more correctly speaking, I believe that I should have some advantage, and that it is the true position for recalling one's love in sonnets."

Having no imagination of the richer kind to vary the expression of such feeling as she possessed, she exercises her ingenuity in inventing subjects of complaint. She resembles Faulkland in the "Rivals," who fancies that his mistress's melancholy is assumed to excite his sympathy, and that her gaiety when he is out of spirits is a proof of her indifference. In letter after letter she goes on refining on sentiment till it is well-nigh lost in logical distinctions or metaphysical analysis. In a postscript to one of them she adds:

"Do not set about correcting yourself in anything. I like you to talk elms, rivulets, sparrows, etc.: it affords me a most agreeable occasion for contradicting you, confounding you, tormenting you: *it is, I believe, what most contributes to the salutary operation of the waters.*"

How lightly she regarded the tie is shown by La Harpe, when he relates that, having made up her mind, by way of change and for the sake of excitement, to try devotion, she began by setting down the different things she was prepared to renounce, and concluded the list with: "As for *rouge* and the President, I will not do them the honour of giving them up." Latterly the intimacy became a mere matter of habit, and ceased to be a source of gratification to either. On the 22nd of February, 1769, Voltaire, who detested him, writes to her:

"So the President's watch is out of order? It is the fate of all who live long. . . . I am told that the President declines apace. I am sorry for it, but one must submit to one's destiny. Pray, tell the shattered President how much I am interested in his amiable soul."

She writes to Walpole, on the 13th of June, 1770:

"Yesterday I dragged the President to a concert. Mademoiselle le Maure was singing. He did not hear her any more than the instruments that accompanied her. He kept asking me every minute if I heard anything. He supposes me deaf as well as blind, and as old as himself: on this last point he is not far wrong."

Why did she drag him to a concert, except, as he always complained, to "tyrannise" him. He was then eighty-six and she seventy-three. On Sunday, the 25th of November, 1770, she writes:

"What I announced in my last letter has come to pass. The President died yesterday at seven in the morning. I felt sure he was dying since Wednesday: he had not on that day, nor since, either suffering or consciousness: never was end more gentle: he became extinct. Madame de Jonsac's grief has appeared extreme: mine is more moderate. I had so many proofs of his lack of friendship, that I believe I have only lost an acquaintance: however, as this acquaintance was of very long standing, and all the world believed us intimate (except a few who know some of my subjects of complaint), I receive compliments of condolence on every side. It only rests with myself to believe that I am much loved; but I have renounced the pomps and vanities of this world, and you have made me a perfect proselyte: I have all your scepticism as to friendship."

As Walpole's proselyte, she had simply renounced one set of vanities for another, probably a worse; and as for disbelief in friendship, her whole correspondence is based upon an exaggerated notion of its reality. A scene which took place at the President's death-bed may have had something to do with her bitterness of tone:

"She asked him if he remembered Madame de Castelmoron. The sound of this name roused the President, who replied that he well remembered it. She then asked him if he had loved her more than Madame du Deffand. "What a difference!" exclaimed the dying man. And then he set himself to make the panegyric of Madame de Castelmoron, and always by comparing her excellent qualities with the vices of Madame du Deffand. This dotage lasted half an hour, with everybody listening, without its being possible for Madame du Deffand to silence her panegyrist, or change the conversation. It was the song of the swan."

Until the rupture with Mademoiselle de Lespinasse, D'Alembert was one of the most intimate and valued of her friends. The correspondence with or relating to him is replete with literary interest; and his letters bear ample testimony to his truthfulness, independence, and self-respect. He had need of these qualities; for, in regard to birth, he lay under the same disadvantage as Mademoiselle de Lespinasse, whilst his person and voice went far to justify the reply to a fanatical admirer who, in the height of his fame, pronounced him to be a god, "Allons donc! si c'etait un Dieu, il commencerait par se faire homme." There was another depreciating and somewhat profane remark on his personal appearance, which may have suggested Lord Byron's on Curran and Corinne: "I saw him (Curran) presented to Madame de Stael at Mackintosh's: it was the grand confluence between the Rhone and the Saône, and they were both so d——d ugly that I could not help wondering how the best intellects of France and Ireland could have taken up respectively such residences." So long as D'Alembert and Madame du Deffand remained friends, all his literary projects are communicated to her, and his precise state of mind at critical epochs of his career is laid bare:

"March 10, 1753.—I am now immured for a long time to come, and likely enough for ever, in my sad but very dear and very peaceable geometry. I am quite satisfied with finding a pretext for doing nothing more, in the storm my book has raised against me.[1] I have, however, neither attacked nor designated anybody, more than the author of

[1] "Essai sur les Gens de Lettres."

'Le Mechant' and twenty others, against whom no one has broken out. But there is only luck and ill-luck. I need neither the friendship of these people, since assuredly I have no wish to ask them for anything, nor their esteem, since I have resolved never to live with them; so I let them do their worst. I have already made 500 livres clear profit by my book; which may amount to 2000 when the impression is sold; but only half has been yet. Adieu, Madame; hasten your return. Do you know this of geometry, that with it one dispenses with a great many things?"

She took an active part in his election to the Academy, in opposition to another great lady, who strenuously exerted herself for Bourdaloue. Formont writes, December 4, 1763:

"I am enchanted with the election of D'Alembert; it seemed that he had only to show himself and it was a settled affair. However, you needed all the talents you have for negotiation; but one is not surprised when one reflects that you had to do with the illustrious, the learned D. de Ch. (Duchesse de Chaulnes). . . .

"Since D'Alembert is very glad to be of the Academy, he must for the present compose works intelligible to the vulgar. He has done enough to be admired by the calculators: it is time for him to think of pleasing the amiable ignoramuses, for whom he is made as much as for the others. I have written to him to-day, and I will write to-morrow to the President."

The letter of Formont to D'Alembert throws light on the literary and social cabals of the period.

"She (the Duchesse de Chaulnes) thinks, perhaps, that you are wanting in some qualities which she deems indispensable to a great man. She has said that you were but a child: she believes that even in a seraglio you would drag along an everlasting infancy. I do not believe it, at all events; and I am persuaded that you will come well out of whatever you may undertake, even the compliment you are about to make to the Academy, which appears to me a more difficult operation than that of contenting a Duchess.

And these six black balls? Who are those people? Six pious persons apparently, who are frightened at the philosophers; as if Newton had not commented the Apocalypse, and Locke the Epistle to the Galatians!

"Seriously, my dear friend, I am delighted they have done you justice. I am sorry for the Academy and for the nation, that you have not been elected by acclamation; but that of all France and of all Europe will be an ample recompense."

None of her correspondents, except Voltaire, relate current events, some of which now sound strange enough, with more discriminating liveliness than D'Alembert:

"Paris, December, 1752.—I entreat you to spare your eyes: it is a real evil to have weak sight; but it is not an evil, it is sometimes a good, not to see many people. It would be one in truth not to hear all the follies which are committed here, and the billets of confession, and the Archbishop, and the Parliament. We have been much occupied during a fortnight with a sister Perpétue, of the community of Saint Agatha, to whom the Parliament wished the sacraments to be administered, and to whom they were refused by the Archbishop. The temporalities of the Archbishop were under seizure for twenty-four hours. (They would have found it no easy matter to discover his spiritualities.) The King has nullified the seizure, and hindered the convocation of the Peers. The sister Perpétue is better: she has caused the Parliament to be informed that she was no longer in danger, that she was grateful to them for their intentions; and the whole affair has ended in an interchange of compliments.

"We are threatened with another schism on music. People pretend that I am at the head of the Italian faction; but I have no exclusive taste, and I shall always approve what is agreeable in French music. It is true I believe we are a hundred leagues from the Italians in this article. The Parliament wishes to send them back their Constitution; we should at least take their music in exchange. . . .

"I have already had the honour to tell you that you

could keep my letters, and let Formont read them, but he alone; very few have seen them, and you alone have a copy of them. *It is, of all that I have done in my life, the only thing I should wish to subsist when I am no more.*"

In February 1753, D'Alembert writes that the outcry against his book is prodigious, and that it is not so much the evil he has said of the great, as the good he has said of Italian music, that has made him a host of enemies :

"I fancied one might like, down to puppets inclusively, without doing wrong to anybody; but I deceived myself. A powerful and formidable faction, headed by MM. Géliotte and the President Henault, are going barking from house to house against me. Judge of the impression this has made on me, and how much I should need my stoicism on this occasion if I had not thought I ought to keep it for more important conjunctures.

* * * * *

"I have made a sufficiently stupid bargain with my publishers: it is, that they shall undertake the cost, and that we shall share the profits. I have as yet received nothing. I will tell you what I get; there is no appearance of its being much, nor any more appearance of my continuing to work in this line. I will do geometry, and read Tacitus. It strikes me that people are very anxious I should be silent, and in truth I demand no better. When my little fortune no longer suffices for my subsistence, I will retire to some place where I can live cheap. Adieu, Madame. Esteem, as I do, men according to their worth, and nothing will be wanting to your happiness. I hear of Voltaire, reconciled with the King of Prussia, and Maupertius relapsed. *Ma foi!* men are well nigh mad, beginning with the wise."

He recurs again and again to his beloved geometry, which his friends are constantly entreating him to give up :

" If you did but know what a sweet retreat this geometry is to idleness! And then the fools do not read you, and consequently neither blame nor praise; and do you count this advantage for nothing? In any case, I have geometry for a year at the very least. Ah! what fine things I am employed on that nobody will read."

After stating that he had received only 500 livres out of the 2000 he had expected from his book, he says:

"With all that, I have more money in prospect than I can spend. How foolish it is to torment oneself for things which do not render one more happy. One had better say at once, 'Could I not do without it?' And this is the recipe I have long been in the habit of following."

To Madame du Deffand belongs the saying, sometimes attributed to Voltaire, that "L'Esprit des Lois" of Montesquieu might have been more accurately entitled "De l'Esprit *sur* les Lois;" a saying, perhaps, more pointed than true.[1] Montesquieu was one of her correspondents, and the man, with his habits and modes of thought, is depicted in his letters. He was obviously fond of trifling:

"Château de la Brede, June 15, 1741.—I promised you to write, but what could I tell you that you would care about? Now that I have only sad objects, I occupy myself with reading romances: when I am happier, I shall read the old Chronicles, to temper the good and the evil. But I feel that there is no reading which can replace a quarter of an hour of those suppers which made my delight. . . . Here they talk of nothing but vineyards, and poverty, and lawsuits, and I am happily foolish enough to accuse myself of all that; that is to say, to interest myself in it. But I forget that I am wearying you to death, and that the thing in the world which does you most harm is *ennui*; and I ought not to kill you, as the Italians kill, by a letter."

---

[1] "Madame du Deffand was right in calling his book 'De l'Esprit *sur* les Lois.' It cannot, I think, be defined better . . . . The author is always thinking, and sets others thinking."—*Voltaire to the Duc d'Uzès*, September 14, 1752.

"September 12, 1741.—You say, Madame, that nothing is happy, from the angel to the oyster. We must distinguish. The seraphim are not happy: they are too sublime. They are like Voltaire and Maupertius; and I am persuaded that, there on high, they do their best to get each other into trouble. But you cannot doubt that the cherubim are happy. The oyster is not so unhappy as we: he is swallowed without suspecting it; but as for us, we are told beforehand that we are going to be swallowed, and made aware that we shall be digested eternally. I could speak to you who are *gourmande* of those creatures who have three stomachs: the devil is in it if there is not one good amongst the three. I return to the oyster: he is unhappy when some prolonged disease causes him to become pearl: this is precisely the happiness of ambition."

It would seem from his next letter (September 13, 1742) that she was already in dread of blindness:

"I begin with your postscript. You say that you are blind. Do you not see that you and I elsewhere were little rebel spirits condemned to darkness? What ought to console us is, that those who see clearly are not more luminous on that account. . . .

"It is very singular that a lady who has a Wednesday has no news. I will do without it. I am nearly overwhelmed with business: my brother is dead. I never read a book; I walk a great deal; I think often of you. *Je vous aime.*[1] I present my respects."

The animated and sustained correspondence with Voltaire did not begin till after the death of "the divine Emilie," Madame la Marquise du Chatelet, who died of childbirth at the beginning of September, 1749. The event gave occasion for

---

[1] It is a defect, often remarked, in the French language, that it has only one word for liking and loving. "J'aime Julie; J'aime un gigot." The "Je vous aime" of Montesquieu is untranslatable. He meant something more than liking and less than loving. On the other hand, we have no word for *esprit*.

more than one scandalous story; and the scene at her death-bed, between her husband, St. Lambert, and Voltaire, as currently told, must be familiar to our readers. Voltaire writes, the 10th of September, 1749:

"That unhappy little daughter of whom she was brought to bed, and who has caused her death, did not interest me enough. Helas, Madame, we made a joke of this event; and it is in this unhappy tone, that I wrote by her order to her friends. If anything can aggravate the horrible condition in which I am, it would be to have treated with gaiety an adventure the result of which poisons the remainder of my miserable life. I have written to you on her lying-in, and I announce her death. It is to the sensibility of your heart that I have recourse in my despair. They are carrying me to Cirey with M. du Chatelet (the husband). Thence I return to Paris, without knowing what will become of me, and *hoping to rejoin her soon.* Permit me on arriving to have the mournful consolation of speaking of her and of weeping at your feet for a woman who, with all her weaknesses, *had a respectable soul.*"

He must have been hard pushed for sympathy when he wrote thus, for he was well aware that there was no love lost between the two ladies, and he must certainly have seen the portrait of the dear defunct addressed to herself by Madame du Deffand. The lurking satire is so obvious, that the writer was compared to the surgeon who not only attended a friend carefully during a last illness, but dissected him.

The most interesting of his letters to her are from Prussia and Switzerland. In one dated Potsdam, May 1751, after stating that he had promised the King to remain with him till September, he continues:

"One must keep one's word with kings, and especially with this one. Besides, he inspires me with so much ardour for work, that if I had not learnt to occupy myself I should learn it of him. I have never seen a man so laborious. I should blush to be idle, when I see a King who governs four hundred leagues of country all the morning, and who cultivates letters all the afternoon. There is the secret of avoiding the *ennui* of which you speak; but for that, you should have the phrenzy for work like him, and like me his poor servitor. When new books arrive from Paris, crammed with *esprit* which no one understands, bristling with old saws brushed and rebroidered with new glitter, do you know, Madame, what we do? We do not read them. All the good books of the past age are here; and that is quite right. We re-peruse them to preserve us from the contagion. Take care of yourself; don't eat too much. I foresaw, when you were so ill, that you would live long. Above all, don't get disgusted with life; for taking it all in all, after having long dreamed about it, one finds that there is nothing better."

The graceful mockery of his style is particularly remarkable in such passages as the following:

"I only regretted in your eyes, Madame, the loss of your beauty, and I knew you were philosopher enough to console yourself; but if you have lost your sight, I pity you infinitely. I will not propose to you the example of M. de S., blind at twenty, always and even too gay. I agree with you that life is not good for much; we only endure it by dint of an almost invincible instinct which Nature has given us; she has added to this instinct the bottom of Pandora's box, hope.

"It is when this hope absolutely fails us, as when an insupportable melancholy gets possession of us, that one triumphs over the instinct which makes one hug the chains of life, and that one has to leave this badly-built house, which one despairs of repairing. It is what has been done recently by two persons of the country I inhabit. One of these two philosophers was a girl of eighteen, whose head had been turned by the Jesuits, and who, to get rid of them, has gone to another world. It is a course which I shall not adopt, at least so soon, for the reason that I have annuities from two sovereigns, and I should be inconsolable if my death enriched two crowned heads. If, Madame, you have annuities from the King, take great care of yourself: eat little, go to bed early, and you will live a hundred years."

He is fond of reverting to this topic:

"If I am not mistaken, I advised you to live to exasperate those who pay you annuities. As for me, it is almost the only pleasure I have left. I picture to myself, when I feel the approach of an indigestion, that two or three princes will inherit from me: then I take courage through pure malice, and I conspire against them with rhubarb and sobriety."

The critical remarks interspersed in his letters are always suggestive, if not always sound:

"Do you know Latin? No: this is why you ask me if I like Pope better than Virgil. Ah, Madame, all our modern languages are dry, poor, and without harmony, in comparison with those spoken by our first masters, the Greeks and the Romans: we are but village fiddles. How, moreover, can you expect me to compare epistles to an epic poem —to the loves of Dido, to the burning of Troy, to the descent of Æneas into hell? I believe the 'Essay on Man' by Pope to be the first of didactic poems: but do not let us place him alongside of Virgil. You only know Virgil by translations; but poets cannot be translated. *Can one translate music?*"

Referring to translations in another place, he says: "We translate the English as badly as we fight against them by sea."

The Duc de Richelieu was so renowned for his successes with the fair sex, that as the highest tribute that could be paid to a woman of sense and virtue, Madame de Flamarens, it was proposed to give her for epitaph: "*Elle fut belle: elle aima son mari, et elle resista à Richelieu.*" What a comment on the morals of her age! In allusion to the Duc's reputation in this respect, Voltaire, after remarking that he will have a large share of her favour if he takes Port-Mahon, adds: "This Isle of Minorca was formerly called the Isle of Venus; it is no more than just that it should surrender to M. de Richelieu."

Nothing can be better than his remarks on reading, which, he shows, should be sustained and pursued with a given object, to afford either instruction or a relief from *ennui:*

"But you, Madame, do you pretend to read as one makes conversation? take up a book as one asks the news, read it, and lay it down? take up another which has no connection with the first, and leave it for a third? In this case you have no great pleasure. To have pleasure, you need a little passion; you need a great object which interests you, a fixed desire of instruction which occupies the soul continually. This is difficult to find, and does not come of its own accord. You are disgusted: you only wish to be amused, I see it well, and amusements are still very rare. If you were fortunate enough to know Italian, you would be sure of a good month of pleasure with Ariosto; you would be transported with joy; you would see the most elegant and the most flowing poetry, ornamented without effort by the most fruitful imagination with which nature has ever gifted man. Every romance becomes insipid alongside of Ariosto; all is flat before him, and above all, the translation of our Mirabeau.

In a subsequent letter he says that Ariosto is his god; that all poems weary except his:

"I did not like him enough in my youth; I did not know Italian. The Pentateuch and Ariosto now make the charm of my life. But, Madame, if I ever make a tour to Paris, I should prefer you to the Pentateuch."

* * * * *

"A burgomaster of Middlebourg, whom I don't know, wrote to me a short time since to ask me, as a friend, if there is a God; if, in case there is one, he cares about us; if matter is eternal; if it can think: if the soul is immortal. He begged me to reply by return of post. I receive such letters every week; I lead a pleasant life."

In January 1764 he writes to tell her that one of her *bons-mots* is quoted in the notes of "La Pucelle." There is no *bon-mot* which has struck deeper root, or to this day is more familiar in men's mouths, although few, perhaps, are acquainted with its history as related by Voltaire. Having occasion to mention Denis, Bishop of Paris, he proceeds to state that the Abbé Heldouin was the first who wrote that this bishop, having been decapitated, carried his head between his arms from Paris to the abbey which bears his name. Crosses were afterwards erected at all the places where the Saint stopped on his way. When the Cardinal of Polignac related this history to Madame du Deffand, and added that Denis had no trouble in carrying his head except to the first station, she replied: "I can well believe it; in affairs of this kind, *Il n'y a que le premier pas qui coûte.*"[1]

The germ of a famous saying of Voltaire's may be found in his letter to her of November 21, 1766:

"The juridical assassination of the Calas, and the murder of the Chevalier de la Barre, have not done honour to the Velches in foreign countries. Your nation is divided into two species: the one of idle monkeys who mock at everything, and the other of tigers who tear. The more progress reason makes on one side, the more on the other does fanaticism grind its teeth."

His moral sense was neither strong nor discriminating, notwithstanding his burning hatred of bigotry and persecution, or he would hardly have been seduced by any amount of flattery or

[1] "La Pucelle," note to canto i.

cajolery into making light of the crimes by which the Empress Catherine won her way to the throne:

"There is a woman who is founding a great reputation, the Semiramis of the North, who marches fifty thousand men into Poland to establish toleration and liberty of conscience. It is a unique thing in this world's history and, I warrant you, will go far. I boast of being a little in her good graces. I am her knight towards and against all. *I know well that she is reproached with some trifles on the subject of her husband,* but these are family matters with which I do not meddle; and besides, it is not bad to have a fault to repair; this engages her to make great efforts to force the public to esteem and admiration; and assuredly her wretched fellow of a husband would not have done any of the great things my Catherine is doing every day."

Madame du Deffand does not appear to have been quite as much revolted by the tone of this letter as she should have been, for she mentions it to the Duchesse de Choiseul as a very agreeable one, and it was left to the Duchesse to expose its fallacies and bad taste:

"What! Voltaire finds something to laugh at in an assassination! And what an assassination! That of a sovereign by his subject! that of a husband by his wife! This woman conspires against her husband and her sovereign, deprives him of his empire and his life in the cruellest manner, and usurps the throne over her own son; and Voltaire calls these things family quarrels!"

Voltaire could never get Madame du Deffand to go completely along with him in his religious (or anti-religious) flights, although he himself stopped short of the conclusions at which the leading freethinkers of Paris had arrived. They said of him, "c'est un bigot: il est déiste." But there was one remark of hers on which he was able to fix as indicating her wavering state of mind on such subjects:

"'The things which cannot be known to us are not necessary to us.' Great *mot*, Madame; great truth! and, what is more, very consolatory."

Notwithstanding her sceptical turn, Madame du Deffand took part against the philosophers, who regarded her with fear and suspicion. There are numerous traces of their ill-will in the correspondence between Voltaire and D'Alembert; and Voltaire, at the very period when we should have supposed him the most attached of her friends, indulges in the grossest abuse. Writing to D'Alembert, March 3, 1766, and referring to a report of his own marriage to Mademoiselle de Lespinasse, he says:

"I live actually in the same house with her, where there are besides ten other lodgers; this it is which has occasioned the current report. I have, moreover, no doubt of its being confirmed by Madame du Deffand, to whom, it is said, you write fine letters (*I do not know why*). She knows well that there is no marriage; but she wishes to have it believed that there is something else. An old and infamous *catin* like her does not believe in virtuous women: happily she is known and believed as she merits."

On July 2, 1770, D'Alembert writes from Paris to Voltaire, in Switzerland:

"I know, my dear master, that people write to you from Paris (to try to poison your pleasure) that it is not to the author of 'La Henriade,' of 'Zaire,' etc., that we raise this monument, but to the destroyer of religion. Do not believe this calumny. And to prove to you and to all France how atrocious it is, it is easy to engrave on the statue the titles of your principal works. Rest sure that Madame du Deffand, who has written you this atrocity, is much less your friend than we are: that she reads and applauds the writings of Fréron; and that she cites from them with praise the malicious things aimed at you. I have more than once been witness of this. Do not then believe the malicious things she writes to you."

The hollowness of feeling which underlies the warm professions of friendship in this correspondence is absolutely repulsive. But there is one striking exception. The letters of the Duchesse de Choiseul bear internal testimony to her solid worth and truth of character; and they are not less remarkable for their range and variety than for their good sense. There is a novel by Emile Souvestre, entitled, "Les Réprouvés," in which all the warm-hearted people come to grief, and the cold-hearted calculating people monopolise all the honours and riches of this world. But the balance is restored in the next, when, all hearts being laid bare, in those of the prosperous appears a serpent, and in those of the reprobates (*les réprouvés*) a star. Madame de Choiseul had some such theory in her mind when she wrote:

"You are right, the cold hearts are *réprouvés*. I don't know whether they will burn in the other world, but I am sure they are frozen in this: they are dead before they are born. Life is in the fire: youth burns for pleasure; sensitive hearts for love; the ambitious for glory; the virtuous for honour, for what is good—that good by which we enjoy and make others enjoy. Those who in any walk whatever have acquired celebrity, those who from the remote ages have transmitted their names to our time, were all animated with this divine fire: it extends existence in the present; it perpetuates it in ages to come. Those whose names are dead to posterity, were dead already for their contemporaries."

Yet examples abound of names and reputations fully alive to contemporaries which are now a dead letter except to what Mr. Carlyle calls the Dry-as-dusts. She continues:

"Don't believe, then, these cold souls and narrow minds who tell us that the best spirits of antiquity are those who are not known to us, for the very reason that they are unknown: they make goodness passive; it is the goodness of fools; it consists in not doing harm; but the true goodness is the result of all the virtues, and the active virtues, because they all tend to produce good. Let people say what they will, one is still more celebrated by the good than by the evil which one does to mankind. The first divinities on earth have been the first benefactors of humanity."

This, it will be remembered, was the subject of Lord Melbourne's prize essay at Cambridge, and there still remains much to be said on both sides.[1]

Horace Walpole's acquaintance with Madame du Deffand began in 1765, and his first impression was far from favourable. He writes to Seymour Conway from Paris, October 6, 1765:

"There are two or three houses where I go quite at my ease, am never asked to touch a card or hold dissertations. Nay, I don't pay homage to their authors. Every woman has one or two planted in her house, and God knows how they water them. The old President Henault is the pagod at Madame du Deffand's, an old blind debauchee of wit, where I supped last night. The President is very near deaf, and much nearer superannuated. He sits at table by the mistress of the house, who formerly was *his*. She inquires after every dish on the table, is told who has eaten of which, and then bawls the bill of fare of every individual into the President's ears. In short, every mouthful is proclaimed, and so is every blunder I make against grammar."

In a letter of November 14, 1765, he speaks

---

[1] Ante, vol. i. p. 338.

much in the same tone of her and her society; but on December 2, 1765, he writes to Selwyn:

"In return for your kind line by Mr. Beauclerk, I send you a whole letter; but I was in your debt before for making over Madame du Deffand to me, who is delicious; that is, as often as I can get her fifty years back. But she is as eager about what happens every day as I am about the last century. I sup there twice a week, and bear all her dull company for the sake of the Regent."

Selwyn, who passed a good deal of his time at Paris, was the connecting link between the best French and English society. He introduced Gibbon to Madame de Geoffrin, as well as Walpole to Madame du Deffand, who speaks thus of him in a letter to Crawford, February 13, 1767:

"I am far from thinking Mr. Selwyn stupid, but he is often in the clouds. Nothing strikes or rouses him but ridicule, and he catches it on the wing. He has grace and finesse in what he says, but he does not understand continuous conversation; he is absent, indifferent; he would be frequently *ennuyé*, without a very good recipe which he has against *ennui*; it is, to fall asleep when he likes. It is a talent that I much envy him; if I had it, I should make great use of it. He is malicious (*malin*), without being wicked (*méchant*); he is officious, polite; besides his Lord March, he loves nothing. One would be at a loss to form any tie with him; but one is glad to meet him, to be in the same room with him, although one has nothing to say to him."

In reference to Selwyn's habit of dozing in society, Gilly Williams writes:

"We hear of your falling asleep standing at the old President's, and knocking him and three other old women into the fire. Are these things true? . . . Cannot we get you an hospital in this island, where you can pass your evenings with some sensible matrons? And if they are not quite blind, they may have some natural infirmity equivalent to it."

About the same time (1766) Lord March writes to Selwyn to say that Lady Hertford made a thousand inquiries about him; "asked how long you intended to stay (at Paris), and hoped you would soon be tired of blind women, old Presidents, and Premiers (the Duc de Choiseul)."

To return to Walpole: in a letter to Gray, dated Paris, January 25, 1766, after a lively sketch of Madame Geoffrin, he proceeds:

"Her great enemy, Madame du Deffand, is now very old and stone-blind, but retains all her vivacity, wit, memory, judgment, passions, and agreeableness. She goes to operas, plays, suppers, and Versailles; gives suppers twice a week; has everything new read to her; makes new songs and epigrams, aye, admirably, and remembers every one that has been made these fourscore years. She corresponds with Voltaire, dictates charming letters to him, contradicts him, is no bigot to him or anybody, and laughs at both the clergy and the philosophers. In a dispute, into which she easily falls, she is very warm, and yet scarce ever in the wrong. Her judgment on every subject is as just as possible; *on every point of conduct as wrong as possible;* for she is all love and hatred, passionate for her friends to enthusiasm, still anxious to be loved, I don't mean by lovers, and a vehement enemy, but openly.

"As she can have no amusement but conversation, the least solitude and *ennui* are insupportable to her, and put her into the power of several worthless people, who eat her suppers when they can eat nobody's of higher rank, wink to one another, and laugh at her; hate her because she has forty times more parts, and venture to hate her because she is not rich."

In a letter to Crawford, March 6, 1766, after speaking of her as the most generous friendly being upon earth, he says:

"I converse with Mesdames de Mirepoix, Boufflers, and

Luxembourg, that I may not love Madame du Deffand too much, and yet they do but make me love her the more. But don't love, pray don't love me. Old folks are but old women, who love their last lovers as much as they did their first. I should still be liable to believe you, and I am not at all of Madame du Deffand's opinion, that one might as well be dead as not love somebody. I think one had better be dead than love anybody. Let us compromise this matter; you shall love her, since she likes to be loved, and I will be the confidant. We will do anything we can to please her. I can go no further. I have taken the veil, and would not break my vow for the world."

Whenever he talks of going to Paris, it is to see his charming, his dear old blind woman; and his fondness for her society was a topic of pleasantry amongst his friends.

"My Lady Shelburne has taken a house here (Twickenham), and it has produced a *bon-mot* from Mrs. Clive. You know my Lady Suffolk is *deaf*, and I have talked much of a charming old passion I have at Paris who is *blind*. 'Well,' said Mrs. Clive, 'if the new Countess is but *lame*, I shall have no chance of ever seeing you.'"

He was close on fifty, and Madame du Deffand seventy, when their correspondence began; and considering that she had never seen him, one would have thought that it might have been established and sustained upon a rational footing, undisturbed by suspicion, distrust or irritability on either side. But he was morbidly sensitive to ridicule, and she had grown into the confirmed habit of exaggerating sentiment till it became ridiculous. There is a French proverb: "En amour trop n'est jamais assez." She acted as if this was equally true of friendship, which, under her treatment, became as she advanced in years more absorbing, more unreasonable, more exacting than love. Yet this was not owing to the warmth, but rather to the coldness of her heart, which required a succession of stimulants to quicken its action and prevent her blood from stagnating. We are reminded of Madame de Stael's German Baron, who jumped over the chairs and tables "pour se faire vif." She spoke from sorrowful experience when she told Walpole that one might as well be dead as not love somebody. This incapacity for loving was her curse, the source and origin of her constant longing for excitement, of her ever-present sense of the wearing wasting monotony of life.

Struck by the fondness of Madame de Genlis for the infant Pamela, she said, "Then you love this child very much?" "Yes, Madame." "That is very fortunate; I have never been able to love anything." Yet she is as eloquent, in the gushing strain, on the affections, as if her whole soul was made up of tenderness, and she rings the changes on fancied neglect till she has well-nigh driven Walpole mad. In refining and expatiating on her own wounded sensibility, in reproducing it in every imaginable shape, she displays a command of language, a fertility of resource, an abundance of illustration, that recall Petrarch's sonnets and Tennyson's "In Memoriam."

"I fancied the other day," she writes to Walpole, "that I was in a garden, of which you were the gardener; that, seeing the approach of winter, you had torn up all the flowers you thought out of season, although there were some not yet quite faded—as violets, daisies, etc.—and that you had left only a certain flower, which has neither odour nor colour, called *immortelle*, because it never fades. It is the emblem of my soul, from which results a great privation of thoughts and imagination, but where there remains a great constancy, esteem, and attachment."

This was not at all in his way, and he accuses

her of writing like a Portuguese nun. Felton Hervey had jocularly given out that he himself was in love with her, and she with Walpole. On hearing this, Walpole is furious, and writes in a tone the severity of which may be guessed from her reply.

"My friend, my only friend, in God's name let us make peace. I had rather believe you mad than unjust. Be neither one nor the other. If I was wrong I would own it, and you would forgive me. But in truth I am not guilty; I never speak of you. Your English who are satisfied with me, think to show their gratitude by speaking of my esteem for you. Those who love you, think they give you pleasure: those who do not love you, seek to annoy you, if they see that this displeases you; but I am sure that good Hervey thought he was doing wonders. I forgive him, despite of the evil he has done me."

* * * * *

"When I receive a severe letter from you, full of reproaches, of suspicions, of coldness, I am wretched for eight days; and when at the end of this term I receive one still more cross, I lose my head altogether."

Ten days afterwards, April 14, 1770, she writes:

"I am as satisfied with the letter I have just received as a *pendu* would be to obtain his pardon; but the cord has hurt my neck, and if I had not received prompt relief, it was all over with me. Let us forget the past. I had rather be thought guilty, than risk troubling the peace afresh. I am well with everybody."

It inevitably results from the peculiar character of their friendship that the prospect of meeting is clouded with apprehension, and seems, on the whole, to afford her more pain than pleasure. She promises him that her first care will be to banish every topic that might ruffle his tranquillity, to make no allusion to the past, and not enter into explanations which would be equally useless and fatiguing.

"I will not make you sit up late: you shall fix the hour of supper, and have the entire regulation of my conduct during all the days you can give me. On your side, I earnestly entreat you not to let me see any fear or distrust; and let there be between us neither complaints, nor reproaches, nor restraint, nor embarrassment; so that I may really during some weeks be happy and taste pleasure. Prepare yourself to find me much aged: it is not of the exterior that I speak; that signifies nothing: it is of the soul, which is much depressed. If you reanimate it, you will perform a miracle."

This was in June, 1771, when she was seventy-five. A few months before, she had written:

"It is singular that at my age there are so many things which appear new to me, and which cause much surprise. It is, in truth, a pity that I have so little time left to profit by them. Perhaps I should not utilise them as I imagine; and if I was not a dupe in certain respects, I should be so in others. I have been so up to the present time, through too much confidence; I should become so through too much distrust. But what is sure is, that I have acquired a fund of the deepest contempt for mankind. I do not except the women: quite the contrary; I find them much worse than the men. It would be very pleasing to have a friend to whom one could confide all one's observations, all one's remarks; but it is impossible. . . .

"When I think of all the people I know, even those with whom I live daily, that are called my friends, there are none, men or women, who have the slightest spark of sentiment for me, nor I for them: there are some of those whom I see the most frequently in whom I discover a jealousy, an envy, the effects of which I am unceasingly occupied in counteracting. Their vanity, their pretensions, make most people unsociable. Am I wrong in thinking it a misfortune to be born? You suffice, however, to prevent me from being miserable; but mark well the kind of happiness I owe to you, and with how many crosses it is accompanied."

A judge of the old school (Littledale), when a leading counsel pressed the adjournment of the Court on account of the lateness of the hour, replied: " Why, Mr. ——, we must be *somewhere*." The remark was pregnant with meaning, whether the legal dignitary saw it or not. There are few who, at given hours or intervals, have not wished to be nowhere; or whom the necessity of being somewhere has not led into difficulty or harm. " How happy one would be," exclaims Madame du Deffand, "if one could throw off oneself as one can throw off others; but one is perforce with oneself and very little in accord with oneself." In other words, one must always be somewhere; and no human being ever suffered more from this law of nature than this remarkable woman, because, highly gifted as she was with every intellectual quality and surrounded by troops of what (as the world goes) might fairly be termed friends, she wanted both faith and heart.

Walpole should have made a more ample allowance for her weakness; but that he was not fairly chargeable with the unhappiness she laid to the charge of his coldness or unkindness, is made evident by the fact of her victimising Crawford much in the same manner. It was the prayer of the poet—

" That the sunshine of love may illumine our youth,
And the moonlight of friendship console our decline."

But moonlight, clear steady moonlight, was too calm, soothing, composing, for her. She would have preferred it struggling through clouds, and relieved by occasional flashes of lightning or other indications of a storm. The quarrels of lovers are the renewal of love. Improving upon this maxim, she acted as if the quarrels of friends were the soul, the essence, the charm, the mainstay of friendship. At all events, there must be an uncertainty and a misunderstanding, or rather a constant succession of misunderstandings, or the interest was at an end. With her, the sentiment was so purely factitious, that it might be compared to whipt syllabub or manufactured champagne, which is nothing without the froth. She was in her element when she could write to a friend as she wrote to Crawford from Paris, March 8, 1766:

"To say the truth, I do not know in what tone I shall write to you. I do not know what I think. I know still less what ought to be said. I do not know if I am content with your letter: I do not know if its date and all it contains are really true. I do not know what is the opinion you have of me. I do not know if it is not a constraint and an effort for you to write to me: I do not know whether you would not be glad never to hear more of me. I do not know whether it is not your design never to return here. I do not know whether I ought not to forget you. I do not know whether I ought not to take literally what Mr. Walpole says to me about friendship. Finally, I do not know how I stand with you: I only know that you say very flattering things to me, and that they have more the air of politeness than of friendship."

Continuing in this strain till she has worked herself into a flurried conviction that they are never to meet again, she continues:

"I ought to have expected it; I ought to be prepared for it; and it is not your fault nor Mr. Walpole's if I have deceived myself. I shall soon lose him: I will not permit myself to be angry at it. I will no longer permit myself any examination, any distinction, any preference, any sentiment. All that only serves to make one unhappy; and what, moreover, is peculiar to me, it makes me ridiculous. I wish, say you, lovers, and passionate ones, in my friends. Ah, my God, what thoughts! what ideas! How have I been able to give rise to them? Such is my state of mind, monsieur: judge of what I can say."

In her next letter to him June, 1766, she is a little more reasonable:

"You will always be my little Crawford, behave as you may. First, because I love you, and I love you because I esteem you, and because I believe you love me when you remember me, which, in truth, very rarely comes to pass. Secondly, because you have induced me to love Mr. Walpole, with whom I get on very well, notwithstanding all the hard things and atrocious affronts with which he fills his letters. One page transports me with fury, and all of a sudden another makes me burst with laughter. No one has ever been more original; no one resembles him. . . .

"You are going to Scotland, then? I pity you. I know all the power of *ennui*, and the impossibility of surmounting it; but you must not think, my dear sir, that it is better to ruin oneself than to feel wearied with oneself, unless one is resolved to hang oneself instead of dying of hunger. You have a very bad head. What is to be done for it? I know nothing about it. I wish you could fall desperately in love with a reasonable woman. I see but this remedy for you. You love play to madness, without loving money. You would be fully capable of engaging in affairs whilst detesting them. You have all the *esprit* one can have, without any curiosity, without any desire to know anything: in a word, were it not for Lord Ossory, to whom I suppose you are still attached, I should be under serious apprehension lest you should be found in the Thames or hanging from a tree."

It was the current belief at the time that he was one of the most devoted adorers of Georgiana, Duchess of Devonshire.

M. de Lescure, forming rather an undue estimate of the comparative merit of the letters to Walpole, remarks:

"Madame du Deffand only begins to think when she begins to feel. It is her affection for Walpole which has awakened in her the passion, the eloquence, the style, all the qualities that the President Henault had allowed to sleep. This tardy and senile love—which is the only emotion, the only drama, of her existence—has inspired, one may say, the genius of Madame du Deffand. Before, it was a woman of a great *esprit*. After, it is a great writer."

A great writer (if a great writer at all) only in the sense in which Madame de Sévigné was a great writer; that is, a great letter-writer. There was one marked analogy between these two ladies: an ill-requited attachment—an exaggerated, almost morbid, sentiment—was the main source of inspiration in each. In the one case, the rock from which the waters were to come was struck by the cold, unsympathising daughter: in the other, by the harsh, fastidious, warmth-repelling friend.

Madame du Deffand's style has never attracted a tithe of the enthusiastic admiration lavished on her predecessor in the same line; and her fame mainly rests on the tradition of her conversational powers, and on her association with the master-spirits of her age. It is their letters, even more than her own, that give value and interest to the seven volumes of correspondence now before us. But hers abound in spirited narrative and apt illustration; they are light without being superficial; above all, they are easy, natural, and unstudied. Where she appears to have taken pains, and to have had something resembling a literary aspiration, was in the portraits which she drew of her friends; but, as these were intended to be shown (indeed, were generally addressed) to the sitters, they are probably more remarkable for grace of expression and delicacy of touch than for truth. Amongst the many similar portraits of herself by contemporaries, that from the pen of the President Hénault is the most worthy of attention, because no one knew her better, and because it was not meant to see the light in his lifetime.

"The heart, upright, noble, and generous, unceasingly occupied in being useful and in imagining the means—how many people, and considerable people, had reason to say it! the intellect sound, an agreeable imagination, a gaiety which made her young again (I speak of later times, for she had once a charming face), the mind accomplished, and taking no pride in anything of all this at the age when she only thought of diverting herself. It were much to be wished that what she has written should not be lost: Madame de Sévigné would not be the only one to cite."

She composed songs, and sang them. In a letter to Walpole, dated March 10, 1771, when she was seventy-five, she describes a supper given by the King of Sweden (Gustavus III.), then at Paris, and apparently to her :

"I found with the King the two Duchesses (d'Aiguillon, *mère* and *régnante*), and MM. de Sestain and de Creuz. The King busied himself with getting me a good arm-chair, and made me change that in which they had placed me for a more convenient one. He would fain have had a tub.[1] The big Duchess set to singing the song I had made on my tub, telling the King that it was of my composition. . . . We supped: after supper they spoke of the Chevalier de Bouflers. They made me sing *L'Ambassade;* and then Madame d'Aiguillon told the King to ask me for the song of "The Philosophers;" after which she whispered him that it was by me; and the King, she, and all the company cried out as one does at the end of a new play, The Author, the Author, the Author. The party broke up at midnight. I cannot tell you how kind Madame d'Aiguillon was, and all the care she took to bring me out."

Her longing for society increased with her years. "Que la chère soit bonne," was her repeated injunction to her cook; "j'ai besoin de monde plus

[1] *Tonneau*, the name given by her to an easy-chair of peculiar construction which she occupied at home.

que jamais." On the 15th November, 1777, she writes to Crawford:

"As if it was not enough to be blind, I have now the dread of becoming deaf. I have seen the Abbé de Saint-Julien: you may take for granted that he said all he could imagine to console me, but faith and hope are not my principal virtues."

June 2, 1778, to Madame de Choiseul:

"Picture to yourself, dear grandmama, that, to extreme old age, and to blindness, is added deafness. . . . It is too many miseries at once: I have not the courage to support them. In this situation the death of Voltaire has made, I own, little impression on me, and I am not in a condition to relate any circumstance of it."

Still she bore up gallantly, and her deafness must have been slight, for, on October 8, 1779, she writes to Walpole, that she has been reading (i.e. having read to her) the "Théâtres" of Corneille, Racine, and Voltaire, remarking that she finds the last "greatly inferior, not at all worthy to rank with the two others: all his personages are no other than himself." In the same letter she congratulates Walpole on having refurnished his house, and asks jocularly, whether, if she were to come to England, he could take her in.

She died on September 23rd, 1780. What she said of the President's mode of dying was true of her own. She went out, or became extinguished, like a lamp, without pain or consciousness, showing at no time any apprehension of death. Her religious state has been questioned. La Harpe, speaking of a spiritual director who had been in attendance on her, says that, "be his qualifications what they might, she did not keep him six months. The ascetic language of these pious intercommunications was not in the tone of her ordinary conversation, nor in harmony with her soul." So, when the *curé* of Saint-Sulpice came to see her in her last illness, she said, "Monsieur le Curé, you will be satisfied with me; but spare me three things: no questions, no reasons, no sermons." This is partially confirmed by Wiart, her private secretary, in a letter to Walpole, giving a detailed account of her last illness and death. She was buried, he states, in the Church of Saint-Sulpice, her parish, according to her request.

"But they would not suffer any marks of distinction to be paid to her. *These gentlemen were not perfectly satisfied.* However, her Curé saw her every day, and had even commenced her confession, when she lost her head and was not able to receive the sacraments; but M. le Curé behaved admirably. He did not believe her end so near."

The master-passion strong in death was never more strikingly exemplified than in her. Her last words were as characteristic as the "More Light" of Goethe, the "Aber" (But) of Frederic Schlegel, the "Give Dayrolles a chair" of Chesterfield, or the "Life is a poor vanity" of Locke. They were "Vous m'aimez donc?" addressed in a mixed tone of surprise and incredulity to the secretary, who knelt dissolved in tears at her bedside. She died doubting the existence, the bare possibility, of the feeling or faculty which helps, more than any other, to expand the heart, to refine the intellect, to soften and sweeten life, to grace and elevate humanity!

HOLLAND HOUSE.[1]

(*From the Quarterly Review, October*, 1873.) [2]

As Henry Bulwer (Lord Dalling) was leaving Holland House one evening with a friend, after pausing at point after point till they reached the corridor, he said: "I have seen most of the palaces and palatial residences of Europe, and if I were told to choose one to live in for the remainder of my life, I should choose this." His companion quietly added:

"And I said to myself if there's peace in the world,
A heart that is *humble* might hope for it here."

All things considered, it is certainly the pearl of metropolitan or suburban houses. Take Northumberland House, Devonshire House, Chesterfield House, Cambridge House, Lansdowne House, Stafford House: extend the area so as to comprise Sion House, Strawberry Hill, and Hatfield. Where have you such a continuous stream of historical, literary and political associations, reaching nearly three centuries back? Which of them calls up so many striking scenes, characters and incidents, or can be re-peopled by no extraordinary effort of memory or imagination with so many

[1] *Holland House*. By Princess Marie Liechtenstein. In 2 vols. London. 1873.
[2] Some passages of this Essay are reprinted from a notice of the same book in "The Times" of October 28, 1873, by the writer.

brilliant groups of statesmen, orators, poets, artists, beauties, wits—with the notabilities of both hemispheres during six or seven generations, including (not, we hope, terminating with) our own?

Then, for what Henry Bulwer was thinking of at the moment, for what more peculiarly addresses itself to the sense of material enjoyment and the eye, for the combination of comfort with space, splendour, luxury and refinement in the interior arrangements, Holland House stands equally unmatched. There is a real charm, an irresistible attraction, in the proportions, harmony of colouring, and disposition of the rooms—in the exquisite tone and keeping of the pictures, busts, decorations, hangings, china, the Elizabethan staircase of dark oak, and the quaintly constructed hall. The late Lord de Mauley asked one of a party of excursionists whom he met in a gallery at Chatsworth, to tell him where he was, as, after a week's stay in the house, he had lost his way. This could hardly happen at Holland House: although it is large enough to have a winter and summer set of sitting-rooms and (without counting the library) ten or eleven reception-rooms open to the guests.

Considering the variety of almost indispensable qualifications, it required no common courage and self-reliance in a young woman settled abroad to undertake the exhaustive treatment of such a subject in all its aspects. But Princess Marie Liechtenstein had gifts and opportunities which, used as she was capable of using them, went far towards counterbalancing her disadvantages. Quick-witted and highly educated, the adopted child of one of the most refined and charming of her sex, observant, sympathising, appreciating, she had been cradled in Holland House, nurtured in its traditions, and imbued from infancy with the genius of the place. "*Je ne suis pas la rose, mais j'ai vécu près d'elle.*" Although she had seen only a surviving relic or two of its celebrities, her impressions from constantly hearing about the rest of them, were vivid: she had a speaking acquaintance with their portraits: her knowledge, if secondhand or hearsay, came from the best sources: the family archives were open to her; and she must be supposed to have laid under contribution all the best informed friends and connections of the house.

When Sir James Mackintosh was asked by a Frenchwoman what he had done that people should think him so superior, "I was obliged," he says, "as usual to refer to my projects." Among these was a history of Holland House, as well as a complete History of England. The notes made for the more ambitious project were turned to good account by Macaulay: those on Holland House have been well employed by the Princess.

This accomplished lady has a cultivated taste for the fine arts, along with a keen sense of natural beauty: and she writes about objects of virtù with the ease and confidence of a connoisseur. Her industry and discriminating research are shown by the number and variety of scattered facts and notices she has brought together from every quarter; and although the amount of original matter is less than may have been anticipated, and some of the moral reflections and sentimental touches might have been spared, she has produced a curious and valuable work; enabling us to do for almost every room in the mansion what the brilliant essayist has done for the gallery—make them the scenes of a succession of *tableaux vivants*, in which words reproduce character and expression as vividly as the pencil or the brush. It is a work which will lie long on the drawing-table before it is promoted to the library, for the illustrations are numerous and choice. They consist of five steel engravings of portraits, and between sixty and seventy woodcuts. The quarto edition also contains forty Heliotype illustrations, which are really beautiful specimens of the art.

The difficulty of writing a book, or even an essay, on a historic site, rises in exact proportion to the eminence of the celebrities that have flung a halo round the spot. What is best worth telling is familiarly known already: if we venture on the slightest digression, the chances are that we find ourselves on the beaten track of biography; and the utmost we can hope is, that some traits or incidents may acquire an air of novelty by being, so to speak, localised. The safest course, therefore, is to keep as strictly as possible to the subject, and place the minor notabilities, the "associate forms" that have hitherto rested in comparative obscurity, in broad relief.

Despite of Pope's warning, when ladies get hold of a little learning, they experience no sense of danger. They are apt to think it new to others because it is new to them. In the course of her introductory account of Kensington, the Princess discourses trippingly about Domesday Book, Saxon derivations, allodial proprietors, hides and virgates of land, and the pedigree of the De Veres; who held the manor till 1526, when it passed through co-heiresses into the families of Neville, Wingfield, and Cornwallis. In 1610, we find it the property of Sir Walter Cope, gentleman of the bedchamber to James I., who (in 1607), before acquiring the manor, had built the centre and turrets of what was then Cope Castle.

"As for the ancient Manor House, even its site is unknown; and Sir Walter Cope not mentioning such a habitation in his will, we may conclude that it was destroyed before the present house was built; in the building of which, indeed, some of its materials were perhaps used.

"The first stone is often lost sight of beneath what follows; so the name of Cope is superseded by that of Holland, and Cope Castle by Holland House. But it may be now time to say with Vidocq: *Trouvez-moi la femme.* We find her in Sir Walter Cope's daughter and heiress, Isabel, who married Sir Henry Rich, created in 1622 Baron Kensington, sent to Spain by James I. to assist in negotiating a marriage between Prince Charles and the Infanta, and made Earl of Holland in 1624. He it was who added to the building its wings and arcades; and, more than this, he employed the best artists of the time in decorating the interior."

This Earl of Holland, described by Clarendon as "a very handsome man of a lovely and winning presence, and gentle conversation," played a busy and conspicuous rather than a distinguished part during the reign of Charles I. and the commencement of the Great Rebellion. He stood so high in favour with the Court, especially with Queen Henrietta, whose marriage he had negotiated, that he was named General of the Horse in the army raised against the Scotch Covenanters in 1639. His retreat from Dunse having met with disapproval, he published, in 1643, "A Declaration made to the Kingdom," which has been called a bad apology for bad conduct; and in 1647, he fully justified the worst suspicions entertained of his disloyalty, by lending Holland House for a meeting between Fairfax and sundry disaffected Members of Parliament.

The year following, having rejoined the royalists, he was taken in arms for the king at St. Neots, imprisoned in Warwick Castle, and condemned to death by a high court of justice improvised for the trial of himself and others similarly situated. He was beheaded in Palace Yard on the 9th March, 1648–9, meeting death with a firmness which had been wanting in the leading passages of his life. Warburton (in a note on Clarendon's history) says that he lived like a knave and died like a fool. He appeared on the scaffold dressed in a white satin waistcoat and a white satin cap with silver lace. After "some divine conference" with a clergyman for nearly a quarter of an hour, and an affectionate leave-taking with a friend, he turned to the executioner and said, "Here, my friend, let my Cloaths and my body alone, there is ten pounds for thee, that is better than my cloaths, I am sure of it. And when you take up my head, do not take off my cap."

"Then going to the front of the Scaffold, he said to the People, *God bless you all, God give all happiness, to this Kingdom, to this People, to this Nation.* Then laying himself down, he seemed to pray with much affection for a short space, and then lifting up his head (seeing the Executioner by him) he said, *Stay while I give the signe,* and presently after stretching out his hand, and saying, Now, now; just as the words were coming out of his mouth, the Executioner at one blow severed his head from his body."

"Such," adds the Princess, "was the end of Henry Rich, first Earl of Holland, who owed Holland House to his wife, and to whom Holland House owes its name. The portrait we give of him . . . is from an old print, and may excite more interest than admiration." She says that he received all that was clever and fashionable at Holland House, not confining himself to his own countrymen; and Bassompierre, who came over in 1626 about some Court matter, thinks it worth recording that he dined at the Earl of Holland's— "*à Stintinton.*"

It is surmised, rather than stated, that the next

inhabitant of the house was Fairfax: that Lambert fixed his head-quarters there in July 1649; and that Cromwell and Ireton held conferences on State affairs in a field forming part of the property; choosing (on account of Ireton's deafness) a spot where there was no danger of their being overheard. "Eventually, however, the widowed Countess of Holland was allowed to live once more in her own home; *and if devotion to a late husband can be proved by opposition to his enemies*, Lady Holland was a devoted widow, for she encouraged acting in Holland House when theatres were shut by the Puritans."

This was a somewhat anomalous mode of showing conjugal devotion to a dear deceased, and it would seem that the widowed Countess simply fell in with the practice prevalent among the nobility and gentry in the neighbourhood of the metropolis, of lending their houses to the players, who, without such connivance, must have starved. Her son, the second Earl of Holland, who became, by succession to a cousin, fifth Earl of Warwick in 1673, made Holland House his principal residence. His son and successor, Edward, married Charlotte, daughter of Sir Thomas Middleton, of Chirk Castle, and she was the Countess of Warwick who married Addison in 1716. The event was thus announced in the "Political State of Great Britain" for that year:

"About the beginning of August, Joseph Addison, Esq., famous for many excellent Works, both in Verse and Prose, was married to the Right Honourable Charlotte, Countess of Warwick, Relict of Edward late Earl of Warwick, who died in 1701, and Mother to the present Earl, a Minor."

The marriage is thus mentioned by Johnson:

"This year (1716) he married the Countess Dowager of Warwick, whom he had solicited by a very long and anxious courtship, perhaps with behaviour not very unlike that of Sir Roger to his disdainful widow; and who, I am afraid, diverted herself often by playing with his passion. . . . His advances at first were certainly timorous, but grew bolder as his reputation and influence increased; till at last the lady was persuaded to marry him, on terms much like those on which a Turkish princess is espoused, to whom the Sultan is reported to pronounce, 'Daughter, I give thee this man for thy slave.' The marriage, if uncontradicted report can be accredited, made no addition to his happiness. It neither found nor made them equal. She always remembered her own rank, and thought herself entitled to treat with very little ceremony the tutor of her son."

That his advances were "certainly timorous" is mere matter of inference. So little is known of the courtship and the prior relative position of the couple, that it is a disputed point whether Addison had been the young Earl's tutor. Johnson's sole authority was Spence's Anecdotes. Two letters from Addison to Lord Warwick in 1708 prove that he was not his domestic tutor. These are dated from Sandy End, a hamlet of Fulham. Macaulay, referring to the marriage, says that Addison had for some years occupied at Chelsea a small dwelling, once the abode of Nell Gwynn; and that he and the Countess, being country neighbours, became intimate friends. The son of a dignified clergyman, and at the height of literary celebrity, he was guilty of no extraordinary presumption in aspiring to her hand. He was made Secretary of State in 1717, and the traditions do not bear out the theory that he quietly accepted the humble part assigned him by the lexicographer. He is reported to have asserted his independence to the extent of joining the little senate to which he gave laws at Button's or of taking his ease at a neighbouring house of entertainment without her leave, and to have driven her, in her jealous or irritable moods, to the humiliating expedient of watching or keeping guard over him. The common belief that they did not live a very comfortable life is conveyed by the quaint remark, that their house, though large, could not contain a single guest—Peace. But he left her the whole of his fortune, "a proof" (remarks Mackintosh) "either that they lived on friendly terms, or that he was too generous to remember their differences." He also confided his daughter to her affectionate care by his will.

He breathed his last in what is now the Dining Room. This was the scene of the parting interview with Gay, when, having sent for him he implored his forgiveness—Gay never knew for what—and of the still more memorable scene with the young Earl of Warwick, whom he summoned to his bedside to "see how a Christian could die!" Walpole cynically remarks, " Unluckily he died of brandy!" His complaints were asthma and dropsy; and he no more died of brandy than Pitt died of port, although his constitution equally required stimulants. There is a tradition that a bottle of wine was placed at each end of the gallery or dining-room when he paced up and down in the act of composition or meditation. The Princess says, a bottle of port at one end and a bottle of sherry at the other; in which case he might have been acting on the same principle as Sir Hercules Langrishe, who, on being asked, " Have you finished all that port (three bottles) without assistance?" made answer, "Not quite: I had the assistance of a bottle of Madeira."

Speaking of Addison's connexion with Holland House, Macaulay says, " His portrait still hangs there. The features are pleasing; the complexion is remarkably fair; but in the expression we trace rather the gentleness of his disposition than the force and keenness of his intellect." This was written in 1843. In 1858 there appeared a pamphlet raising a strong presumption that it is not a portrait of Addison.[1]

The young Earl of Warwick died in 1721, and the estates of the Rich family devolved on his cousin, William Edwardes, raised to the Irish peerage by the title of Baron Kensington in 1776. Between 1721 and 1749 Holland House was occupied by a succession of distinguished tenants:— Sir John Chardin, the Persian traveller: William Penn: Shippen, the downright Shippen of Pope; and Van Dyck, being those most known to fame. Penn, according to the Mackintosh MS., writes that, during his residence here in the reign of James II., "he could hardly make his way down the front steps of the house, through the crowds of suitors, who besought him to use his good offices with the King." It was during this affluence of visitors and inevitable notoriety that Macaulay supposes him to have made a secret journey into Somersetshire to negotiate the pardons of the maids of Taunton on behalf of the maids of honour. In the same MS. it is set down that Van Dyck resided two years at Holland House and painted two fine portraits here.

Atterbury's daughter, Mrs. Morice, once inhabited Holland House, in which a room was kept for the prelate and his library was deposited for safe custody. Another reminiscence, dating farther back, is that William III., soon after his arrival in England in 1689, came to look at

[1] "Joseph Addison and Sir Andrew Fountayne; or, the Romance of a Portrait." Simpkin, Marshall, and Co. Macaulay makes no allusion to an original portrait painted by Kneller in 1716; although an engraving of it forms the frontispiece of the "Life of Addison," by Lucy Aikin, the book he was reviewing.

Holland House, with a view to its conversion into a palace; and a wide field of speculation is laid open as to whether it would have gained or lost in renown or interest by being so honoured. Its connection with the Fox family began in 1749, when it was let on lease, at a rent of 182*l*. 16*s*. 9*d*., to the first Lord Holland, who became virtually the proprietor in 1767.

To show by how few links a tradition might be handed down for more than two hundred years, Lord Lansdowne (the third Marquis) used to say that his father had intimately known a man who had intimately known one who had witnessed the execution of Charles I. This was Stephen Fox, the founder of the family, alleged to have been one of the royal pages in 1648. But Richard, Lord Holland (the third), only partially confirms the story. His clear and succinct account of his ancestor begins : "Sir Stephen Fox, mentioned for his honesty by Clarendon and for his riches by Grammont, was the founder of our family, and seems, notwithstanding some little venial endeavours of his posterity to conceal it, to have been of a very humble stock. He was born in 1627. He owed his introduction at Court to Lord Percy, his favour with Charles II. to Lord Clarendon, and his general success in the world to integrity, diligence, and abilities in business."[1] According to the Princess, "he is said to have belonged to the children's choir in Salisbury Cathedral."

There is a French story, entitled "L'Art de Plaire," in which the hero wins all hearts, unites

---

[1] "Memorials and Correspondence of Charles James Fox." Edited by Lord John Russell; vol. i. p. 2. Lord Holland goes on to state as a usage in Sir Stephen's family, that during the whole of the 30th January, the wainscot of the house used to be hung with black, and that no meal of any sort was allowed till after midnight.

all voices, and succeeds in every undertaking, by dint of a nameless fascination, without birth, fortune or even what are commonly understood by personal advantages. This might pass for a description of Stephen Fox:

"He was endowed, even in his youthful days, with a certain amount of that inexplicable power called charm, which attracted the notice, and thus gained him the protection, of Bishop Duppa. His next patron was the Earl of Northumberland's brother, Henry, Lord Percy, who entertained him in Paris after the battle of Worcester. Lord Percy was at that time Chamberlain of Charles's household; and through him Stephen became known to the exiled king, after whom he named one of his sons, and in whose service he discharged various financial and confidential commissions."

By good luck, or most probably through superior energy in procuring intelligence, he was the first to announce the death of Cromwell to Charles the Second:

". . . Mr. Fox received the news of that Monster's Death, six Hours before any Express reach'd Brussels; and while the King was playing at Tennis with the Archduke Leopold, Don John, and other Spanish Grandees, he very dutifully accosted His Majesty, upon the Knee, with the grateful Message; and beg'd leave to call him really King of Great Britain, &c., since he that had caus'd him to be only Titularly so, was no longer to be number'd among the Living; which so ingratiated him afresh with that Prince, who received him with an Air of Pleasantry, that from thenceforward he was admitted into the King's most secret Thoughts, and was advised with more like a Privy Counsellor, than a Servant of an inferior Rank."

The prominent points of his career may be learned from the "Diary" of his intimate friend, Evelyn, who makes frequent and always honourable mention of him. Besides several other lucrative appointments, he was made Paymaster-General of the Forces, and managed to accumulate a large fortune, "honestly got and unenvied; which is next to a miracle." So says Evelyn, who adds that he was "as humble and ready to do a courtesy as ever." What is more, he was as ready to do good; it being mainly through his exertions that the project for the establishment of Chelsea Hospital, popularly attributed to Nell Gwynn, was taken up in good earnest by the *poco curante* king. After recapitulating the heads of the plan as communicated by Sir Stephen, Evelyn sets down:

"I was therefore desired by Sir Stephen (who had not only the whole managing of this, but was, as I perceived, himself to be a grand benefactor, *as well it became him who had gotten so vast an estate by the soldiers*) to assist him, and consult what method to cast it in, as to the government. . . ."

One reason he assigned for his labours in this work is reported to have been that "he could not bear to see the common soldiers, who had spent their strength in our service, to beg at our doors."

Sir Stephen held office under Charles II., James II., William III., and Queen Anne, without being a trimming politician; for he was excepted by name from the general pardon proffered by James II. in 1692. He died in 1716, in his eighty-ninth year, at his villa of Chiswick, where Charles James Fox died in 1806, and Canning in 1827. He was twice married, and left nine sons and two daughters. The second marriage took place in 1703, when he was seventy-six. His eldest son by this marriage afterwards became Earl of Ilchester, and the younger was Henry Fox, the first Lord Holland, with whom we have next to deal as the first of the family brought into connexion with Holland House.

The Princess, with the allowable partiality of a biographer, is bent on making him out an eminent statesman, as well as a warm-hearted man, an affectionate husband and father, and a deservedly popular member of society. In point of fact, he was a good debater, although a bad speaker; but his strength lay more in his shrewdness, his tact, his masculine good sense, his moral (or immoral) courage, and his familiarity with the springs of parliamentary action, than in his debating powers. He had the very qualities most needed by a trading politician in corrupt, unsettled times; and it may be safely predicated that no arrangement or combination of his making or proposing was ever with his consent prevented or impeded by a principle. He broke off the treaty with the Duke of Newcastle for the management of the House of Commons in 1754, because they could not come to terms touching the secret-service money to be employed in bribery; and it was the promise of a peerage, not congeniality of views, that induced him to desert the Duke of Cumberland and join Lord Bute.

There is no rival or competitor with whom he contrasts more disadvantageously than with the "great commoner," the born orator, the man of sudden impulses and electrical effects, the lofty model of proud disinterestedness. A single point of comparison is enough. Each was Paymaster of the Forces when the proceeds of the place were mainly regulated by the conscience of the holder. Pitt refused to receive more than the regular salary. Fox's profits were so exorbitant that he was denounced by the citizens of London, in an address, as the defaulter of unaccounted millions; and from what is known of his expenses and accumulations, he could not have pocketed less than half a million sterling in his eight years' tenure of the place. Macaulay calls him a needy political adventurer, and says that he was regarded by the nation as a man of insatiable rapacity. The public estimate of him was indicated by a couplet on the death of Wolfe:

"All conqu'ring cruel death, more hard than rocks,
    Thou shouldst have spared the *Wolfe* and took the *Fox*."

Gray's satire (suppressed in the earlier editions of his works) on Lord Holland's seaside villa began:

"Old, and abandon'd by each venal friend,
    Here H—d form'd the pious resolution
To smuggle a few years, and strive to mend
    A broken character and constitution.
"On this congenial spot he fixed his choice;
    Earl Godwin trembled for his neighbouring sand;
Here sea-gulls scream, and cormorants rejoice,
    And mariners, though shipwreck'd, dread to land."

The correspondence (printed from the Holland House MSS.), which grew out of his abortive treaty with the Duke of Newcastle, throws light on the still unsettled question of when the Cabinet was first constituted as now, or named by the Prime Minister without the direct personal interference of the Sovereign. The following letter from Fox, then Secretary of War, was delivered by Lord Waldegrave to the King, December 10th, 1754:

"SIR,—Infinitely thankfull for Your Majesty's Command receiv'd by Ld Waldegrave to explain myself in writing; I must begin by humbly asking Pardon for having mistaken Your Majesty. I now understand Your Majesty do's not intend to have any Leader in the House of Commons and I receive Your Majesty's Pleasure on this head with all that Duty and Submission that becomes me. What Your Majesty requires, I understand, is that on all occasions as well not relative as relative to the Army, I should act with Spirit in support of Your Majesty's Service in the H. of Commons; And, Your Majesty bids me put in writing what will enable me to obey these y^r Commands.

"Thinking then no more of taking the Lead; but of obeying Your Majesty's Commands only, I answer—That, in the present State of the H. of Commons, I desire no Change of Employment, no pecuniary Advantage, but some such Mark only of Your Majesty's Favour as may enable me to speak like one well inform'd and honour'd with Your Majesty's Confidence in regard to the Matters I may be speaking of. This then, Sir, is what I desire, and can desire for no other purpose than to enable me to attempt what You command, confining myself to Your Majesty's own Views, and to the very Manner Your Majesty shall command me to pursue them in.

"I am, &c., &c., &c."

The King's reply is dated Dec. 12th, 1754.

"December 12th, 1754.

"It is the King's Pleasure, that Lord Waldegrave should acquaint Mr. Fox, that His Majesty is graciously pleased to condescend to His Request of being admitted into His Cabinet Council: But that, in order to avoid future Difficulties, and Inconveniences, His Lordship should acquaint Mr. Fox, that this Advancement to the Cabinet Council, is not intended, by the King, in the least, to interfere with, or derogate from, the Priority, belonging to His Majesty's Secretary of State in the House of Commons; And that It is not His Majesty's Intention, to confer any Power, or Confidence, independent of such Ministers, as His Majesty shall think fit to entrust with the Conduct of His Affairs."

He had been sworn of the Privy Council on being made Secretary-at-War in 1746.

His marriage was the most remarkable episode

of his private life. It made a noise that is hardly intelligible unless we bear in mind the social prejudices then in full force. When his engagement with Lady Caroline Lennox, eldest daughter of the second Duke of Richmond, became known to her noble parents, their indignation knew no bounds: they would not hear of such a *mésalliance;* and they took the most decided steps for compelling the young lady to break it off. She was peremptorily commanded to receive another suitor; and the hour for the formal introduction of the chosen individual had been fixed, when she adopted the perilous measure of cutting off her eyebrows.

There is an English novel ("Cyril Thornton"), in which the hero, returning from the Peninsular war with a terribly disfiguring wound across the face, is thrown over by his affianced bride on that account. There is a French novel ("La Vigie de Koatven," by Sue), in which the heroine destroys her beauty in order to revenge herself on a treacherous lover, and, during a voyage in pursuit of him, gets thrown overboard as a witch. Lady Caroline was more fortunate. She escaped the presence of the hated suitor, and did not repel the favoured one. She eloped, and was secretly married to Fox on the 1st May, 1744. The letters of condolence, instead of congratulation, which poured in upon the Duke and Duchess from persons of social or political eminence, are amusing from their absurdly inflated professions of regret. A fortnight after the great event Sir Charles Hanbury Williams writes:

"MY DEAR FOX,—Time that overcomes, eats up, or buries, all things Has not as yet made the least impression upon the story Of the Loves of Henry Fox and Caroline. It still lives grows and flourishes under the Patronage of their Graces of Newcastle and Grafton, and Mr. Pelham.

But in spite of them the Town grows cool and will take the tender Lovers' parts.

"Ld Carteret diverts himself with this. He says he was call'd up by the Duke of Newcastle to him by the D: of Dorset, as he was going thro' the rooms at Kensington, and told that they two were talking upon this most unfortunate affair, and that they shou'd make no secret of it to him, that they were both greatly affected with it. Upon this says Carteret; I thought our fleets or our armys were beat, or Mons betrayed into the hands of the French. At last it came out that Harry Fox was married, which I knew before. This, says He, was the Unfortunate affair. This was what he was concerned about. Two people to neither of which he was any relation were married against their Parents' consent! And this Man is Secretary of State!"

* * * * *

"Nobody has done Lady Caroline more justice than Miss Pelham. She says she is her friend and cant give her up. She speaks well of her and you to those that dont like it. Answers all their objections; and particularly upon its being said you was no Gentleman, She reply'd thus, 'Upon that head I will appeal to the company whether, if Lord Ilchester had been unmarried and had offer'd himself to the D: of R——'s daughter the D: and D^{ss} wou'd not have jump'd at the Match, and How Mr. Fox comes to be a worse Gentleman than Ld Ilchester I cant tell.'"

The guilty, yet happy, pair were not forgiven till after the birth of a son in 1748, when (March 26th) the Duke indites a solemn epistle, beginning:

"Whitehall, Saturday, 26 March [1748].

"MY DEAR CAROLINE,—Altho' the same reason for my displeasure with you, exists now, as much, as it did the day you offended me, and that the forgiving you is a bad example to my other Children, yett they are so young, that was I to stay till they were settled, the consequence might in all likelyhood be that wee should never see you so long as wee lived, which thoughts our hearts could not bear. So the conflict between reason and nature is over, and the tenderness of parents has gott the better and your Dear Mother and I have determin'd to see and forgive both you and Mr. Fox."

His Grace stipulates, however, that their conduct is not to grow into an example or a precedent:

"One thing more of the greatest consequence to the future hapiness of my familly I must mention and recommend to you, which is that I trust to Mr. Fox's honor, probity, and good sense, as well as to yours, that your conversation ever hereafter with any of my children, especially with my dear March, may be such as not to lead them to thinke children independent of their parents."

Henry Fox was raised to the peerage in 1763, Lady Caroline having been created Baroness Holland in 1762.

The Princess says that he had stipulated for an earldom, and that when only a barony was conferred upon him, he reproached Lord Bute for a breach of faith, who replied that it was only a pious fraud. "I perceive the fraud, my Lord," was the retort, "but not the piety." Lord Stanhope says that the subject of altercation was whether Fox should retain the office of Paymaster, which Lord Bute maintained he had promised to resign on being made a peer. "Both parties now appealed to Lord Shelburne, who, in the preceding autumn, had been the negotiator between them. Lord Shelburne, much embarrassed, was obliged to own that he had in some degree extenuated or exaggerated the terms to each, from his anxiety to receive, at all events, the support of Fox, which he thought at that period essential to the Government. These misrepresentations Lord Bute, now forgiving, called "a pious fraud."[1] The lady's version agrees with Lord Russell's, but Lord Stanhope's strikes us to be the most probable; for we can hardly conceive Lord Bute admitting a palpable breach of faith and calling it a pious fraud.

[1] ".History," vol. v. p. 40.

Moreover, Fox kept the place till he was compelled to surrender it by George Grenville in 1765.

Walpole, contrasting the father's style of speaking with the son's, says, that Lord Holland "was always confused before he could clear up the point, fluttered and hesitated, wanted diction, and laboured only for one forcible conclusion." Yet in the debate on the Marriage Bill of 1753, inspired doubtless by personal recollections, he spoke with clearness and vivacity, breaking through all bounds of parliamentary or official restraint. The Bill was introduced by the Lord Chancellor (Hardwicke) with the approval of the Prime Minister (Pelham), and Fox was Secretary at War. But he attacked the measure and the framers in language that provoked Charles Yorke (the Chancellor's son) to exclaim: "It is new in Parliament, it is new in politics, it is new in ambition." Fox retorted, "Is it new in Parliament to be conscientious? I hope not. Is it new in politics? I am afraid it is! Is it new in ambition? It certainly is to attack such authority." He held up a copy of the Bill, in which he had marked the alterations with red ink; and on the observation of the Attorney-General "How bloody it looks!" he retorted: "Thou canst not say *I* did it. Look what a rent the *learned* Casca made" (pointing to the Attorney-General). "Through this, the well-beloved Brutus stabbed" (alluding to Mr. Pelham).

We need hardly say that these graphic details are not given in the meagre parliamentary reports. They are mostly taken by Coxe from the correspondence of Dr. Birch, and from a note of Lord Hardwicke's counter-attack on Fox, who, finding he had gone too far, had endeavoured to deprecate the Chancellor's resentment by an apology.

"Yielding, then, to the impulse of wounded feelings, he

repelled the attacks which had been levelled against him in the House of Commons. The conduct of Mr. Charles Townsend he ascribed to youth and inexperience, and directed the whole force of his invective against Mr. Fox.

" 'It is not, indeed, surprising,' he said, 'that young men in the warmth of their constitution should be averse to regulations which seem to interfere with their impassioned and sanguine pursuits; but it is extraordinary to see grave and solemn persons convert a law, so essential to the public good, into an engine of dark intrigue and faction, and into a pretext for forming a party, and trying its strength. Their opposition, however, has produced a result which they little expected; for it has raised a zeal in favour of the Bill, which has ensured its success.'

" He then indignantly animadverted upon the profligacy of the principles avowed by the enemies of the measure. Alluding to the apology of Mr. Fox, he said, ' With regard to my own share in this torrent of abuse, as I am obliged to those who have so honourably defended me, so I despise the invective, and I despise the recantation. I despise the scurrility, for scurrility I must call it, and I reject the adulation.' "[1]

A few months after his elevation, October 5, 1763, Fox writes to Selwyn, that his object in going to the Upper House was to cut up any further views of ambition by the roots. The rest of his life (observes Lord Russell) was passed in some favour with the Court, but (after the resignation of his place) in no ostensible position in office or in the House of Lords. A singular remark is quoted of his dying hours, which at least shows composure and good humour: "If Mr. Selwyn calls again," he told his servant, "let him in. If I am alive I shall be very glad to see him, and if I am dead he will be very glad to see me." In allusion to what are aptly termed the mortuary tastes of Selwyn, who never missed an execution

[1] Coxe—"Memoirs of the Pelham Administration;" vol. ii. p. 267.

if he could help it, Lord Holland had written to him on a preceding occasion:

"Yorke was very ugly whilst he lived, how did he look when he was dead?   "Yours ever,
                                "HOLLAND."

It would be superfluous to dwell on the public career of Charles James Fox; but there are a few particulars of his early life which are less familiarly known and strikingly illustrate the formation of his character.[1] The boundless indulgence with which he was brought up, and the temptations to which he was systematically exposed from boyhood, not merely account for the errors of his maturer years, but greatly enhance our admiration of the qualities of head and heart that could go through such an ordeal essentially unimpaired. " Mr. Fox's children were to receive no contradiction. Having promised Charles that he should be present when a garden wall was to be flung down, and having forgotten it, the wall was built up again, that he might perform his promise." Lord Holland (Charles's nephew), after quoting this passage from the Reminiscences of Sir G. Colebrook, remarks: "This was perhaps foolish, but the performance of a promise was the moral inculcated by the folly, and that, *ce me semble*, is no bad lesson."

"Charles is dreadfully passionate; what shall we do with him?" said Lady Caroline. "Oh, never mind," replied Mr. Fox; "he is a sensible little fellow, and will learn to curb himself." Charles overheard this conversation, and adverting to it in after life, said: "I will not deny that I

[1] The Early History of Charles James Fox has recently been made the subject of a work so planned and executed as to give the charm of novelty even to much that was already familiarly known. (*The Early History of C. J. Fox. By George Otto Trevelyan, M.P.* 1880.)

was a very sensible little fellow, a very clever little boy, and what I heard made an impression on me, and was of use to me afterwards." This is related by Lord Russell. The three following instances are given, we take for granted on good authority, in the book before us:

"Once the *enfant terrible* wished to break a watch. 'Well!' said the father, 'if you must, I suppose you must.'

"At another time, Lord Holland, as Secretary of State, was preparing some important papers, when Charles, going into the study, read, criticised, and burnt a despatch which was ready to be sealed. The father, without even reprimanding his boy, calmly got ready another copy of the despatch from the official draft.

"Charles James in his childhood does not seem to have shown his mother much more deference than he showed his father. One day he heard her make a mistake in Roman history, and, asking her, with utter contempt, what *she* knew about the Romans, he went on to explain how she was wrong."

Before he was fourteen he was taken by his father to Paris and Spa, where he made his first acquaintance with the gaming-table. After a brief interval at Eton (where he was flogged) he was taken a second time to Paris, where (says Lord Russell), "according to family traditions, he was indulged in all his youthful passions, and when he showed any signs of boyish modesty and shame, was ridiculed for his bashfulness by his injudicious and culpable father." In a letter, dated July 25th, 1765, the father writes:—" Charles has been here, but is now at Oxford, studying very hard, after two months at Paris, which he relished as much as ever. Such a mixture in education was never seen, but, extraordinary as it is, seems likely to do well." It certainly enabled him to make himself familiar with foreign languages and literature, whilst becoming a good classic; but what were the odds that, with such desultory habits and in the midst of every variety of seduction, all power of steady application and solid acquirement would be lost? It was about this time that he and a fellow-student set out to walk from Oxford to Holland House without a penny in their pockets. On arriving, his first exclamation to his father, who was taking his coffee, was, "You must send half-a-guinea or a guinea, without loss of time, to the ale-house keeper at Nettlebed, to redeem the gold watch you gave me some years ago, and which I have left in pawn there for a pot of porter."

The mother was less confident than the father of the success of his system, and is reported by her sister, the Duchess of Leicester, to have said to him soon after Charles left Oxford: "I have been this evening with Lady Hester Pitt, and there is little William Pitt, not eight years old, and really the cleverest child I ever saw, and brought up so strictly and properly in his behaviour, that, mark my words, that little boy will be a thorn in Charles's side as long as he lives." The result in each of these contrasted systems equally sets all calculation at defiance.

On the 8th February, 1772, Gibbon writes to Holroyd in reference to a debate on the Church Establishment:

"By-the-bye, Charles Fox prepared himself for that holy war by passing twenty-two hours in the pious exercise of hazard: his devotion cost him only about 500*l.* per hour —in all 11,000*l.*"

On December 6th, 1773, the same to the same:

"You know Lord Holland is paying Charles' debts. They amount to 140,000*l.* At a meeting of the creditors, his agent declared that, after deducting 6000*l.* a year settled on Ste (the eldest son), and a decent provision for his old age, the residue of his wealth amounted to no more than 90,000*l.*"

Walpole mentions another separate payment of 20,000*l.* for the debts of Stephen and Charles. In April 1772, Charles brought in a Bill to amend the Marriage Bill which his father had so vehemently opposed; and Walpole, after commending the ease, grace, and clearness of his speech, says:

"He was that very morning returned from Newmarket, where he had lost some thousand pounds the preceding day. He had stopped at Hockeril, where he found company —had sat up all night drinking, and had not been in bed when he came to move his Bill, which he had not even drawn. This was genius, was almost inspiration."

During the first three years of his parliamentary career, Charles Fox, as if impatient (as Walpole remarks) to inherit his father's unpopularity, professed the same arbitrary principles; and it was his motion to commit Woodfall, accompanied by a fierce denunciation against the City and the Press, that caused Lord North, at the King's suggestion, to send the well-known note:

"His Majesty has thought proper to order a new Commission of Treasury to be made out, in which I do not see your name.—NORTH."

This dismissal was fortunate for his fame. It threw him into opposition, compelled him to take the Liberal side on all great questions, and eventually led to his being the chosen champion, the pride and boast, of the Whig party.

He is the grand illustration of the Fox family, but if required to specify the persons to whom Holland House is most indebted for its fame, we should name his nephew Henry Richard, Lord Holland, and Elizabeth Vassall, Lady Holland, who has left a more marked impression of her individuality than any woman of her age. The distinctive qualities of both may be accurately learned from this work, although the authoress lies under the disadvantage of having never seen either of them; and she has also hit off, with intuitive justness of appreciation, the composition, aspect, tone, and constantly-varying, curiously-contrasted character of their society:

"Lord Holland enjoyed the Continent, and, when he left it, was all the more fit for his own home. After enjoying, and profiting by, his travels, he returned to England in 1796, and restored Holland House.

"He restored it in two ways: he restored it practically, under Mr. Saunders, fitting it up at great expense for his own habitation; and he restored it intellectually by bringing together those wits and geniuses who invested it with greater brilliancy than it had enjoyed even in the days of Addison.

"The circle of Holland House was a cosmopolitan one, and Holland House was among houses what England is amongst nations—a common ground, where all opinions could freely breathe.

"Much as people are wont to regret the number of their years, who would not gladly now be half a century older to have formed part of that circle, and heard the brilliant passages of wit and intellect which passed, and too often passed away, within those walls! A list furnished by Elizabeth, Lady Holland, to Sir James Mackintosh, helps us in enumerating some of the names which have thus immortalised the house."

This list includes almost all the celebrities of the Whig party, and most of the distinguished foreigners who visited England for half a century: with only one Tory, Lord Eldon, the very last whom we should have expected to find at Holland House.

The Princess has attempted to range them in a kind of *catalogue raisonné*, in which the character, or chief title of fame, is dashed off in a pointed sentence or two, or at most a paragraph, *e.g.*:

"Talleyrand, the diplomatic wit and witty diplomatist, who cared not which party he supported, provided it was the stronger.

"Madame de Staël, who in graceful French painted Italy, and in solid French digested German literature.

"Whishaw, whose sense made his opinions valuable to have and difficult to obtain."

Others are described by their *bons mots*:

"Then there was Luttrell, whose idea of the English climate was, 'On a fine day, like looking up a chimney; on a rainy day, like looking down it.' Luttrell, the epicure, who once, marvellous to relate, let the side-dishes pass by; but it was in order to contemplate a man who had failed to laugh at Sydney Smith's jokes. He himself, too, had plenty of original wit: he expressed a dislike for monkeys because they reminded him so of poor relations; and upon being asked whether a well-known bore had made himself very disagreeable, he answered musingly, 'Why, he was as disagreeable as the occasion would permit.'"

These *mots* of Luttrell are quoted from familiar memoirs. But one at p. 158 is new:

"She (Lady Holland) was rather fond of crowding her dinner-table. Once, when the company was already tightly packed, an unexpected guest arrived, and she instantly gave her imperious order: 'Luttrell! make room!' 'It must certainly be *made*,' he answered, 'for it does not *exist*.'"

One of the most graceful passages in the book is the tribute to Miss Fox, sister of the third lord. "Simplicity and purity of heart were hers; her very contact imparted goodness; her presence, sunshine. A woman in the best sense of the word; such was the dear 'Aunty' of that family." She was the early, the only, love of Jeremy Bentham, who, in his eightieth year, wrote to her reminding her of a flower she had given him on the lawn at Bowood. "From that day not a single one has passed (not to mention nights) in which you have not engrossed more of my thoughts than you could have wished." Bowring, who was present when he received her answer, describes him as singularly mortified and depressed by its coldness. In the Yellow Drawing-room of Holland House may still be seen what the Princess terms "souvenir d'amitié, understood though not expressed": a cameo ring, containing Jeremy Bentham's hair and profile, with the words, *Memento for Miss Fox* engraved upon it, with the dates of his birth and death:

"Not very unlike her, in goodness and kindliness, was her brother, the master of Holland House. Devoted to literature and art, he welcomed authors and artists with cordial affability. Well versed in the politics of Europe, he entertained statesmen and diplomatists of all nations with cosmopolitan fairness. Himself a wit and a humorist, he greeted with fellow-feeling the most brilliant men of the day. But while he enjoyed and preferred the society of choice spirits, while with him absence could not extinguish friendship, his benevolence and courtesy made him extend a kind reception to all who came to Holland House.

* * * * *

"In a very different way did Lady Holland wield her sceptre. Beautiful, clever, and well informed, she exercised a natural authority over those around her. But a habit of contradiction—which, it is fair to add, she did not mind being reciprocated upon herself—occasionally lent animation, not to say animosity, to the arguments in which she engaged. It is easy for some natures to say a disagreeable thing, but it is not always easy to carry a disagreeable thing off cleverly. This Lady Holland could do."

Two years have not yet elapsed since we gave a sample of her peculiarities;[1] but fresh instances are constantly recurring. Such was her strength of volition, that it required no slight degree of moral courage to resist her commands or refuse her most unreasonable wishes. Returning by the Great Western from Chippenham, after a visit to Bowood, she took Brunel in the carriage with her, and made him slacken the pace of the express train to less than twenty miles an hour in spite of the protestations of the passengers.

She insisted on Dickens telling her how "Nicholas Nickleby" was to end, before he had half developed or haply conceived the plot. She had a superstitious dread of lightning; and there is a story of her dressing up her maid in her own clothes to attract the bolt intended for herself. She had an equal dread of fire, which induced Sydney Smith to hurry to her with the model of a fire-escape, the efficacy of which he was prepared to guarantee on condition that the person resorting to it was first reduced to a state of nudity. He recommended it by the example of a clerical friend who, haunted by the same fear, had provided himself with one, and being awakened in the dead of the night by a knocking and ringing which he took for an alarm of fire, let himself down, after throwing off his night-shirt, on the steps before his door, where his wife and daughters (kept late at a ball) were knocking and ringing to be let in.

Lady Holland once called up a celebrated beauty, told her to kneel down on a footstool, and after pulling off her wreath and disarranging her hair in the operation, said, "There, my dear, now

---

[1] "Quarterly Review," Jan. 1872. Art. "Sir Henry Holland's Recollections," reprinted by the writer in "Biographical and Critical Essays. Second Series."

you look decent; those roses were quite out of keeping with your style." And she was right, though rude.[1]

One summer's day Lord Holland came down to dinner in a white waistcoat, which certainly loomed large on his portly figure, suggesting (as Luttrell whispered in an aside) the image of a turbot standing on its tail. She declared she would not sit down to dinner till he changed it, and he had no alternative but to comply. She was certainly no respecter of persons, and was brusque without reference to rank. A dinner-party in Great Stanhope Street was breaking up, and Lord Duncannon (the late Earl of Bessborough) had left the room, when she called out, "Mr. H., call back Lord Duncannon." Mr. H. went to the top of the staircase and told his lordship that he was wanted. On his presenting himself in the doorway she said, " The Duchess of Sutherland can't dine here to-morrow, and I want another woman. Bring one of your girls." He withdrew with an assenting bow.

The authoress relates that once when this imperious dame told Sydney Smith to ring the bell, he asked whether he had not better sweep the room too. Familiar as he was with her ways he would scarcely have taken offence at such a trifle, since some one must ring the bell for a lady unless she is to get up and ring it herself. But they had an occasional tiff, and a visitor at Combe Florey who found him sedulously attending to the comforts of a sucking-pig, was informed that it was intended for a peace-offering to Lady Holland.

She has been heard pressing Dutch herrings on an epicure, on the ground that they came over in

---

[1] Mrs. Norton was fond of telling this story, of which she was the heroine.

the Ambassador's bag; and a most appetising odour they must have communicated to the despatches. The introduction of the dahlia into England is said to be owing to her culinary research. Having been much gratified somewhere in the South of Europe by her first acquaintance with Palestine soup, and ascertaining that the main ingredient was the Jerusalem artichoke, she procured what she supposed to be a root of it, and forwarded it (probably by a King's Messenger) to her gardener at Holland House. When a beautiful flower came up instead of a succulent vegetable, she gazed on it with a feeling near akin to that of the foxhunter who complained that the smell of the violets spoilt the scent. But the value of her acquisition began to break upon her when the London seedsman who came to look at it offered thirty guineas for a root. Another version is, that a root was given to her at Valentia in 1804 by a botanist, who had just received it, an unknown rarity, from South America. At all events, there was ample justification for the graceful verses of her lord:

> "The dahlia you brought to our isle,
> Your praises for ever shall speak,
> In gardens as sweet as your smile,
> And colours as bright as your cheek."

She was an aristocrat to the tips of her fingers, and spoke contemptuously of the riband of the Bath as "a thing that was got by deserving it,"—an objection, by the way, to which it is not invariably exposed. The Garter was the only English order to her taste.

The excellence of Lady Holland's dinners was in no small respect owing to her habit of levying contributions on guests who inhabited districts famous for the venison, the poultry, the game, or any other edible. The praises of the *mouton des Ardennes* having been sounded at her table when M. van de Weyer was present, she commissioned him to procure her some. He sent an order for half a sheep, which was left at the Foreign Office in Brussels, directed to him and marked *très-pressé*. The clerks, taking it for a bundle of despatches, forwarded it by a special messenger. The affair got wind, and for more than a week the Belgian journals rang the changes on the Epicurean habits of his Excellency, who happened to be deservedly famous for his dinners.

We were present at a violent altercation between her and Motteux (the former proprietor of Sandringham) on the knotty point whether prunes are an improvement in cock-a-leeky soup: he *pro*, she *con*.

She made Byron seriously unhappy by telling him he was getting fat. "But (he comforted himself by adding) she is fond of saying disagreeable things." In the same spirit Talleyrand accounted for her inconveniently early dinner hour: "*C'est pour gêner tout le monde.*" She told Lord Porchester (the late Earl of Carnarvon), "I am sorry to hear you are going to publish a poem. Can't you suppress it?" She had more sense than wit, but like most people who affect a saucy roughness, she occasionally said a good thing. Speaking of the "Rejected Addresses," Monk Lewis remarked to her: "Many of them are very fair, but mine is not at all liked: they have made me write burlesque, which I never do." "You don't know your own talent," was the encouraging reply.

Jekyll was dining at Holland House in company with the Duke of York, when his Royal Highness showed strong symptoms of irritation at something said by Lady Jersey. It was his well-known habit to resort to brandy as a restorative for his nervous system in such an emergency, and Jekyll, leaning across, said, "Will your Royal Highness excuse the infirmity of an old man, and do me the honour of taking brandy with me instead of wine." "With the greatest pleasure, Mr. Jekyll: I feel very much obliged to you." When the brandy was called for, it was not forthcoming: there was literally none in the house; and Lady Holland with difficulty suppressed her anger till his Royal Highness was gone, when she turned to Jekyll and burst out, "You asked for it on purpose on the chance of finding that there was none."—"I, Lady Holland! I suppose that anything could be wanting at Holland House! I fully believed that, if I had called for a slice of broiled rhinoceros with cobra sauce, it would have been brought to me on the instant."

Among the reminiscences of that far-famed dinner table there is another which may be thought worth preserving.

Sir James Mackintosh was travelling in Switzerland when he got into a dispute about a change of horses with a German baron, who vowed he would have satisfaction on the spot were he not on his way to attend the deathbed of his wife, but insisted on Mackintosh's card that the demands of honour might be satisfied when the conjugal duty had been discharged. Mackintosh gave his card, glad to be quit of the business at so easy a rate, and thought no more of it till, some three months afterwards when he was dining at Holland House, an envelope sealed with an enormous coat-of-arms was placed before him, and was found to contain a formal cartel from the Baron, who had come all the way from the South of Germany to redeem his pledge. The party burst into a hearty laugh on learning the nature of the communication, and their merriment was not diminished by the lugubrious look of Mackintosh, who had no wish whatever to measure swords or exchange shots with the Teuton. As he was not to be put off, however, Sir Robert Wilson was deputed to wait upon him and arrange the matter amicably, which he did so successfully that the next day but one the two adversaries dined together with the same party at Holland House.

Allen was called her "pet atheist," and she showed no extraordinary reverence for the Church ritual when, at Florence, she caused the Burial Service to be performed by a beneficed clergyman (who, we hope, was not privy to the secret) over the body of a kid, having first given out that the funeral was that of a daughter by her first husband, whom his family had threatened to take from her. That daughter grew up to be a charming woman, and till her death in 1849 was familiarly known as "the kid" among her friends.

Lady Holland's passion was not singularity, but power. Her invitations were commands, and latterly she would go nowhere unless the party was made for her. There was to be no rule without an exception in her favour. She was peremptory in stipulating for *les petites entrées*, and superbly indifferent about *les grandes*. On the evening of a grand concert at Lansdowne House, Lord Lansdowne, after dining at Brookes', went home to dress. He had half got through the operation—*i.e.*, (to use his own words in telling the story) he was "between two shirts," when the door of the adjoining room flew open, a rustling of silk—*frou frou*—met his ear, and a female figure, which he failed to recognise, glided by. It was

Lady Holland, who, to avoid entering like other people, had come early, made her way to Lady Lansdowne's dressing-room opening into Lord Lansdowne's, and insisted on remaining there till the company were assembled, and then entering the music-room through the private door at the end.

The Princess was apparently not aware that a register of the dinners was kept as regularly as a merchant's ledger by Allen. It was in the possession of General Fox shortly before his death, and opposite the record of a dinner including the Prince of Wales (George IV.) and Sydney Smith is a marginal note by the General, stating that this was the dinner at which their celebrated passage of arms occurred. The subject of discussion being who was the wickedest man that ever lived, Sydney Smith said, addressing the Regent: "The Regent Orleans, and *he* was a *prince*." The Regent sharply replied: "I should give the *pas* to his tutor, the Abbé Dubois, and *he* was a *priest*."

In his diary, during the year 1813, Lord Byron writes: "Why does Lady Holland always keep that damned screen between the whole room and the fire? I, who bear cold no better than an antelope, and never yet found a sun quite *done* to my taste, was absolutely petrified, and could not even shiver. All the rest, too, looked as if they were just unpacked, like salmon, from an ice-basket, and set down at table for that day only. When she retired, I watched their looks as I dismissed the screen; and every cheek thawed and every nose reddened with the anticipated glow."

His attack on the Hollands, as he afterwards felt and admitted, was ill-directed and unjust.

"Blest be the banquets spread at Holland House,
  Where Scotchmen feed and critics may carouse!
  Long, long beneath that hospitable roof
  Shall Grub-street dine, while duns are kept aloof."

There was never the slightest taint of Grub Street, and any notion of social inequality was set at rest by (to use Macaulay's words) " that frank politeness which at once relieved all the embarrassment of the youngest and most timid writer or artist who found himself for the first time among ambassadors and earls."

The Princess's task becomes one of extreme delicacy when she arrives at the last Lord Holland and the present mistress of the domain, associated as they are with recent events and living contemporaries; but her execution is marked by fineness of touch and tact, and her frank tributes of gratitude and admiration are neither fulsome nor forced:

" We may not perhaps speak of the fourth Lord Holland as of a great statesman, as of a great philosopher; but (we humbly crave pardon of those whose opinion is otherwise) fame is not the link we would care to place between ourselves and the loved ones we have lost. Suffice it for us that we loved and, alas! lost him; *suffice it for all who had the happiness of knowing him that they were ever received by him with courteous kindness when they were happy; with noble generosity and graceful delicacy when fortune did not favour them.*

This is a noble panegyric; and by a rare felicity it may be applied to each successive proprietor and mistress of Holland House for three generations, not excepting Elizabeth, Lady Holland, of whom Moore sets down in his journal: " She is a warm and active friend, and I should think her capable of highmindedness upon occasions." The occasions were when a friend was in trouble,—had undergone affliction or suffered wrong.

There is another entry in Moore's journal which, after what we have said of her eccentricities, it is no more than bare justice to her to quote:

"*July 6th*, 1821.—By-the-bye, I yesterday gave Lady Holland Lord Byron's 'Memoirs' to read; and on my telling her that I rather feared he had mentioned her name in an unfair manner somewhere, she said, 'Such things give me no uneasiness: I know perfectly well my station in the world; and I know all that can be said of me. As long as the few friends that I *really* am sure of speak kindly of me (*and I would not believe the contrary if I saw it in black and white*), all that the rest of the world can say is a matter of complete indifference to me.'"

How much unhappiness would be avoided by resolving, like her, never to believe the alleged unkindness of a friend. All of us must be conscious of dissatisfied, uncongenial moments when we may let drop words utterly at variance with our genuine feelings. These are repeated without the modifying words or circumstances: then come complaints and explanations: the credulous hope of mutual minds is over; and a true, valued, really attached friend is irretrievably estranged.

In comparing periods there is an important peculiarity to be marked. During what is commonly deemed its brightest, the Holland House circle (besides its political complexion) was principally composed of men: the dinner was the rallying-point; and the number of guests on any given evening rarely exceeded what might have been casually collected at a country house. It was reserved for the present mistress of this historic mansion to throw it open to the whole of the great world without distinction of party: to invest it with a fresh set of associations; to blend female loveliness and grace with masculine sense, learning, genius and wit within its walls.

Memorable as are the interchanges of mind between orators and statesmen, artists and authors, in the library, not less memorable will be more than one of those afternoon receptions, when the old Dutch Garden resembled the garden of Florence in "Boccaccio," with its bevies of cavaliers and dames, in the gayest of dresses and the most picturesque of attitudes: when a table, heaped with fruit and flowers, was placed for royalty and the representatives of royalty in the open air before the refreshment-room, where a genuine Neapolitan *acquaiuolo* was plying his craft with the shrill accompaniment of its cries: when the far-famed Countess of Castiglione moved through the brilliant throng with the air of a goddess: when the leaders of both Houses were exchanging grave courtesies on the lawn: when Lord and Lady Russell and Lady Palmerston were talking to the Comte and Comtesse de Paris in a group, which the Prince of Wales had just quitted to engage in animated conversation with Longfellow.

We can understand why no allusion is made to these more modern scenes in the work before us, but the omission leaves the general impression incomplete.

At the conclusion of the historical part the character of the book changes, and it assumes somewhat the tone of a handbook, but a handbook like Ford's for Spain, or Palgrave's for Central Italy, in which we are conducted over classic or consecrated ground by the light of knowledge and taste.

In the chapter entitled "The Grounds," after pausing in the avenue to catch a glimpse of the south front, our attention, on reaching the entrance-sweep, is directed to the two stone piers by Inigo Jones, through which, after ascending a double flight of steps, we reach a terraced walk. A few paces to the left bring us in front of a lawn which slopes up gradually into a hill crowned by an old cedar-tree struck by lightning. "On the same lawn are other cedar-trees, younger and more strong; but the old cedar-tree crowning the hill stands there proud of its age, proud of its mutilations, like the veteran warrior, whose shattered arm and the scarred brow command the sympathetic enthusiasm of those around him."

There is a summer house called "Rogers' Seat," with which his memory is associated in complimentary verses by Luttrell and an inscription by Lord Holland:

"Here Rogers sat, and here for ever dwell,
With me, those Pleasures that he sings so well."

After being conducted through the Dutch garden, we are taken to a spot called the Moats, the scene of the fatal encounter between Captain Best and Lord Camelford. Best was reputed the best shot in England; and it was for this very reason that Lord Camelford forced on the duel, although consciously and confessedly in the wrong. It took place on the morning of the 7th March, 1804 : he fell on receiving the first fire, and was carried to Little Holland House, where the wound was examined and declared mortal. He expired on the evening of the 10th.

Best always reverted to the catastrophe with regret. The late Hon. and Rev. Fitzroy Stanhope used to relate that, being second to a sporting clerical friend in a duel that was to come off on a Sunday morning when the shops were shut, he asked Best (then in the rules of the King's Bench Prison for debt) to lend them his pistols, which he positively declined, saying: "No, no, my pistols have already more than enough to answer for."

There is a piece of water belonging to the

Moats in which the Duc and Duchesse d'Aumale used to fish with the last Lord Holland; and we arrive in due course at an alley called the "Alley Louis Philippe," the exiled King having lingered under the shelter of its trees during a visit to Holland House in 1848. At the end of the adjoining walk stands the statue of Charles James Fox (a cast of that in Bloomsbury Square), with the motto: "*Cui Plurimæ consentiunt Gentes Populi Primarium fuisse Virum.*" In the English translation *plurimæ* is rather freely rendered by *all*.

The Green Lane, called Nightingale Lane so long as there was a tradition of a songster,[1] "is a long avenue, like an immense gallery arched with trees and carpeted with grass, the distant light at the end softening down into that misty blue so peculiar to dear England." It has much of the wild charm of a forest glade, and the romance of its evening gloom is deepened by a touch of the supernatural:

"But we will avoid the possible charge of concocting a ghost story, by relating the event *verbatim* from 'Aubrey's Miscellanies'":—

"' The Beautiful Lady *Diana Rich*, Daughter to the Earl of *Holland*, as she was walking in her Father's Garden at *Kensington*, to take the fresh Air before Dinner, about Eleven a Clock, being then very well, met with her own Apparition, Habit, and every thing, as in a Looking-glass. About a Month after, she died of the Small-pox. And 'tis said, that her Sister, the Lady *Isabella* (*Thinne*,) saw the like of her self also before she died. This Account I had from a Person of Honour.'

"A third sister, Mary, was married to the first Earl of Breadalbane, and it has been recorded that she also, not long after her marriage, had some such warning of her approaching dissolution.

---

[1] An inscription on a pillar records that the swallows abandoned Holland House in 1876.

"And so the old tradition has remained—and who would wish to remove it? Belonging to past times, it should be respected. But whether we respect tradition or not, it is as a received fact, that whenever the mistress of Holland House meets herself, Death is hovering about her."

On entering the house we find almost every room invested with some special attraction, and a bare inventory of the contents calls up a throng of images. "Stop, for thy tread is on an empire's dust." Stop, for you cannot look around you without your gaze alighting on some memorial or relic of genius or greatness,—the writing-table of Addison: the watch and walking-stick of Fox: the candlesticks of Mary, Queen of Scots: the hair, ring, and snuff-box of Napoleon: the autographs of the Empress Catherine, Voltaire, Rousseau, Petrarch, Savonarola, Lope de Vega, Gonsalvo de Cordova. Then the pictures are something more than fine specimens of art. They point a moral or adorn a tale. Either the painter or the subject is commonly associated by some curious incident with the house. The "Sir Joshua Room" (chap. xx.) contains eleven of his masterpieces. One of these is the portrait of the first Lord Holland mentioned by Cotton. It is said that Lord Holland when he received this portrait could not help remarking that it had been hastily executed, and making some demur about the price, asked Reynolds how long he had been painting it. The offended artist replied, "All my life, my Lord."

Another is the picture of Lady Sarah Lennox, Charles Fox, and Lady Susan Strangeways. Lady Sarah is leaning out of a window at Holland House: Lady Susan, standing below with Fox, is offering her a dove; Fox, under fourteen at the time, in a blue coat and a paper in his hand, looks old for his age. But the ladies are the grand objects of interest: each of them being destined to play the part of a heroine of romance.

Lady Susan's story is soon told. In April 1764, she eloped with an actor, named O'Brien, with whom she had kept up a correspondence, occasionally sending him money, for eighteen months. He had learned to counterfeit Lady Sarah's (her cousin's) hand so well that her father (Lord Ilchester) had delivered several of his letters to her. The first discovery of the intrigue is described by Walpole:

"Lord Cathcart went to Miss Read's, the paintress: she said softly to him, "My lord, there is a couple in the next room that I am sure ought not to be together, I wish your lordship would look in.' He did, shut the door again, and went directly and informed Lord Ilchester. Lady Susan was examined, flung herself at her father's feet, confessed all, vowed to break off—but—what a *but!*—desired to see the loved object, and take a last leave. You will be amazed—even this was granted. The parting scene happened the beginning of the week. On Friday she came of age, and on Saturday morning—instead of being under lock and key in the country—walked downstairs, took her footman, said she was going to breakfast with Lady Sarah, but would call at Miss Read's; in the street, pretended to recollect a particular cap in which she was to be drawn, sent the footman back for it, whipped into a hackney chair, was married at Covent-garden church, and set out for Mr. O'Brien's villa at Dunstable. My lady—my Lady Hertford! what say *you* to permitting young ladies to act plays, and go to painters by themselves?"

He goes on to say that Lord Ilchester was distracted: that it was the completion of disgrace: that even a footman were preferable. "The publicity of the hero's profession perpetuates the mortification. *Il ne sera pas milord, tout comme un autre.* I could not have believed that Lady

Susan would have stooped so low. She may, however, still keep good company, and say, 'nos numeri sumus'—Lady Mary Duncan, Lady Caroline Adair, Lady Betty Gallini—the shopkeepers of next age will be mighty well born."

The husbands of these three ladies respectively were Dr. Duncan, a physician, afterwards created a baronet; Mr. Adair, a surgeon; and Sir John Gallini, a professor of dancing. O'Brien was an amusing fellow, who, in the course of time, achieved the distinction of being made the butt of the wits. A practical joke they played on him may have originated the operation of tarring and feathering: one of the very few inventions to which the Americans can lay claim. Having made him dead drunk, they stripped him, smeared him all over with currant jelly, and rolled him in a feather bed. Waking the next morning in a semi-intoxicated state, he staggered to a pier-glass, and gazing on his own reflected image, exclaimed: "A bird, by G—d."[1]

Lady Susan also played the part of confidant in the romance of her cousin, the outline of which is familiar enough. But the true and complete story could not be told without the narratives of Mr. Henry Napier (her son) and the first Lord Holland (her brother-in-law), which form part of the Holland House MSS.[2]

---

[1] Lord Stanhope speaks of tarring and feathering as first practised at Boston in 1770 ("Hist." vol. v. p. 397). In Foote's "Cozeners," O'Flanagan is to have a tide-waiter's place in North America: "And a word in your ear, if you discharge well your duty, you will be found in tar and feathers for nothing. . . . . When properly mixed they make a genteel kind of dress, which is sometimes worn in that climate; it is very light, keeps out the rain, and sticks extremely close to the skin."

[2] The story is told by Mr. Jesse as well as could be told from the information within his reach. "Memoirs of the Life and Reign of George III.," vol. i. ch. iv., his main authorities being Walpole and the Grenville Papers.

Mr. Napier begins with the marriage of her mother, *née* Lady Sarah Cadogan, to the second Duke of Richmond:

"'This marriage was made to cancel a gambling debt, the young people's consent having been the last thing thought of: the Earl of March was sent for from school and the young Lady from her nursery; a clergyman was in attendance, and they were told that they were immediately to become man and wife! The young lady is not reported to have uttered a word; the gentleman exclaimed: "*They surely are not going to marry me to that dowdy!*" The ceremony, however, took place, a post-chaise was ready at the door, and Lord March was instantly packed off with his Tutor to make the "Grand Tour," while his young wife was returned to the care of her Mother, a Dutch-woman, daughter of William Munter, Counsellor of the Courts of Holland.'"

He returns after spending some years abroad, and instead of going to claim his bride, repairs to the Opera and amuses himself with examining the company through his glass:

"'He had not been long occupied in this manner, when a very young and beautiful woman more especially struck his fancy, and, turning to a gentleman beside him, he asked who she was. "You must be a stranger in London," replied the gentleman, "not to know the toast of the Town, the beautiful Lady March!" Agreeably surprised at this intelligence, Lord March procceded to the box, announced himself, and claimed his bride, the very dowdy whom he had so scornfully rejected some years before, but with whom he afterwards lived so happily that she died of a broken heart within the year of his decease, which took place at Godalming, in Surrey, in August 1750, when my mother was only five years and a few months old.'"

Lady Sarah was in her sixteenth year and residing under her eldest sister's care at Holland House, when George the Third, who had been caught by her appearance before his accession to the throne, became seriously attached to her. Her charm in his eyes, in addition to her extraordinary loveliness, was her truthfulness. "Once he pressed her to say something, and she refused because it would have been telling an untruth. 'But,' said the King, 'you would not mind a white lie?' 'Yes, I would, Sir.'"

She did not encourage his passion, nor, strange to say, appear to be much flattered by it. One evening at a private Court Ball, at which she was not present, the King entered into conversation with Lady Susan, and asked her when she meant to leave town. On her saying she intended to remain for the coronation, he told her: 'There will be no coronation until there is a Queen, and I think your friend is the fittest person for it: tell your friend so from me." This was tolerably plain speaking. "When my mother next saw him at Court," Mr. Napier continues, "he took her alone into a recess of one of the large windows and said: 'Has your friend told you of my conversation with her?'—'Yes, Sir.' 'And what do you think of it? Tell me, for my happiness depends on it!' '*Nothing, Sir,*' was my mother's reply: upon which he left her abruptly, exclaiming pettishly, '*Nothing comes of Nothing.*'"

Walpole says: "Though he [Fox] went himself to bathe in the sea (possibly to disguise his intrigues), he left Lady Sarah at Holland House, where she appeared every morning in a field close to the great road (where the King passed on horseback), in a fancied habit, making hay."

It is not at all probable that she would have exhibited herself in this fashion; and there is a story that the King once passed rather unexpectedly and inopportunely when she was romping or flirting in the hayfield. Lord Holland says that about this time she was indulging in a silly flirtation with Lord Newbottle, afterwards Marquis of Lothian; who speedily lost all favour in her eyes by the want of feeling he betrayed when she fractured her leg out riding in Somersetshire. The King, on the other hand, manifested the most genuine anxiety, " and (adds Mr. Napier) had not the impropriety of such a proceeding been strongly urged, would instantly have set off to visit her!" When told of this her heart was touched. "If she now (writes Lord Holland) ever thinks of Newbottle, it is to vex and hate herself for the foolish transaction I have before related." Her chances of ascending a throne rose rapidly. One day she was entering the Presence Chamber when Lady Barrington, who was famous for her fine back, drew her aside, and said: " Do, my dear Lady Sarah, let me take the lead and go in before you this once: for you will never have an opportunity of seeing my beautiful back again." She announces her disappointment in a letter to Lady Susan:

"[July 7, 1761.]

" MY DEAREST SUSAN,— . . . To begin to astonish you as much as I was I must tell you that the ——— is going to be married to a Princess of Mecklembourg and that I am sure of it. There is a Council to-morrow on purpose. The orders for it are *urgent* and *important* business; does not your Chollar (*sic*) rise at hearing this? But you think I dare say that I have been doing some terrible thing to deserve it, for you would [not] easily be brought to change so totally your opinion of any person, but I assure you I have not. . . . I shall take care to shew that I am not mortified to anybody, but if it is true that one can vex anybody with a reserved cold manner, he shall have it I promise him."

Her information was correct. The intended marriage with the Princess Charlotte was announced to the Council on the 8th. The first time afterwards (July 16th), when she and the King met,

" She answered short; with dignity and gravity, and a cross Look, neither of which things are at all natural to her." According to her brother-in-law, however, she was simply piqued:

"'To many a Girl H. M.'s Behaviour had been very vexatious. But L^y Sarah's Temper and affections are happily so flexible and light that the sickness of her Squirrel immediately took up all her Attention, and when in spite of her nursing it dy'd I believe it gave her more concern than H. M. ever did. That Grief however soon gave way to the care of a little Hedge-Hog that She sav'd from destruction in the field and is now her favourite.'"

She was one of the bridesmaids at the Royal wedding, and Walpole writes to Conway: "With neither features nor air, Lady Sarah was by far the chief angel." Her portraits do not convey the impression of perfect beauty; neither do those of the Gunnings. "Her Beauty (says her brother-in-law) is not easily describ'd, otherwise than by saying She had the finest Complexion, most beautifull Hair, and prettyest Person that ever was seen, with a sprightly and fine Air, a pretty Mouth, and remarkably fine Teeth, and excess of Bloom in Her Cheeks,—little Eyes."

Both were carefully watched during the ceremony. The King was calm till the officiating Archbishop came to the words, "And as Thou didst send Thy blessing upon Abraham and Sarah, to their great comfort, so vouchsafe," etc., when his emotion was perceptibly betrayed. Mr. Napier, not noticing this incident, writes:

"The King appeared mentally absent but never took his eyes off Lady Sarah during the whole ceremony; the Queen, then and ever after was very gracious and attentive to my mother; but as all the young Bridesmaids were drawn up in a line near her Majesty, with Lady Sarah at their head very richly dressed, Lord Westmoreland, a very old Jacobite follower of the Pretender's, who was purblind, and had never appeared at Court since the Hanoverian succession, was persuaded by his friends to honour the marriage of a *native* Monarch by his presence. Passing along the line of ladies, and seeing but dimly, he mistook my Mother for the Queen, plumped down on his knees and took her hand to kiss! She drew back startled, and deeply colouring, exclaimed, 'I am not the Queen, Sir.' This little incident created a laugh and a little gossip; and when George Selwyn heard of it, he comically enough observed, 'O! you know he always loved *Pretenders*.'"

Many years afterwards, the King being present with the Queen at the theatre during a performance of Mrs. Pope, who had been thought to bear a strong resemblance to Lady Sarah, he murmured, half aloud, "She is like Lady Sarah still."[1]

The "Sir Joshua Room" contains pictures by Murillo, Velasquez, Jacob Jansen, G. Morland, two Turners, a Wouvermans, and a Van de Velde—the four last-named having belonged to Charles Fox. We quote the Princess's remarks on the Murillo, "The Vision of St. Antony of Padua," as an admirable specimen of art-criticism:

"According to tradition, St. Antony was expounding the mystery of the Incarnation, when the Infant Saviour came down and stood upon his book. In the present instance, though, St. Antony is praying, not expounding, and two features are to be particularly noticed in the picture: that St. Antony seems to ignore the *visible* Presence of Him whom he is adoring, and that the Divine Infant impresses no weight upon the book—as indeed a *spiritual* presence would not—yet Murillo is guilty of allowing the *spiritual* form to throw a *shadow!* Nor is this the only instance in which Murillo has fallen into this error, an error which, so far as we are aware, has escaped criticism. Curious indeed that one who so often shines forth as a heaven-inspired artist, one whose choice of subjects proves that his thoughts

---

[1] Lady Sarah was twice married. Her first husband (whom she married in June 1762) was Sir Charles Bunbury; her second (whom she married in 1781), the Honourable George Napier. She died in 1826.

dwelt constantly in another world, should have overlooked this essential and very beautiful distinction between the spirit and the flesh, and should have given to the one such a marked attribute of the other. But if the great painter has thus not always proved himself an accurate poet, a great poet has in similar circumstances proved himself a true painter. Dante, throughout his glorious journey, keeps in sight this spiritual indication :

"'Ora, se innanzi a me nulla s' adombra,
Non ti maravigliar, più che de' cieli,
Che l' uno all' altro 'l raggio non ingombra.'

"Or as Longfellow renders it :

"'Now if in front of me no shadow fall,
Marvel not at it more than at the heavens,
Because one ray impedeth not another.'"

There is another art-criticism susceptible of practical application. The subject is a portrait of Mary Augusta, Lady Holland (the present), by Watts:

"Watts pronounces this his finest piece of colouring. On a canvas which measures 85 inches by 61, Lady Holland is represented as standing in a corner of the GILT ROOM. The massive plaits of her auburn hair are displayed, without rudeness, by her back being turned to a looking-glass! Utilizing a looking-glass thus, was, at that time, very new in painting; nor are there many artists to this day who, having the idea, would care to profit by it. But photography, which can afford to give details without making them *extras*, has hackneyed the looking-glass idea into a looking-glass trick, and reduced it to the condition of a fine melody popularized on barrel-organs. In the picture before us, the looking-glass not only contributes a second view, but gives us variety in reflection. Everything is well managed. The drawing is good, the arrangement effective; and as for the colouring: what is dark, is rich; what is light, is pure; what is shade, is harmonious."

The "Fourth West Room" contains three pictures by Hogarth, one of which, a portrait of Henry, first Lord Holland, may be connected with an anecdote printed without the name. A nobleman having refused to take or pay for his portrait, painted to order, was thus addressed:

"Mr. Hogarth's dutiful respects to Lord ——, finding that he does not mean to have the picture which was drawn for him, is informed again of Mr. Hogarth's necessity for the money; if, therefore, his Lordship does not send for it in three days, it will be disposed of, with the addition of a tail and some other little appendages, to Mr. Hare, the famous wild-beast man; Mr. Hogarth having given that gentleman a conditional promise of it for an exhibition of pictures, on his Lordship's refusal."

The harshness and repulsiveness of Lord Holland's features are commemorated by more than one parliamentary sarcasm, and we have already seen him haggling with Reynolds. A similar threat was actually put in execution by a painter named Du Bost, some sixty years since. Failing to extract an extravagant price for a picture of Mr. and Mrs. Hope, of Deepdene, he exhibited it for money in Pall Mall, as "Beauty and the Beast," till her brother entered the room and cut it to pieces. An action was brought, and tried before Lord Ellenborough, who held that, the picture being a libel, the plaintiff could only recover damages for the loss of the canvas and the paint. *Semble* (as the Year Books have it) that he was therefore entitled to no damages at all.[1]

The modern artist of whom we are most frequently reminded in Holland House is Watts; a painter whose best portraits, instinct with mind and character, are historic pictures as well as likenesses. There are portraits by him of Guizot, Thiers, Jerome Buonaparte, the Duc d'Aumale, Sir Antonio Panizzi, Mr. Cotterell, Mr. Cheney, the Princess Lieven, the Countess Castiglione, the third Lord Holland, Elizabeth Lady Holland, and

[1] Du Boste *v.* Beresford.—Campbell's "Nisi Prius Reports," vol. ii. p. 511.

Mary Augusta Lady Holland, taken in a Nice hat at Florence in 1843. "This picture is charmingly painted, and gives us the present hostess of Holland House presiding, as it were, over one of its most sociable rooms, with a smile which lights up her face as much as the ray of sunshine lights up the picture."

The portrait of the Princess de Lieven is one of extraordinary merit, and it is added that Watts ranks it amongst his best. It gives occasion for a slight, but striking, biographical notice, most of the particulars of which are taken from a manuscript in the possession of Lady Holland:

"In appearance dignified, in manners simple, with the intellect of a man and the pliability of a woman, well dressed, and always suitably to her years, she presented in herself a general concentration of charms; and these, wherever she went, she seemed unwittingly to dispense without self-privation. Her style in writing harmonized with her other qualities, and was always in harmony with her subject. She could be grave, gay, learned, sarcastic. One generally loves doing what one does well; she wrote well and loved to use her pen. She has been very aptly said to combine 'la raison de la Rochefoucauld avec les manières de Madame de Sévigné.' But with all this she had no taste for reading, except the newspapers; and her ignorance upon some common subjects would have been marvellous even in a schoolboy."

* * * *

"Her end was touching and dignified. Naturally nervous about herself, she had dreaded the slightest indisposition; but when she heard that her doom was sealed, she looked death calmly in the face, and conformed to the last rites of the Protestant Church. Feeling the supreme moment at hand, she requested that Guizot and his son would leave her bedside, in order that they might be spared the painful sight of her agony. She had, however, still strength enough to address Guizot, her old and devoted friend, tracing in pencil these words: 'Merci de vingt ans d'amitié et de bonheur.'"

Speaking of Cleyn, in his "Anecdotes of Painting," Walpole says: "There is still extant a beautiful chamber adorned by him at Holland House with a ceiling in grotesque, and small compartments on the chimneys, in the style and not unworthy of Parmeggiano." This is "The Gilt Room." All the decorations and paintings in it have been restored by Watts, who found no traces of any painting on the chimney-piece; and the old ceiling, having fallen in, was replaced during the minority of the third Lord Holland. On Mayday, 1753, an entertainment was given in this room, of which a singular reminiscence has been preserved in the shape of a list of the company and an account of their proceedings. There were twenty-one couples of dancers: Mr. George Selwyn dancing with Miss Kitty Compton, the Earl of Hillsborough with Lady Caroline Fox, the Duke of Richmond with Miss Bishop, Captain Sandys with the Countess of Coventry, &c. Lady Albemarle, Lady Yarmouth, Mrs. Digby, and Mr. Fox played two pools at quadrille. Five gentlemen and four ladies "cut in at whist," including the Duke and Duchess of Bedford, Lady Townshend, and Mr. Digby. Five played cribbage. Eight, including Mr. H. Walpole and Mr. Calcraft, "only looked on." Lord Bateman and the Earl of Holderness "danced minuets only:"

"The Card Players play'd but a little while.

"The Card Tables (in Number three) were in Lady Caroline's Dressing Room. The Balcony, as well as the Gilt Room, was lighted up, and they Danced a little while in both.

"Tea, Negus, &c., at which Mrs. Fannen Presided, in the Tapestry Room. At One We all went down to a Cold Supper, at Three Tables in the Saloon, and three in the Dining Room.

"Supper was remov'd at each Table with a Desert (*sic*), and Ice.

"All sate down, Lady Townshend, Lady Fitzwilliams, Duke of Marlbro', and Mr. Legge, only Excepted who went before Supper.

"Danced after Supper.

"No Dancer went before three, or stay'd after Five.

"The Tables Prepar'd in the Supper Rooms held Fifty-six. A Corner Table was plac'd Extraordinary for Six Men, Besides. Sate down to Supper in all Sixty-two.

"Lord Digby, and Mr. Bateman did not sup, but walk'd about admiring."

After a bit of moralising in her manner, the Princess winds up her entertaining chapter of " The Gilt Room " in these words:

"And so the brilliant medal has its reverse: for now, in spite of being still sometimes filled by a joyous, laughing crowd, the Gilt Room is said to be tenanted by the solitary ghost of its first lord, who, according to tradition, issues forth at midnight from behind a secret door and walks slowly through the scenes of former triumphs with his head in his hand. To add to this mystery, there is a tale of three spots of blood on the side of the recess whence he issues, three spots of blood which can never be effaced."

There is a celebrated passage in one of Macaulay's Essays, in which he eloquently expatiates on the impressions which survivors of a nearly extinct generation may retain of the Library. "They will remember how the last debate was discussed in one corner and the last comedy of Scribe in another; while Wilkie gazed with modest admiration on Sir Joshua's Baretti, while Mackintosh turned over Thomas Aquinas to verify a quotation, while Talleyrand related his conversations with Barras at the Luxembourg, or his ride with Lannes over the field of Austerlitz."

This *tableau* strikes us as a somewhat inadequate one, and we hardly understand why the brilliant historian should have singled out and limited himself to Wilkie, Mackintosh, and Talleyrand, when he had so long and luminous a beadroll of equal or greater celebrities to choose from and group as he thought fit. Charles James Fox, Grey, Grenville, Monk Lewis, Sheridan, Windham, Romilly, Tierney, Parr, Horner, Jeffrey, Sydney Smith, Luttrell, Byron, Moore, Rogers, Thurlow, Eldon, Lyndhurst, Brougham, Melbourne, Grattan, Curran, Davy, Lawrence, Landseer, Canova, Chantrey, Washington Irving, Alexander and William von Humboldt, Pozzo di Borgo, Molé, Guizot, Lord and Lady Palmerston, the Prince and Princess de Lieven, Madame de Staël—all these might have been seen conversing in that library within living memory. There are enough to fill every niche in that "venerable chamber" if we were to set about re-peopling it with the illustrious dead; and there is barely a room in the mansion, or a spot in the grounds, which is not associated with some hallowed image or cherished memory.

Macaulay might have expatiated in much the same strain on "The Library Passage," where many an illustrious guest has lingered over the prints, portraits, photographs, and autographs on the walls. Here is the so-called portrait of Addison, with his last autograph: a miniature of the Empress Catherine, with her autograph; the miniature of Robespierre, on the back of which may be read, in the handwriting of Charles Fox: "*Un scélérat, un lâche et un fou.*"

"But before quite leaving the LIBRARY PASSAGE we must not forget to look at the windows. In the southern window is a pane of glass removed from the window of what we believe used to be Rogers's dressing-room in the East Turret. Upon this pane of glass are cut some lines by Hookham Frere. They date from October 1811, and run as follows:

"'May neither fire destroy nor waste impair
Nor time consume thee till the twentieth Heir,
May Taste respect thee and may Fashion spare.'

"To which we add a devout Amen! and to which Rogers is reported to have said, 'I wonder where he got the diamond.'"

"The Breakfast Room" was the scene of the well-authenticated anecdote of Lord Brougham, who slept at Holland House the night before the delivery of his principal speech on the Queen's trial. On coming down to breakfast Lord Holland saw his guest busily writing at a side table, and found that, instead of preparing for the grand effort, he was drawing the clauses of his Education Bill. The plaster statuette in the Picture Room was bought by himself about a year before his death; and when, in his latter years, he came to spend an hour or two at Holland House, he would often sit moodily down, and, missing the friendly faces of bygone days, he has more than once burst into tears.

The "Yellow Drawing-room" alone boasts relics and memorials enough to excite the envy of the richest and most fortunate collector; and the chapter devoted to it contains matter of historical value, which we pass over with regret. "The Miniature Room" and the "Print Room," also, are eminently suggestive and rich. But it is as much as we can do to afford space for "Allen's Room;" and Lady Holland's "pet atheist" is an indispensable figure in our group. He was recommended, in 1801, by Sydney Smith to Lord Holland, who wanted a "clever young Scotch medical man" to accompany him to Spain. They suited each other so well that he was domesticated in Holland House. "To Lady Holland he must have been a friendly factotum. He almost always attended her on her drives, was usually invited out with her and Lord Holland to dinner, and in Holland House sat at the bottom of the table and carved. In this performance Lady Holland was apt to fidget him by giving him directions, and he would assert his independence by laying down the knife and fork and telling her she had better do it herself!"

His character has been carefully drawn by Lord Brougham, who raises the question why " with his great talents, long experience, many rare accomplishments, and connection with statesmen," he was never brought into public life; an injustice or neglect which his lordship thinks can be accounted for " in no other way than by considering it as a fixed and settled rule that there is a line drawn in this country between the ruling caste and the rest of the community." May it not be accounted for by the habits and disposition of the man who was content to pass his whole life in a dependent position. Would not the same line (had it existed) have excluded Horner and Lord Brougham himself? Moreover, Allen's intellectual efforts never attracted much attention beyond a limited circle. He died in 1843. The year before his death, Sydney Smith writes to Lady Holland:

"I am sorry to hear Allen is not well; but the reduction of his legs is a pure and unmixed good; they are enormous,—they are clerical! He has the creed of a philosopher and the legs of a clergyman; I never saw such legs,—at least belonging to a layman."

"Yet a few years, and the shades and structures may follow their illustrious masters. The wonderful city, which, ancient and gigantic as it is, still continues to grow as fast as a young town of logwood by a water privilege in Michigan, may soon displace those turrets and gardens which are associated with so much that is interesting and noble, with the courtly magnificence of Rich, with the loves of Ormond, with the counsels of Cromwell, with the death of Addison."[1] If we are not misinformed, arrangements have been made that will prevent these turrets and gardens from being speedily displaced. But we tremble when we think of the fate of the Northumberland House lion: of Fonthill dismantled and coming down with a crash: of the ring of the auctioneer's hammer in the princely halls of Stowe: of the dispersion of the art-treasures of Strawberry Hill, just as it was about to derive fresh lustre from taste and munificence. If, then, the stately fabric we have been commemorating, with its priceless contents, must perish, so much the greater will be the debt of gratitude due from future generations to those who afford the means of keeping it permanently present to the mind's eye. *Non omnis moriar.* Though lost to sight, to memory dear. Good copies are nearly as effective as originals in supplying food for reflection, in appealing to the imagination and the heart. Heinrich Heine said of a celebrated poem that, if suddenly destroyed, it might be completely reproduced from a translation which he named. Thanks to the work before us, with its graphic delineations and descriptions, if Holland House were to be burnt down or swallowed up to-morrow, its most inspiring elevating associations would survive, and everything in it or about it, capable of material reproduction, might be reproduced.

[1] "Macaulay's Essays." We have found no trace of the loves of Ormond at Holland House.

STRAWBERRY HILL.[1]

(*From the Quarterly Review, October,* 1876.)

HOLLAND HOUSE and Hatfield are examples of historic houses which were great and noble from the foundation and can boast a far-ascending and richly-associated past. Holland House recalls a succession of statesmen and orators, interspersed and relieved by poets, historians and essayists, prominent among whom rises the honoured shade of Addison pacing up and down the library. Hatfield is redolent of royal reminiscences, and we can fancy the Virgin Queen seated under the traditional oak, with the grave Cecil in respectful attendance by her side. Strawberry Hill cannot bear a momentary comparison with either in antiquity, original splendour, or illustration. Its historic, artistic, and literary interest is the creation of one man. It stole obscurely into existence as a cottage under the name of "Chopped Straw Hall," having been built by a retired coachman (Lord Bradford's),

---

[1] 1. *A Description of the Villa of Mr. Horace Walpole, Youngest Son of Sir Robert Walpole, Earl of Orford, at Strawberry Hill, near Twickenham. Middlesex. With an Inventory of the Furniture, Pictures, Curiosities, &c.,* Strawberry Hill: printed by Thomas Kirkgate, MDCCLXXXIV.

2. *The Letters of Horace Walpole, Earl of Orford.* Edited by Peter Cunningham. Now first Chronologically arranged. In Nine Volumes. London, MDCCCLXI.

who was supposed to have acquired the necessary funds by feeding his noble master's horses with a cheap substitute for oats. At a subsequent stage it had just so much connection with the drama as could be derived from being tenanted by Colley Cibber when he wrote " The Refusal," and just so much of the odour of sanctity or divinity as could be conferred by the residence of Talbot, Bishop of Durham, who rented it for eight years. It could boast of two noble occupants, the Marquis of Carnarvon and Lord John Sackville, prior to Walpole, but his immediate predecessor was Mrs. Chenevix, the celebrated toy-woman. The manner in which he came into possession is specified in his " Short Notes of My Life ":

"In May, 1747, I took a small house near Twickenham for seven years. I afterwards (1748) bought it by Act of Parliament, it belonging to minors; and have made great additions and improvements to it. In one of the deeds I found it was called Strawberry Hill."

He hastens to announce his new possession in his characteristic style to his friends. To Mr. (afterwards Sir Horace) Mann, June 5, 1747, he writes:

"The house is so small, that I can send it you in a letter to look at: the prospect is as delightful as possible, commanding the river, the town, and Richmond Park; and being situated on a hill descends to the Thames through two or three little meadows, where I have some Turkish sheep and two cows, all studied in their colours for becoming the view. This little rural *bijou* was Mrs. Chenevix's, the toy-woman *à la mode*, who in every dry season is to furnish me with the best rain water from Paris, and now and then with some Dresden-china cows, who are to figure like wooden classics in a library: so I shall grow as much a shepherd as any swain in the Astræa."

To the Hon. H. Seymour Conway.

"Twickenham, June 8, 1747.

"You perceive by my date that I am got into a new camp, and have left my tub at Windsor. It is a little plaything-house that I got out of Mrs. Chenevix's shop, and it is the prettiest bauble you ever saw. It is set in enamelled meadows, with filigree hedges:

"A small Euphrates through the piece is roll'd
And little finches wave their wings in gold.

"Two delightful roads, that you would call dusty, supply me continually with coaches and chaises: barges as solemn as Barons of the Exchequer move under my window; Richmond Hill and Ham walks bound my prospect; but, thank God! the Thames is between me and the Duchess of Queensberry. Dowagers as plenty as flounders inhabit all around, and Pope's ghost is just now skimming under my window by a most poetical moonlight. I have about land enough to keep such a farm as Noah's when he set up in the ark with a pair of each kind; but my cottage is rather cleaner than I believe his was after they had been cooped up together forty days. The Chenevixes had tricked it out for themselves: up two pair of stairs is what they call Mr. Chenevix's library, furnished with three maps, one shelf, a bust of Sir Isaac Newton, and a lame telescope without any glasses. Lord John Sackville *predecessed* me here, and instituted certain games called *cricketalia*, which have been celebrated this very evening in honour of him in a neighbouring meadow."

Limited as was the accommodation, he seems to have been perfectly satisfied with it at starting: indeed, more than satisfied: for in the May of the following year he advises his friend, George Montagu, to come there after his own place, Roel, in Gloucestershire, "which you would not be able to bear after my paradise;" and June 7, 1748, he writes to Mann:

"I am now returning to my villa, where I have been making some alterations: you shall hear from me from Strawberry Hill, which I have found out in my lease is the old name of my house: so pray never call it Twickenham again. I like to be there better than I have liked being anywhere since I came to England."

These alterations were confined to the garden and the grounds. The bare notion of converting the cottage into a castle had not yet occurred to him; and it may be as well to show, by a short sketch of his early years, what manner of man he was when he planned the quaint, fanciful, so-called Gothic structure, which, with its decorations and embellishments, was henceforth to form the main object of his life and largely co-operate in the establishment of his fame.

Horace (christened Horatio) Walpole, the third son of Sir Robert Walpole and Catherine (*née*) Shorter, was born in Arlington Street on October 15, 1717. His mother was a beautiful woman, fond of admiration: scandal had been already busy with her name, and common rumour assigned the honour of his paternity to Carr, Lord Hervey, the elder brother of Pope's Sporus. Sir Robert was not remarkable for delicacy of sentiment or speech, and we see no reason to discredit a traditional story (told by Lord Wharncliffe) of his remarking, after Horace had given decided proofs of ability at school, that, whether the lad had or had not the right to the name he went by, he was likely to do it honour.[1] He was educated until his tenth year with his cousins, the four younger sons of Lord Townshend, under Mr. Weston, a son of the Bishop of Exeter. On April 26th, 1727, he went to Eton, where Mr. Bland, son of the Master, and afterwards Provost, was his tutor. Whilst still at Eton, May 1731, he was entered at Lincoln's Inn, being in-

---

[1] "Letters and Miscellaneous Works of Lady Wortley Montague," vol. i. p. 33.

tended for the law; but (he says) he never went there, not caring for the profession.[1] In his "Reminiscences," after mentioning that he was extremely weak and delicate, and extravagantly indulged by his mother on that account, he states that a longing to see the King suddenly took possession of him:

"This childish caprice was so strong that my mother solicited the Duchess of Kendal to obtain for me the honour of kissing his Majesty's hand before he set out for Hanover. A favour so unusual to be asked for a boy of ten years old, was still too slight to be refused to the wife of the First Minister for her darling child; yet not being proper to be made a precedent, it was settled to be in private, and at night. Accordingly, the night but one before the King began his last journey, my mother carried me at ten at night to the apartment of the Countess of Walsingham on the ground-floor towards the garden at St. James's. Notice being given that the King was come down to supper, Lady Walsingham took me alone into the Duchess's ante-room, where we found alone the King and her. I knelt down, and kissed his hand. He said a few words to me, and my conductress led me back to my mother."

We have here the courtier in embryo, the germ of that fondness for Courts and Court ceremonials which clung to him through life. His genius for forming friendships was another of the distinctive qualities which were developed in boyhood. The famous *partie quarrée* which met at Strawberry Hill was anticipated by the "quadruple alliance" at Eton, consisting of Gray, West, Ashton, and himself. Like the three Mousquetaires of Dumas, they were known to each other by nicknames: Tydeus, Orosmanes, Almanzor, and Plato. Contemporaneous with these three, and very nearly on

[1] "Short Notes of my Life." Eliot Warburton, quoting no authority, says he went to Eton in 1726.—"Memoirs of Horace Walpole," vol. i. p. 61.

a par with them in his early affections, were George Montagu, Seymour Conway, George Selwyn, and Sir Charles Hanbury Williams. In fact, the enduring friendships he formed with so many of his schoolfellows are a conclusive answer to the charges of selfishness and insensibility that have been heaped upon him. It was a favourable report of the Eton master that drew from Sir Robert the remark already quoted on his proficiency; but there are more decisive proofs of his having made good use of his time—of his having, at all events, acquired a taste for classical reading, one of the most enviable attainments which a public school can confer. Writing to West, at Oxford, from King's College, Cambridge, in December, 1735, a few months after leaving Eton, and referring to the paucity of topics of interest in the University, he says:

"But why may not we hold a classical correspondence? I can never forget the agreeable hours we have passed in reading 'Horace' and 'Virgil,' and I think they are topics which never grow stale. Let us extend the Roman empire, and cultivate two barbarous towns (Oxford and Cambridge) o'errun with rusticity and mathematics. The creatures are so used to a circle, that they plod on in the same eternal round, with their whole view confined to a *punctum cujus nulla est pars.*"

"That ever you should pitch upon me for a mechanic or geometric commission"—is the commencement of a letter to Mann in 1759—"I will tell you an early anecdote in my own life, and you shall judge." It is that when he first went to Cambridge he studied mathematics under the blind Professor Sanderson, who at the end of a fortnight's attendance said to him, "Young man, it is cheating you to take your money; believe me, you never can learn these things—you have no capacity for them." He was ready (he owns) to cry with mortification; and determined to confound the Professor. Conceiving that he had talents for anything in the world, he engaged a private tutor, who came to him once a day for a year. The result was, that he learnt just enough to confirm his distaste. He got on no better with logic:

"I have been so used to the delicate food of Parnassus, that I can never condescend to apply to the grosser studies of Alma Mater. Sober cloth of syllogism suits me ill; or what's worse, I hate clothes that one must prove to be of no colour at all. . . . Great mathematicians have been of great use, but the generality of them are quite unconversable. I tell you what I see, that, by living amongst them, I write of nothing else; my letters are all parallelograms, two sides equal to one side, and every paragraph an axiom that tells you nothing but what every mortal almost knows."

His dislike to the studies of the University did not prevent him from cherishing the recollection of his residence at King's College:

"Though I forget Alma Mater," he writes in 1780, "I have not forgot my Almæ Nutrices, wet or dry, I mean Eton and King's. I have laid aside for them, and left them in my will, as complete a set as I could of all I have printed."

He sustained an irreparable loss in the second year of his residence by the death of his mother—an event rendered the more poignant by the second marriage of his father, with Maria Skerrett. This lady had borne a daughter to the Premier prior to wedlock, and her reputation fully justified the sarcasm that he took her to wife because he had tried all other ways of robbing the public and exhausted them. "I continued at Cambridge," we read in the "Short Notes," "though with long intervals, till towards the end of 1738, and did not leave it in form till 1739, in which year, March 10th, I set out on my travels with my friend, Mr. Thomas Gray, and went to Paris." From Paris they went with his cousin, Conway, to Rheims, where they stayed three months to learn French:

"You must not wonder (he writes from Rheims to West) if all my letters resemble dictionaries with French on one side and English on t'other. I deal in nothing else at present, and talk a couple of words of each language alternately from morning to night."

On quitting Rheims they crossed the Alps at Mont Cenis, and proceeded to Genoa, Parma, Placentia, Modena, Bologna, and Florence, where they stayed three months, "chiefly for the sake of Mr. (afterwards Sir) Horace Mann, the English Minister." After visiting Rome and Naples he returned to Florence in June, 1740, where he resided in Mann's house till the following May, leaving no ground for the sarcasm (although they did not subsequently meet for forty years) that the solidity of their friendship was in an inverse ratio to their proximity. They got on equally well together from the commencement of their intimacy, and there is nothing extraordinary in their so doing. They were on a footing of social equality: they lived the same life with the same people: the diplomatist would naturally lay himself out to please the son of the Premier; and Walpole, had he been ever so disposed, could hardly have been captious or supercilious to one in the position of his host.

His relations with Gray were of a totally different character, and the wonder is not that they quarrelled and separated before the conclusion of the tour, but that they ever planned such an expedition in concert or kept together for a week. Gray was the son of a London money-scrivener, and his going to Eton was owing to the accident of his uncle being one of the assistant-masters of the school. His habits were studious, pensive, and recluse, and he had neither inclination nor aptitude for the amusements or society in which Walpole delighted and shone. The classic lore, the speculative philosophy, the polite literature, which were the sport, the pastime, the playthings, of the one, were the serious absorbing occupation of the other; and Walpole, we suspect, was not long in discovering that he had made the same mistake in choosing Gray for a travelling companion which Lord Byron made when he invited Leigh Hunt to be his guest in Italy.

"You would be as much amazed (he writes) at us as at anything you saw; instead of being deep in the liberal arts and being in the gallery every morning, as I thought of course I would be, we are in all the idleness and amusements of the town. . . .

"I have seen nothing but cards and dull pairs of Cicisbeos. I have literally seen so much love and pharaoh since being here, that I believe I shall never love either again as long as I live. Then I am got into a horrid lazy way of a morning. I don't think I should know seven o'clock in the morning again if I was to see it."

This was written from Florence in October and November, 1740. Gray seems to have quietly taken his own line when they were stationary, but so soon as they resumed their travels, the incompatibility broke out. They parted company at Reggio, the first place they visited after leaving Florence; and Gray started for Venice with Whithed and Chute; whither Walpole also repaired soon afterwards with Lord Lincoln and Spence, but he did not rejoin Gray, who returned to England alone in the summer of 1741. It is highly honourable to Walpole that, on a calm review of the circumstances, he took the principal blame of the misunderstanding upon himself:

"I am conscious (he wrote to Mason after Gray's death) that in the beginning of the difference between Gray and me the fault was mine. I was young, too fond of my own diversions, nay, I do not doubt, too much intoxicated by indulgence, vanity, and the insolence of my situation as a Prime Minister's son, not to have been inattentive to the feelings of one, I blush to say it, that I knew was obliged to me. . . . I treated him insolently. He loved me, and I did not think he did. I reproached him with the difference between us, when he acted from the conviction that he was my superior. Forgive me if I say that his temper was not conciliating."

We learn from Mason, who gives the same account of the disagreement, that "in the year 1744 a reconciliation was effected between them by a lady who wished well to both parties." That the reconciliation was complete in 1747 is shown by Gray's letters to Walpole of that year, especially one of March 1, enclosing the ode "On the Death of a Favourite Cat, Drowned in a Tub of Gold Fishes." The cat came to this untimely end in Arlington Street; but the bowl or tub (of blue and white china) stood on a pedestal in the small cloister at Strawberry Hill, with a label containing the first stanza of the ode:

> "'Twas on this lofty vase's side,
> Where China's gayest art has dy'd
> The azure flow'rs that blow:
> Demurest of the tabby kind,
> The pensive Selima reclin'd,
> Gaz'd on the lake below."[1]

[1] The bowl and pedestal were knocked down to the Earl of Derby at the sale in 1842 for 42*l.*

Walpole's letters during his protracted tour, averaging hardly one a month, confirm the account of his idleness, but they are not deficient in lively observation or in thought:

"I have made," he writes, "no discoveries in ancient or modern arts. Mr. Addison travelled through the poets, and not through Italy; for all his ideas are borrowed from the descriptions and not from the reality. He saw places as they were, not as they are."

Walpole saw them as they were, and his reflection at Rome was that before a great number of years was elapsed it might not be worth seeing, as from the combined ignorance and poverty of the Romans, everything was neglected and falling to decay; "the villas are entirely out of repair, and the palaces so ill kept that half the pictures are spoiled by damp." At the villa Ludovisi, an oracular head of red marble, colossal, with vast holes for the eyes and mouth, was shown to him as *un ritratto della famiglia* (a family portrait). In a postscript to the letter mentioning this, Gray adds: "*Apropos du Colisée*, if you don't know what it is, the Prince Borghese will be very capable of giving you some account of it, who told an Englishman that asked what it was built for: 'They say it was for Christians to fight tigers in.'" At the same time Walpole was rapidly qualifying for a virtuoso, and his intermittent mania for collecting was at fever heat in Rome, when (April, 1740) he wrote: "I am far gone in medals, lamps, idols, prints, &c., and all the small commodities to the purchase of which I can attain; I would buy the Coliseum if I could."

From Florence, July 9, 1740, he writes to Conway, in Ireland:

"Let us see: you are come back to stand for some place,

that will be about April. *'Tis the sort of thing I should do, too*, and then we should see one another, and that would be charming; but it is a sort of thing I have no mind to do, and then we shall not see one another."

Here we have the tone of his set. George Selwyn was opposed at Gloucester by a timber merchant, whom Gilly Williams calls "a d—d carpenter," whilst Lord Carlisle asks: "Why did you not set his timber-yard on fire? What can a man mean who has not an idea separated from the footsquare of a Norway deal plank by desiring to be in Parliament? But these beasts are monstrously obstinate, and about as well bred as the dogs they keep in their yards."

Walpole was nominated for Callington, a Government borough, and chosen in his absence at the general election of June, 1741, when the tone of languid indifference with which he anticipated the event was speedily exchanged for one of ill-disguised anxiety. His father's fall was impending, and something more than tenure of office was at stake, when half-mockingly he writes (Dec. 10th) to Mann:

"I look upon it now that the question is, Downing Street or the Tower. Will you come and see a body, if one should happen to lodge at the latter? There are a thousand pretty things to amuse you—the lions, the armoury, the crown, and the axe that beheaded Anna Bullen. I design to make interest for the room where the two princes were smothered. . . . If I die there, and have my body thrown into a wood, I am too old to be buried by robin-redbreasts, am I not?"

A week later, December 17th, to the same:

"Say a great deal for me to the Chutes. How I envy your snug suppers? I never have such suppers! Trust me, if we fall, all the grandeur, all the envied grandeur, of our house will not cost me a sigh; it has given me no pleasure while we had it, and will give me no pain when I part with it. My liberty, my ease, and choice of my own friends and company will sufficiently counterbalance the crowds of Downing Street. I am so sick of it all, that if we are victorious or not, I propose leaving England in the spring."

We can readily believe that it was a positive relief to him when things came to a crisis. The first decisive defeat sustained by Sir Robert was on the question whether an election petition should be received. He was beaten by a majority of one, 236 to 235, and after a brief hesitation intimated his intention to resign so soon as the necessary arrangements could be completed. After recapitulating what had occurred, Horace writes, Feb. 4, 1742:

"For myself I am quite happy to be free from all the fatigue, envy, and uncertainty of our late situation. I go everywhere, indeed, to have the stare over, and to use myself to neglect, but I meet nothing but civilities."

The uncertainty was not yet over, for impeachments were threatened, and motions for Committees of Inquiry were eagerly pressed. It was on one of these, March 23, 1742, that he made his maiden speech:

"I am now (he writes to Mann) going to tell you what you will not have expected—that a particular friend of yours opposed the motion, and it was the first time he ever spoke. As the speech was very favourably received and has done him service, I prevailed with him to give me a copy—here it is."

The most remarkable thing about it is that he should have thought it calculated to do him credit as a composition. Poor and commonplace as it reads, the circumstances under which it was delivered secured it a favourable reception, and Pitt, the great commoner, highly commended him for making it, adding that, if it was becoming in him to remember that he was the child of the accused, the House ought to remember too that they are the children of their country.

In the "Short Notes" he says that the speech was published in the magazines, but "was entirely false, and had but one paragraph of the real speech in it." Parliamentary reporting was then strictly prohibited by both Houses; and speeches were published in feigned names from rough notes or hearsay. The famous reply of Pitt to "old" Horace Walpole was composed by Johnson, who was not even present at the debate.

With the exception of a copy of Latin verses at Cambridge, the earliest composition acknowledged in the "Short Notes" was a squib, entitled "The Lessons for the Day: being the First and Second Chapters of the Book of Preferment." This was written in July, 1742, when Mr. Coke, coming in whilst he was writing it, "took a copy and dispersed it till it got into print, but with many additions, and was the original of a great number of things of that sort." There can be no reasonable doubt that it got into print (like Pope's letters) by the connivance of the writer, or that the additions were by him. About the same time he wrote a "Sermon on Painting" for the amusement of his father, who had it preached by his chaplain. It was printed in the "Ædes Walpolianæ." In 1743 he contributed a paper to a weekly journal, called "Old England," a parody on some scenes in Macbeth, in ridicule of the new Ministry; and a squib in ridicule of Lord Bath.

His father died on March 28, 1745, and on the 29th he writes a letter of four closely-printed pages, in which, after disposing of the melancholy event in a sentence as "only to be felt, never to be talked over, by those it touches," he displays, if possible, more than ordinary spirit and vivacity in supplying his correspondent with the current news and gossip. Although he fully appreciated Sir Robert's best qualities, there was little congeniality or sympathy between the father and the son—the one delicate in constitution and refined to fastidiousness; the other, robust, rude, frank, hearty and coarse. From early manhood, moreover, Horace was in a great measure emancipated from paternal influence and control by pecuniary independence. When he was between eighteen and nineteen he obtained the place of Inspector of Imports and Exports, which he resigned in about a year on receiving the patent place of Usher of the Exchequer, then reckoned worth 900*l.* a year. It subsequently turned out worth a great deal more; the returns given in by his deputy for a single year being 4200*l.* This he protests was an exceptional year; but the annual proceeds certainly averaged more than half that sum, to which must be added those of two other patent places, Clerk of the Estreats and Comptroller of the Pipe, granted to him in boyhood. His father left him the house in Arlington Street,[1] 5000*l.* in money, and shares in a patent place held for two lives, which raised his income to not far from 5000*l.* a year.

In 1746, besides two or three contributions to the "Museum," a magazine, he wrote "The Beauties," which (he says) "was handed about till it got into print very incorrectly." In 1747 he printed, to give away, 200 copies of "Ædes Walpolianæ," being an account of the collection at Houghton. In the same year he wrote "Letters

---

[1] No. 18, now the property of Mr. Pender, M.P.

to the Whigs," in answer to a "Letter to the Tories," written, he believed, by Mr. George Lyttleton. In connection with this controversy he mentions a quarrel he had with the Speaker (Onslow), who had ruled that he and his friends could only be heard on the amendments to a Bill.

"The Speaker supporting this, I said: 'I had intended to second Mr. Potter, but should submit to his (the Speaker's) *oracular* decision, though I would not to the complaisant peevishness of anybody else.'

"The Speaker was in a great rage and complained to the House. I said: 'I begged his pardon, but had not thought that submitting to him was the way to offend him.'"

All these things, he frankly owns, were only excusable by the lengths to which party had been carried against his father, "or rather were not excusable at all."

We have now brought him down to the point at which we left him delighted, after a year's experience, with his recent acquisition. All his hopes, wishes, plans and prospects, all his objects of interest or affection, will henceforth be found centred in or clustering round it. The history of Strawberry Hill will be his history; which is tantamount to saying that it will be the history of the aristocratic and fashionable world—the only world he really cared about—with occasional glimpses of contemporary literature and politics, for half a century.

But there is another point of view from which he and his cherished creation must be contemplated. A far prouder position has been assigned to them than mere eminence in the social annals of England could confer. They stand confessedly in nearly the same relation to the Gothic Revival in which Brunelleschi and the Church of Santa

Maria dei Fiori at Florence stood to the Renaissance. One writer of established and well-merited reputation writes thus:

"The first person who, in England at least, seems to have conceived the idea of a Gothic Revival was the celebrated Horace Walpole. He purchased the property at Strawberry Hill in 1753, and seems shortly afterwards to have commenced rebuilding the small cottage which then stood there. The Lower Cloister was erected in 1760-61, the Beauclerc Tower, and Octagon Closet, and the North Bedchamber, in 1770. We now know that these are very indifferent specimens of the true Gothic Art, and are at a loss to understand how either their author or his contemporaries could ever fancy that these very queer carvings were actual reproductions of the details of York Minster or other equally celebrated buildings from which they were supposed to have been copied.

"Whether correct or not, they seem to have created quite a *furore* of Mediævalism among the big-wigged gentry who strutted through the saloons, and were willing to believe the Middle Ages had been reproduced; which they were with as much correctness as in the once celebrated tale of the 'Castle of Otranto.'"[1]

This is clear enough as to the main point—the first conception of the Revival. But the account of the building is imperfect: the purchase is post-dated by six years: the other dates are inaccurate: neither Walpole nor his contemporaries lay under the delusion so contemptuously imputed to them, and we fail to recognize the familiar forms of his visitors under the description of "big-wigged gentry who strutted through the saloons."[2]

---

[1] "History of the Modern Styles of Architecture," etc. By James Fergusson, Fellow of the Royal Institute of British Architects. 1862, p. 313.

[2] "The library, and refectory or great parlour, were entirely new built in 1753; the gallery, the round tower, great cloyster, and cabinet, in 1760 and 1761; the great north bedchamber in 1770; and the Beauclerc Tower, with the hexagon closet, in 1776."—*A Description of the Villa*, p. 2.

The services rendered by Walpole to architecture and art are more precisely and less grudgingly stated by Mr. C. L. Eastlake:

"If in the history of British art there is one period more distinguished than another for its neglect of Gothic, it was certainly the middle of the eighteenth century. . . . The old antiquarians were dead or had ceased from their labour. Their successors had not yet begun to write. An interval occurred between the works of Dugdale and Dodsworth, of Herbert and Wood, on the one side, and those of Grose, Bentham, Hearn, and Gough, on the other—between the men who recorded the history of Mediæval buildings in England, and the men who attempted to illustrate them. In this interval one author (Walpole) appeared who did neither, but to whose writings and to whose influence as an admirer of Gothic art, we believe, may be ascribed one of the chief causes which induced its present revival. . . .

"It is impossible to peruse either the letters or the romances of this extraordinary man without being struck by the unmistakable evidence which they afford of his Mediæval predilections. His 'Castle of Otranto' was, perhaps, the first modern work of fiction which depended for its interest on the incidents of a chivalrous age, and it thus became the prototype of that class of novel which was afterwards imitated by Mrs. Radcliffe, and perfected by Sir Walter Scott.

"The position which he occupies with regard to art resembles in many respects that in which he stands as a man of letters. His labours were not profound in either field. But their result was presented to the public in a form which gained him rapid popularity both as an author and a *dilettante*. . . .

"Walpole's Gothic, in short, though far from reflecting the beauties of a former age, or anticipating those which were destined to proceed from a redevelopment of the style, still holds a position in the history of English art which commands a respect, for it served to sustain a cause which had otherwise been wellnigh forsaken."[1]

[1] "A History of the Gothic Revival." By Charles L. Eastlake, Architect, etc. Ch. iii. 1872.

Whether that cause was worth sustaining, whether the revival has done good upon the whole, is still a question; and a controversy has arisen strongly resembling that which arose some fifty years since between the Classicists and Romanticists in France. Mr. Fergusson evidently thinks that there would be small matter for regret if Strawberry Hill had never risen above the rank of a cockney villa, or had shared the fate of Fonthill Abbey, built upon the same principle but with far more grandeur and effect.

"The fashion (he remarks) set by so distinguished a person as Horace Walpole was not long in finding followers, not only in domestic but in religious buildings. Although London was spared the infliction, Liverpool and other towns in Lancashire which were then rising into importance were adorned with a class of churches which are a wonder and a warning to all future ages. . . . The idea at that time seems to have been that any window that was pointed, any parapet that was nicked, any tower that had four strange looking obelisks at its angles, was essentially Gothic; and proceeding on this system, they produced a class of buildings which, if they are not Gothic, have at least the merit of being nothing else. The same system was carried into Domestic Architecture, and it is surprising what a number of castles were built which had nothing castellated about them except a nicked parapet and an occasional window in the form of a cross, with a round termination at the end of each branch. . . . Lambton, Lowther, Inverary, Eglinton, and fifty others, represent this class."

Viewed with reference to the wants and requirements of modern life, a modern castle may be as much an anachronism as a tournament; and the Gothic style would hardly have become so popular for Protestant places of worship, had it not fallen in with the ritualistic tendency, with that fondness for Roman Catholic (mostly mediæval) forms and ceremonies which distinguishes a section of the Anglican Church. But all the abuses and corruptions of that style cannot obscure the fact that we are indebted to it for some of the most beautiful specimens of ecclesiastical architecture: for (amongst others) the cathedrals of Cologne, Strasburg, Rheims, Amiens, Milan, Salisbury, and Lincoln; and whatever objections may be urged against its adoption for new buildings, no admirer of the poetical or picturesque, no one imbued with a genuine love of art or respect for antiquity, will consider any amount of care or money expended in the restoration or preservation of existing and time-honoured structures, of any age or order, misapplied.

The Gothic revival, be it remembered, did not stand alone. It led to a Saxon, a Norman, a Tudor revival; and the impulse thus communicated came just in time to save what was left of many a venerable mansion, crumbling abbey, or dismantled castle, from devastation or decay. When, about a hundred years since, Rhyddlan Castle, in North Wales, fell into the possession of Dr. Shipley, Dean of St. Asaph, the massive walls had been prescriptively used as stone quarries, to which any neighbouring occupier who wanted building materials might resort; and they are honeycombed all round as high as a pickaxe could reach. How often might a baronial hall have been found doing duty as a stable, or an exquisitely carved pointed window giving light to a barn! "To what base uses we may return, Horatio!" How often was the traveller's glance attracted to the spot— .

> "Where longs to fall yon tottering spire
> As weary of th' insulting air,
> The poet's dream, the warrior's fire,
> The lover's vows, are sleeping there."

Now we rarely pass through a rural district without seeing signs of renovation or encountering a bazaar for the restoration of a church.

It will be the enduring praise awarded by common consent to Walpole, that the work of devastation has been checked, and the stealthy unobserved action of decay's effacing fingers arrested, through his instrumentality. Yet, if it had been foretold to him when he set about enlarging his cottage, that he was about to form an epoch in architecture or æsthetics, no one would have been more surprised or amused at the prophecy than himself. Its aggrandisement was gradual, and the form it ultimately assumed was, in a great measure, the result of caprice or accident; certainly not of any complete or original conception or design. It was much the same with the " Castle of Otranto," which he dashed off on the spur of the occasion, without the smallest suspicion that he was founding a new school of romance.

He may have been in one of his mocking or desponding moods, but we believe he spoke his real feeling in July, 1761, when he wrote :

"I am writing, I am building —both *works that will outlast the memory of battles and heroes!* [The Italics are his.] Truly, I believe, the one will as much as the other. My buildings are paper like my writings, and both will be blown away in ten years after I am dead. If they had not the substantial merit of amusing me while I live, they would be worth little indeed."

In June, 1748 :

"Mr. Churchill and Lady Mary have been with me two or three days and are now gone to Sunning. I only tell you this, to hint that my house will hold a married pair : indeed it is not quite large enough for people who lie, like the patriarchs, with their genealogy, and menservants, and maidservants, and oxen and asses, in the same chamber with them."

He expresses no intention of enlarging it, and when, later in the same year, he speaks of improvements, he is alluding merely to the grounds. In October, 1748, he writes:

"I am all plantation, and sprout away like any chaste nymph in the 'Metamorphoses.'"

On December 16th:

"I am extremely busy planting here: I have got four more acres, which make my territory prodigious in a situation where land is so scarce and villas as abundant as formerly at Tivoli and Baiæ. I have now about fourteen acres, and am making a terrace the whole breadth of my garden on the brow of a natural hill with meadows at the foot, and commanding the river, the village, Richmond-hill, and the Park, and part of Kingston; but I hope never to show it you."

This terrace is the lawn on which recently and frequently has been assembled all that is most brilliant and distinguished in society by birth, rank, beauty, genius or accomplishment. It still commands the same prospect, or rather would command it but for the trees, which only allow glimpses of the river and the various objects in the distance or on the banks. It may be doubted, however, whether this is not one of the instances in which glimpses, by leaving scope for the imagination and creating constant variety, are not more effective than full views.

His hope never to show his villa to Mann is explained in a letter referring to the possibility of that gentleman's recall:

" You see my villa makes me a good correspondent;

how happy I should be to show it you, if I could, with no mixture of disagreeable circumstances to you! I have made a vast plantation! Lord Leicester told me the other day that he heard I would not buy some old china, because I was laying out all my money in trees. 'Yes,' said I, 'my Lord, I used to love *blue* trees, I now love *green* ones.'"

He had a good deal of difficulty in completing his purchase, and so far on as May 18, 1749, Mrs. Chenevix brought him a deed to sign, and her sister Bertrand, the wife of the fashionable toyman of Bath, for a witness:

"I showed them my cabinet of enamels, instead of treating them with white wine. The Bertrand said, 'Sir, I hope you don't trust all sorts of ladies with this cabinet.' What an entertaining assumption of dignity!"

The first we hear of the contemplated castle is (September 28, 1749) in describing a chapel at Chenies, in Buckinghamshire:

"It is dropping down in several places without a roof, but in half the windows are beautiful arms in painted glass. As these are so totally neglected, I propose making a push and begging them of the Duke of Bedford. They would be magnificent for Strawberry Castle. Did I tell you that I had found a text in Deuteronomy to authorize my future battlements?—'When thou buildest a new house then shalt thou make a battlement for thy roof, that thou bring not blood upon thy house, if any man fall from thence.'"

We need hardly say that this is a somewhat strained interpretation of the text; the battlements of a castle, with a high-peaked roof, having a different purpose from the battlements of a flat-roofed house in the East. In the following January the matured intention is distinctly announced in the postscript of a letter to Mann:

"P.S.—My dear Sir, I must trouble you with a commission which I don't know whether you can execute. I am going to build a little Gothic castle at Strawberry Hill. If you can pick me up any fragments of old painted glass, arms, or anything, I shall be exceedingly obliged to you. I can't say I remember any such things in Italy, but out of old châteaux I imagine one might get it cheap, if there is any."

He was fully aware of the irregularity, incongruity, and departure from the recognised principles of architecture, of which he was about to set the example ; but what he wanted was not an imposing structure or commodious house, but one in which his peculiar taste might be indulged, and his heterogeneous collection be ranged without appearing very much out of place :

"I shall speak more gently to you, my dear child (he writes to Mann, February 25, 1750), though you don't like Gothic architecture. The Grecian is only proper for magnificent and public buildings. Columns and all their beautiful ornaments look ridiculous when crowded into a closet or a cheese-cake house. The variety is little, and admits no charming irregularities. I am almost as fond of the *Sharawaggi*, or Chinese want of symmetry, in buildings, as in grounds or gardens. I am sure, whenever you come to England, you will be pleased with the liberty of taste into which we are struck, and of which you can have no idea."

As his sole building fund consisted of savings out of income, much of which was frittered away in small purchases, the castle progressed slowly. We hear nothing more of it till March, 1753, when he writes :

"Mr. Chute and I are come hither for a day or two to inspect the progress of a Gothic staircase, which is so pretty and so small that I am inclined to wrap it up and send it you in my letter. As my castle is so diminutive, I give myself a Burlington air and say that, as Chiswick is a model of Grecian architecture, Strawberry Hill is to be so of Gothic."

"March 27, 1753.

"Adieu! I am all bricks and mortar. The castle at Strawberry Hill grows so near a termination, that you must not be angry if I wish you to see it. Mr. Bentley is going to make a drawing of the best view, which I propose to have engraved, and then you shall have at least some idea of that sweet little spot—little enough, but very sweet."

His correspondent, Mann, seems to have stood in need of a more precise idea of the castle than could be conveyed by letters, for on April 27, 1753, Walpole writes:

"I thank you a thousand times for thinking of procuring me some Gothic remains from Rome, but I believe there is no such thing there. I scarcely remember any morsel in the true taste of it in Italy. Indeed, my dear sir, kind as you are about it, I perceive you have no idea what Gothic is. You have lived too long amidst true taste to understand venerable barbarism. You say, 'you suppose my garden is to be Gothic too.' That can't be: Gothic is merely architecture; and as one has a satisfaction in imprinting the gloom of abbeys and cathedrals on one's house, so one's garden, on the contrary, is to be nothing but *riant*, and the gaiety of nature. . . . I was going to tell you that my house is so monastic, that I have a little hall decked with long saints in lean-arched windows and with taper columns, which we call the 'Paraclete,' in memory of Eloisa's cloister."

He refers to Eloisa's cloister as described by Pope:

"Where awful arches make a noonday night,
And the dim windows shade a solemn light."

"May 22, 1753. (To George Montagu.)

"We emerge very fast out of shavings, and hammerings, and pastings; the painted glass is full blown in every window, and the gorgeous saints that were brought out for one day on the festival of St. George Montagu, are fixed for ever in the tabernacles they are to inhabit."

The armoury never came to much, but it was seriously contemplated. In April, 1753, referring to the probable visit of an Italian Prince, he states that by next spring he hopes to have rusty armour, and arms with quarterings enough to qualify for Grand Master of Malta; in June, that the armoury bespeaks the ancient chivalry of the lords of the castle. In a detailed description of the house as it stood, June 12, 1753, beginning at the little parlour with the bow window, he says:

"From hence under two gloomy arches, you come to the hall and staircase, which it is impossible to describe to you, as it is the most particular and chief beauty of the castle. Imagine the walls covered with (I call it paper, but it is really paper painted in perspective to represent) Gothic fretwork; the lightest Gothic balustrade to the staircase, adorned with antelopes (our supporters) bearing shields; lean windows fattened with rich saints in painted glass, and a vestibule open with three arches on the landing-place, and niches full of old coats-of-mail, Indian shields made of rhinoceros' hides, broad-swords, quivers, long bows, arrows, and spears, all *supposed* to be taken by Sir Terry Robsart (an ancestor) in the holy wars. . . . The bow-window room, one pair of stairs, is not yet finished, but in the tower beyond it is the charming closet where I now write to you. . . . I must tell you, by the way, that the castle, when finished, will have two-and-thirty windows enriched with painted glass."

He goes on to say that the only two good chambers he shall have, an eating-room and a library, were not yet built. The gallery and round tower were not yet so much as meditated. Even in this unfinished state the castle began to attract attention, and on March 2, 1754, the hero of Culloden paid him a visit. We quote from a letter to Bentley:

"The weather grows fine, and I have resumed little flights to Strawberry. I carried George Montagu thither, who was in raptures, and screamed, and hooped, and hollaed, and danced, and crossed himself a thousand times over. But what will you say to greater honours which Strawberry has received? Nolkejumskoi[1] has been to see it, and liked the windows and staircase. I can't conceive how he entered it. I should have figured him, like Gulliver, cutting down some of the largest oaks in Windsor Forest to make joint-stools, in order to straddle over the battlements and peep in at the windows of Lilliput. I can't deny myself this reflection, even though he liked Strawberry, as he has not employed you as an architect."

The Princess Emily was more difficult, or was at less pains to look pleased:

"June 10, 1755.

"Princess Emily has been here. 'Liked it?' 'Oh, no!' I don't wonder, I never liked St. James's."

But her Royal Highness ought to have come prepared to like it, or not have come at all:

"She (the princess) was so inquisitive and so curious in prying into the very offices and servants' rooms, that her [equerry] Captain Bateman was sensible of it, and begged Catherine not to mention it. He addressed himself well, if he hoped to meet with taciturnity! Catherine immediately ran down to the pond, and whispered to all the reeds, 'Lord! that a princess should be such a gossip!' In short, Strawberry Hill is the puppet-show of the time."

A great breakfast to the "Bedfort Court," in the preceding month, is thus described:

"There were the Duke and Duchess, Lord Tavistock and Lady Caroline, my Lord and Lady Gower, Lady Caroline Egerton, Lady Betty Waldegrave, Lady Mary Coke, Mrs. Pitt, Mr. Churchill, and Lady Mary, Mr. Bap. Leveson, and Colonel Sebright. The first thing I asked Harry" (his butler) "was: 'Does the sun shine?' It did; and

[1] Cant name for the Duke of Cumberland.

Strawberry was all gold, and all green. I am not apt to think people really like it, that is, understand it; but I think the flattery of yesterday was sincere. I judge by the notice the Duchess took of your drawings. Oh! how you will think the shades of Strawberry extended! Do you observe the tone of satisfaction with which I say this as thinking it near?"

He was already growing into authority on ornamental building:

"Sir Charles Hanbury Williams told me that, on the Duke of Bedford's wanting a Chinese house at Woburn, he said, 'Why don't your Grace speak to Mr. Walpole? He has the prettiest plan in the world for one.' 'Oh!' replied the Duke, 'but then it would be too dear.'

"I hope this was a very great economy, as I am sure ours would be a very great extravagance; only think of a plan for little Strawberry giving the alarm to thirty thousand a year! My dear Sir (to Bentley), it is time to retrench. Pray send me a slice of granite no bigger than a Naples biscuit."

It was shortly after the entertainment to the Bedford Court that Strawberry Hill received a compliment a little in excess of its claims at that time:

"My Lord Bath, who was brought hither by my Lady Hervey's and Billy Bristow's reports of the charms of the place, has made the following stanzas, to the old tune which you remember of Rowe's ballad on Dodington's Mrs. Strawbridge: *e.g.*,

I.

"Some talk of Gunnersbury,
    For Sion some declare;
And some say that with Chiswick-house
    No villa can compare;
But all the beaux of Middlesex,
    Who know the country well,
Say, that Strawberry Hill, that Strawberry
    Doth bear away the bell."

"Can there be an odder revolution of things, than that the printer of the 'Craftsman' should live in a house of mine, and that the author of the 'Craftsman' should write a panegyric on a house of mine?"

The "Craftsman" was the principal organ of the Opposition to Sir Robert Walpole. The coincidence is repeated in a note to the "Description of Strawberry Hill;" but in a preceding letter, April, 1753, he writes:

"I am now assured by Franklyn, the old printer of the 'Craftsman,' that Lord Bath never wrote a 'Craftsman' himself, only gave hints for them. Yet great part of his reputation was built on those papers."

Walpole's mind, if we are to accept Macaulay as a judge, was "a bundle of inconsistent whims and affectations. His features were covered with mask within mask: when the outer disguise of obvious affectation was removed you were still as far as ever from seeing the real man." We entirely agree with Miss Berry that this is a complete misunderstanding and misrepresentation of the character. Artificial, fastidious, capricious, frivolous, finical, if you like: affected, not. He was what he appeared to be, what he showed himself. He never pretended to like things which he did not like, or to be capable of things of which he was incapable, or to know what he did not know, or to be in any respect better or worse than he was. The real man is constantly before our eyes. Mere change of mood or inconsistency is not affectation; and nothing can be more natural or more in keeping than the air of mock seriousness with which he blends the grave with the gay. What mask does he throw off when he writes thus to Mann?—

"Forgive me, my dear child, you who are a Minister, for

holding your important affairs so cheap. I amuse myself with Gothic and painted glass, and am as grave about my own trifles as I could be at Ratisbon. I shall tell you one or two events within my own small sphere, and you must call them a letter. I believe I mentioned having made a kind of *armoury*. My upper servant, who is as full as dull as his predecessor, whom you knew, Tom Barney, has had his head so filled with *arms*, that the other day, when a man brought home an old chimney-back, which I had bought for belonging to Harry VII., he came running in, and said, ' Sir, sir ! here is a man who has brought some more *armour !* ' "

" Serious business," it is objected, " was a trifle to him, and trifles were his serious business." Did he ever pretend that they were not? He was quite in earnest when he exclaimed : " How I have laughed when some of the Magazines have called me the learned gentleman. Pray, don't be like the Magazines." His opinions of his literary contemporaries were mostly prejudiced and wrong, but they were his real opinions.

It was one of Johnson's sagacious maxims never to tell a story or repeat anything against yourself, lest people should repeat it to your disadvantage without giving you credit for your frankness. If Walpole had acted on this maxim, he would have blunted the edge of many a sarcastic comment. When Macaulay said he had " the soul of a gentleman usher," this was no more than what (according to Miss Berry) he had often said of himself : " that, from his knowledge of old ceremonials and etiquettes, he was sure that, in a former state of existence, he must have been a gentleman-usher about the time of Elizabeth." It was a current joke amongst his friends—

" Who had he lived in the Third Richard's reign,
 Had been Lord Steward or Lord Chamberlain." [1]

[1] Mason to Walpole.

The style of his letters was not less natural because it was playful and discursive: because, instead of saying what he had to say in plain direct language, he draws upon a fertile fancy and richly-stored memory for allusions and illustrations which arrest attention and invest the commonest incidents with a charm. If to be invariably read with pleasure be the object of style, Walpole's must be pronounced inimitable in its way. He has never been excelled in the art of making something out of nothing. Thus, on June 11th, 1755, he writes to Bentley:

"About four arrived such a flood that we could not see out of the windows; the whole lawn was a lake, though situated on so high an Ararat; presently it broke through the leads, drowned the pretty, blue bedchamber, passed through ceilings and floor into the little parlour, terrified Harry, and opened all Catherine's water-gates and speech-gates. I had just time to collect two dogs, a pair of bantams, and a brace of gold-fish, for, in the haste of my zeal to imitate my ancestor Noah, I forgot that fish would not easily be drowned. In short, if you chance to spy a little ark with pinnacles sailing towards Jersey, open the skylight, and you will find some of your acquaintance. You never saw such desolation! A pigeon brings word that Mabland (Lord Radnor's) has fared still worse; it never came into my head before that a rainbow office for insuring against water might be necessary."

Fine gentleman as he was, he was far from exclusive in his company, and he exults in the notabilities of his neighbourhood without reference to their rank:

"Nothing (he writes in 1755) is equal to the fashion of this village. Mr. Muntz says we have more coaches than they have in half France. Mr. Pritchard has bought Ragman's castle, for which my Lord Lichfield could not agree. We shall be as celebrated as Baiæ or Tivoli; and if we have not such sonorous names as they boast, we have very famous people; Clive and Pritchard, actresses; Scott and Hudson, painters; my Lady Suffolk, famous in her time; Mr. H——, the impudent lawyer that Tom Hervey wrote against; Whitehead, the poet, and Cambridge, the everything."

We learn from Boswell that Johnson had a very high opinion of Mrs. Clive's comic power, and conversed more with her than with any of the other players. He said, "Clive, sir, is a good thing to sit by; she always understands what you say." And she said of him, "I love to sit by Dr. Johnson, he always entertains me." The same congeniality existed between her and Walpole. Occupying "Little Strawberry," which he christened Cliveden, she was his nearest neighbour and the frequent subject of remark. His regret at her temporary absence (Nov. 1754) is elicited by a sarcastic allusion to her proximity:

"I never came up the stairs without reflecting how different it is from its primitive state, when my Lady Townshend all the way she came up the stairs, cried out, 'Lord God! Jesus! what a house! It is just such a house as a parson's, where all the children lie at the foot of the bed.' I can't say that to-day it puts me much in mind of another speech of my lady's, 'That it would be a very pleasant place, if Mrs. Clive's face did not rise upon it and make it so hot.' The sun and Mrs. Clive seem gone for the winter."

Lady Townshend was the original of the Lady of Quality in "Peregrine Pickle," and Lady Bellaston in "Tom Jones." She was ill-conducted and coarse, but had a great deal of wit, which unluckily was of the same character as the late Lady Aldborough's. Many of her (Lady Townshend's) best *bons mots*, scattered over the Walpole MS. at Strawberry Hill, are hopelessly unfit for publication.

In illustration of Mrs. Pritchard's vulgarity, Johnson told Boswell that she always said *gownd;* but we find her frequently one of Walpole's guests:

"Our dinner passed off very well; the Clive was very good company; you know how much she admires Ashton's preaching. She says she is always vastly good for two or three days after his sermons; but by the time Thursday comes, all their effect is worn out. I never saw more decent behaviour than Mrs. Pritchard."

Garrick rented a large house at Hampton, and in Aug. 1755, Walpole writes to Bentley:

"I have contracted a sort of intimacy with Garrick, who is my neighbour. He affects to study my taste; I lay it all upon you; he admires you. He is building a grateful temple to Shakespeare; I offered him this motto: *Quod spiro et placeo, si placeo, tuum est* (That I breathe and please, if I please, is yours). The truth is, I make the most of my acquaintance to protect my poor neighbour at *Clivden*—you understand the conundrum, *Clive's den.*"

He forgot that the sound of this name was already poetically linked to other scenes and associations:

"Gallant and gay, in Cliveden's proud alcove,
The bower of wanton Shrewsbury and love."

On Dec. 24, 1754, to Bentley:

"I am here quite alone; Mr. Chute is setting out for his Vine; but in a day or two I expect Mr. (Gilly) Williams, George Selwyn, and Dick Edgecumbe. You will allow that, when I do admit anybody within my cloister, I choose them well. My present occupation is putting up my books; and thanks to arches, and pinnacles, and pierced columns, I shall not appear scantily provided."

Portraits of this trio of friends (who, with himself, constituted the famous *partie quarrée* of

Strawberry Hill) form the "Conversation" by Reynolds, bought at the sale by the late Lord Taunton.

It was nearly five years after he was putting up his books in his completed library that he writes (July 8, 1759):

"The weather is sultry; this country never looked prettier. I hope our enemies will not have the heart to spoil it! It would be a great disappointment to me, who am going to make great additions to my castle; a gallery, a round tower and a cabinet, that is to have all the air of a Catholic chapel—bar consecration."

In May, 1761, he begs his friend Montagu not to imagine that the Gallery will be *prance-about-in-able* by the beginning of June, as he does not propose to finish it till next year. In the following December:

"My Gallery advances, and I push on the works there; for pictures, and baubles, and buildings look to me as if I realised something. I had rather have a bronze than a thousand pounds in the Stocks, for if Ireland or Jamaica are invaded, I shall still have my bronze; I would not answer so much for the funds, nor will buy into the new loan of glory. . . .

"Crassus, the richest man on t'other side their (the Roman) Temple Bar, lost his army and his life, and yet their East India Bonds did not fall an obolus under par. I like that system better than ours. . . .

"How Scipio would have stared if he had been told that he must not demolish Carthage, as it would ruin several aldermen who had money in the Punic *actions!*"

The Gallery was finished in the autumn of 1763, and on October 3 he writes:

"I have given my assembly to show my Gallery, and it was glorious; but happening to pitch upon the Feast of Tabernacles, none of my Jews would come, though Mrs.

Clive proposed to them to change their religion; so I am forced to exhibit once more. For the incoming spectators, the crowd augments instead of diminishing. . . .

"My next assembly will be entertaining; there will be five countesses, two bishops, fourteen Jews, five papists, a doctor of physic, and an actress (Mrs. Clive); not to mention Scotch, Irish, East and West Indians!"

Some of the fine ladies pressed hard for a ball. Not for the universe! What! "Turn a ball, and dust, and dirt, and a million of candles into my charming new Gallery." They compounded for a dinner, which came off June 13, 1764. The French and Spanish ambassadors, four other foreigners of distinction, Lord March and George Selwyn, were among the guests:

"The refectory never was so crowded, nor have any foreigners been here before that comprehended Strawberry. . . . They really seemed quite pleased with the place and the day; but I must tell you, the treasury of the abbey will feel it, for without magnificence, all was handsomely done. I must keep *maigre;* at least till the interdict is taken off from my convent. I have kings and queens, I hear, in my neighbourhood, but this is no royal foundation. Adieu! your poor beadsman,

"The Abbot of Strawberry."

It was now no longer a castle but an abbey, or more correctly speaking, it partook in tolerably equal proportions of both—*templum in modo arcis;* although it was crowded with articles which would have harmonised equally well with a Grecian temple, a Turkish mosque, or a Chinese pagoda, and which would have been hopelessly inappropriate in a regularly constructed mediæval building of any kind. What would a baron or abbot of the olden time have made of the printing-press which was formally installed in the new building on its completion? Among the movements of the distinguished party that dined with him in June, 1764, he sets down: "Thence they went to the printing house and saw a new fashionable French song printed." In the "Short Notes" he records:

"*June* 25 (1757).—I erected a printing-press at my house at Strawberry Hill.
"*August* 8.—I published two Odes, by Mr. Gray, the first production of my press."

In a letter to George Lord Lyttelton, August 25, 1757, he goes fully into the merits and demerits of these Odes, "The Progress of Poesy" and "The Bard," which were little relished or appreciated by the general public:

"Your Lordship sees that I am no enthusiast to Mr. Gray: his great lustre hath not dazzled me, as his obscurity seems to have blinded his contemporaries. Indeed, I do not think that they ever admired him, except in his Churchyard, though the Eton Ode was far its superior, and is certainly not obscure. The Eton Ode is perfect: those of more masterly execution have defects, yet not to admire them is total want of taste."

Sir George Cornewall Lewis used also to maintain that the "Ode to Eton College" was for its length the most perfect poem in the language since Pope, and decidedly superior to the "Elegy." This is an instance of the misleading tendency of subjective criticism. It was as old Etonians that he and Walpole felt and spoke, forgetting that individual gratification should never be made the unqualified test of excellence.

The dilettante style of publication by a private press exactly suited Walpole: it distinguished him from the common herd of authors, and enabled him to feel the pulse of a select circle of readers before definitively exposing himself to the risks of free criticism. But in resorting to it he necessarily laid aside the anonymous, and he shrank from doing this when he did not see his way clearly to a success. Neither the "Castle of Otranto," nor his "Historic Doubts," were printed at Strawberry Hill. The title of the first edition of his romance ran thus:

"The 'Castle of Otranto,' a story translated by William Marshal, Gent., from the original Italian of Onuphrio Muralto, Canon of the Church of St. Nicholas at Otranto. Printed for Thomas Lownds, in Fleet Street, 1765."

Finding it take, he hastened to lay aside the anonymous. On sending a copy to the Rev. William Cole, he takes occasion to explain the circumstances under which it was composed:

"Your partiality to me and Strawberry have, I hope, inclined you to excuse the wildness of the story. You will even have found some traits to put you in mind of this place. When you read of the picture quitting its panel, did not you recollect the portrait of Lord Falkland, all in white, in my Gallery? Shall I even confess to you, what was the origin of this romance! I waked one morning, in the beginning of last June, from a dream, of which, all I could recover was, that I had thought myself in an ancient castle (a very natural dream for a head filled like mine with Gothic story), and that on the uppermost banister of a great staircase I saw a gigantic hand in armour. In the evening I sat down, and began to write, without knowing in the least what I intended to say or relate. The work grew on my hands, and I grew fond of it—add, that I was very glad to think of anything rather than politics. In short, I was so engrossed with my tale, which I completed in less than two months, that one evening, I wrote from the time I had drunk my tea, about six o'clock, till half an hour after one in the morning, when my hand and fingers were so weary, that I could not hold the pen to finish the sentence, but left Matilda and Isabella talking, in the middle of a paragraph. You will laugh at my earnestness;

but if I have amused you, by retracing with any fidelity the manners of ancient days, I am content, and give you leave to think me as idle as you please."

Walpole was at daggers drawn with Warburton. In letters to third persons, each, unconscious of the *tu quoque*, designates the other as a coxcomb. Referring to an explanatory communication from the Bishop in Oct. 1762, Walpole writes:

"After this I would as soon have a controversy with a peacock, or with an only daughter that her parents think handsome. The fowl, the miss, and the bishop, are alike incorrigible. The first struts naturally; the second is spoiled; reason itself has been of no use to the last."

Referring to the cause of the quarrel, an "oblique fling" in the "Anecdotes of Painting," Warburton (Feb. 17, 1762) had written to Garrick:

"It is about Gothic edifices, for which I shall be about *his pots*, as Bentley said to Lord Halifax of Rowe. But I say it better; I mean the galley-pots and washes of his toilet. I know he has a fribble-tutor at his elbow, as sicklied over with affectation as himself."

This quarrel was smoothed over by Walpole's declaring, on his honour, that in the offending passage he had not Warburton in his thoughts. But Warburton was not really satisfied with this formal disavowal, and four years afterwards calls Walpole an insufferable coxcomb.[1] We are puzzled, therefore, what to make of the exaggerated pane-

---

[1] Letter to Hurd, Nov. 16, 1766. In a letter to the same correspondent (Feb. 7, 1757), Warburton, who was prone to strong language, writes: "Expect to hear that the churches are all crowded next Friday, and that on Saturday they buy up Hume's new Essays, the first of which is the 'Natural History of Religion;' for which I will trim the rogue's jacket" . . . "a wickeder heart, and more determined to do public mischief, I think I never knew." Could this have been Macaulay's precedent when, speaking of Mr. Croker, he said, "See whether I do not dust that varlet's jacket for him" and calls him "a bad, a very bad, man"?

gyric on the "Castle of Otranto" in a note by Warburton on these lines of Pope:

> "The peers grew proud in horsemanship t'excel
> Newmarket's glory rose as Britain's fell;
> The soldiers breathed the gallantries of France,
> And every flow'ry courtier wrote romance."

"Amid all this nonsense," runs the note, "when things were at the worst, we had been entertained with what I will venture to call a masterpiece in the Fable; and a new species likewise. The piece I mean is the 'Castle of Otranto.' The scene is laid in Gothic chivalry; where a beautiful imagination, supported by strength of judgment, has enabled the author to go beyond his subject and effect the full purpose of the ancient tragedy; that is, to purge the passions by pity and terror, in colouring as great and harmonious as in any of the best dramatic writers."

Such a criticism from Warburton is little less surprising than the more discriminating one of Sir Walter Scott, who sums up the merits of the work in these words: "This romance has been justly considered not only as the original and model of a peculiar species of composition attempted and successfully executed by a man of great genius, but as one of the standard works of our lighter literature."

It is no longer read except as a curiosity, and commonly laid down with a feeling of disappointment. The characters excite little interest: there is no local colouring; no lifelike representation of manners; and the machinery on which the whole plot turns—" an enormous helmet, a hundred times more large than any casque made for a human being," with sword and gauntlet to match—is too material and palpable to inspire awe or terror. It is, moreover, out of keeping with the period. The superstitious credulity of the middle ages lent itself to any amount of the supernatural in the shape of haunted chambers, skeletons clanking chains, portraits stepping out of frames, statues descending from pedestals, or deceased barons taking their nightly walk in corridors; but a knight sixty or seventy feet high (and the wearer of the helmet could have been no less) must be relegated to the primitive age when Jack the Giant-killer flourished. At the same time there is no denying that the romance had the grand attraction of novelty, and originated the school of which "The Mysteries of Udolpho" and "The Romance of the Forest" were the pride. The rise and decline of this class of prose fiction are cleverly hit off in one of Haynes Bayley's lyrics:

> "Oh, Radcliffe, thou once wert the charmer
>   Of maids who sate reading all night,
> Thy heroes were knights clad in armour,
>   Thy heroines damsels in white;
> But gone are such terrible touches,
>   Our lips in derision we curl,
> Unless we are told how a duchess
>   Conversed with her cousin the earl."

But it was not the fashionable novel or silver-fork school which succeeded Mrs. Radcliffe's or drove her and her imitators from the field. This good service had been most effectually performed already by Scott, who went to the fountain-head for his inspiration, whose mind was thoroughly saturated with that mediæval lore with which Walpole's was slightly and superficially tinged. Mediævalism was only one, and not the most pronounced, of his innumerable tastes, fancies and pursuits. As for the warlike spirit of chivalry, he had not a spark of it. He would have regarded a combat or encounter in which hard knocks were interchanged, like the "certain lord, neat, trimly dressed," who angered Hotspur by talking so like a waiting gentlewoman of guns, and drums, and wounds. He preferred the silken barons to the iron barons. His forte lay in chronicling the gossip of Courts, or in transporting his readers behind the scenes when a political intrigue was in progress. He was more of a Saint-Simon than a Bayard. Although he counted a suit of Francis I.'s armour amongst his choicest treasures, he would have been more in his element handing Louis XIV. a shirt at Versailles than in helping Francis to a fresh horse at Pavia.

It is a singular fact that in the whole nine volumes of letters there is only one allusion to Froissart, and that one a sneer at Lady Pomfret for translating the "Chronicles." His loyalty, considered as a sentiment, was on a par with his chivalry. "On each side of my bed," he writes in 1756, "I have hung Magna Charta, and the warrant for King Charles' execution, on which I have written 'Major Charta'; as, I believe, without the latter, the former by this time would be of small importance." The degree of his patriotism may be inferred from his well-known remark: "I should like my country well enough if it were not for my countrymen." His lukewarmness towards the Church is betrayed by his readiness to desecrate her shrines, and the complacency with which he anticipates her fall:

"Bishop Luda must not be offended at my converting his tomb into a gateway. Many a saint and confessor, I doubt, will be glad soon to be *passed through*, as it will, at least, secure his being *passed over*. When I was directing the east window at Ely, I recollected the lines of Pope:

"'How capricious were Nature and Art to poor Nell!
   She was painting her cheeks at the time her nose fell.'

"Adorning cathedrals where the religion itself totters, is very like poor Nell's mishap."

His "Epistle in Verse" to West begins:

"The greatest curses any age has known
Have issued from the temple or the throne."

Without attaching undue weight to a flash of cynicism or a pleasantry, it must be admitted that he was wanting in the exalted feelings which dignify the finest models of prose fiction; and with the Author of Waverley before our eyes, we see little reason to regret that the "Castle of Otranto" was his first and last incursion into the region of mediæval or historical romance.

A list, purporting to be complete, of the productions of the Strawberry Hill press is printed in the quarto edition of his works.[1] They are twenty-six in number, besides small pieces of verse and loose sheets; and it is surprising that he contrived to print so much with an establishment at no time exceeding a man and a boy. On March 15, 1759, he writes:

"At present, even my press is at a stop; my printer, who was a foolish Irishman, and who took himself for a genius, and who grew angry when I thought him extremely the former, and not the least of the latter, has left me, and I have not yet fixed upon another."

The next whom he engaged, Thomas Kirkgate, remained with him till his (Walpole's) death, March, 1797. The name of this faithful servant figures on the title-pages of all the productions of the Strawberry Hill press in his time, and is indissolubly coupled with it. Yet no provision

[1] Vol. ii. pp. 515, 516. Copies of all are in the collection of Walpolean books and manuscripts at Strawberry Hill, which Lord Carlingford and Lady Waldegrave have spared no pains or expense to complete.

was made for him, and his " Printer's Farewell" begins :

> "Adieu ! ye groves and Gothic towers,
> Where I have spent my youthful hours;
> Alas ! I find in vain :
> Since he who could my age protect,
> By some mysterious sad neglect,
> Has left me to complain."[1]

He survived his employer more than thirteen years, dying June 16th, 1810. As Walpole was in the habit of selling copies of his privately printed books through the booksellers, he escaped none of the ordinary trials of authorship, especially in his dealings with the trade, who, he complains, treated him worse because he was a gentleman. It was the same with the critics, towards whom he struggles to appear indifferent, like Pope, with one of Cibber's lampoons before him, declaring " These things are my diversion," while his features writhed with pain ; or like Sir Fretful Plagiary exclaiming : " Ha ! Ha ! Ha ! very pleasant. Now another person would be vexed at this." Referring to his "Anecdotes of Painting," May 14, 1759, he writes :

> "For *nobler* or any other game, I don't think of it ; I am sick of the character of author; I am sick of the consequences of it; I am weary of seeing my name in the newspapers ; I am tired with reading foolish criticisms on me, and as foolish defences of me ; and I trust my friends will be so good as to let the last abuse of me pass unanswered. It is called 'Remarks' on my Catalogue, asperses the Revolution more than it does my book, and, in one word, is written by a nonjuring preacher, who was a dog-doctor."

---

[1] "Memorials of Twickenham, Parochial and Topographical." By the Rev. R. S Cobbett, M.A., etc. etc. : a carefully executed compilation, containing much valuable matter.

After reading Shenstone's letters, he writes:

"Poor man! he wanted to have all the world talk of him for the pretty place he had made, and which he seems to have made only that it might be talked of."

Then his own similar weakness breaks upon him:

"The first time a company came to see my house, I felt his joy. I am now so tired of it that I shudder when a bell rings at the gate. . . . I own I was one day too cross. I had been plagued all the week with staring crowds; at last, it rained a deluge. 'Well,' said I, at last, 'nobody will come to-day.' The words were scarcely uttered when the bell rang; a company desired to see the house. I replied, 'Tell them they cannot possibly see the house, but they are very welcome to walk in the garden.'"

If he had been under any illusion on this subject, his exact state of mind would have been laid bare for him by Madame du Deffand:

"Oh! vous n'êtes point fâché qu'on vienne voir votre château; vous ne l'avez pas fait singulier; vous ne l'avez pas rempli de choses précieuses, de raretés; vous ne bâtissez pas un cabinet rond, dans lequel le lit est un trône, et ou il n'y a que des tabourets, pour y rester seul ou ne recevoir que vos amis. Tout le monde a les mêmes passions, les mêmes vertus, les mêmes vices; il n'y a que les modifications qui en fond la différence; amour propre, vanité, crainte de l'ennui, etc."

Another material drawback to the enjoyment of a suburban residence in Walpole's time was the liability to be robbed. He relates that one night in the beginning of November, 1749, as he was returning in his chariot from Holland House by moonlight, about ten at night, he was attacked by two highwaymen in Hyde Park, and the pistol of one of them going off accidentally, razed the skin under his eye, left some marks of shot on his face, and stunned him. He wrote an account of the adventure in "The World,"[1] and made light of it to Mann; complaining that "the frequent repetition has been much worse than the robbery." The capture and exploits of the robber who shot him are mentioned in a letter of August 2, 1750:

"I have been in town for a day or two, and heard no conversation but about M'Lean, a fashionable highwayman, who is just taken, and who robbed me among others; as Lord Eglinton, Sir Thomas Robinson of Vienna, Mrs. Talbot, etc. He took an odd booty from the Scotch earl, a blunderbuss, which lies very formidably upon the justice's table. He was taken by selling a laced waistcoat to a pawnbroker, who happened to carry it to the very man who had just sold the lace. His history is very particular, for he confesses everything, and is so little of an hero, that he cries and begs, and I believe, if Lord Eglinton had been in any luck, might have been robbed of his own blunderbuss. His father was an Irish dean; his brother is a Calvinist minister in great esteem at the Hague."

"September 1, 1750.
"M'Lean is still the fashion: have not I reason to call him my friend? He says, if the pistol had shot me, he had another for himself. Can I do less than say I will be hanged if he is?"

He was robbed again (October, 1781) near his own house in company with Lady Browne, who, after the highwayman had left them, expressed great uneasiness lest he should return, as she had given him a purse with only bad money which she carried on purpose. In 1782, when this state of things was at its worst, Walpole complains that no one can stir out after sunset without servants with blunderbusses; and, referring to the consequent difficulty of making up his card-table, remarks: "If partridge-shooting is not turned

[1] No. 103, republished amongst his works. He there states that M'Lean wrote him two letters of apology, and proposed a friendly meeting at midnight, which he declined.

into robber-shooting, there will be an end of all society."

"A painful incident in his domestic life was the discovery of the body of his man-servant, who had been missing for some days, hanging on a tree in the grounds near the chapel. The man had committed suicide after a petty robbery of one or two spoons or forks."[1] We cannot help fancying that this must have affected Walpole much as a similar incident affected the late Sir John (Mr. Justice) Williams, who, on entering his chambers late at night found his head caught between the legs of his clerk, who was *sus. per col.* in the passage. On hiring another he gravely said to him, " I have only one stipulation to make : if you hang yourself—which you can do or not, as you think fit—do not hang yourself in my chambers."

Whilst Walpole's building was still in progress, the saddening conviction grew upon him that the place was too damp, which is not surprising, considering how frequently it was flooded when the river flowed in full volume and was banked back by the old bridges :

" I revive after being in London an hour like a member of parliament's wife. It will be a cruel fate, after having laid out so much money on this place, and building it as the nest of my old age, if I am driven from it by bad health."

He goes to Bath to take the waters, and cannot endure it :

" The river (Avon) is paltry enough to be the Seine or Tyber. Oh ! how unlike my lovely Thames ! . . . I sit down by the waters of Babylon and weep, when I think of thee, oh Strawberry ! "

" Memorials of Twickenham," p. 307.

The late Lord Derby, after trying some sherry which was recommended as a cure for the gout, said that he preferred the gout. A friend of ours, on consulting the late Sir Henry Holland, was told that he would get well if he dined at four and went to bed at ten. "Oh!" was the reply, "I don't come to a physician to tell me *that*. I want to know how I am to get well if I dine at eight and go to bed at one." Like Lord Derby and our friend, Walpole preferred the disease to the remedy. He writes from Bath, October 18, 1766:

"If I can but be tolerably well at Strawberry, my wishes are bounded. If I am to live at watering-places, and keep what is called *good hours*, life itself will be indifferent to me. I do not talk very sensibly, but I have a contempt for that fictitious character styled philosophy. *I feel what I feel, and I say I feel what I do feel.*

His apprehensions of being compelled to leave the banks of the Thames proved groundless, and in April, 1768, we find him coaxing Montagu to settle there:

"I thought you would at last come and while away the remainder of life on the banks of the Thames in gaiety and old tales. I have quitted the stage, and the Clive is preparing to leave it. We shall neither of us ever be grave; dowagers roost all around us, and you could never want cards or mirth."

In May, 1769, he writes that Strawberry has been in great glory, and that he has given a festino there which will almost mortgage it. The party was principally made up of diplomatists and distinguished foreigners:

"They arrived at two. At the gates of the castle I received them, dressed in the cravat of Gibbons's carving, and a pair of gloves embroidered up to the elbows that had belonged to James I. The French servants stared, and firmly believed this was the dress of English country gentlemen. After taking a survey of the apartments, we went to the printing-house, where I had prepared the enclosed verses, with translations by Monsieur de Lille, one of the company. The moment they were printed off, I gave a private signal, and French horns and clarionets accompanied this compliment. We then went to see Pope's grotto and garden, and returned to a magnificent dinner in the refectory."

No locality hallowed by being the abode of genius has suffered so much from Vandalism as Pope's Villa. Sir William Stanhope, the purchaser after Pope's death, began with the garden:

"The poet (writes Walpole) had valued himself on the disposition of it, and with reason. Though containing but five square acres, enclosed by three lanes, he had managed it with such art and deception that it seemed a wood, and its boundaries were nowhere discoverable. It is true, it was closely planted, and consequently damp. Refined taste went to work: the vocal groves were thinned, modish shrubs replaced them, and three lanes broke in; and if the Muses wanted to tie up their garters, there is not a nook to do it without being seen."

After it had undergone a series of changes, it was bought in 1807 by Lady Howe, who pulled down the house and built a new one on the site. This shared the fate of its predecessor, and was replaced by one of a style partaking so much of the Chinese that it was said to have been copied by the tea-merchant who built it from one of his chests. Nothing of Pope's creation now remains but the grotto, sarcastically described by Johnson: "A grotto is not often the wish or pleasure of an Englishman, who has often more need to solicit than exclude the sun; but Pope's excavation was requisite as an entrance to his garden, and as some men try to be proud of their defects, he extracted an ornament from an inconvenience, and vanity produced a grotto where necessity enforced a passage." The passage is under a public road which separates the front garden from the house. The entrance at the river end alone presents any semblance of the grotto so enthusiastically celebrated by Pope in poetry and prose.[1]

Walpole is never tired of telling stories of the sightseers, who were by turns his pleasure and his plague. He overheard one of them, on being shown the bows and arrows in the armoury, ask the housekeeper, "Pray, does Mr. Walpole shoot?"

"Lady Charleville, my neighbour, told me three months ago, that, having some company with her, one of them had been to see Strawberry. 'Pray,' said another, 'who is that Mr. Walpole?' 'Lord!' cried a third, 'don't you know the great epicure, Mr. Walpole?' 'Pho!' said the first, 'great epicure! you mean the antiquarian.' There, Madam, surely this anecdote may take its place in the chapter of local fame."

Local fame is singularly precarious. The only tradition we could gather of Pope's garden was that a fine cedar was planted by a famous man a long time ago. An elderly, well-to-do inhabitant of Beaconsfield, of whom we inquired where Burke had lived, made answer: "Pray, sir, was he a poet?" During a pilgrimage which Rogers and his friend Maltby made to Gerrard Street, Soho, to discover the house once occupied by Dryden, they came upon a house-agent, who, scenting a job, eagerly responded to their inquiry: "Dryden —Mr. Dryden—is he behindhand with his rent?"

A favourite excursion from Chevening, in the late Earl Stanhope's time, was to Holwood, to the spot, "at the foot of an old tree just above the

---

[1] The villa, delightfully situated on the river, now belongs to Mr. Henry Labouchere, M.P. for Northampton.

steep descent into the vale of Keston," where Pitt and Wilberforce meditated the suppression of the Slave Trade.[1] Some twelve or fourteen years since, when the head-gardener had, as usual, conducted the party to the traditional spot, one of them ventured to suggest that it materially differed from the description, the vale being some way off. This remark came upon the Earl like Edie Ochiltree's "I mind the bigging o't," on the Antiquary; but another spot with the requisite qualification was speedily discovered, to which the tradition was transferred, nothing the worse for the change, by the amiable and accomplished nobleman, who forthwith set up a tablet to perpetuate it.

On August 30, 1768, Walpole writes to the Rev. W. Cole:

"When the Round Tower is finished, I propose to draw up a description and catalogue of the whole house and collection, and I think you will not dislike lending me your assistance."

On June 7, 1771, to Mann:

"The Round Tower is finished and magnificent, and the State Bed-chamber proceeds fast; for you must know the little villa is grown into a superb castle. We have dropped all humility in our style."

The "Description and Inventory" was not printed till 1774. It was reprinted in 1784, with additions, engraved illustrations and a Preface, from which (copies being rare) we shall extract the most remarkable passages:

"It will look (he begins), I fear, a little like arrogance in a private man to give a printed description of his villa and collection, in which almost everything is diminutive. It is not, however, intended for public sale, and originally

---

[1] "Life of Wilberforce," by his Sons, vol. i. p. 151.

was meant only to assist those who should visit the place. A farther view succeeded; that of exhibiting specimens of Gothic architecture as collected from standards, in cathedrals, and chapel-tombs, and showing how they may be applied to chimney-pieces, ceilings, windows, balustrades, loggias, etc. The general disuse of Gothic architecture, and the decay and alterations so frequently made in churches, give prints a chance of being the sole preservatives of that style."

After stating that the collection was made out of the spoils of many renowned collections, he says :

"Such well-attested descent is the genealogy of objects of vertu, not so noble as those of the peerage, but on a par with those of race-horses. *In all these, especially the pedigrees of peers and rarities, the line is often continued by many insignificannt ames.*"

This is Horace Walpole all over. If a sneer at his own order or royalty lay in his way, he was sure to pick it up and make the most of it. The collection of miniatures and enamels, he goes on to say, is the largest and finest in any country:

"The historic pictures, including several Holbeins, must be dear to the English antiquary. . . . To virtuosos of more classic taste, the small busts of Jupiter Serapis in basaltes and of Caligula in bronze, and the silver bell of Benvenuto Cellini, will display the art of ancient and modern sculpture; how high it was carried by Greek statuaries, appears in the eagle."

In a concluding paragraph he states and meets the objection that a collection thus composed is out of keeping with the building:

"In truth, I did not mean to make my house so Gothic as to exclude convenience and modern refinements in luxury. The designs of the inside and outside are strictly ancient, but the decorations are modern. Would our ancestors, before the reformation of architecture, not have deposited in their gloomy castles antique statues and fine pictures, beautiful vases and ornamental china, if they had possessed them?"

Most probably they would, for the simple reason that they had nowhere else to put them, at all events nowhere else where they would be safe. But if our ancestors had not wanted these gloomy strongholds for other purposes, they would not have built them to receive statues, pictures, and objects of vertu; or fitted up interiors to resemble a cloister or an aisle. Conscious of the fallacy, he breaks off:

"But I do not mean to defend by argument a small capricious house. It was built to please my own taste, and in some degree to realise my own visions. I have specified what it contains; could I describe the gay but tranquil scene where it stands, and add the beauty of the landscape to the romantic cast of the mansion, it would raise more pleasing sensations than a dry list of curiosities can excite; at least, the prospect would recall the good-humour of those who might be disposed to condemn the fantastic fabric, and to think it a very proper habitation of, as it was the scene that inspired, the author of the 'Castle of Otranto.'"

This tone disarms criticism, and we believe it to be his natural tone; for talk as he may, he almost always returns to and settles in good sense.

The two principal events of his life, after the completion of his building projects, were his accession to the earldom by the death of his nephew, December 15, 1791, and his acquaintance with the Berrys (Mary and Agnes), which began in the winter of 1787-88. The first notice of them occurs in a letter to the Countess of Ossory. After describing their persons, dress, and manners, he proceeds:

"The first night I met them I would not be acquainted, having heard so much in their praise that I concluded they would be all pretension. The second time, in a very small company, I sat next to Mary, and found her an angel both inside and out. Now I do not know which I like best, except Mary's face, which is formed for a sentimental novel, but is ten times fitter for a fifty times better thing—genteel comedy. This delightful family comes to me almost every Sunday evening, as our region is too *proclamatory* to play at cards on the seventh day. I do not care a straw for cards, but I do disapprove of this partiality to the youngest child of the week; while the other poor six days are treated as if they had no souls to save. I forgot to tell you that Mr. Berry is a little merry man with a round face, and you would not suspect him of so much feeling and attachment. I make no excuse for such minute details; for, if your ladyship insists on hearing the humours of my district, you must for once indulge me with sending you two pearls that I found in my path."

They were the comfort of his declining years; and it was for them he wrote his "Reminiscences." He was never happy when away from them, and in November, 1791, he installed them in Little Strawberry, which he bequeathed to them for their joint lives at his death.

His accession to the earldom inspired his "Epitaphium Vivi Auctoris," in 1792, beginning:

"An estate and an earldom at seventy-four,
  Had I sought them or wished, 'twould add one fear more,
That of making a countess when almost fourscore!"

It is believed that he was ready to make a countess (when still nearer four score) by marrying Miss Mary Berry, with the sole view of giving her the title and a jointure which he was empowered to charge on the estate.

He died at his house in Berkeley Square, March 2, 1797, in his eightieth year; having devised Strawberry Hill, with its contents, to Mrs.

Damer for life, with remainder in fee to the Countess Dowager of Waldegrave, his niece. Through her it came to George Edward, the seventh Earl Waldegrave, who (September 28, 1840) married Frances (*née*) Braham, widow of Mr. J. J. Waldegrave, and, dying September 28, 1846, devised to her in fee the whole of his property, including Strawberry Hill. Pecuniary embarrassments, real or supposed, led to the sale of the entire collection (with the exception of the family portraits[1] and some choice china) in 1842.

Referring to the treasures of art collected at Fonthill, Mr. Eastlake remarks that some idea of their value may be formed from the fact that in 1819, at the sale of the abbey and its contents to Mr. Farquhar, 7200 copies of the catalogue at a guinea each were sold in a few days. The large sale of this catalogue, which served as a ticket of admission, was mainly owing to the general eagerness to see a place which had been carefully secluded from view. Connoisseurs and collectors, with the *élite* of the fashionable world, had enjoyed free access to Strawberry Hill; but, making full allowances on this ground, we are at a loss to account for the comparative indifference with which it was regarded by the general public. The private view began on the 28th of March; the public were admitted on the 4th of April, and the sale began on the 25th. The views, public and private, were thinly attended; and on the first and most of

[1] The intention was to reserve the whole of the family portraits, but four were sold by mistake, and, much to her regret, Lady Waldegrave was unable to recover them. They are thus described in the Catalogue: A three-quarter length portrait of Sir Robert Walpole, afterwards Earl of Orford, etc.: A *ditto* of Catherine, first wife of Sir Robert Walpole, in white, copied from Sir Godfrey Kneller's picture, by Jarvis: A *ditto* of Maria Skerret, second wife of Sir Robert Walpole, in blue, and in the dress of a shepherdess, by Jarvis: A *ditto* of Robert Walpole, second Earl of Orford, etc., in a red velvet dress, by Richardson.

the succeeding days of the sale the renowned auctioneer's audience was principally composed of professional bidders and dealers. The tone taken by the leading journal had doubtless contributed towards this result:

"There are not, perhaps, a dozen things in the house which evince any refined taste, or taste of a high order, in him by whom they were collected. There is nothing whatever of the highest class of art in the whole collection, not one single solitary object by which national taste can be improved, or from the contemplation of which a pure feeling of art can be produced." [1]

Can the writer have gone over a single department of the collection, or even have read the catalogue? He summarily disposes of the whole of the historical relics in this fashion:

"Old hats, old clothes, old gloves, and old rubbish, dignified by whatsoever name their owner may rejoice to give them, are still rubbish: those by whom they are collected are little better than antiquated dealers in slops; and those who wish to buy may be supplied at half the expense of a trip to Strawberry Hill, by the recognized retailers of rubbish in Mayfair or Rosemary Lane."

Under the generic term "rubbish" are comprised Queen Elizabeth's glove, the tortoiseshell jewelled comb of Mary Queen of Scots, the spur with which William III. pricked his charger through the Boyne, the clock which was Henry VIII.'s wedding-present to Anne Boleyn, the watch of Fairfax, the hat of Wolsey, etc., etc. As for the trappings of chivalry:

"The good knights are dust,
And their swords are rust,
And their souls are with the Lord, we trust."

[1] The "Times," April 25, 1842.

What are their coats of mail, helmets, and gauntlets but so many stone of old iron? And what (by a parity of reasoning may be asked) are the ruins of Iona but ruins? or what is the plain of Marathon but a plain? Johnson's noble apostrophe is the reply. Historic relics appeal to the same sympathies as historic localities:

> "Struck with the seat that gave Eliza birth,
> We kneel and kiss the consecrated earth."

Why not her glove? Is it not linked with the same associations? Does it not similarly recall the lion-hearted Queen who flung foul scorn at Tilbury, or the old coquette who signed the death-warrant of Essex? Far from laughing at Mr. Charles Kean for purchasing the dagger of Henry VIII. and the scarlet hat of Wolsey, we should have been strongly tempted to bid against him. Sentiment apart, historic relics have a positive value as illustrations of manners and customs; but if they are one and all to be set down as rubbish, the celebrated collection of the Hôtel de Cluny, at Paris, might as well be flung into the Seine.

By way of counterpoise to the depreciation of the journalist, the noble owner was fortunate enough to engage the services of the late George Robins, the prince of auctioneers, who carried the peculiar eloquence of his profession to a point which almost entitles him to be regarded as the founder of a school. The swelling periods in which Macaulay described the procession of peers at the trial of Warren Hastings were pronounced by Sir George Cornwall Lewis to be an excellent specimen of the genuine George Robins style; and a still happier adaptation of that style was the paragraph in which Lord Beaconsfield brought vividly before the mind's eye the array of large-acred squires who sealed the doom of Sir Robert Peel's Government in 1846.[1]

Nor will any judicious critic deem these comparisons invidious after reading the prefatory remarks to the Catalogue, in which Mr. Robins speaks in his own proper person. For example:

"Whether he considers the hallowed recollections that surround a pictorial and historical abode, so dear to its distinguished originator, and so often and so tenderly referred to in his letters and writings, or the extreme rarity and value of the collection contained in it, rich in all that can delight the antiquarian, the scholar, the virtuoso, or the general lover of art, so perfect and unapproachable in all its details that each will quit it with the fixed opinion that his peculiar tastes were those to which the energies, the learning, and the research of the noble founder were directed; when there pass before him in review, the splendid gallery of paintings teeming with the finest works of the greatest masters;[2] matchless enamels, of immortal bloom, by Petito, Boit, Bordice, and Zincke; chasings, the workmanship of Cellini and Jean de Bologna; noble specimens of Faenza Ware, from the pencils of Robbia and Bernard Palizzi; glass, of the rarest hues and tints, executed by Jean Cousin and other masters of the fifteenth, sixteenth, and seventeenth centuries; Limoges Enamels, of the period of the Renaissance, by Leonard and Courtoise; Roman and Grecian antiquities in bronze and sculpture; Oriental and European china, of the choicest forms and colours; exquisite and matchless missals, painted by Raphael and Julio Clovis; magnificent specimens

---

[1] "They trooped on: all the men of metal and large-acred squires whose spirit he had so often quickened and whose counsels he had so often solicited in his fine Conservative speeches in Whitehall Gardens: Mr. Bankes, with a parliamentary name of two centuries, and Mr. Christopher from that broad Lincolnshire which Protection had created. . . . and Devon had sent there the stout heart of Mr. Buck, and Wiltshire the pleasant presence of Walter Long," etc.—*Life of Lord George Bentinck.*

[2] Holbein, Rembrandt, Vandyck, Giorgione, Annibale Caracci, Poussin, Canaletto, Watteau, Van Eyck, Mytens, Zucchero, Lely, Kneller, Reynolds, Romney, etc.

of cinque-cento armour; miniatures illustrative of the most interesting periods of history; a valuable collection of drawings and manuscripts; engravings in countless numbers and of infinite value; a costly library, extending to fifteen thousand volumes, abounding in splendid editions of the classics; illustrated, scarce and unique works, with ten thousand other relics of the arts and histories of bygone ages; he may well feel overpowered at the evident impossibility of rendering to each that lengthened notice which their merits and their value demand."

This is a magnificent sentence, in linked richness long drawn out: indeed, one of the longest in the language; yet, considering the weight of the matter, it cannot be censured for redundancy.

Judging merely from the abridged reports in the newspapers, we should say that Mr. Robins's opening address, delivered from a state chair that had belonged to the great cardinal, was on a par with his prefatory remarks:

"He concluded by saying that he should have considered it sacrilege to have altered the disposition or arrangement of a single lot; that those who did him the honour to bid should live for ever in his heart, and that he would charge them no rent for the tenancy. This eloquence produced good prices."[1]

The prices were far from good. With the marked catalogue now before us, we should say they were surprisingly low. The Sèvres porcelain, for example, did not sell for a tenth of what it would fetch now. Fancy this lot knocked down at 4*l*.:

"A cabinet cup and saucer, embellished with strawberries, a present from Madame du Deffand, and a ditto with wreath of flowers and gold border."

The whole contents of the China Room, 140 lots, went for 648*l*. 15*s*. 6*d*. The sale realised

[1] The "Times," April 26, 1842.

33,450*l*. We speak within compass when we say that it would now realise three times that sum.

When the last blow of the auctioneer's hammer had sounded, the guardian genius of poor, stripped, despoiled, desecrated, degraded Strawberry must have resembled the White Lady of Avenel when her golden zone had dwindled to the fineness of a thread; and only too appropriate in the mouth of the owner, when, as its uncontrolled mistress, she paced the denuded gallery, would have been the words of Moore's song:

> "I feel like one who treads alone
> Some banquet hall deserted,
> Whose lights are fled, whose garlands dead,
> And all but he departed."

But she had head, heart, imagination, energy, and a will as resolute as Warren Hastings when he made it the set purpose of his life to regain and reinstate his ancestral home of Daylesford. Animated instead of depressed by the self-imposed task of repairing what seemed irreparable, with views opening and plans expanding as she went on—she restored, renovated, improved, added, acquired and annexed to give breathing-room, till the villa had grown into a first-class country-house in a land where country-houses are palaces, and this without destroying or materially impairing the distinctive character which the founder had so perseveringly impressed upon it or (what would be still worse) producing inside or outside an impression of incongruity.

This is not the place for details. But take up a position on the south-east side so as to command a complete view of the portions constructed at four different periods, and you will find that they slide into each other without a break. Enter the house, pass through the gallery, round-room and ante-room, into the finely-proportioned richly-furnished drawing-room with the famous Reynolds (the three Ladies Waldegrave) confronting you, and you will see nothing to remind you abruptly or disagreeably of the fact that you have been passing from one epoch of internal decoration to another. The transition is softened down and rendered less perceptible by the adoption of a happy thought of the celebrated Marquise de Rambouillet, who had a room devoted to portraits of her friends. The walls of the gallery at Strawberry Hill are now exclusively occupied by portraits of intimate friends and illustrious or distinguished visitors, including the Prince and Princess of Wales, whose grace, affability, and charm of look and manner, faithfully reflected, would most assuredly have cured Walpole, had he fallen beneath their influence, of his dislike to royal visitors.

First come, first served. Those to whom places have been assigned form only a section of the illustrious or distinguished visitors and friends. When an increase of the peerage was proposed at the Restoration, Buckingham remarked that, if every Cavalier with a claim were created, the House of Lords must meet on Salisbury Plain. To carry out Lady Waldegrave's original plan, it might have become necessary to extend the gallery by roofing over the lawn.[1]

[1] Besides the portraits of the Prince and Princess of Wales in a single picture, the gallery contains separate portraits of the Duc and Duchesse d'Aumale, the late Earl and Countess of Clarendon, Earl Russell, Earl Grey, Viscount Palmerston, Mr. Gladstone, Viscount Halifax, the Marchioness of Clanricarde, the late Countess of Morley, Lord Lyndhurst, M. Van de Weyer, Bishop Wilberforce, Viscount Stratford de Redcliffe, the Duchess of Sutherland and the late Duchess, the Duchess of Westminster, Lady Churchill, Lady Augusta Sturt, the Countess of Shaftesbury, the Marchioness of Northampton, Madame Alphonse de Rothschild, Lady Selina Hervey, the Hon. Mrs. F. Stonor, Sir Thomas May, the Countess

All Walpole's smaller rooms have been preserved pretty nearly as he left them, although their destination has been changed. It was in the narrow passage leading from the hall to the Beauty Room (now a bedroom) that a late Chancellor of Ireland, his thoughts reverting to the natural enemies of his youth, exclaimed : " What a capital place if a man was pursued by bailiffs ! "

Walpole was constantly haunted by the fear that his creations and collections would not be respected by his successors, whatever indulgent friends might think or say of them :

" I wish," he writes to Montague in 1755, "you would visit it (Strawberry Hill) when it is in its beauty, and while it is mine. You will not, I flatter myself, like it so well when it belongs to the *Intendant* of Twickenham, when a cockle shell walk is made across the lawn, and everything *without* doors is made regular, and everything *within* modern and *riant;* for this must be its fate."

"May, 1772.

" In short, this *old, old, very old* castle, as his prints called Old Parr, is so near being perfect, that it will certainly be ready by the time I die to be improved with Indian paper, or to have the windows let down to the ground by some travelled lady."

"May 4, 1774. (To Cole.)

" Consider, Strawberry is almost the last monastery left, at least in England. Poor Mr. Bateman's is despoiled. Lord Bateman has stripped and plundered it, has advertised the site, and is dirtily selling by auction what he neither would keep nor sell for a sum that is worth while. Surely it is very indecent for a favourite relation, who

Spencer, the Countess Somers, and Lady Waldegrave herself. The next addition, we believe, will be the charming *habituée* (the Duchess of Manchester) who, at a ball given by Lady Waldegrave at the Secretary's Lodge, Dublin, caused an old Irish gentleman to exclaim: "I have come fifty miles to attend this ball, and I would have come a hundred to look at that beautiful Duchess." This compliment may pair off with that of the drayman who asked Georgiana, Duchess of Devonshire, to let him light his pipe at her eyes.

is rich, to show so little remembrance and affection. I suppose Strawberry will share the same fate. It has already happened to two of my friends."

His melancholy forebodings have been partly realised:

" Jove heard and granted half the suppliants' prayer,
  The rest the winds dispersed in empty air."

His collection has been dispersed through both hemispheres. But the fixed (we can hardly say, solid) fabric of his creation, his monastic castle or castellated monastery, the historic Strawberry Hill, has risen with renovated splendour from its temporary prostration; and—thanks to the taste, spirit, munificence, and cordial graceful abounding hospitality of an accomplished highly gifted woman —has regained and surpassed all the interest, attraction, and celebrity which it possessed in his lifetime and which he sorrowfully foretold would die with him.

NOTE.—Since this was written, Strawberry Hill has again undergone an eclipse by the untimely loss of the presiding genius, a woman whose true value, admired and esteemed as she was in her lifetime, was not fully felt and recognised till she died. It would be difficult to name a death which has caused so lively and general a sensation of regret, which has created a blank in so many circles, which so frequently elicits the reflection that somebody or something would be different and better had she lived.

BYRON AND TENNYSON.[1]

(*From the Quarterly Review, October,* 1871.)

The book before us is a biographical and critical essay on the noble poet and his works, containing a conscientiously accurate summary of his life and an impartial estimate of his genius. It will help to correct many erroneous notions, and it offers the opportunity which we have long coveted of analysing and (if possible) fixing the existing state of opinion regarding him, in especial relation to the living poet whose name is most frequently pronounced in rivalry.

"Byron, indisputably the greatest poetical genius that England has produced since Shakespeare and Milton." Such is the commencement of the notice of Byron in the last edition of the "Conversations-Lexicon," and we have ascertained by careful inquiry that it may be accepted as the exact representative of enlightened Germany upon this as upon most other subjects of thought, speculation or philosophy. Herr Elze says, "In the four head-divisions of poetry, English literature has produced four unapproached men of genius: Shakespeare in the dramatic: Milton in the reflecting, so far as this can be regarded as a peculiar

[1] *Lord Byron.* Von Karl Elze. Berlin, 1870.

species: Scott in the epic: and Byron in the lyrical—the lyrical understood in the widest sense as subjective poetry." The intended supremacy is clear, although the lines of demarcation are not so well defined as could be wished. Turning to the rest of the continent, whether north or south—to Russia and Poland, to France, Italy, and Spain—and consulting the highest authorities dead and living, printed and oral, we arrive at a similar conclusion. The result of our persevering researches and persistent interrogatories is everywhere throughout Europe, that Byron is deemed the greatest poet that England has produced for two centuries; and although the same unanimity may not be found across the Atlantic as to the amount of his pre-eminence, although he does not there rise so high above his competing predecessors or contemporaries as to dwarf or overshadow them, he takes precedence by common consent of all.

"Tennyson, one of the most distinguished modern English lyrical poets." Such is the commencement of the notice of Mr. Tennyson in the Lexicon; and that it will startle his English admirers, we infer from its first effect upon ourselves. But tame and depreciatory as this description may sound to ears ringing with the music of his verse, it is one which would be deemed just and adequate by the bulk of the reading public of Germany, or the reading public of any country that knew him chiefly by translation. It would not satisfy the reading public of the United States, where his popularity is little inferior to that which he enjoys in England, but with this material difference. It is not an exclusive popularity. It coexists with the popularity of other poets whose influence is deemed antagonistic to him amongst us, especially with that of Byron;

and the main object of this article is to bring the English mind into better agreement with the Anglo-American mind on this subject, or, in other words, to reclaim a befitting and appropriate pedestal for Byron without disturbing Mr. Tennyson or his school. It is the comparative, not the positive, reputation of the author of the " Idylls " that we dispute. Let him be read and applauded as much as ever, by all means: let the due meed of praise be ungrudgingly continued to those of his immediate contemporaries who cluster round him as their chief, or have adopted him as their model, or, essentially unlike as they are, have repaired to the same altar for their fire; but let the fitting honour be also vindicated and reserved for those whom they have temporarily superseded in popular estimation, far more by an accidental concurrence of opinions and events than by merits which will stand the test of time and command the judgment of posterity.

Foreign nations, in their independence of local influences, resemble and represent posterity: foreign nations have already given their verdict in the cause which we propose to bring before the home tribunal; and before appealing from that verdict on the ground that foreign nations mostly know the productions of the contrasted poets by translation, it would be well to meditate on this passage of Goethe:

"I honour both rhythm and rhyme, by which poetry first becomes poetry, but the properly deep and radically operative—the truly developing and quickening, is that which remains of the poet, when he is translated into prose. The inward substance then remains in its purity and fullness; which, when it is absent, a dazzling exterior often deludes with the semblance of, and, when it is present, conceals."[1]

[1] "Aus meinem Leben: Dichtung und Wahrheit," Th. 3, B. 11. "It

Whether a poet is translated into verse or prose, he will be appreciated in his new form in proportion to the amount of thought, reflection, palpable imagery, or, what Goethe calls "inward substance," embodied in the original. Grace or felicity of expression, idiomatic ease, and rhythm, must almost necessarily be lost; or, if replaced, should be set down to the credit of the translator, whose language is his own. Dryden said of Shakespeare, that if his embroideries were burnt down, there would be silver at the bottom of the melting-pot. If Mr. Tennyson were submitted to such a process, the residuum would be comparatively small. His greatest beauties are confessedly untranslatable; they are too delicate, too evanescent, too bloomlike. Speaking of the female characters in the "Poems," M. Taine says: "I have translated many ideas and many styles. I will never try to translate a single one of these portraits. Every word is like a tint, curiously heightened or softened by the neighbouring tint, with all the hardihood and the success of the happiest refinement. The least alteration would spoil all."[1]

Is, then, Mr. Tennyson's English fame enough? Is his title to rank as the first English poet of his epoch conclusively established by the fact that a majority of the rising generation of both sexes within this realm insist on so regarding him? We make bold to think not. It rests on divine

would be a most easy task to prove that not only the language of a large portion of every good poem, even of the most elevated character, must necessarily, except with reference to the metre, in no respect differ from that of good prose, but likewise that some of the most interesting parts of the best poems will be found to be strictly the language of prose when prose is well written." (*Wordsworth*, Preface to the "Lyrical Ballads.") The obvious inference is that the best poems are those which —*cæteris paribus*—will best bear literal or prose translation.

[1] "Histoire de la Littérature Anglaise," vol. iv. 434.

authority that no man is a prophet in his own country. But many a man has been a poet in his own country whose poetry had no exchangeable value, and could only live in a particular atmosphere. Were these necessarily first-class poets? This is a question which we will endeavour to illustrate before proceeding further, for all sound criticism depends upon the principles involved in it.

Our estimate of books and men are far more frequently subjective than objective. We judge them rather by our own feelings, prejudices, and passions, than by their inherent or individual qualities; and no man is a fair judge of either who does not habitually analyse his impressions as they are caught up or imbibed. Approval and disapproval are too frequently confounded with liking and disliking, with being pleased or displeased. The most cultivated intellects are not exempt from this liability to error, and should be equally on their guard against it. We once heard an eminent scholar and statesman (Sir G. C. Lewis) maintain that Gray was the first of modern English poets; and in the course of the ensuing discussion it was made clear that his admiration was mainly owing to the rush of youthful associations which a recent perusal of the "Ode to Eton College" had brought back. We strongly suspect that an analogous solution might be given of what we have heard cited as a proof of Mr. Tennyson's pathos, namely, that an ex-ambassador, Lord Stratford de Redcliffe, of resolute will and masculine understanding, by no means given to the melting mood, burst into tears during the reading of "Elaine" aloud to a party at a country house. A word, a phrase, may have loosened the floodgate of association:

"And as a fort to which beleaguers win
Unhop'd for entrance through some friend within,

One clear idea, centr'd in the breast,
By memory's magic lets in all the rest."

It is one of Chamfort's aphorisms that "what makes the success of numerous works, is the affinity between the mediocrity of the ideas of the author and the mediocrity of the ideas of the public." Literary history so abounds with instances of adventitious and ill-deserved popularity, that Wordsworth, discontented with the limited circulation of his own poems and deriving cold comfort from (what he called) the parallel case of Milton, was wont to contend that popularity, far from being a proof of merit, implied that unworthy sacrifices must have been made and solid fame bartered for it. He forgot that most of the great writers who have now taken rank amongst the classics of their respective countries, attained their proud pre-eminence at starting or early enough to enjoy it to the full, and that genius, tremulous with the glowing and agitated atmosphere around and about it, may shine with as bright and sustained a light as if it had shrunk away from the haunts of crowded life to draw inspiration from the grotto or the lake. All we maintain is that local or temporary popularity is unsatisfactory and inconclusive as a test: that it may prove the forerunner of permanent and world-wide reputation, or it may not.

Fancy has been amused by conjecturing " with what temper Milton surveyed the silent progress of his work, and marked its reputation stealing its way in a kind of subterranean current through fear and silence." Its reputation did not burst forth in full brilliancy till he had been forty years in his grave, and shows what invaluable services may occasionally be rendered by retrospective criticism in compelling the complete recognition of genius. Addison devoted eighteen papers of the "Spectator," interspersed with numerous extracts, to "Paradise Lost," and thereby (in Johnson's words) "has made Milton a universal favourite, with whom readers of every class think it necessary to be pleased."[1]

With Byron the progress of fame has been reversed. He rose in splendour, and his meridian is obscured by clouds. He states that the morning after the publication of the first and second cantos of "Childe Harold," he awoke and found himself famous. These cantos would have made a name at any time, but their effect was undeniably enhanced by the choice of topics, and the state of the public mind. "The Comedy of the *Visionnaires*," wrote Madame de Sévigné, "delighted us much: we found it the representation of everybody; each of us has his or her visions shadowed out." "Childe Harold," on his first appearance had thus much in common with this forgotten Comedy. He had a word for everything and everybody that was uppermost in men's thoughts: theories of government for the political speculator, of social progress for the moralist, classical reminiscences for the scholar, and never ending sentiment for the fair. He dealt swashing blows right and left at Whigs and Tories, aristocracy and democracy. He described the scenes on which all English eyes and interests were fixed. He lingered on the battle-fields where English laurels had been won. He sang of the Tagus and the Guadalquivir, of Talavera and Albuera. He

---

[1] "Life of Addison," Johnson's Works, vol. vii. p. 142. In the "Life of Milton," vol. vi. p. 173, he says: "'Paradise Lost' is one of the books which the reader admires and lays down, and forgets to take up again. None ever wished it longer than it is. Its perusal is a duty rather than a pleasure."

denounced the devastating ambition of Napoleon, and mingled the denunciation with a sneer at the fools who were pouring out their blood like water to maintain their own domestic despots on their thrones. War is thus grandly personified:

> "Lo! where the Giant on the mountain stands,
>   His blood-red tresses deep'ning in the sun,
>   With death-shot glowing in his fiery hands,
>   And eye that scorcheth all it glares upon;
>   Restless it rolls, now fix'd, and now anon
>   Flashing afar,—and at his iron feet
>   Destruction cowers, to mark what deeds are done;
>   For on this morn three potent nations meet,
> To shed before his shrine the blood he deems most sweet.
>
> *   *   *   *   *
>
> "There shall they rot—Ambition's honour'd fools!
>   Yes, Honour decks the turf that wraps their clay!
>   Vain Sophistry! in these behold the tools,
>   The broken tools, that tyrants cast away
>   By myriads, when they dare to pave their way
>   With human hearts—to what?—a dream alone.
>   Can despots compass aught that hails their sway?
>   Or call with truth one span of earth their own,
> Save that wherein at last they crumble bone by bone?

Or take the glowing sketch of the Maid of Saragossa, in her contrasted moods of tenderness and heroism:

> "Ye who shall marvel when you hear her tale,
>   Oh! had you known her in her softer hour,
>   Mark'd her black eye that mocks her coal-black veil,
>   Heard her light, lively tones in Lady's bower,
>   Seen her long locks that foil the painter's power,
>   Her fairy form, with more than female grace,
>   Scarce would you deem that Saragoza's tower
>   Beheld her smile in Danger's Gorgon face,
> Thin the closed ranks, and lead in Glory's fearful chase.
>
> "Her lover sinks—she sheds no ill-timed tear;
>   Her chief is slain—she fills his fatal post;
>   Her fellows flee—she checks their base career;

> The foe retires—she heads the sallying host:
> Who can appease like her a lover's ghost?
> Who can avenge so well a leader's fall?
> What maid retrieve when man's flush'd hope is lost?
> Who hang so fiercely on the flying Gaul,
> Foil'd by a woman's hand, before a batter'd wall?"

To idealise modern warfare, or invest it with an air of chivalry in verse, is no common feat. Addison's "Campaign" is barely redeemed by a single image (the angel), and the author of "Marmion," whose Flodden Field stirs the blood like a trumpet-tone, became tame and prosaic at Waterloo. Byron makes the dragoon's sabre glitter like Arthur's sword Excalibur, and by mere dint of imagination gives to a modern fortification, bristling with cannon, the picturesqueness of a mountain side or valley crowned with rocks. Here is Cintra, the natural object to be described:

> "The horrid crags, by toppling convent crown'd,
> The cork-trees hoar that clothe the shaggy steep,
> The mountain-moss by scorching skies imbrown'd,
> The sunken glen, whose sunless shrubs must weep,
> The tender azure of the unruffled deep,
> The orange tints that gild the greenest bough,
> The torrents that from cliff to valley leap
> The vine on high, the willow branch below,
> Mix'd in one mighty scene, with varied beauty glow."

Here is Morena, the material and mechanical:

> "At every turn Morena's dusky height
> Sustains aloft the battery's iron load;
> And, far as mortal eye can compass sight,
> The mountain-howitzer, the broken road,
> The bristling palisade, the fosse o'erflow'd,
> The station'd bands, the never-vacant watch,
> The magazine in rocky durance stow'd,
> The holster'd steed beneath the shed of thatch,
> The ball-piled pyramid, the ever-blazing match."

We shall come to descriptive passages of far higher grasp and richer colouring; but those we have just quoted illustrate a quality in which no modern poet has rivalled the noble author. Not the least of the attractions of "Childe Harold," especially to the young, lay in the self-revealings, the avowal of over-indulged and yet unsuppressed passions, the premature feeling of satiety, and the deep all-pervading despondency:

"To sit on rocks, to muse o'er flood and fell,
  To slowly trace the forest's shady scene,
Where things that own not man's dominion dwell,
  And mortal foot hath ne'er or rarely been;
To climb the trackless mountain all unseen,
  With the wild flock that never needs a fold;
Alone o'er steeps and foaming falls to lean;
  This is not solitude; 'tis but to hold
Converse with Nature's charms, and view her stores unroll'd.

"But midst the crowd, the hum, the shock of men,
  To hear, to see, to feel, and to possess,
And roam along, the world's tired denizen,
  With none who bless us, none whom we can bless;
Minions of splendour shrinking from distress!
  None that, with kindred consciousness endued,
If we were not, would seem to smile the less
  Of all that flatter'd, follow'd, sought, and sued;
This is to be alone; this, this is solitude!"

When it is remembered that the writer was young, noble, and handsome—that his career, short as it had been, was involved in mystery—that the keen-edged falchion which he had unsheathed in his satire was ready at any moment to leap again from the scabbard—no wonder that he speedily became the idol, in due course the spoiled child, of the fashionable world and was by common consent enrolled amongst—

"the few
Or many, for the number's sometimes such,

> Whom a good mien, especially if new,
> Or fame, or name, for wit, war, sense, or nonsense,
> Permits whate'er they please, or did not long since."

Intoxicating as all this was, and intensely as it was for a time enjoyed by him despite of his morbid melancholy, he seems to have had an instinctive consciousness that he could not depend on these two cantos of "Childe Harold" any more than on "Hours of Idleness," or "English Bards and Scotch Reviewers," for permanent reputation, and that he had in him something better that must come out. Admiration is catching and imitative. When a book has once attracted marked attention, people buy and read in self-defence, whether they derive pleasure from it or not. The odds are, that many readers did not derive much pleasure from "Childe Harold," which has no story, and is mainly discursive on themes which it requires reading and reflection to follow out. But the case was widely different when he entered upon that series of tales which includes "The Giaour," "The Bride of Abydos," "The Corsair," "Lara," "The Siege of Corinth," and "Parisina." Then he was read with rapt interest throughout the length and breadth of the land; then he was scrambled for at the circulating libraries; then his applauding public comprised the indiscriminating many as well as the select and discriminating few.

They concurred in this instance, and they were right in concurring. Their delight in a story and a plot was simply a return to the wholesome taste of the olden times, the golden ages of poetry, the days of Homer and the Homeridæ, the Troubadours, the Minnesingers, the Bards, who were neither more nor less than story-tellers in verse, and bound, like the lady in the "Arabian Nights," to be provided with an inexhaustible supply. The only wonder is, that the reign of the didactic, speculative, and descriptive poets was prolonged till it was interrupted by Scott and terminated by Byron. The taste for exciting or sensational fiction may be meretricious or carried to excess: both mental and bodily stimulants must be used with caution; but to inspire breathless and sustained interest is one of the rarest and most enviable faculties of inventive genius, and it is hard on a poet to be denied credit for the beauties he scatters by the way because we are hurried along too fast and in too satisfied a state to dwell upon them; because we first read for the story, and then re-read for the imagery and thought. Nor, on re-reading either Scott's or Byron's rhymed romances, is it always to the episodes that we turn for genuine poetry. To blend passion and sentiment with rushing events and actions is their charm. In "The Giaour," for example:

> "On—on he hasten'd, and he drew
> My gaze of wonder as he flew:
> Though like a demon of the night
> He pass'd, and vanish'd from my sight,
> His aspect and his air impress'd
> A troubled memory on my breast,
> And long upon my startled ear
> Rung his dark courser's hoofs of fear.
> He spurs his steed; he nears the steep,
> That, jutting, shadows o'er the deep;
> He winds around; he hurries by;
> The rock relieves him from mine eye;
> For well I ween unwelcome he
> Whose glance is fix'd on those that flee;
> And not a star but shines too bright
> On him who takes such timeless flight.
> He wound along; but ere he pass'd
> One glance he snatch'd, as if his last,
> A moment check'd his wheeling speed,
> A moment breathed him from his steed,

A moment on his stirrup stood—
Why looks he o'er the olive wood?

"He stood—some dread was on his face,
Soon Hatred settled in its place :
It rose not with the reddening flush
Of transient Anger's hasty blush,
But pale as marble o'er the tomb,
Whose ghastly whiteness aids its gloom.
His brow was bent, his eye was glazed ;
He raised his arm, and fiercely raised,
And sternly shook his hand on high,
As doubting to return or fly ;
Impatient of his flight delay'd,
Here loud his raven charger neigh'd—
Down glanced that hand, and grasped his blade ;
That sound had burst his waking dream,
As Slumber starts at owlet's scream.
The spur hath lanced his courser's sides ;
Away, away, for life he rides.
'Twas but an instant he restrain'd
That fiery barb so sternly rein'd ;
'Twas but a moment that he stood,
Then sped as if by death pursued ;
But in that instant o'er his soul
Winters of Memory seem'd to roll,
And gather in that drop of time
A life of pain, an age of crime.
O'er him who loves, or hates, or fears,
Such moment pours the grief of years :
What felt *he* then, at once opprest
By all that most distracts the breast ?
That pause, which ponder'd o'er his fate,
Oh, who its dreary length shall date !
Though in Time's record nearly nought,
It was Eternity to Thought ! "

Although we write principally for those who are not familiar with Byron, we will give them credit for having fallen in, at some time or other in their lives, with the renowned episodes of " He who hath bent him o'er the dead," and "Know'st thou the land," but there is another (in the "Giaour") which we have reason to believe is less known and unappreciated:

> "As rising on its purple wing
> The insect-queen of eastern spring,
> O'er emerald meadows of Kashmeer
> Invites the young pursuer near,
> And leads him on from flower to flower
> A weary chase and wasted hour,
> Then leaves him, as it soars on high,
> With panting heart and tearful eye:
> So Beauty lures the full-grown child,
> With hue as bright, and wing as wild;
> A chase of idle hopes and fears,
> Begun in folly, closed in tears.
> If won, to equal ills betray'd,
> Woe waits the insect and the maid;
> A life of pain, the loss of peace,
> From infant's play, and man's caprice:
> The lovely toy so fiercely sought
> Hath lost its charm by being caught,
> For every touch that woo'd its stay
> Hath brush'd its brightest hues away,
> Till charm, and hue, and beauty gone,
> 'Tis left to fly or fall alone,
> With wounded wing, or bleeding breast,
> Ah! where shall either victim rest?
> Can this with faded pinion soar
> From rose to tulip as before?
> Or Beauty, blighted in an hour,
> Find joy within her broken bower?
> No: gayer insects fluttering by
> Ne'er droop the wing o'er those that die
> And lovelier things have mercy shown
> To every failing but their own,
> And every woe a tear can claim
> Except an erring sister's shame."

The four concluding lines are nearly as familiar as Scott's "Oh, woman, in our hours of ease," as

Moore's "Oh, ever thus from childhood's hour." But a short time since, on their being quoted in a numerous group, a lady, not long past her meridian, turned round to a friend of her own standing with the remark, "You and I are the only persons present who know where those lines come from." She proved right. The analogy between beauties and butterflies as objects of chase is obvious enough; and (it may be said) the incident which gave rise to the "Rape of the Lock" was only a piece of not over-refined gallantry. It is the exquisite workmanship and the delicate handling which give choice works of fancy their value and their charm.

What ineffably enhances the effect of Byron's narratives and descriptions, however rapid and condensed or however replete with thought and feeling, is the idiomatic ease of the language, its lucid clearness, and the utter absence of inversion, affectation, or obscurity. You are never obliged to dig for his meaning, never obliged to construe or translate his sentences; whilst there are modern poets who make you work as hard as if you were solving a problem or discovering an acrostic, not unfrequently reminding you of the Irishman's horse, which (he said) was very difficult to catch and when caught not worth having. Mr. Browning is one of the most incorrigible offenders in this line; and this is the more provoking, because he is a man of truly original genius. A patient diver into the depths of his rich and capacious mind has always a fair chance of bringing up pearls. Certainly the most extensively popular of Mr. Tennyson's minor poems is "Locksley Hall," and we can hardly err in attributing the marked preference given to it by the uninitiated, to the spirit, vivacity, and simplicity of the language, and the natural unbroken flood of thought. It reads as if it had been thrown off spontaneously and impulsively, unlike so many of his most admired poems, where the *limæ labor* may almost invariably be traced.

Byron's command of language is equally observable in every variety of metre which he attempted, and on the appearance of "The Corsair," critics of all parties hastened to recognise and applaud the flexibility of the heroic couplet in his hands. This poem abounds in passages of beauty and force, the only puzzle being what range of feelings is most strikingly expressed. The parting scene with Medora is replete with the pathos of tenderness :

> She rose—she sprung—she clung to his embrace,
> Till his heart heaved beneath her hidden face,
> He dared not raise to his that deep-blue eye,
> Which downcast droop'd in tearless agony.
> Her long fair hair lay floating o'er his arms,
> In all the wildness of dishevell'd charms ;
> Scarce beat that bosom where his image dwelt
> So full—*that* feeling seem'd almost unfelt !
> Hark—peals the thunder of the signal-gun !
> It told 'twas sunset—and he cursed that sun.
> Again—again—that form he madly press'd,
> Which mutely clasp'd, imploringly caress'd !
> And tottering to the couch his bride he bore,
> One moment gazed—as if to gaze no more :
> Felt—that for him earth held but her alone,
> Kiss'd her cold forehead—turn'd—is Conrad gone ?"

What a startling picture of Remorse is presented by Conrad imprisoned, chained, and destined to the stake :

> "There is a war, a chaos of the mind,
> When all its elements convulsed—combined—
> Lie dark and jarring with perturbed force,
> And gnashing with impenitent Remorse ;

That juggling fiend—who never spake before—
But cries ' I warn'd thee ! ' when the deed is o'er.
No single passion, and no ruling thought
That leaves the rest as once unseen, unsought ;
But the wild prospect when the soul reviews—
All rushing through their thousand avenues.
Ambition's dreams expiring, love's regret,
Endanger'd glory, life itself beset ;
The joy untasted, the contempt or hate
'Gainst those who fain would triumph in our fate ;
The hopeless past, the hasting future driven
Too quickly on to guess if hell or heaven ;
Deeds, thoughts, and words, perhaps remember'd not
So keenly till that hour, but ne'er forgot ;
Things light or lovely in their acted time,
But now to stern reflection each a crime ;
The withering sense of evil unreveal'd,
Not cankering less because the more conceal'd—
All, in a word, from which all eyes must start,
That opening sepulchre—the naked heart
Bares with its buried woes, till Pride awake,
To snatch the mirror from the soul—and break."

The scene in which Conrad throws off his disguise is instinct with fire :

"Up rose the Dervise with that burst of light,
Nor less his change of form appall'd the sight :
Up rose that Dervise—not in saintly garb,
But like a warrior bounding on his barb,
Dash'd his high cap, and tore his robe away—
Shone his mail'd breast, and flash'd his sabre's ray !
His close but glittering casque, and sable plume,
More glittering eye, and black brow's sabler gloom,
Glared on the Moslems' eyes some Afrit sprite,
Whose demon death-blow left no hope for fight.
The wild confusion, and the swarthy glow
Of flames on high, and torches from below ;
The shriek of terror, and the mingling yell—
For swords began to clash, and shouts to swell—
Flung o'er that spot of earth the air of hell !
* * * * *

> He saw their terror—from his baldric drew
> His bugle—brief the blast—but shrilly blew;
> 'Tis answered—'Well ye speed, my gallant crew!
> Why did I doubt their quickness of career?
> And deem design had left me single here?'
> Sweeps his long arm—that sabre's whirling sway
> Sheds fast atonement for its first delay;
> Completes his fury, what their fear begun,
> And makes the many basely quail to one.
> The cloven turbans o'er the chamber spread,
> And scarce an arm dare rise to guard its head:
> Even Seyd, convulsed, o'erwhelm'd with rage, surprise,
> Retreats before him, though he still defies.
> No craven he—and yet he dreads the blow,
> So much Confusion magnifies his foe!"

How many a chilled, crushed, ill-mated heart will beat in unison with Gulnare's, when she indignantly exclaims—

> "My love stern Seyd's! Oh—No—No—not my love—
> Yet much this heart, that strives no more, once strove
> To meet his passion—but it would not be.
> I felt—I feel—love dwells with—with the free.
>
> *   *   *   *   *
>
> Oh! hard it is that fondness to sustain,
> And struggle not to feel averse in vain;
> But harder still the heart's recoil to bear,
> And hide from one—perhaps another there.
> He takes the hand I give not—nor withhold—
> Its pulse nor check'd—nor quicken'd—calmly cold:
> And when resign'd, it drops a lifeless weight
> From one I never loved enough to hate.
> No warmth these lips return by his imprest,
> And chill'd remembrance shudders o'er the rest."

In the dedication of this poem to Moore (dated January 7th, 1814), Byron speaks of it as the last production with which he shall trespass on public patience for some years. On the 9th of April he writes: "No more rhyme for—or rather *from*

—me. I have taken my leave of that stage, and henceforth will mountebank it no longer." That very evening a Gazette Extraordinary announced the abdication of Fontainebleau, and in the diary for the 10th we find: "To-day I have boxed one hour—written an Ode to Napoleon Buonaparte, copied it—eaten six biscuits—drunk four bottles of soda-water, and idled away the rest of my time." The ode was a decided failure, and although published anonymously was made the occasion of some bitter criticisms and personalities, depreciatory of both genius and character, which cut him to the quick, and on the 29th of the same month he came to the determination not only to write no more, but to purchase back the whole of his copyrights, and suppress every line he had ever written. "For all this," he said in the letter to Mr. Murray enclosing a draft for the purchase-money, "it might be as well to assign some reason. I have none to give except my own caprice, and I do not consider the circumstance of consequence enough to require explanation."

This outburst of pique and pettishness did not last longer than forty-eight hours, at the end of which he requests Mr. Murray to tear the draft and go on as usual. In the May following he set to work on "Lara," which was published in August 1814, in the same volume with Rogers' "Jacqueline." This union of Larry and Jacquey (as he christened them) caused a good deal of merriment and surprise at the indiscretion of the graver poet in trusting his innocent heroine in the company of a retired pirate and his paramour, Kaled, a lady who did not stand upon trifles and wore small clothes. Continuations rarely answer when a work has been accepted as complete; and "Lara," a continuation of the "Corsair," formed no exception to the rule. Neither the conception nor execution can be commended; but that the rich vein which had been worked so prodigally remained unexhausted, was proved by " The Siege of Corinth," and " Parisina," composed in 1815, and published, the first in January, and the second in February, 1816. The opening of " Parisina " may be taken as a specimen of the graceful versification of the poem:

> " It is the hour when from the boughs
>   The nightingale's high note is heard;
> It is the hour when lovers' vows
>   Seem sweet in every whisper'd word;
> And gentle winds, and waters near,
> Make music to the lonely ear.
> Each flower the dews have lightly wet,
> And in the sky the stars are met,
> And on the wave is deeper blue,
> And on the leaf a browner hue,
> And in the heaven that clear obscure,
> So softly dark, and darkly pure,
> Which follows the decline of day,
> As twilight melts beneath the moon away."

The subject of this poem—an incestuous passion—would have been forgiven him, as many an admitted error or offence against propriety had been condoned in consideration of youth and genius, in the heyday of his popularity. Then, his countrymen and countrywomen could see nothing wrong, where now they could see nothing right. The crisis had arrived: a terrible reaction had set in, and it was not the less terrible because it was irrational and indefensible. What had the literary or fashionable world to do with a domestic quarrel? What could they possibly know about the merits of one that was only whispered about in a one-sided shape by the friends of the wife?

When an attempt was made to drive Kean from the stage for a breach of the Seventh Commandment with the wife of an alderman, there were law proceedings to testify against him; but where were the *pièces justificatives* when the cry was raised against Byron?

The most brilliant of our essayists and historians has declared that he knew no spectacle so ridiculous as the British public in one of its periodical fits of morality. "In general, elopements, divorces, and family quarrels pass with little notice. We read the scandal, talk about it for a day, and forget it. But once in six or seven years our virtue becomes outrageous. We cannot suffer the laws of religion and decency to be violated. We must make a stand against vice. Accordingly, some unfortunate man, in no respect more depraved than hundreds whose offences have been treated with lenity, is singled out as an expiatory sacrifice." Byron was so singled out and, it so happened, singled out at a time when he was undergoing the utmost extent of humiliation to which a haughty spirit could be exposed by pecuniary embarrassment. The letters from his wife to his sister prove that the presence of bailiffs in his house maddened him, and that he was on the verge of downright insanity for some weeks. It is astonishing that he passed unscathed (intellectually, we mean) through the fiery furnace. He not only passed through it with his genius unimpaired, but refreshed, renewed, and re-invigorated by the shock. The life he led prior to this violent disruption of all the social and domestic ties which bound him to England, was distracting and enervating; and the half-formed resolution to write no more may have been prompted by an inward consciousness that his mind wanted rest or change.

In the remarkable novel of "Gerfault," the hero, a dramatic author and poet in the flood-tide of fame, suddenly finds his creative powers giving way. The brain has been overworked, and will no longer answer to the call. He is advised to try either counter-irritation or repose. He prefers counter-irritation, and fortune so far favours him that he gets involved in an intrigue with a married woman, which ends in a frightful catastrophe. The husband falls by his hand in an abnormal kind of duel, and the wife commits suicide. His share in the catastrophe, attributed to an unforeseen casualty, is unsuspected, and he departs for the East under a flourish of trumpets from the journalists, who hope that "the glowing climes of Asia will prove a mine of new inspirations for the celebrated poet who has gloriously marked out his place at the head of our literature." Their hopes are realised. He returns improved, though saddened; with genius heightened and enriched, but clad in mourning garb. "He is daily congratulated on this black chord recently added to his lyre, the vibrations of which surpass in mortal sadness the sighs of Renè and the reveries of Obermann. None are aware that his bitterly-passionate pages are written under the inspiration of a funereal vision; and that this melancholy and sombre colour, which they take for the phantasy of imagination, has been tempered with blood and brayed in the heart."

Byron's lyre was similarly re-strung, the chief difference being that the source of his renewed inspiration was patent to the world. It is impossible not to see and feel the changed and deepened hue of the despondency with which all his writings are imbued. His tone, after leaving England for the last time, is no longer that of the satiated epicure, the sufferer from fancied sorrows, but the expression of genuine sadness, of hopeless despondency, welling up from the depths of the heart; and his despairing or reproachful communings with Nature often remind us, by their sublime intensity, of Lear:

> "I tax not you, you elements, with unkindness,
> I never gave you kingdoms, call'd you children,
> You owe me no subscription."

Manfred's apostrophe is pitched in the same exalted key:

> "Ye toppling crags of ice!
> Ye avalanches, whom a breath draws down
> In mountainous o'erwhelming, come and crush me!
> I hear ye momently above, beneath,
> Crash with a frequent conflict; but ye pass,
> And only fall on things that still would live;
> On the young flourishing forest, or the hut
> And hamlet of the harmless villager."

The Third and Fourth Cantos of "Childe Harold," immeasurably superior to the First and Second, abound in instances:

> "Thy sky is changed!—and such a change! Oh night,
> And storm, and darkness, ye are wondrous strong,
> Yet lovely in your strength, as is the light
> Of a dark eye in woman! Far along,
> From peak to peak, the rattling crags among
> Leaps the live thunder! Not from one lone cloud,
> But every mountain now hath found a tongue,
> And Jura answers, through her misty shroud,
> Back to the joyous Alps, who call to her aloud!

> "And this is in the night:—Most glorious night!
> Thou wert not sent for slumber! let me be
> A sharer in thy fierce and far delight,—
> A portion of the tempest and of thee!
> How the lit lake shines, a phosphoric sea,

And the big rain comes dancing to the earth!
And now again 'tis black,—and now, the glee
Of the loud hills shakes with its mountain-mirth,
As if they did rejoice o'er a young earthquake's birth."

"The 'fierce and far delight' of a thunder-storm," wrote Scott, "is here described in verse almost as vivid as its lightnings. The live thunder 'leaping among the rattling crags'—the voice of mountains, as if shouting to each other—the plashing of the big rain—the gleaming of the wide lake, lighted like a phosphoric sea—present a picture of sublime terror, yet of enjoyment, often attempted, but never so well, certainly never better, brought out in poetry."

"Byron," says Herr Elze, "reaches the highest pinnacle when he succeeds in blending his individual woe with the universal; when he pours himself out into Nature, and finds in her the occasion for recollections of and reflexions on the world's history. For this reason, the two last Cantos of 'Childe Harold' belong to his richest and greatest productions."

The fine stanzas on the "Ocean" should be read in connection with the Storm in "Don Juan":

"Roll on, thou deep and dark blue Ocean—roll,
  Ten thousand fleets sweep over thee in vain;
  Man marks the earth with ruin—his control
  Stops with the shore; upon the watery plain
  The wrecks are all thy deed, nor doth remain
  A shadow of man's ravage, save his own,
  When, for a moment, like a drop of rain,
  He sinks into thy depths with bubbling groan,
Without a grave, unknell'd, uncoffin'd, and unknown.

*   *   *   *   *

"Thy shores are empires, changed in all save thee—
  Assyria, Greece, Rome, Carthage, what are they?

> Thy waters wash'd them power while they were free,[1]
> And many a tyrant since; their shores obey
> The stranger, slave, or savage; their decay
> Has dried up realms to deserts :—not so thou;—
> Unchangeable, save to thy wild waves' play,
> Time writes no wrinkle on thine azure brow;
> Such as creation's dawn beheld, thou rollest now.

* * * * *

> "And I have loved thee, Ocean! and my joy
> Of youthful sports was on thy breast to be
> Borne, like thy bubbles, onward: from a boy
> I wanton'd with thy breakers—they to me
> Were a delight; and if the freshening sea
> Made them a terror—'twas a pleasing fear,
> For I was as it were a child of thee,
> And trusted to thy billows far and near,
> And laid my hand upon thy mane—as I do here."

It is from an instinctive yearning for natural grandeur and beauty, that, after an admirable comparative sketch of Voltaire and Rousseau, he breaks off:

> "But let me quit man's works, again to read
> His Maker's, spread around me."

And no mortal man ever read them more reverently, or penetrated more deeply into their recondite meanings, or drew from them a finer moral, or breathed round them an atmosphere so charged with the electricity of thought. It is here that he may defy comparison with any writer since Wordsworth; and yet it is with Nature's works that the Tennysonians claim to be most conversant. They disclaim the mechanical and artificial. The description of natural objects—of hills, dales, trees, flowers, meadows, and rivulets—is their

---

[1] This is the correct reading. The older editions have—
  "Thy waters wasted them while they were free,"
but upon reference to the poet's MS. (in Mr. Murray's possession) we find that he wrote the line as printed above.

forte; and their master's use of these materials in his own manner is irreproachable: whether it be the Gardener's daughter, with the shadow of the roses trembling on her waist; or the Miller's daughter, leaning over her "long green box of mignonette"; or the Lady of Shalott, with "the leaves upon her falling light"; or the silvery cloud that lost its way in Œnone's glen; or the hollow ocean-ridges, as seen from Locksley Hall. Nothing, generally speaking, can be more appropriately selected, or more artistically employed, than these gems of rural scenery. When they are not a picture in themselves, they form an admirable setting to one: they are always fresh and sweet, always redolent of innocence and simplicity; and it is the reader's, not the poet's fault, if the wicked reflection will occasionally arise:

"Oh, Mirth and Innocence, oh, Milk and Water,
  Ye happy mixtures of these happy days."

Mr. Tennyson's Nature differs from Byron's as a flower-piece by Van Huysum or an English landscape by Creswick differs from a Salvator Rosa or a Gaspar Poussin. In the elaborate minuteness of his finish, he may be compared to the painters of the pre-Raphaelite school, who (by a perverse abuse of power) convert their backgrounds into foregrounds, and make you look more at the roses and apple-blossoms than at the damsels who are embowered in them. Minute details are ruinous to great effects, and the poet who rises to sublimity must always rank above the one who simply attains to prettiness. The quality of the aspiration must cast the balance, assuming the execution to be equal. When Mr. Tennyson is moralising on a bending lily or describing the ripple of the rivulet, Byron is apostrophising a crashing forest or an avalanche, or pouring out his whole mind and soul in unison with the roar of the cataract and the mountain capped with snow. He rises far the highest, and he continues longest on the wing.

In poetical description of a natural object, what can be better than the rivulet in " The Island " ?

> " A little stream came tumbling from the height
> And straggling into ocean as it might,
> Its bounding crystal frolicked in the ray,
> And gushed from cliff to crag with saltless spray,
> Close on the wild, wide ocean,—yet as pure
> And fresh as Innocence, and more secure;
> Its silver torrent glittered o'er the deep
> As the shy chamois' eye o'erlooked the steep,
> While, far below, the vast and sullen swell
> Of ocean's Alpine azure rose and fell."

Mr. Ruskin remarks on these lines : " Now I beg leave, with such authority as an old workman may take concerning his trade, having also looked at a waterfall or two in my time, and not unfrequently at a wave, to assure the reader that here *is* entirely first-rate work. Though Lucifer himself had written it, the thing itself is good, and not only so but unsurpassingly good, the closing line being probably the best concerning the sea yet written by the race of the sea-kings."

We know from long experience that it is useless to refer. To produce the desired impression, or maintain the given argument, we must quote; and we shall quote three of the stanzas on Rome and the Coliseum as a specimen of the poet's power of enveloping the wrecks of vanished empires, the emblems of human vanity, with the halo which he flings around the rocks and valleys of the Alps:

> " Oh Rome! my country! city of the soul!
> The orphans of the heart must turn to thee,

Lone mother of dead empires! and control
In their shut breasts their petty misery.
What are our woes and sufferance? Come and see
The cypress, hear the owl, and plod your way
O'er steps of broken thrones and temples, Ye!
Whose agonies are evils of a day—
A world is at our feet as fragile as our clay.

* * * * *

"Arches on arches! as it were that Rome,
Collecting the chief trophies of her line,
Would build up all her triumphs in one dome,
Her Coliseum stands; the moonbeams shine
As 'twere its natural torches, for divine
Should be the light which streams here, to illume
This long-explored but still exhaustless mine
Of contemplation; and the azure gloom
Of an Italian night, where the deep skies assume

" Hues which have words, and speak to ye of heaven,
Float o'er this vast and wondrous monument,
And shadow forth its glory. There is given
Unto the things of earth, which Time hath bent,
A spirit's feeling, and where he hath leant
His hand, but broke his scythe, there is a power
And magic in the ruin'd battlement,
For which the palace of the present hour
Must yield its pomp, and wait till ages are its dower."

The Pantheon, St. Peter's, the Venus de' Medici, the Laocoon, the Gladiator—all the finest creations of architecture and sculpture that Italy can boast—are similarly invested with the brightest or deepest hues of poetry. But we can only find room for the Apollo:

"Or view the Lord of the unerring bow,
The God of life, and poesy, and light—
The sun in human limbs arrayed, and brow
All radiant from his triumph in the fight;
The shaft hath just been shot—the arrow bright
With an immortal's vengeance; in his eye
And nostril beautiful disdain, and might

And majesty, flash their full lightnings by
Developing in that one glance the Deity.

"But in his delicate form—a dream of Love,
Shaped by some solitary nymph, whose breast
Long'd for a deathless lover from above,
And madden'd in that vision—are exprest
All that ideal beauty ever bless'd
The mind with in its most unearthly mood,
When each conception was a heavenly guest—
A ray of immortality—and stood,
Starlike, around, until they gather'd to a god!"

There is hardly any variety of poetic power that may not be illustrated from "Don Juan." In the opinion of most competent judges, it forms the copestone of Byron's fame. But it confirmed the worst charges that had been levelled against the spirit, tone, and tendency of his writings, and thereby strengthened the bigoted opposition, against which we are at this moment struggling, to the full recognition of his genius by his countrymen. The epithet "meanest," attached to the name of a great philosopher, has been merged and forgotten in "wisest," "brightest." The recent attempt of an accomplished scholar and critic (Elwin) to gauge a great poet (Pope) by his personal weaknesses has fortunately failed; but the spirit which denied Byron a place in Westminster Abbey is abroad and stirring; and it is melancholy to reflect what an amount of narrow-minded sectarian hostility was brought into mischievous activity by Mrs. Stowe. Hardly an American or foreign journal of note took her part, whilst a majority of the most influential English journals sided with her.

The run against Byron cleared the course for the new comers, but an unusually long interval elapsed before any fresh poet arose to replace him, although several candidates were started or pretenders set up.

> "Sir Walter reigned before me, Moore and Campbell
> Before and after; but now grown more holy,
> The Muses upon Sion's hill must ramble
> With poets almost Clergymen, or wholly.
> * * * * *
> Then there's my gentle Euphues;[1] who they say
> Sets up for being a sort of *moral me;*
> He'll find it rather difficult some day
> To turn out both, or either, it may be.
> Some persons think that Coleridge hath the sway;
> And Wordsworth hath supporters, two or three."

Then came Keats, the alleged victim of a critique:

> "Tis strange the mind that very fiery particle
> Should let itself be snuffed out by an article."

It was the "literary lower empire" when (1830) Tennyson made his first appearance, diffident and sensitive, in the arena:

> "First Fear his hand, its skill to try,
> Amid the chords bewilder'd laid,
> And back recoil'd, he knew not why,
> Ev'n at the sound himself had made."

His reception was not encouraging, despite of an applauding circle of young friends; and his earliest poems, if not actually withdrawn, were suffered to remain out of print for some years, by way of testing the patience of the general public, or to punish them. It was not till after the collected edition of 1842 that he began to be looked upon as the poet of the epoch, or was talked of for the laureate throne.[2] Except amongst the

---

[1] Barry Cornwall (Procter).

[2] "When Tennyson published his first poems, the critics spoke ill of them. He was silent: during ten years no one saw his name in a review,

older race of critics, who remained obdurate and unappreciating, the finer qualities of his genius were then frankly recognised at once. With an inexhaustible fancy, an exquisite perception of moral and natural beauty, a well stored and highly cultivated mind, a trained eye for observation, a rich vocabulary, and a familiarity with rythmical composition acquired in a long apprenticeship to the craft, what more was wanting to entitle him to the throne? He wanted spontaneity and continuity: his productions were laboured and disconnected: little interest was felt beyond that of picking out the abounding pearls and rubies at random strung: the incidents were commonplace: the reflections lay upon the surface: the groundwork was too thin for the embroidery: the foundations were not broad or strong enough for the superstructure: there was no linked sweetness long drawn out: no sustained rush or flow, although we were met at every turn by fountains or jets that sparkled in the moonlight or flashed in the sun. Why did he not carry out the fine conception of "The Poet":

"Dower'd with the hate of hate, the scorn of scorn,
  The love of love.
      *   *   *   *   *
  And bravely furnished all abroad to fling
  The winged shafts of truth,
  To throng with stately blooms the breathing spring
      Of Hope and Youth."

nor even in a catalogue. But when he appeared again before the public, his books had made their way alone and underground, and at the first bound he passed for the greatest poet of his country and his time."— (Taine, vol. iv. p. 432.) Mr. Tennyson's first publication was in 1830: his second in 1832: his third in 1842. As the first and second comprised many of the minor poems most distinctive of his genius, it would be curious to inquire to what change in the public mind it was owing that what was coldly or slightly received in 1830 and 1832 elicited such enthusiastic applause in 1842.

To realise a noble dream like this there must be a set purpose, an appointed goal, a comprehensive plan, an intense earnestness, a pride of genius which will not consent to be frittered away, which will not complacently accept exaggerated congratulations and applause even for the production of such charming specimens of the poetic art as "Œnone," "The Miller's Daughter," "A Dream of Fair Women," "Locksley Hall," or (a formidable rival to "Christabel") "The Lady of Shalott."

Most of Byron's poems were the result of a sudden inspiration, eagerly followed up: he struck, and continued striking, whilst the iron was hot. He never, like Pope, stopped waiting for his imagination for weeks; and he compared himself to the tiger, which, when the first spring fails, withdraws into the jungle with a growl. Mr. Tennyson leaves the impression of a diametrically opposite habit. We can conceive him working doggedly against the grain, and overlaying a description, a narrative, or a train of thought, which he had better have left as it originally suggested itself or left alone altogether. "The Palace of Art" is overdone; "The Two Voices" is weakened by dilution: the best of the "May Queen" is "The Conclusion"; and there are verses in "The Miller's Daughter" which, diffusely sentimental, ill-harmonise with such as these:

> "I loved the brimming wave that swam
>   Thro' quiet meadows round the mill,
> The sleepy pool above the dam,
>   The pool beneath it never still,
>
> "The meal-sacks on the whiten'd floor,
>   The dark round of the dripping wheel,
> The very air about the door
>   Made misty with the floating meal."

Amongst Byron's memoranda, we find: "What is Poetry? The feeling of a Former world and Future." This is inconsistent with his general theory. In one of his letters, he says, in allusion to Wordsworth, Coleridge, and Barry Cornwall, "The pity of these men is that they never lived in high life nor in solitude: there is no medium for their knowledge of the busy or the still world." In another, after declaring a strong passion to be the poetry of life, he asks: "What should I have known or written, had I been a quiet, mercantile politician or a lord in waiting?"

The highest quality of the highest genius is to dispense with exact knowledge of what it paints or shadows forth, to grasp distant ages by intuition like Shakespeare, or to pierce the empyrean with the mind's eye like Milton. But when a poet habitually mixes up his individuality with external objects, or draws largely on his own impressions and reminiscences, the tone of his poetry will necessarily be much influenced by his commerce with the world; and as Mr. Tennyson is fond of appearing in his own person in his works, he certainly lies under some disadvantage in this respect. He has never undergone the hard schooling of adversity: he has never stood with his household gods shattered round him: he has never been the mark of the public contumely. His bitterest complaint against the world is that the tourists have driven him from the Isle of Wight to Surrey: he has never (we are persuaded) been the slave of guilty passion, nor (we would fain hope) the heartbroken victim of female inconstancy. It is fortunate for him that he has not: but what his domestic life has gained in sobriety, his poetry has lost in intensity; and his voice is mild as the sucking dove's when he communes with Nature or rails against mankind. In "Locksley Hall," for example, the desperate resolution to retire to some island in the "shining Orient," partakes a little of the bathos :

> "There methinks would be enjoyment more than in this march of mind,
> In the steamship, in the railway, in the thoughts that shake mankind.
> There the passions cramp'd no longer shall have scope and breathing-space ;
> I will take some savage woman, she shall rear my dusky race.
> Iron-jointed, supple-sinew'd, they shall dive, and they shall run,
> Catch the wild goat by the hair, and hurl their lances in the sun ;
> Whistle back the parrot's call, and leap the rainbows of the brooks,
> Not with blinded eyesight poring over miserable books."

The parody is really little more than an imitation :

> "There the passions, cramp'd no longer, shall have space to breathe, my cousin ;
> I will take some savage woman—nay, I'll take at least a dozen.
> There I'll rear my young Mulattoes, as the bondslave brats are reared ;
> They shall dive for alligators, catch the wild goats by the beard,
> Whistle to the cockatoos, and mock the hairy-faced baboon,
> Worship mighty Mumbo Jumbo in the Mountains of the Moon."[1]

Laboured writing is liable to incongruities which are rarely, if ever, found in the impulsive and spontaneous. We raise no ornithological objec-

---

[1] "The Book of Ballads," edited by Bon Gaultier,—"The Lay of the Lovelorn."

tions to "The Dying Swan"; but, assuming the poem to be allegorical, surely the comparison to a mighty people rejoicing is out of keeping and overstrained:

> "The wild swan's death-hymn took the soul
> Of that waste place with joy
> Hidden in sorrow: at first to the ear
> The warble was low, and full and clear;
> And floating about the under-sky,
> Prevailing in weakness, the coronach stole
> Sometimes afar, and sometimes anear;
> But anon her awful jubilant voice,
> With a music strange and manifold,
> Flow'd forth on a carol free and bold:
> *As when a mighty people rejoice*
> *With shawms, and with cymbals, and harps of gold,*
> *And the tumult of their acclaim is roll'd*
> *Through the open gates of the city afar,*
> *To the shepherd who watched the evening star.*
> And the creeping mosses and clambering weeds,
> And the willow-branches hoar and dank,
> And the wavy swell of the soughing reeds,
> And the wave-worn horns of the echoing bank,
> And the silvery marish-flowers that throng
> The desolate creeks and pools among,
> Were flooded over with eddying song."

In one of the fine stanzas on Waterloo and the associated events in the Third Canto of "Childe Harold," as originally written, were these lines:

> "Here his last flight the haughty eagle flew,
> Then tore with bloody beak the fatal plain."

Reinagle sketched a chained eagle grasping the earth with its talons. On hearing this, Byron wrote to a friend, "Reinagle is a better poet and a better ornithologist than I am: eagles, and all birds of prey, attack with their talons, and not with their beaks, and I have altered the line thus:

"Then tore with bloody talon the rent plain."

"This is, I think, a better line, besides its poetical justice." Would Mr. Tennyson, on being assured, on the high authority of Mr. Gould, that swans never sing, be prepared to pay a similar tribute to poetical justice and truth?—or would he abide by the popular and time-honoured error?

When Byron (in "Don Juan") describes the career of a young noble and the life of May Fair, he writes *con amore* from personal knowledge of his subject, but when Mr. Tennyson takes us, in Will Waterproof's "Lyrical Monologue," to the "Cock" in Fleet Street, it is obvious that he has no acquaintance with the old waiter, and no real sympathy with the frequenters of the place. He is more at home in the drawing-room than the tavern, and the high-born coquette is admirably hit off:

"I know you, Clara Vere de Vere,
    You pine among your halls and towers;
The languid light of your proud eyes
    Is wearied of the rolling hours.
In glowing health, with boundless wealth,
    But sickening of a vague disease,
You know so ill to deal with Time,
    You needs must play such pranks as these.

"Clara, Clara Vere de Vere,
    If Time be heavy on your hands,
Are there no beggars at your gate,
    Nor any poor about your lands?
Oh! teach the orphan-boy to read,
    Or teach the orphan-girl to sew,
Pray Heaven for a human heart,
    And let the foolish yeoman go."

In graceful play and redundancy of fancy, Mr. Tennyson's "Mermen" and "Mermaid" rival Mercutio's Queen Mab:

> "I would be a merman bold:
>   I would sit and sing the whole of the day;
>   I would fill the sea-shells with a voice of power,
>   But at night I would roam abroad and play
> With the mermaids in and out of the rocks,
>   Dressing their hair with the white sea-flower,
> And holding them back by their flowing locks;
>
> I would kiss them often under the sea,
> And kiss them again till they kiss'd me—
>   Laughingly, laughingly.
> And then we would wander away, away,
> To the pale-green sea-groves straight and high,
>   Chasing each other merrily."

We see no harm in these submarine gambols; but exception might be taken, without an excess of prudishness, to "The Sisters," in which sensual passion is coarsely blended with the sense of injured honour and revenge:

> "I kiss'd his eyelids into rest:
> His ruddy cheek upon my breast.
>   The wind is raging in turret and tree.
> I hated him with the hate of hell,
> But I loved his beauty passing well—
>   O the earl was fair to see!"

We shall not differ much with Mr. Tennyson's discriminating admirers when we say that his fame might rest on "In Memoriam," like that of Petrarch on his Sonnets. It is wonderful,—the variety of shapes in which the living and breathing spirit blends with the departed; in how many moods and tones they hold colloquy beyond the grave; what wealth of imagery is brought to gild the thronging memories; how we are made to taste the full luxury of woe! The Muse evoked by "Il Penseroso" appears and reappears in her "sweetest, saddest plight"; different, yet the same. There is no iteration; and the surprise of novelty enhances the melancholy pleasure to the last. Compare, for example, the manner in which the individual grief is illustrated in No. VIII., beginning "A happy lover who has come," with the swelling tide of feeling and lofty prophetic spirit of CV. on Christmas Eve:

> "Ring out the grief that saps the mind,
>   For those that here we see no more;
> Ring out the feud of rich and poor,
>   Ring in redress to all mankind.
>
> "Ring out a slowly dying cause,
>   And ancient forms of party strife;
> Ring in the nobler modes of life,
>   With sweeter manners, purer laws.
>
> "Ring out the want, the care, the sin,
>   The faithless coldness of the times;
> Ring out, ring out my mournful rhymes,
>   But ring the fuller minstrel in."

Petrarch's Sonnets do not raise him to the level of Dante, Tasso, or Ariosto: the highest place in every branch of creative genius must be reserved for those who combine breadth and comprehensiveness of design with felicity of execution: who, in short, idealise on a grand scale; and Mr. Tennyson's historic or pre-historic fragments (like the "Morte d'Arthur" and "Sir Lancelot and Queen Guinevere") were compared to the studies of a painter like Leonardo da Vinci or Raphael preparing for the "Last Supper" or "The Transfiguration." It was probably to justify this hopeful and flattering comparison that he chose a larger canvas, concentrated his powers, and produced his more ambitious poems, "The Princess," "The Idylls of the King," and "The Holy Grail."

The Princess is entitled "A Medley"; and a medley it is of the most heterogeneous sort; in which poetry and prose, fact and fiction, science and romance, ancient and modern customs and modes of thinking, are flung together without blending; so as to resemble a Paris masquerade in which a crusader waltzes with a grisette, Henry the Fourth flirts with Marie Antoinette, and a Psyche who has lost her Cupid requests an animated milestone to escort her to the supper-room.

A beautiful Princess, betrothed to a beautiful Prince, is prematurely smitten with the now growing doctrine of woman's rights; and forswearing all thoughts of marriage, she founds a university, with female professors and 600 pupils, within whose pure precincts no male creature is to set foot under pain of death. The Prince, having obtained her royal father's permission to try his fortune in bringing her to reason, sets out with two friends, and arrives one fine evening at a rustic town close to the boundary of the liberties:

> "There enter'd an old hostel, call'd mine host
> To council, plied him with his richest wines,
> And show'd the late-writ letters of the king."

The host looked rather blank at first, but when, like the Governor in the "Critic," he was tempted with a pecuniary bribe—"A thousand pounds, there thou hast touched me nearly,"—he began to thaw:

> "'If the king,' he said,
> 'Had given us letters, was he bound to speak?

> The king would bear him out;' and at the last—
> The summer of the vine in all his veins—
> 'No doubt that we might make it worth his while.
> She once had past that way; he heard her speak;
> She scared him; life! he never saw the like;
> She look'd as grand as doomsday and as grave;
> And he, he reverenced his liege-lady there;
> *He always made a point to post with mares;* [1]
> His daughter and his housemaid were the boys:
> The land he understood for miles about
> Was till'd by women; *all the swine were sows,
> And all the dogs—*"
>   But while he jested thus,
> A thought flashed thro' me which I clothed in act,
> Remembering how we three presented Maid,
> Or Nymph, or Goddess, at high tide of feast,
> In masque or pageant at my father's court,
> We sent mine host to purchase female gear;
> He brought it, and himself, a sight to shake
> The midriff of despair with laughter, holp
> To lace us up, till, each in maiden plumes
> We rustled: him we gave a costly bribe
> To guerdon silence, mounted our good steeds,
> And boldly ventured on the liberties."

This is the plot, which is carried out in a poem of 183 pages, and, in refinement and delicacy, is quite in keeping with the old host's facetiousness. Three young gentlemen—one of whom is described as "of temper amorous, as the first of May"—are to be domesticated for an indefinite period in a female college, like Achilles in the court of Lycomedes; and—*honi soit qui mal y pense*—let no one, remembering his adventure with Deodamia, entertain or hint a suspicion of the consequences, or the Tennysonians will set him down for a

---

[1] Not a very delicate conceit; which may pair off with that of the lady who placed her male and female authors on different shelves. On being told this, Lord Lyndhurst remarked: "Probably she did not wish to add to her library."

Philistine. The trio are received with an appropriate address by the Princess:

> "At those high words, we conscious of ourselves
> Perused the matting; then an officer
> Rose up, and read the statutes, such as these:
> Not for three years to correspond with home;
> Not for three years to cross the liberties;
> Not for three years to speak with any men;
> And many more, which hastily subscribed,
> We enter'd on the boards: and 'Now,' she cried,
> 'Ye are green wood, see ye warp not. Look, our hall!
> Our statues! *not of those that men desire,*
> *Sleek Odalisques, or oracles of mode,*
> Nor stunted squaws of West or East; but she
> That taught the Sabine how to rule, and she
> The foundress of the Babylonian wall,
> The Carian Artemisia strong in war,
> The Rhodope, that built the pyramid,
> Clelia, Cornelia, with the Palmyrene
> That fought Aurelian, and the Roman brows
> Of Agrippina.'"

We remember the time when it was considered the depth of ill-breeding and bad taste to allude to Odalisques or Anonymas in good society, it being assumed that matrons and damsels of high degree were not aware of the existence of such a class. It is rather strange, therefore, that the Princess should be so familiar with male objects of desire. There is one line in the Princess's speech which does not sound or look like a verse:

> "Ye are green wood, see ye warp not. Look, our hall."

We have marked other lines in other places which we are equally unable to reconcile to either eye or ear as verses, *e.g.*:

> "For when the blood ran lustier in him again."
> * * * * *
> "His eyes glisten'd: she fancied, is it for me?"
> * * * * *

"Would she had drowned me in it, where'er it be."

* * * * *

"For agony, who was yet a living soul."

The undergraduates (including the new arrivals) attend lectures and listen to a discourse such as Mr. John Stuart Mill might have delivered on his favourite subject: to another that smacks of Darwin and Tyndall: to a third worthy of Lyall or Murchison. Between the lectures they converse with their fellow collegians on the topics that puzzled Milton's angels; and one of their pleasantest evening rambles ends thus :

> "And then we turn'd, we wound
> About the cliffs, the copses, out and in,
> Hammering and clinking, chattering stony names
> Of shale and hornblende, rag and trap and tuff,
> Amygdaloid and trachyte, till the Sun
> Grew broader toward his death and fell, and all
> The rosy heights came out above the lawns."

They transgress the boundary, and become aware that the University police includes Proctors and their attendant (in college phrase) Bulldogs.

> "Scarce had I ceased when from a tamarisk near
> Two Proctors leapt upon us, crying 'Names.'
>
> * * * * *
>
> They haled us to the Princess where she sat
> High in the hall: above her droop'd a lamp,
> And made the single jewel on her brow
> Burn like the mystic fire on a mast-head,
> Prophet of storm : a handmaid on each side
> Bow'd toward her, combing out her long black hair
> Damp from the river; and close behind her stood
> Eight daughters of the plough, stronger than men,
> Huge women blowzed with health, and wind, and rain,
> And labour. Each was like a Druid rock ;
> *Or like a spire of land that stands apart*
> *Cleft from the main, and wail'd about with mews.*"

The avowal of the intruders' sex leads to a scene of confusion—

> "And so she would have spoken, but there rose
> A hubbub in the court of half the maids
> Gather'd together: from the illumined hall
> Long lanes of splendour slanted o'er a press
> Of snowy shoulders, thick as herded ewes,
> And rainbow robes, and gems and gemlike eyes,
> And gold and golden heads; they to and fro
> Fluctuated, as flowers in storm, some red, some pale,
> All open-mouth'd, all gazing to the light,
> Some crying there was an army in the land,
> And some that men were in the very walls,
> *And some they cared not;* till a clamour grew
> As of a new-world Babel, woman-built,
> And worse-confounded: high above them stood
> The placid marble Muses, looking peace."

A companion picture to this has been painted by Byron in his description of the group of young ladies amongst whom Don Juan, disguised like the Prince, was unexpectedly introduced:

> "Many and beautiful lay those around,
>   Like flowers of different hue, and clime, and root,
> In some exotic garden sometimes found,
>   With cost, and care, and warmth induced to shoot.
> One with her auburn tresses lightly bound,
>   And fair brows gently drooping, as the fruit
> Nods from the tree, was slumbering with soft breath,
> And lips apart, which show'd the pearls beneath.

> "One with her flush'd cheek laid on her white arm,
>   And raven ringlets gather'd in dark crowd
> Above her brow, lay dreaming soft and warm;
>   And smiling through her dream, as through a cloud
> The moon breaks, half unveil'd each further charm,
>   As, slightly stirring in her snowy shroud,
> Her beauties seized the unconscious hour of night
> All bashfully to struggle into light.

"This is no bull, although it sounds so; for
  'Twas night, but there were lamps, as hath been said.
A third's all pallid aspect offer'd more
  The traits of sleeping sorrow, and betray'd
Through the heaved breast the dream of some far shore
  Beloved and deplored; while slowly stray'd
(As night-dew, on a cypress glittering, tinges
  The black bough) tear-drops through her eyes' dark
    fringes.
"A fourth as marble, statue-like and still,
  Lay in a breathless, hush'd, and stony sleep;
White, cold, and pure, as looks a frozen rill,
  Or the snow minaret on an Alpine steep."

In grouping, colouring, and expression, Byron's picture strikes us, to be decidedly the finer of the two. We need hardly say that there are many graceful flights of fancy, many pleasing bits of description, many happy epithets, many fine thoughts, scattered over "The Princess"; but the prosaic so predominates over the poetic element, that it fairly passes our comprehension how it ever passed muster as a whole. Byron certainly contrived to mix up an extraordinary variety of heterogeneous subjects in "Don Juan"; but "Don Juan" was composed in a mocking, laughing spirit: it runs over with wit and humour; and we should feel much obliged to any one who would point out either wit or humour in "The Princess."

These faults of subject and construction were carefully eschewed in "The Idylls of the King," published in 1859, which raised the author to the seventh heaven of popular favour. He was reported to have realised seven or eight thousand pounds by this small volume in a year. It was literally one which no library, drawing-room, or boudoir, could be without. It was the common topic of conversation amongst the higher classes;

and the votaries of the dainty artificial style in composition raised shouts of triumph at its undeniable success. The malcontents were obliged to hold their tongues, or murmured aside with Old King Gama in "The Princess":

> "These the women sang;
> And they that know such things—I sought but peace;
> No critic I—would call them masterpieces:
> They mastered me."

Fashion, we repeat, must always have a great deal to do with the popularity of any work of art that appeals to an acquired taste and affects independence of the ordinary sources of interest. Canning said that whoever pretended to prefer dry champagne to sweet, lied. This was going a little too far; but the preference is confined to a limited circle of connoisseurs with educated palates; and those who honestly prefer blank verse to rhyme are not more numerous than those who honestly prefer dry champagne to sweet. Then, again, Mr. Tennyson's tales of chivalry had none of the attractiveness of Scott's. The main narrative in each would merely have formed an episode in the genuine epic or regular romance. Although drawn from the same repository of traditional lore, and steeped in the same carefully-prepared dye, "The Idylls," four in number, look like so many pieces of rich tapestry, worked after a pattern for separate panels. The more we study them, the more forcibly are we impressed with the fertility of the author's fancy, the purity and elevation of his general tone of mind, his insight into the best parts of human nature, his comparative ignorance of the worst, and the poverty of his inventive faculty in constructing or embellishing a fictitious narrative. Surely the adventures that befell

Geraint and Enid, when she is undergoing her trials, might have been varied with advantage. Her first transgression of his strict command to precede him without speaking, is caused by the discovery of three knights in ambush. These, duly warned by her, he slays, strips of their armour, binds it on their horses, each on each,

> "And tied the bridle-reins of all the three
> Together, and said to her, 'Drive them on
> Before you;' and she drove them thro' the waste."

Her second transgression occurs exactly in the same manner. She gives timely notice of three lurking robbers, and identically the same action is repeated. He kills them all, binds their armour on their horses, and issues exactly the same order to the uncomplaining wife:

> "He follow'd nearer still: the pain she had
> To keep them in the wild ways of the wood,
> Two sets of three laden with jingling arms,
> Together, served a little to disedge
> The sharpness of that pain about her heart."

He has a third encounter with an entire troop, whom he disperses with equal ease, after unhorsing their leader; and when he is supposed dying from his wounds, with his head in Enid's lap, he is suddenly roused by her sharp and bitter cry against an insult offered her by his enemy:

> "This heard Geraint, and grasping at his sword,
> (It lay beside him in the hollow shield),
> Made but a single bound, and with a sweep of it
> Shore thro' the swarthy neck, and like a ball
> The russet-bearded head roll'd on the floor.
> So died Earl Doorm by him he counted dead."

We are content to read tales of chivalry in the same spirit as "Don Quixote." A knight of the

Round Table (or the Table Round, as the exigencies of verse require it to be called throughout) would not be worth his salt if he could not demolish any number of assailants by his single arm, or cut off a giant's head at a sweep; but we cannot help thinking that "Enid's" task was beyond her strength, and that more appropriate and more original machinery might have been hit upon to place in broad relief the depth, purity, humility, and devotedness of a true woman's love, which we take to be the intended moral of "Enid." There is hardly an incident in the combats which may not have been suggested by "Ivanhoe." The lances of the assailants splinter against the breast of Geraint, as they splintered against the breast of Richard in Sherwood Forest; and Geraint sinks down, from the effects of a concealed wound, like Ivanhoe.

This is repeated in "Elaine," where Lancelot is similarly wounded in the *mêlée*, and leaves the field (like the Black Knight) without claiming the prize. But in the development of fine feeling, relieved by natural weakness, "Elaine" is unsurpassed. It was a difficult and delicate subject,— the unresisted sway of an unrequited passion over a pure-minded girl, the slave of her imagination and her heart, who falls in love with Lancelot, as Desdemona fell in love with Othello, for the deeds he had done and the soul that beamed in his face:

> "He spoke and ceased : the lily maid Elaine,
> Won by the mellow voice before she look'd,
> Lifted her eyes, and read his lineaments.
> The great and guilty love he bare the Queen,
> In battle with the love he bare his lord,
> Had marr'd his face, and mark'd it ere his time.
> Another sinning on such heights with one,
> The flower of all the west and all the world,

> Had been the sleeker for it: but in him
> His mood was often like a fiend, and rose
> And drove him into wastes and solitudes
> For agony, who was yet a living soul.
> Marr'd as he was, he seem'd the goodliest man,
> That ever among ladies ate in Hall,
> And noblest, when she lifted up her eyes.
> However marr'd, of more than twice her years,
> Seam'd with an ancient swordcut on the cheek,
> And bruised and bronzed, she lifted up her eyes
> And loved him, with that love which was her doom."

It is the conventional thing for a damsel never to tell her love, but "let concealment, like a worm i' the bud, feed on her damask cheek." Elaine does tell her love, and no sullying thought or suspicion is awakened by her burst of uncontrollable self-sacrificing tenderness:

> "Then suddenly and passionately she spoke:
> 'I have gone mad. I love you: let me die.'
> 'Ah, sister,' answer'd Lancelot, 'what is this?'
> And innocently extending her white arms,
> 'Your love,' she said, 'your love—to be your wife.'
> And Lancelot answer'd, 'Had I chos'n to wed,
> I had been wedded earlier, sweet Elaine:
> But now there never will be wife of mine.'
> 'No, no,' she cried, 'I care not to be wife,
> But to be with you still, to see your face,
> To serve you, and to follow you thro' the world.'"

Lancelot's gentle words, soothing and flattering, but chilling and withering, prove her death-blow. She dies, after lingering through some touching pages, of that rare and (some think) apocryphal disease, a broken heart; and her image on her bier has taken permanent rank, in painting and poetry, with that of Ophelia floating down the brook:

> "In her right hand the lily, in her left
> The letter—all her bright hair streaming down—

> And all the coverlid was cloth of gold
> Drawn to her waist, and she herself in white
> All but her face, and that clear-featured face
> Was lovely, for she did not seem as dead
> But fast asleep, and lay as tho' she smiled."

The mixed emotions of Lancelot, and the Queen's jealous forebodings, equally exhibit the poet's mastery of the springs of thought and action; and we are almost tempted to ask why is not "Elaine" a chapter of a great drama or epic, with unity of action, a beginning, a middle, and an end? in which all the incidents should have a bearing on the plot, and all the characters should co-operate towards one common object of interest. Why are we eternally tantalised with specimens or fragments of a never-to-be-completed whole? Is it the power that is wanting, or the will? or is the will ever wanting where there consciously and indisputably exists the power?

The absence or limited quality of creative genius in Mr. Tennyson is thus mentioned by M. Taine:

> "He is born a poet, that is, a builder of aerial palaces and imaginary castles. But the personal passion, and the absorbing pre-occupations which ordinarily master the hand of his peers, have failed him: he has not formed the plan of a new edifice in himself: he has built after all the others: he has simply chosen amongst the most elegant forms, the most ornate, the most exquisite. The utmost that can be said is that he has amused himself in arranging some cottage, thoroughly English and modern. If, in this recovered or renewed architecture, we look for the trace of him, we shall find it here and there in some frieze more finely sculptured, in some more delicate and graceful rosette; but we shall not find it marked and clear, except in the purity and elevation of the moral emotion that we shall carry away on leaving his museum."

The chronological succession of Mr. Tennyson's

Arthurian poems, or parts of poems, proves that he never conceived or comprehended the Arthurian period as a whole. The "Morte d'Arthur" was amongst his earlier productions: "The Coming of Arthur" (including the birth and marriage) amongst his last. He seems to have picked out a legend here and there as he wanted one for a subject, without regarding its connection with the rest.

"Guinevere" is not even a short act of a drama. It consists of two scenes: one, in which the guilty Queen gives utterance to grief and repentance, mingled with bitter anger at those whose evil tongues and malice had brought her to shame: a second, in which the blameless King pardons and utters a parting blessing over her. Both are replete with pathos and tenderness, with noble thoughts, with the purest essence of Christian charity and love; and the morality that breathes through them is in parts etherealised and sublimated till it becomes poetry. Thus, in the institution of the Round Table:

> "I made them lay their hands in mine and swear
> To reverence the King, as if he were
> Their conscience, and their conscience as their King.
> To break the heathen and uphold the Christ,
> To ride abroad redressing human wrongs,
> To speak no slander, no, nor listen to it,
> To lead sweet lives in purest chastity,
> To love one maiden only, cleave to her,
> And worship her by years of noble deeds,
> Until they won her; for indeed I know
> Of no more subtle master under heaven
> Than is the maiden passion for a maid,
> Not only to keep down the base in man,
> But teach high thought, and amiable words
> And courtliness, and the desire of fame,
> And love of truth, and all that makes a man."

The figure of the King is Miltonic in its shadowy awe-inspiring outline as he moves off:

> "And more and more
> The moony vapour rolling round the King
> Who seem'd the phantom of a Giant in it,
> Enwound him fold by fold, and made him gray
> And grayer, till himself became as mist
> Before her, moving ghost-like to his doom.

Poor Guinevere's best excuse for her infidelity to the blameless King was that he was too good for her:

> "I thought I could not breathe in that pure air,
> That pure serenity of perfect light,
> I wanted warmth and colour which I found
> In Lancelot."

It is to be feared that many readers have felt like Guinevere; and (we speak from actual observation) when dame or damsel is seen deep in ".The Idylls," a peep over the shoulder too frequently betrays the fact that it is "Vivien" on whom the absorbing interest is fixed—"the lissome, wanton Vivien," who exerts all her pretty tricks and cajoleries to make a fool of old Merlin, and learn his charm "of woven paces and of waving hands":

> "'O Merlin, do you love me?' and again,
> 'O Merlin, do you love me?' and once more,
> 'Great Master, do you love me?' he was mute.
> And lissome Vivien, holding by his heel,
> Writhed toward him, slided up his knee and sat,
> Behind his ankle twined her hollow feet
> Together, curved an arm about his neck,
> Clung like a snake; and letting her left hand
> Droop from his mighty shoulder, as a leaf,
> Made with her right a comb of pearl to part
> The lists of such a beard as youth gone out
> Had left in ashes."

On her offering to swear that she would never use the charm against himself, he suggests—

> "You might perhaps
> Essay it on some one of the Table Round,
> And all because you dream they babble of you."

Then the vixen flares out:

> "And Vivien, frowning in true anger, said:
> 'What dare the full-fed liars say of me?
> *They* ride abroad redressing human wrongs!
> They sit with knife in meat and wine in horn.
> *They* bound to holy vows of chastity!
> Were I not woman, I could tell a tale.
> But you are man, you well can understand
> The shame that cannot be explain'd for shame.
> Not one of all the drove should touch me: swine!'"

On his challenging her for proof, she retails an amount of current scandal, touching the knights and their ladye loves, confirmatory of Byron's theory that they were no better than they should be, and leading to the conclusion that the blameless King's Court had points in common with that of Charles II.:

> "And Vivien answer'd frowning wrathfully.
> 'O ay, what say ye to Sir Valence, him
> Whose kinsman left him watcher o'er his wife
> And two fair babes, and went to distant lands;
> Was one year gone, and on returning found
> Not two but three: there lay the reckling, one
> But one hour old! What said the happy sire?
> A seven months' babe had been a truer gift.
> Those twelve sweet moons confused his fatherhood.'"

On Merlin's endeavouring to explain this away:

> "'O ay,' said Vivien, 'overtrue a tale.
> What say ye then to sweet Sir Sagramore,
> That ardent man? "to pluck the flower in season,"

So says the song, "I trow it is no treason."
O Master, shall we call him overquick
To crop his own sweet rose before the hour?'"

Then there is a story of Sir Percivale:

"What say ye then to fair Sir Percivale
And of the horrid foulness that he wrought;
The saintly youth, the spotless lamb of Christ,
Or some black wether of St. Satan's fold?
What in the precincts of the chapel yard,
Among the knightly brasses of the graves,
And by the cold Hic Jacets of the dead!"

Well chosen topics for a maid-of-honour's mouth! She crowns all by the affair of Lancelot with the Queen, which sets Merlin meditating:

"But Vivien deeming Merlin overborne
By instance, recommenced, and let her tongue
Rage like a fire among the noblest names,
Polluting, and imputing, her whole self,
Defaming and defacing, till she left
Not even Lancelot brave, nor Galahad clean."

She triumphs in a scene resembling that between Dido and Æneas in the cave:

"Then crying, I have made his glory mine,
And shrieking out, 'O fool!' the harlot leapt
Adown the forest, and the thicket closed
Behind her, and the forest echo'd 'fool.'"

Taken all in all, it strikes us that this poem is quite as objectionable as "Don Juan," and that Vivien's conversation is not more edifying than Julia's letter, whilst in point of feminine delicacy she is decidedly inferior to Haidee.

There is a once popular novel, entitled "Ellen Wareham," by Mrs. Sullivan, in which a woman, believing her first husband (forced on her by her parents) to have died abroad, marries the man of her heart, has a family by him, and is living happily, when the first husband unexpectedly presents himself to insist upon his conjugal rights. There is a more remarkable novel, entitled "André," by George Sand, in which the hero, finding that his young wife, to whom he is devotedly attached, would rather be the wife of a friend, quietly starts for Switzerland and tumbles into a glacier in a way to exclude all suspicion of his having committed suicide to set her free. Mr. Tennyson's "Enoch Arden" is a husband of an intermediate quality between these two. On finding, on his return after a ten years' absence, that his wife has committed bigamy, he neither interferes with her domestic arrangements, nor sets her free till he dies a natural death; when, by way of consolation, she receives a deathbed message to tell her what he has suffered through her fault. His story is made the vehicle for fifty pages of blank verse. There is a fine passage (p. 32) about the island in which Enoch passes a Robinson Crusoe kind of life: there are touches of pathos and bits of poetical description interspersed; but these do not occur often enough to animate the whole, nor to suppress the doubt whether a story, which could be better told in prose, is to take rank as a standard poem on the strength of that manipulation and inversion of language which are now held to constitute blank verse.

We pass over "Maude," "The Holy Grail," etc., etc., as we have passed over "Mazeppa," "Cain," "Marino Faliero," "Sardanapalus," "Werner," and the whole of Byron's minor poems, which would make the reputation of half-a-dozen minor poets of our time, and to spare. We call attention to salient points, to grand features. Strike, but hear: pronounce, but read. Let any real lover of fine poetry, who does not freshly remember them, read once again the Third and Fourth Cantos of "Childe Harold," and then say in what class or category the author is to be placed. It is in the ordinary course of things that the popular taste should veer about: that reputation should follow reputation as star chases star across the sky; and a name with innate buoyancy, if accidentally submerged, may commonly be trusted to rise unaided to the surface and float on with the rest. But it will rise the sooner, if relieved from all adventitious weight; and the weight of prejudice by which Byron's is kept down, has grown with foreign critics into a set topic of national reproach. Goethe pointedly contrasted the dirt and rubbish flung at the noble poet with the glory he had reflected on his country, "boundless in its splendour and incalculable in its consequences."

"Having now," concludes Herr Elze, "traced the literary and political influence of Byron from the southern extremity of the earth to its north-eastern boundary, we come back to his native land, where his influence has hitherto been least, where moral and religious illiberality still stands in the way of an unprejudiced estimation." He thinks that this "blinding bigotry" cannot go further without producing a reaction, and he discerns, or fancies he discerns, a turning-point. There is at all events a standing-point, from which the lever which will restore the balance may be worked. There is a compact body of sound, ripe, critical opinion in this country that has never wavered, and on its sure, if slow, expansion we confidently rely.

NOTE.—A marked change has taken place since this was written. Readers who do not remember the state of the public mind ten years ago will probably be surprised to hear that any vindication was required.

THE REPUBLIC OF VENICE:
ITS RISE, DECLINE, AND FALL.[1]
(*From the Quarterly Review, October*, 1874).

Marc Antonio Barbaro was a Venetian noble of illustrious birth, who filled successively each of the highest offices in the Republic, with the exception of the Dogeship, which he narrowly missed. He was born in 1518 and died in 1595; and adopting him as the type of the patrician of the sixteenth century, the author of the book before us has undertaken to connect or associate with his career a full description of the laws, customs, manners, and policy of the Queen of the Adriatic in the height of her prosperity and the fulness of her pride. Thus, à *propos* of Barbaro's rank, we are treated to a sketch of the patrician order, with its privileges: on his marriage, to a disquisition on Venetian women. His nomination to an embassy suggests the fertile topic of diplomacy; while his candidature for the Dogeship gives occasion for a complete account of this exalted office with its attributes. The conception is ingenious, and the execution leaves little to desire as regards learning, critical acuteness and discriminating research.

[1] *La Vie d'un Patricien de Venise au Seizième Siècle.—Les Doges—La Charte Ducale—Les Femmes à Venise—L'Université de Padoue Les Préliminaires de Lépante*, etc., *d'après les Papiers d'Etat des Archives de Venise.* Par Charles Yriarte. Paris, 1874.

The tone, spirit, and intention of the work are excellent: but it wants life, light, colour, and illustration. The Patrician, instead of being, as we fondly hoped, the centre of a series of animated groups, is too frequently treated as a peg on which dissertations and descriptions might be hung. Except in two or three episodes of his career, he is little better than a lay figure, slenderly draped, without expression or individuality; and as for the romance, poetry, mystery, dramatic or melodramatic interest, traditionally blended with Venetian annals, M. Yriarte's pages are as free from them as if the people under consideration were the prosaic, matter-of-fact Dutch. Yet there is scarcely a prominent incident or turning-point in those annals which does not read more like a fiction than a fact; and so obscurely grand is the subject, that the simplest preface or introduction brings the imaginative faculty into play.

"In the northern angle of the Adriatic is a gulf, called *lagune*, in which more than sixty islands of sand, marsh, and sea-weed have been formed by a concurrence of natural causes. These islands have become the City of Venice, which has lorded it over Italy, conquered Constantinople, resisted a league of all the Kings of Christendom, long carried on the commerce of the world, and bequeathed to nations the model of the most stable government ever framed by man."[1] These are the reflections with which Count Daru introduces his carefully finished and well-proportioned picture of the Republic in all the vicissitudes of her fortunes. The fresh materials accumulated by recent explorers of her archives have rather stimulated than

---

[1] "Histoire de la République de Venise," &c. Par P. Daru, de l'Académie Française. Seconde édition, revue et corrigée. Paris, 1821. In eight vols.

allayed curiosity.[1] She is still vaguely known and imperfectly understood; and we propose, with M. Yriarte's aid, to call attention to such passages in her history and peculiarities in her institutions, as may help to solve the social and political problems presented by them. We shall also show, as we proceed, how far the leading works of fiction of which the scenes are laid in Venice, agree or disagree with the facts.

The islands of the lagune could hardly be said to be inhabited, being merely used as places of occasional resort by fishermen, until towards the end of the fourth or the beginning of the fifth century, when a settled population began to be formed of refugees:

"A few in fear,
Flying away from him whose boast it was
That the grass grew not where his horse had trod,
Gave birth to Venice. Like the waterfowl,
They built their nests among the ocean waves." [2]

The oldest document extant relating to Venetian history, is a decree of the Senate of Padua, A.D.

---

[1] An enduring debt of gratitude is owing from all recent students of Venetian history to M. Armand Baschet. We particularly refer to "Les Archives de Venise, Histoire de la Chancellerie Secrète, &c., par Armand Baschet. Paris, Henri Plon, l'imprimeur-éditeur, Rue Garancière, 1870": a book full of curious information and interesting details. Mr. Rawdon Brown's discriminating researches in the same field are well known.

[2] Rogers's "Italy." These lines are paraphrased, without acknowledgment, from Gibbon. "It is a saying worthy of the ferocious pride of Attila, that the grass never grew on the spot where his horse had trod. Yet the savage destroyer undesignedly laid the foundations of a republic which revived, in the feudal state of Europe, the art and spirit of commercial industry. . . . The minister of Theodoric compares them, in his quaint declamatory style, to waterfowl who had fixed their nests on the bosom of the waves."—("Decline and Fall," chap. xxxv.) In his "Italy," Rogers has throughout treated the historians and chroniclers as Byron accuses "sepulchral Grahame" of having treated the scriptural writers:

"Breaks into blank the Gospel of St. Luke,
And boldly pilfers from the Pentateuch."

421, ordering the construction of a town on Rialto, the largest of the isles, with the view of bringing together in a single community the scattered inhabitants of the rest for the purposes of mutual protection and support. They appear to have been left free to choose their own form of government; for we find that each island had at first its own magistrate: the magistrates of the most considerable being called Tribunes Major, the others, Tribunes Minor, and the whole being equally subject to the council-general of the community; which thus constituted a kind of federal republic.

This lasted nearly 300 years, when it was found that the rising nation had fairly outgrown its institutions. Dangerous rivalries arose among the tribunes. Their divided authority weakened the common action, and their administration became a general subject of complaint. At a meeting of the Council-General, A.D. 697, the Patriarch of Grado proposed the concentration of power in the hands of a single chief, under the title of Doge or Duke. The proposition was eagerly accepted, and they proceeded at once to the election of this chief. "It will be seen (remarks Daru) that the Dogeship saved independence and compromised liberty. It was a veritable revolution, but we are ignorant by what circumstances it was brought about. Many historians assert that the change was not effected till the permission of the Pope and the Emperor was obtained."

The first choice fell on Paolo Luca Anabesto. It was made by twelve electors, the founders of what were thenceforth termed the electoral families.[1] The Doge was appointed for life: he

[1] Badonari, Barozzi, Contarini, Dandoli, Falieri, Gradenighi, Memmi otherwise Monegari, Michielli, Morosini, Polani, Sanudi otherwise Candiani, Thiepoli. All are extinct.

named his own counsellors: took charge of all public business; had the rank of prince, and decided all questions of peace and war. The peculiar title was meant to imply a limited sovereignty, and the Venetians uniformly repudiated, as a disgrace, the bare notion of their having ever submitted to a monarch. But many centuries passed away before any regular or well-defined limits were practically imposed; and the prolonged struggle between the people and the Doges, depending mainly on the personal character of the Doge for the time being, constitutes the most startling and exciting portion of their history.

The first Doge proved a wise and sagacious ruler. He reigned twenty years. The second, Marcello Tegaliano, did equally well. The third, Urso, elected in 726, was restless and ambitious. He seized the first opportunity to engage in warlike operations, and it was under him that the Venetians made their first essay as a military power by land. He took Ravenna by assault, and based such pretensions on his victory, that, after Heraclea (then the capital) had been distracted and split into factions for two years, the people rose, forced their way into his palace, and cut his throat. He had reigned eleven years; long enough to sicken them of Doges for the nonce, so, not wishing to revert to tribunes, they appointed a chief magistrate to be elected annually, under the title of *maestro della milizia*. Five such magistrates were named, and ruled in succession, when the institution came to an untimely end with the fifth. For some unexplained reason or from caprice, the populace rose again, deposed him, and put out his eyes. The Dogeship was then restored in the person of Theodal Urso (son of the last Doge), who quitted Heraclea for Malamocco, which thus became the capital. Unluckily he excited suspicion by constructing a fort at the mouth of the Adige; and a demagogue, named Galba, got a troop of armed men together, fell upon him as he was returning from the works, and subjected him to the same treatment as his predecessor in the magistracy. It thenceforth became the received custom in Venice to put out the eyes of deposed Doges; and Galba, who had contrived to usurp the sovereignty, and hold it for eleven years, found himself deposed, blinded, and an exile in the end.

The next but one obtained such an amount of popularity that he was enabled to get his son Giovanni associated with him in the ducal dignity, which ran considerable risk of becoming hereditary; for Giovanni had *his* son, Maurice, similarly nominated, and the descent might have continued unbroken had they conducted themselves with common prudence or decency. But no sooner were they firmly established, than both father and son threw off the mask, and rivalled each other in the worst and most insulting forms of tyranny, cruelty, and profligacy. A conspiracy was formed. The Emperor Charlemagne and the Pope threatened to interfere; and eventually Giovanni and Maurice, having sought safety in flight, Obelerio, the head of the conspiracy, was proclaimed Doge.

This was in 804. The events of the next five years are involved in obscurity. One thing is clear. Pepin, King of the Lombards, either under the pretence of a request for aid from the new Doge or to enforce some real or assumed rights of his own, declared war against the Republic, and waged it with such impetuosity that his fleet and army, after carrying all before them, were only separated from Malamocco, the capital, by a canal. In this emergency, Angelo Participazio, one of those men who are produced by great occasions to mark an era, proposed that the entire population should remove to Rialto, which was separated by a broader arm of the sea from the enemy, and there hold out to the last. No sooner proposed than done. They hastily embarked their all; and when Pepin entered Malamocco, he found it deserted. After losing a large part of his fleet in an ill-advised attack on Rialto, he gave up the enterprise, and Angelo Participazo was elected Doge in recognition of his services, with two tribunes for counsellors.

One of his first acts was to make Rialto the capital, instead of Malamocco or Heraclea, which had each been the seat of Government at intervals. "There were round Rialto some sixty islets, which the Doge connected by bridges. They were soon covered with houses. They were girt with a fortification; and it was then that this population of fugitives gave to this rising city, which they had just founded in the middle of a morass, the name of Venetia, in memory of the fair countries from which their fathers had been forcibly expatriated. The province has lost its name, and become subject to the new Venice."[1]

This public-spirited Doge could not resist the temptation of perpetuating the dignity in his race. He had two sons, Justinian and John: and during the absence of the eldest on an embassy, he, of his own mere motion and authority, made the youngest co-ruler with himself. But so vehement were the remonstrances of the elder, backed by public opinion, that the junior renounced in favour of the senior, who, moreover, contrived to make his own son Angelo a co-partner, so that the Republic was actually subjected to a

[1] Daru, vol. i. p. 79. There are 72 islands connected by between 350 and 400 bridges.

triumvirate belonging to three generations. The grandson died first, and the son becoming sole Doge by the death of the father in 872, generously shared his power with the brother who had been superseded to make room for him. The most remarkable event in their joint reign was the translation of the body of St. Mark, and the adoption of that saint as the patron saint of the Republic. The original story, as related by the oldest of the Venetian chroniclers, runs thus:

"The King of Alexandria, who was building a magnificent palace, had ordered the most precious marbles to be procured, without sparing even the churches. That of Saint Mark was not excepted, and two holy men, Greek priests, who had the care of it, were groaning over the threatened profanation, when two Venetians, captains of vessels in the port, observed and asked the cause of their distress. On ascertaining it, they pressed to be entrusted with the body of Saint Mark, pledging themselves for its befitting reception by their countrymen. The priests refused till the work of demolition began, then they consented; but it was necessary to keep the transaction secret from the people, who had a great veneration for the remains on account of the daily miracles they worked. The priests carefully cut open the envelope in which the remains were wrapped, and substituted the body of Saint Claudian. Such a perfume was instantly diffused through the Church, and even in the neighbouring places, that the crowd collected about the sacred reliques. There remained the difficulty of conveying them to the ship.

"The historians would not be believed if there was not still to be seen in our Church of Saint Mark a marvellous image which attests the fact. They placed the corpse in a large basket covered with herbs and swine's flesh which the Mussulmans hold in horror, and the bearers were directed to cry *Khawzir* (pork) to all who should ask questions or approach to şearch. In this manner they reached the vessel. The body was enveloped in the sails and suspended to the mainmast till the moment of departure, for it was necessary to conceal this precious booty from those who might come to clear the vessel in the roads. At last the Venetians quitted the shore full of joy. They were hardly in the open sea when a great storm arose. We are assured that Saint Mark then appeared to the captain and warned him to strike all his sails immediately, lest the ship, driven before the wind, should be wrecked upon the hidden rocks. They owed their safety to this miracle."

The arrival of these sacred remains was the signal for a succession of fêtes. The people were wild with enthusiasm, the general belief being that the presence of the Saint guaranteed the lasting prosperity of the Republic; and on many trying occasions this belief or superstition, by inspiring confidence, proved a genuine source of strength. Many a time has the cry of *Viva San Marco* revived the drooping courage of the Venetians when powerful States and monarchs were leagued for their destruction: many a time has it kept them true to their banner on battle-fields strewn with their dead. Yet far from relying exclusively on their patron saint, they established fêtes and ceremonies in honour of several others; and failing to induce the lawful possessors of the body of a much venerated one, Saint Tarasio, to part with it on reasonable terms, they resorted to the strong measure of stealing it, like the old lady mentioned by Fielding, who stole Tillotson's sermons for the sake of religion.[1] The objects of plunder most in request at the sack of Constantinople, in 1204, were the relics; and it is recorded that the Doge Dandolo transmitted (*inter alia*) to Venice a portion of the true Cross, an arm of Saint George, part of the skull of Saint John the Baptist, the bodies of Saint Luke and Saint Simeon, a phial of the Blood

---

[1] "Amongst the pieces of good fortune which increased the reputation of the new Venice in all the Christian world, as well as in the other, was the acquisition of the body of St. Tarasio, stolen from a convent of monks, who refused to sell or part with it."—*Marin*, quoted by *Daru*.

of Christ, a fragment of the pillar at which He was scourged, and a prickle of the Crown of Thorns. The only monuments of art deemed worth transporting were the famous bronze horses.

Another notable epoch in early Venetian history is the grant on which she based her claim to the sovereignty of the Adriatic. In the course of the fierce struggle between Alexander III. and Frederic Barbarossa, the Pope, when his fortunes were at the lowest, took refuge with the Venetians, who, after a vain effort at reconciliation, made common cause with him, and in a naval encounter obtained so signal a victory that the Emperor was compelled to sue for peace and submit to the most humiliating terms. The crowning scene of his degradation has been rendered familiar by the pencil, the chisel, and the pen.

Before entering Venice he was met by six cardinals, who received his oath of submission, gave him absolution, and reconciled him with the Church. He was then conducted by a procession of priests to the Place St. Mark, where, at the door of the cathedral, sat his Holiness, arrayed in his pontifical robes, surrounded by cardinals, prelates, representatives of foreign Powers, and high officers of state. The Emperor, as soon as he came into the sacred presence, stripped off his mantle and knelt down before the Pope to kiss his feet. Alexander, intoxicated with his triumph and losing all sense of moderation or generosity, placed his foot on the head or neck of his prostrate enemy, exclaiming, in the words of the Psalmist, "*Super aspidem et basiliscum ambulabis*" etc. ("Thou shalt tread upon the asp and the basilisk: the lion and the dragon shalt thou trample under foot"). "*Non tibi, sed Petro*" ("Not to thee, but Peter"), cried the outraged and indignant Emperor. "*Et mihi et Petro*" ("To both me and Peter"), rejoined the Pope, with a fresh pressure of his heel.[1]

In return for the good offices of Venice on this occasion, the Pope conferred on the Doges the privilege of being preceded by a lighted taper, a sword, a parasol, a chair of state, a cushion of cloth of gold, banners, and two trumpets. In addition to these barren marks of dignity, Alexander presented the reigning Doge, Ziani, with a ring, saying, "Receive this ring, and with it, as my donation, the dominion of the sea, which you, and your successors, shall annually assert on an appointed day, so that all posterity may understand that the possession of the sea was yours by right of victory, and that it is subject to the rule of the Venetian Republic, as wife to husband."[2]

The Republic ruled the Adriatic (so long as she did rule it) much as Britannia rules the waves—by dint of naval superiority. Her right was stoutly resisted by the other maritime Powers of Italy, especially by the Neapolitans and Genoese; and its real nature was virtually admitted by the celebrated reply of the Venetian ambassador to

---

[1] The spot on which this scene took place was indicated by a marble slab with an inscription in brass:

". . . . in that temple-porch
Did Barbarossa fling his mantle off,
And, kneeling, on his neck received the foot
Of the proud pontiff."

Sismondi (following a contemporary chronicler) narrates the interview without any circumstance of insult, and describes it as concluding with the kiss of peace. There are writers who contend that Alexander was never at Venice, and that the Venetians obtained no victory on his behalf. But the weight of evidence adduced by Daru strikes us to be quite conclusive in favour of his version.

[2] The reported words, which hardly admit of a literal translation, run thus:— "Hunc annulum accipe et, me auctore, ipsum mare obnoxium tibi redditum; quod tu tuique successores quotannis statuto die servabistis; ut omnis posteritas intelligat maris possessionem victoriæ jure vestram fuisse, atque uti uxorem viro, ita illud imperio reipublicæ Venetæ subjectum."

Julius II., when asked where the deed or instrument containing the concession was to be found: "On the back of the grant of the domain of St. Peter by Constantine to Pope Sylvester."

The well-known ceremony of wedding the Adriatic, religiously observed with all its original pomp and splendour during six centuries, was in itself a proclamation and a challenge to the world. It was regularly attended by the papal nuncio and the whole of the diplomatic corps, who, year after year, witnessed the dropping of a sanctified ring into the sea, and heard without a protest the prescriptive accompaniment: *Desponsamus te, mare, in signum veri perpetuique domini* (We espouse thee, sea, in sign of true and perpetual dominion).

> "The spouseless Adriatic mourns her lord,
> And annual marriage now no more renewed;
> The Bucentaur lies rotting unrestor'd
> Neglected garment of her widowhood."

The last Bucentaur, a splendidly-gilt and equipped galley, had been repaired or renewed till the identity might have been made a topic of metaphysical dispute like that of Sir John Cutler's stockings in "Martinus Scriblerus;" but it could hardly have lain rotting when Childe Harold mourned or philosophised over its departed glories, for it was broken up in 1797 by the French.

> "In youth she was all glory,—a new Tyre,
> Her very byeword sprung from victory,
> The 'Planter of the Lion,'[1] which through fire
> And blood she bore o'er subject earth and sea."

Historians have failed or omitted to fix the precise period when this ensign of the lion was

---

[1] "*Plant the Lion*, that is, the Lion of St. Mark, the standard of the Republic, which is the origin of the word pantaloon—pianta-leone, pantalcon, pantaloon."

first adopted by the Republic. But when the two granite columns, still the conspicuous ornaments of the Piazetta of St. Mark, were erected in or about 1172, a winged lion in bronze was placed on one of them, and a statue of St. Theodore, a patron of earlier standing, on the other. These columns, trophies of a successful raid in the Archipelago, had remained prostrate on the quay for more than fifty years, the engineering difficulty of raising them being pronounced insuperable, when a Lombard architect undertook the task, stipulating that he should name his own recompense if he succeeded. Nothing is known of his method except that he wetted the ropes. The recompense he claimed was that games of chance, then prohibited by severe penalties, might be played in the space between the columns. The authorities kept faith, and this anomaly was tolerated for more than four centuries, when it was removed by another and (many will think) a worse. The same locality was devoted to capital executions; so that, rather than break an obsolete pledge, or discontinue a time-honoured custom, these grave and reverend signors established the frequently recurring spectacle of dead or dying malefactors hanging by one leg in the principal square of their city under the windows of their chief magistrate.

Another ceremony, "The Brides of Venice," deeply tinged with romance and celebrated in song, carries us back to a still remoter period, when it was the custom for the marriages of the principal citizens to be celebrated together in the patriarchal church of San Pietro di Castello on the eve of the feast of the Purification:

> "Two and two
> The richest tapestry unrolled before them,
> First came the brides, each in her virgin veil,

> Nor unattended by her bridal maids,
> The two that, step by step, behind her bore
> The small but precious casket that contained
> The dowry and the presents."

The rite is ending, and the entire congregation are on their knees to receive the blessing, when a band of pirates, who had landed the night before and lain in ambush, rush in, and before the bridegrooms, with their "best men," had time to take to their weapons—

> "Are gone again—amid no clash of arms
> Bearing away the maidens and the treasures."

According to Daru and Sismondi, it was the Doge in person who hastily equipped an armament, overtook the pirates, exterminated them to a man, and brought back the brides. Rogers adopts the more romantic version, that they were rescued by the bridegrooms:

> "Not a raft, a plank,
> But on that day was drifting—*in an hour*
> Half Venice was afloat. But *long before*,
> Frantic with grief and scorning all controul,
> The youths were gone in a light brigantine,
> Lying at anchor near the arsenal."

Even the date of the adventure is uncertain. Daru, on a review of the authorities, is clear that it occurred in the tenth century; but Morosini places it in A.D. 668, and it must have occurred when the neighbourhood of the church (now the site of the arsenal) was uninhabited, or the pirates could hardly have landed unobserved.

It was a wonderful advance, allowing even two centuries for its accomplishment, from a state of things in which such an outrage was possible to that in which Venice was able to find means of transport for the whole invading army of the Fourth Crusade, and co-operate in the conquest of the Greek empire on equal terms with the chivalry of Western Europe. The story of this crusade has been admirably told by Sismondi, and forms the subject of one of Gibbon's most celebrated chapters. We shall, therefore, merely recall attention to circumstances which have a marked bearing on the position and resources of Venice at the time.

Geoffrey de Villehardouin, Marshal of Champagne, the contemporary chronicler of the expedition, relates that he formed one of a deputation of six, empowered to treat with the Venetians for the transport of the troops, estimated at 4500 knights with two mounted esquires each, and 20,000 foot soldiers; in rude numbers, about 30,000 men and 13,000 or 14,000 horses. When it is remembered that the French were unable to transport a numerically inferior force to the Crimea in 1854 without leaving their cavalry behind, some notion may be formed of the marine of a country which could not only supply vessels for such an armament, but fit out an auxiliary force to act with it.[1] The terms settled with the Doge, and ratified by acclamation at a grand council or assembly of the people, were four marks per horse and two marks per man, including keep and provisions for nine months, making a sum total of 85,000 marks. It was also stipulated that, on condition of the Venetians joining the expedition with fifty galleys, they should equally share in its fruits.

"Oh, for one hour of blind old Dandolo!" He was past ninety-four when he volunteered to take

---

[1] "The French embarked 24,000 infantry and 70 pieces of field artillery; but since they were straitened in their means of sea transport, the number of horses they allotted to each gun was reduced from six to four. The French embarked no cavalry."—*Kinglake*, "The Invasion of the Crimea," vol. ii. p. 141.

the command in person, but he makes no allusion to his blindness in the speech in which he mentions his age and feebleness, and doubts have been raised whether he was totally deprived of sight, although one of his descendants, amongst other annalists, states distinctly that his eyes were put out when he was ambassador at Constantinople by the Emperor Manuel Comnenus, who is said to have applied the hot iron with his own hands. Villehardouin also, in his account of the first assault, says: " Wonderful prowess must now be told. The Duke of Venice, who was old and saw not at all (*goutte ne voyait*), armed at all points on the prow of his galley, the standard of St. Mark before him, was heard crying to his men to put him on shore." He was landed accordingly, and was carrying all before him, when his victorious course was arrested by the necessity of supporting the French.

He was nominated to replace the dethroned Emperor, but declined or was set aside for reasons of policy which the Venetian electors were the first to appreciate, and he died in little more than a year after the completion of the conquest (June 14, 1205), having lived long enough to be proclaimed "Despot of Romania"—a title annexed to that of Doge and used by his successors till the middle of the fourteenth century with what Gibbon terms the singular though true addition of "Lord of one-fourth and a half of the Roman empire."[1]

The difficulty of maintaining such an extent of dominion became so pressing that, according to two chroniclers, a project was actually brought forward by the Doge, in 1223, for abandoning

---

[1] *Dominus quartæ partis et dimidiæ imperii Romani.* The correct reading is, *imperii Romaniæ*—of the empire of Romania. Daru, Sismondi, and the able author of "Sketches of Venetian History," have fallen into the same mistake as Gibbon. A quarter of Constantinople, and half of the rest of the imperial dominions, were, in fact, allotted to Venice.

Venice and transferring her household gods to Constantinople. His argument in support of this proposal, with those of Angelo Faliero in reply, are reported in the manner of Thucydides; and we are assured that it was only negatived by a majority of one voice, which was termed the voice of Providence. The Venetians wisely abandoned, or granted as fiefs, such of their acquisitions as were not available for ports or commercial depôts. "If, then," concludes Daru, "it be asked what was the fruit of this conquest, we must acknowledge that the result was most important for the Venetians, since it assured the splendour of their republic in giving it the empire of the seas; but for Europe this result was the useless loss of many brave men, the burning of Constantinople, the destruction of precious monuments, the fall of an empire, and a dismemberment which facilitated its speedy conquest by barbarians. The only fruit that Europe appears to have derived from this great revolution is the introduction of millet, some grains of which were sent by the Marquis of Montferrat to his Italian States."

It is not exactly correct to say that the Fourth Crusade assured the empire of the seas to Venice: during more than two hundred years that empire was bravely contested by the Genoese, who more than once reduced the Venetians to the same humiliating position in which the English were placed by the Dutch when Van Tromp sailed up the Thames with the typical broom at his masthead. When, in the war of Chiozza (1378-1381), the Genoese admiral, Doria, reviewed his fleet whilst waiting for orders, he was received in passing from ship to ship with shouts of "*To Venice! To Venice! Viva San Giorgio!*" Nor was this a vainglorious boast, like the French cry of "To Berlin! To Berlin!" The Genoese fought their way victoriously to the verge of the chief lagune, when the Doge hastened in person to sue for peace, bringing with him some Genoese prisoners, whom he proposed to deliver without ransom, presenting at the same time a blank paper to be filled up with any terms, provided the independence of the Republic was respected. "You may take back the prisoners," was the haughty reply of Doria; " ere many hours I hope to deliver both them and their companions. By God above, ye Signors of Venice, you must expect no peace from the Lord of Padua or from our Republic till we ourselves have bridled the horses of your St. Mark. Place but the reins once in our hands, and we shall know how to keep them quiet for the future."[1]

Driven to desperation, the Venetians made good their defence, and after various alternations of fortune consented to a peace which left them entirely denuded of territory on the mainland. Yet it was Genoa, not Venice, whose decline was accelerated by the contest. The Doge of Venice was bearing himself as bravely as ever amongst monarchs, when the Doge of Genoa was giving up his sceptre and sword to the ambassadors of Charles VI. of France in token of vassalage.

During the interval between the decline of Genoa and the rise of the other maritime Powers, Venice very nearly monopolised the carrying trade between Europe and the East, and had become the greatest commercial emporium in the world. Besides a mercantile marine of more than three thousand vessels, the private property of the

[1] "Sketches of Venetian History" (Murray's "Family Library"), vol. i. p. 314. The writer relies on the authority of Chinazzo. Daru has divided the speech between Doria and the lord of Padua (Carrara), who was in league with the Genoese.

citizens, the Government sent annually squadrons of five or six large galleys to call at all the principal ports within the known range of navigation. In the sixteenth century, the arsenal of Venice contained 16,000 workmen and 40,000 sailors. It could turn out a fleet of 85 galleys at the shortest warning. One of the spectacles with which Henry III. of France was entertained, was the building, launching, and equipping of a galley in one day. At the battle of Lepanto, the Venetians had 134 ships, of which 70 were galleys and 6 galeasses. The galley carried from 15 to 20 guns: the galeasse from 60 to 70 of very heavy calibre. It was the six galeasses that decided the battle. So overpowering did the Venetians esteem this class of vessel that the captain's instructions were not to decline an engagement with 25 ordinary ships of war.

Their land forces were considerable. The army which they set on foot in 1509, when menaced by the League of Cambrai, amounted to 30,000 foot and 18,000 horse. There were 5000 soldiers on board their Lepanto fleet. The population of the city never amounted to 200,000; and the question arises where they got men enough for fleets, armies, colonies, commerce, and manufactures. The islands supplied sailors: Dalmatia, soldiers. Italy abounded in mercenary troops who flocked to the standard of the most liberal paymasters: high wages lured the best workmen, as high profits attracted and accumulated capital.

The Venetian system was protective and restrictive. They were no believers in free trade, and their duties on exports and imports by foreigners were in effect prohibitory. We are told of a King of Servia, who, on his departure from Venice, was so startled by the sum he was required to pay for export duty on his purchases, that he solicited the citizenship in order to be excused from paying them. As regards the carrying trade of the Adriatic, when the patriarch of Aquila requested permission to import in a ship of his nation a quantity of wine which he had bought at Ancona, the Republic refused, but offered to carry his wine for him gratis. The Venetians had become so necessary to the Italians, that Robert, King of Naples, was obliged to make peace with them, because his subjects declared themselves too impoverished to pay taxes since the Venetians had discontinued their trade. When, towards the end of the sixteenth century, the English began to trade directly with the Levant, the Venetians took alarm, and requested the interference of the French ambassador at Venice, who writes: "These Signors are excessively displeased that the Queen of England should establish herself in this quarter, since their traffic will be much diminished, as well in the commodities they export as in those they bring back in exchange."

"Thus did Venice rise,
Thus flourish, till the unwelcome tidings came,
That in the Tagus had arrived a fleet
From India, from the region of the Sun,
Fragrant with spices—that a way was found,
A channel opened, and the golden stream
Turned to enrich another. Then she felt
Her strength departing."

This is historically true. It was from their ambassador at Lisbon that the Venetians received the first intelligence of the discovery of the new passage (1497) and the arrival round the Cape of Good Hope of vessels loaded with the richest products of the East. "On hearing this news," says Cardinal Bembo, "the Republic saw that the most important branch of her commerce was slipping away. When she learned that the Portuguese were forming establishments on these coasts, and that they, becoming masters of all the merchandise of Asia, would soon deliver them in Europe at a lower rate than those which arrived by the Red Sea, by the Euphrates, or the Tanais, this jealousy was converted into fury."

They soon afterwards received another heavy blow from the Emperor Charles V., who imposed a duty of 25 per cent. on their imports and exports throughout his dominions, and formally closed his ports against them except on condition that they abandoned their direct trade with Africa and brought to his town of Oran all the merchandise they had to sell to the Moors. In fact, before the end of the sixteenth century, they were no longer able to exert the right of the strongest: they were driven from market after market by the rising maritime Powers of the North; and, jostled between the powerful monarchies into which Europe had settled down, they could only maintain a precarious independence by adroit trimming. The doctrine of the balance of power was thenceforth the sole salvation of the proud Republic till she fell.

We must not forget to mention that the Bank of Venice, which dates from the twelfth century (1157), was by much the oldest establishment of the kind, and that its operations included loans to foreign nations and princes as well as the ordinary business of a national bank. Here, again, its close imitator and rival was Genoa.[1] The Jews

---

[1] "'It is very singular,' I replied, 'that the mercantile transactions of London citizens should become involved with revolutions and rebellions.' 'Not at a', man, not at a',' returned Mr. Jarvie; 'that's a' your silly prejudications. I read whiles in the lang dark nights, and I hae read in "Baker's Chronicle," that the merchants o' London could gar the Bank of Genoa break their promise to advance a mighty sum to the King of Spain,

were permitted to establish a bank at Venice—
which, by the way, broke—but their condition was
pretty nearly such as it is described by Shakespeare. They were compelled to wear a badge,
to pay exceptional taxes, to inhabit a particular
quarter, to be shut up in it from sunset to sunrise,
and might be spat upon with impunity by a
patrician.

The palaces and public buildings show that the
patricians of Venice, collectively and individually,
were amongst the earliest and most munificent
patrons of the fine arts. The country seat of the
Barbaro family was built by Palladio, and the walls
and ceilings were painted in fresco by Paul Veronese. With the exception of Florence, no Italian
State did more for the revival and encouragement
of learning, literature, and science. Venice was
one of the claimants of the invention of printing,
and, within a few years after it became known,
160 printing presses were at work in the city alone.
Giving her credit for the University of Padua, of
which she became mistress in 1405, she could
boast of having protected and pensioned Galileo,
besides employing Sarpi as her advocate and
Bembo as her historiographer: Petrarch was
residing at Venice when Boccaccio came to visit
him: and although Tasso was born in the kingdom of Naples, he was the son of a Venetian
citizen and educated at the Venetian university.
Freedom of thought was rigidly proscribed; no
political allusion was safe: Dante, banished by
Florence, would have been drowned or strangled
at Venice; but she was tolerant of religious
speculation and permitted no tyranny except her
own. Even the Inquisition was kept within

---

whereby the sailing of the Grand Spanish Armada was put off for a hail
year.'"—*Rob Roy.* The Bank of Genoa was established in 1407.

bounds; very fortunately for art, as may be collected from one of M. Baschet's discoveries,—the *procès-verbal* of a sitting (July 18, 1573) at which Paul Veronese was interrogated touching one of his pictures of the Last Supper:

"Q. In this picture of the Supper of our Lord, have you painted people?—A. Yes. Q. How many have you painted, and what is each doing?—A. To begin,—Simon, the master of the hotel; then, below him, an upper servant, whom I suppose to have come there for his amusement and to see after the disposition of the table. There are several other figures of which I have no distinct recollection, considering that it is a long time since I painted this picture. Q. What is the meaning of the figure whose nose is bleeding?—A. It is a servant whose nose has been set bleeding by an accident. Q. And those men armed, and dressed in the German fashion, with halberds in their hands?—A. It is here necessary that I should speak a score of words. Q. Speak them.—A. We painters take the same license as the poets and the jesters, and I have represented the halberdiers eating and drinking at the bottom of the staircase, all ready, moreover, to discharge their duty; for it appeared to me becoming and possible that the master of the house, rich and magnificent, as I have been told, should have such attendants. Q. And that one dressed as a buffoon, with a parrot on his wrist,—with what view have you introduced him into the picture?—A. He is there as an ornament, as is customary. Q. Who are those at the table of our Lord?—A. The Twelve Apostles. Q. What is St. Peter, who comes first, doing?—A. He is carving the lamb to be passed to the other part of the table. Q. And the one next to him?—A. He is holding a plate to receive what St. Peter may give him. Q. And the third?—A. He is picking his teeth with a fork. Q. Who are really the persons whom you admit to have been at this Supper?—A. I believe there were none besides Christ and his apostles; but when I have a little room left in a picture, I adorn it with figures of invention."

He escaped with a reprimand and a command to substitute a Madeleine for a dog.

M. Yriarte devotes a chapter to the magnificent reception of Henry III. of France, in June 1574. But he has omitted the detail which most fastened on the imagination of the author of " Vathek " :

"When Henry III. left Poland to mount the throne of France, he passed through Venice and found the Senate waiting to receive him in their famous square, which by means of an awning stretched from the balustrades of opposite palaces was metamorphosed into a vast saloon, sparkling with artificial stars, and spread with the richest carpets of the east. What a magnificent idea! The ancient Romans in the zenith of power and luxury never conceived a greater. It is to them, however, that the Venetians are indebted for the hint, since we read of the Coliseum and Pompey's theatre being sometimes covered with transparent canvas to defend the spectators from the heat or sudden rain, and to tint the scene with soft agreeable colours."[1]

Whatever may have been the case in more modern times, the early prosperity of Venice was in no respect owing to her form of government, which was of the rudest and most fluctuating kind. "We have now," says Daru, arriving at 1172, "run over the history of fifty Doges. We have seen five abdicate, nine exiled or deposed, five banished with their eyes put out, and five massacred. Thus nineteen of these princes had been driven from their thrones by violence. If there was ample room for complaints of their abuse of their power, there was no less subject for regret and shame at the manner in which it had been overthrown." The early constitution of Venice might have been described, like that of Russia, as a monarchy tempered by assassination. The method of election was no more subjected to fixed rules than the authority conferred by it. Some Doges, as we have seen, nominated their successors.

[1] "Italy," etc. By the author of "Vathek" (Beckford), vol. i. p. 113.

Others were elected by a voluntary assembly of the people. At the election of Domenico Silvo by the people on the shore of San Nicolò del Lido, 1069, a great number came armed in their boats and, without landing, began shouting vociferously "*Vogliamo il Silvo, e lo approviamo*"—(We will have Silvo, and we approve of him). When the election was not the direct act of the people, the Doge was presented for popular approval in St. Mark's. It is passing strange, therefore, to find M. Yriarte so carried away by enthusiasm for his subject as to exclaim: "We may almost say that, for the Venetians, the age of indispensable struggles, of barbarism, of inevitable disorders, has not existed. They will be a people almost without transition, and one of the most powerful in the world. Their magistracies will be already instituted, whilst the greater part of the people of Europe are still sunk in barbarism. Their collection of laws will give evidence from the first of their love of justice, and their rapid instinct of civilisation."

The first of their laws for regulating the authority of the Doge was that of 1032, which assigned him two counsellors, whose assent was necessary to his acts, and required him on important occasions to convoke such of the citizens as he might think proper to deliberate on the interests of the State. These were called the *pregadi*. The nomination being discretionary with the Doge, they exercised no practical control: and, according to Sismondi, the formation of a much more important body, of that which was to assume the sovereignty and contain the whole Republic in itself, was posterior by one hundred years to this first limitation of the ducal authority. "After the unfortunate expedition of the Doge Vital Micheli, after he had exposed his fleet to contagion and lost the flower of his soldiers, a sedition broke out against him on his return, and he was killed by a plebeian. An interregnum of six months preceded the election of his successor; and this time was employed in laying the foundations of a government which should prevent the public weal from being again endangered by the misconduct of one man. Without abolishing the assemblies, a Council of 480 members was formed and invested (conjointly with the Doge) with the entire sovereignty."[1]

They were elected annually by twelve tribunes or electors representing the six sections or divisions of the city, who were originally chosen by the people; but the Grand Council first usurped the right of choosing their own electors, and then passed a succession of decrees, the general effect of which was to render ineligible all who, or whose ancestors, had not already sat in it. The change was gradual. The first Council was elected in 1172: the decree called "The Closing of the Great Council," was passed in 1296; and this was followed up in 1319 by one making the privilege personal and hereditary; it being, moreover, provided that the son might take his seat in the lifetime of the father on attaining his twenty-fifth year. A register was then opened in which the names of the duly qualified persons were enrolled. This was the famous Golden Book, *Il Libro d'Oro*, which, at its commencement, was simply a list of the governing body and included some who were not nobly born, whilst excluding others whose influence or position was inferior to their birth. Indeed, invidious distinctions were sedulously discountenanced, and wholesale additions to the privileged body were occasionally made without regard to pedigree or blood.

[1] "Histoire des Rép. Ital.," vol. ii. p. 345.

When the Republic was hard pressed for money, inscriptions in the Golden Book were sold at the current price of 100,000 ducats; and amongst the thirty heads of families who were admitted after the war of Chiozza, in 1381, as a reward for their services or patriotic sacrifices, we find artisans, wine-merchants, grocers, and apothecaries. Illustrious foreigners were admitted, as they are made free of a corporation amongst us. The form of address to the new member was: *Te civem nostrum creamus.* The honour was not disdained even by crowned heads. Henry IV.'s application for it was accepted as a compliment. Not so that of the Pope Gregory XIII. for one of his illegitimate sons, who passed for a nephew. After long deliberation, he was admitted as a near relative (*strettoparente*) of his Holiness. There was always a wide difference between the members of the Great Council in point of rank: the bearers of historic names, like *gli Elettorali*, being invested with a prestige which secured them a priority in high office as well as social precedence; but all equally belonged to the privileged class: to that aristocracy whose iron yoke, once riveted, neither Doge nor people was ever able to shake off.[1]

In all the other Italian republics, the nobles had been contemporaneously losing ground. "During the last twenty years of the thirteenth century," says Sismondi, "not only were they compelled to share the prerogatives they desired to monopolise: they were absolutely and completely stripped of them. The Priors of Florence were all required to belong to a trade or calling, and exercise it personally. The nine Signors and defenders of the community of Sienna were required to be merchants

---

[1] The original *Libro d'oro* was publicly burned in 1797, but extracts, registers, and other documents are extant, from which its contents might be ascertained.

and people of the middle class." "At Pistoia," says Daru, "the nobles were permanently disqualified for office, and the penalty of the non-noble who incurred degradation was to be inscribed in the book of nobility." At Modena there was a register, called the Book of the Nobles, in which all the *gentlemen* (in the continental sense) were inscribed, along with some of the *roturier* class whom the tribunals had associated with them as guilty of the same disorders; and all the inscribed were disqualified for office in the lump. The same legislation was afterwards carried out at Bologna, Padua, Brescia, Pisa, Genoa, and in all the free cities.[1] The popular hatred, embittered by fear, was especially directed against the feudal or territorial nobility, which never existed in Venice; and the success of the Venetian aristocracy in constituting themselves the sole governing body, was mainly owing to the fact that they were, in the first instance, a genuine and (so to speak) natural aristocracy, comprising nearly all the citizens or heads of families distinguished by birth, public services, personal influence or hereditary wealth. On finding that some families with undeniable claims had been excluded, the Council speedily corrected the error by admitting them.

Prior to the closing of the Council, the principal check on the Doge was the *Promisso Ducale*, or Coronation Oath. To increase its restrictive force, and watch over its observance, the Council named five of their own body, called "Correctors," whose general instructions were to see "that the Doges are the chiefs of the Republic, and not its masters or its tyrants." They ended by making the Doges its passive instruments or slaves. The Doge was

[1] Sismondi, "Hist. des Rép. Ital." vol. iii. pp. 164, 165. Daru, vol. i. pp. 505, 506.

forbidden to open any letter or despatch except in the presence of a certain number of counsellors, or to write any letter, public or private, without showing it to them. He was liable to a penalty of 100 ducats if he left the city for an hour: if his health required change of residence, they were to designate the place to which he might go, and fix the time he might remain. It was provided in 1462 that, if the ambassadors on the day of their reception attempted to touch on any question of State, he must turn the conversation, and in 1521, —apropos of some real or alleged indiscretion of Antonio Grimaldi—that the Doge must always confine himself to evasive expressions or words of mere courtesy in the reception of ambassadors. His sons were excluded from taking any active part in the Council or filling any of the principal offices. The officers attached to his person were similarly excluded from public employments during his reign, and for one year afterwards. The title of Monsignore was proscribed; and he was to suffer no one to bend the knee to him or to kiss his hand. His portrait was not to be hung up in the ducal palace, nor his armorial bearings to figure on public buildings or standards. He was forbidden to marry a foreigner, or to possess fiefs beyond the limits of the State. In 1400, the correctors enacted:

"The advocates of the Commune may prosecute the chief of the State either for a public act or an act of his private life. In the council held by the college, the Doge can never oppose the conclusions of the advocates of the Commune."

The Doges were paid quarterly. Jacopo Tiepolo, 1229–1249, received eight hundred *lire veneti*; Reniere Zeno, 1253–1268, two thousand; Giovanni Dandolo, 1280–1289, three thousand. They had also rents from lands specially assigned for their personal expenses, and other tributary payments. "In 1329," adds M. Yriarte (from whom we copy these figures) "when all this was computed and the times had grown more expensive, the Grand Council fixed the annual appointments at 5200 *lire*. This figure was maintained down to the fall of the Republic. Till 1312 the 'Book of Ducal Promises' contains the clause regulating the appointments; but, dating from this epoch, the chapter relating to the emoluments is suppressed."

Besides the strictest scrutiny into the conduct of the Doge in his lifetime, a sort of coroner's inquest was held over his body after death by commissaries appointed by the Council to inquire how he had managed his fortune, whether he had contracted debts or injured the interests of any one; in which case they acted as liquidators. "There was a law requiring the Chief of the State to pay within eight days for the objects of which he had become the purchaser, but this was almost always a dead letter. The greater part of the inquisitions proved that the Doges had ruined themselves in the service of the State. Twice only the Council were on the point of refusing the public honours to the deceased. Marco Fornarini (1762–1763) who was only a year in power, was so magnificent that he died insolvent; and Paolo Raineri (1779–1789), who had made an immense fortune at Constantinople, left debts to the amount of six millions of ducats. But both instances occurred when the restrictions on expenditure had also become a dead letter."

No qualified person could refuse the Dogeship or resign it without the permission of the Council. In 1368 Andrea Contarini, being elected in spite of his earnest entreaties to be excused, fled to

Padua, and sought refuge with an obscure dependent. The Senate instantly took the decisive step of notifying to him that he must return and accept the office, or expect to see his property confiscated, his name stigmatised, and himself declared a traitor to his country. He came back, submitted to his elevation, and occupied the ducal throne during fifteen years.

Yet the form of election, with its multiplicity of checks, would justify an assumption that the Dogeship was the grand object of ambition, to obtain which all sorts of undue influences would be employed. Thirty members of the Grand Council, chosen by lot, were reduced by lot to nine. The nine chose forty provisional electors, who were similarly reduced to twelve. The twelve chose twenty-five, who were again reduced to nine. Each of these nine proposed five, making a new list of forty-five, which was reduced to eleven; and these eleven produced a list of forty-one, who were to be the definitive electors after each had been submitted to the Grand Council. If any one failed to obtain the absolute majority of suffrages, the eleven were to name another, and so on. When forty-one were approved, they passed into an apartment in which they were shut up till they had elected a Doge. But, unlike our English jury in an analogous position, they were magnificently regaled at the expense of the public: everything they chose to call for was supplied; and, to prevent the semblance of bribery, any article called for by one was scrupulously supplied to the rest. Thus an elector having asked for a rosary, forty-one rosaries were sent in; and another having asked for "Æsop's Fables," the whole city was ransacked till forty-one copies were procured. In 1709 the conclave sate for thirteen days, and the expenses amounted to 59,325 lire (francs); in 1789 the expenses of the same number of electors for six days came to 378,387 lire. Corruption was evidently undermining the fabric which was so speedily to be overthrown by force.

The numbers, seldom under 1200, of the Great Council unfitted it for the direct exercise of its executive powers, which therefore were delegated to the Senate,—a body composed of 120 members of the Council, the Doge, the Council of Ten, the judges, and other high officials invested with executive or administrative authority.[1] This constituted the real government, which acted independently of the Great Council, except when new taxes were to be imposed.

We now come to the most remarkable of Venetian institutions, the Council of Ten, which was the unpremeditated result of exceptional events, instead of being the masterpiece of Machiavellian policy which it passes for. The closing of the Great Council was not effected without producing a good deal of popular indignation, besides exciting the jealousy of the excluded nobles; and the Doge, Pierre Gradenigo, the principal author of the new system, was marked out as the peculiar object of their machinations. Overthrow him, and they would regain the rights and liberties of which they had been robbed. One conspiracy formed by a democratic leader, Marin Bocconio, whilst the obnoxious changes were still in progress, was discovered before the time fixed for its execution, and all engaged in it, or suspected, were arrested, put to the question, and drowned or strangled off-hand.

[1] St. Didier traces the Senate to the *Pregadi*, citizens specially requested to advise the Doge on occasion. M. Baschet estimates the average number of regular members at 220, without including the functionaries who might attend without taking part in their deliberations.

Another, of a later date, proved much more formidable. The ringleaders were patricians: the chief was Tiepolo, who counted two Doges amongst his ancestors, and the numbers engaged were large enough to contend with the whole armed force at the disposal of the State. The opposing factions were fighting hand-to-hand on the place of St. Mark, each waving the same standard and shouting the same cry, when the Doge came upon the scene with fresh troops, which ought to have been encountered by Tiepolo, who accidentally arrived too late to co-operate with his friends. The force he brought with him was strong enough to enable him to make good his retreat to Rialto, where, having secured the boats and broken down the bridges, he held out for some days: when, despairing of the enterprise, he embarked and took refuge beyond the territories of the Republic.

The Doge, who had saved the State by his courage and energy, declared that he only heard of the plot in the course of the night preceding the execution; yet it had been maturing for months: there had been frequent meetings of the conspirators, whose speeches are reported: application had been made to Padua for help, and several hundred persons of all ranks must have been more or less cognisant of what was meditated. The sense of insecurity was such that a kind of dictatorship was created by the nomination of ten members of the Council charged to watch over the safety of the State. "It was armed with all the means, emancipated from all the forms, relieved from all responsibility, and held all heads dependent upon its pleasure." It is true that it was to last only ten days, then ten more, then twenty, then two months; but it was prorogued six times successively for the same time. At the end of one year, it was confirmed for five. Then it found itself strong enough to declare the continuance of its authority for ten years more. At last, in 1325, this terrible magistracy was declared perpetual. What it had done to prolong its duration, it did to extend its attributions. Instituted simply to take cognisance of crimes against the State, it usurped the entire administration.

Giving substantially the same account of it as Daru, Sismondi says that it established despotism, and preserved nothing of liberty but the name; and Hallam, after describing the uncontrolled authority of the Ten in the conduct of affairs, remarks that they were chiefly known as an arbitrary and inquisitorial tribunal, the standing tyranny of Venice. "Excluding the regular court of criminal judicature, not only from the investigation of treasonable charges, but of several other crimes of magnitude, they inquired, they judged, they punished, according to what they called reason of State. The public eye never penetrated the mystery of their proceedings; the accused was sometimes not heard, never confronted with witnesses: the condemnation was secret as the inquiry, the punishment undivulged like both."[1] Yet M. Baschet insists on treating the traditional impression of the Council of Ten as a vulgar prejudice, and thinks he has made out a defence for it by showing that it was steadily upheld by the Great Council on whose authority it had encroached. But this shows merely that the instinct of self-preservation was stronger in the Venetian oligarchy than the love of freedom or the hatred of injustice; and after saying that the State Inquisitors were never anything more than the delegates (*mandataires*) of the Council of Ten, he adds:

[1] "View of the State of Europe during the Middle Ages," chap. iii. part 2.

"Their ministry has always been considered with terror, not without reason. The most absolute mystery prevailed in their procedure. The means at their disposal were unlimited, and the reason of State led to the most terrible expedients as well as to the most cruel necessities. Very much dreaded by the patricians, this tribunal was more than once attacked by them with vehement eloquence in the bosom of the Great Council. The most opposite views were entertained. Some wished its destruction, others its preservation. For some it was the tyranny in the Republic, for others the safeguard. The great debates of March 1762 have continued memorable. The numbers of votes which were the result placed the Conservative party in the right, and it only fell with the Republic."

The Council of Ten consisted, in reality, of seventeen: ten members of the Great Council, the Doge, and his Privy Council of six. The ten were chosen by a complicated system of ballot: they were elected for a year, and could not be re-elected. Their first duty was to elect three chiefs. The Inquisitors, three in number, were chosen two amongst the Ten, one amongst the councillors of the Doge. The two were robed in black, and called the Black Inquisitors; the third in red, and called the Red Inquisitor. They did not act in their own name, nor was the very existence of the tribunal manifested by any outward or visible sign. Their summonses and orders of arrest were signed by one of the regular magistrates. An important part of the business at each meeting of the Council of Ten or the Inquisitors was the examination of the denunciations and complaints found in the Lion's Mouth. M. Daru says there were several of these receptacles; and M. Baschet is confident that the greatest caution was observed in dealing with them, especially when they were anonymous, as, no doubt, the greater part of them were. M. Cantu, who takes the same indulgent view of the proceedings of the Council as M. Baschet, cites a decree of September 11, 1462, requiring the Chiefs to lay the grounds of complaint before the Council within three days, but neutralises it by a later document, showing that the accused were often kept in prison for months and years without any proceedings being taken.[1]

The accused was never confronted with the witnesses, who were sworn to secrecy. " Certain interrogatories were administered in the dark. Was this to inspire terror in the accused, or to prevent his being troubled by the sight of his judges? "[2] M. Baschet is silent as to interrogatories on the rack. Of punishments, he says: " Most of them were terrible; some moderate." Amongst the first, the obscure prison, hanging between the columns of St. Mark, cutting off the hand, beheading, strangling. The most dreadful was the punishment of death mysteriously inflicted and thus pronounced: " That this night the condemned . . . . be conducted to the Canal Orfano,[3] where, his hands being tied and the body weighted, he shall be thrown in by an officer of justice, and that he die there." No net was to be cast in this canal under penalty of death; and if any one exhibited any troublesome curiosity touching the fate of a missing friend, the chances were that he would share the same fate. The recorded sentences found in the Archives are silent as to the crime, *e.g.*:

" Considering what has just been read in this Council, and for reasons of State which can be amply justified, the

---

[1] "Histoire des Italiens." Par M. César Cantu. Paris, 1861. Vol. x. p. 29.

[2] In the torture chamber of Ratisbon is still shown the lattice screen behind which the judge or judges sat during the interrogatory.

[3] A deep channel behind the island of S. Giorgio Maggiore.

Chiefs of this Council provide that, with the greatest and most secret precautions, the Turk Soliman be deprived of life either by poison or drowning."

The execution of this judgment is proved by a memorandum :

"The Chief Captain has vouched for the execution of the annexed order, and the men employed are those whose names are here inscribed. He has given them on the part of the Chiefs of the Council the severest admonition never at any time to reveal this execution under penalty of death."

It appears from another document that the Turk Soliman was drowned. From a document, dated January 15th, 1595, it appears that the Captain Cesar Capuzzimadi had received a hundred ducats from the Venetian Resident at Milan. Then, in less than a month, February 9th, there is a decree of the Ten :

"That to-morrow morning, Captain Cesar Capuzzimadi, Albanian, when he shall present himself before the Chiefs of the Council, be arrested, and that for things which have just been said and read."

On the 15th the Captain is required to produce his defence, which was put to the vote on the 19th, when sentence was passed by fifteen to two :

"It is our will that in the night of Tuesday to Wednesday, which will be the 22nd of the current month, he be strangled in his prison, as secretly as possible, and that his body be buried with the greatest secrecy also by the care of the Chiefs."

The decrees and regulations of the Ten touching State matters were deposited in the Secret Chancery, and carefully guarded. "Greater precautions," observes M. Baschet, "could not be taken to secure the darkest political adventure from indiscretion. The Doge could not enter unattended. Giovanni Rossi relates that a common man used to be chosen as material guardian of these Archives. The last known was Giovanni Polacco, who discharged his duty to perfection. The Government, according to others, were in the habit of seeking out some one who, though faithful and judicious, was grossly ignorant, and who, for greater security, could neither read nor write. The story goes that one day some senator, seeing Polacco writing very near the *Secreta*, expressed the utmost astonishment, and said to him, " What! you know how to write ! " To which the guardian with ready wit replied, " No, Excellence, I am drawing."

A decree of August 8, 1594, shows how the State Inquisitors were employed by the Ten :

"That plenary powers be given to the Inquisitors to find a person who by some prudent means can take away the life of Frà Cipriano of Lucca."

Frà Cipriano was a Venetian monk, who had taken refuge in the Austrian dominions, and was constantly intriguing against the Republic. That poison was frequently employed by the agents of the tribunal in obedience to its orders, and even supplied to them, is beyond dispute. A register has been found in the Archives, entitled *Secreta Secretissima del Consiglio dei Diéci*, containing two documents : one, dated December 14, 1513, relating to a Brother John of Ragusa, who proposes with the greatest secrecy to the three Chiefs " some *admirable* methods of mysteriously causing death :" the other, April 27, 1527, showing that the Council of Ten had resolved to remove the Constable Duc de Bourbon by poison, if he had not saved them the trouble by getting killed in the assault of Rome.

On the 10th March, 1630, Pier Antonio, Venetian Resident at Florence, writes:

"Most excellent and most revered Signors,—I have at length obtained with the greatest secrecy the recipes of two sorts of very potent poison from a person highly skilled in chemistry, who has copies of the greater part of the secrets of the deceased Don Antonio Medici, famous in the same profession, amongst which secrets are these recipes. I transmit them for greater circumspection to the ordinary address of your secretary, under the description of salubrious essences required by him."

So late as 1767, the Proveditor-General of Dalmatia received a packet of poison from the Council of Ten, with directions for its secret and cautious use in ridding them and the world of a person reported "dangerous."

According to the written Statutes of the Inquisitors, if a person had committed any action that it was inconvenient to punish juridically, he was to be poisoned. The patrician who spoke, however slightly, against the Government, was to be admonished twice, and the third time drowned as incorrigible. The vigilance and severity of the tribunal extended over the members of the Council, the Doge, the Inquisitors themselves: only it was provided that such criminals should be proceeded against with the deepest mystery, and that, in case of condemnation to death, poison should be preferred to any other means.

Moore, apostrophising Venice in "Rhymes on the Road," exclaims:

> "Thy perfidy, still worse than aught,
> Thine own unblushing Sarpi taught."

He refers to a set of Maxims drawn up in 1615 by the famous Fra Paolo for the guidance of the Venetian Government, some of which for atrocity throw the "Prince" of Machiavel into the shade, *e.g.* :

"Those who in the municipal councils shall show themselves either bolder or more devoted to the interests of the people must be destroyed or gained at any price. Lastly, if any party leaders are found in the provinces, they must be exterminated under some pretext or another, *but there must be no recourse to ordinary justice. Let poison do the work of the executioner. This is less odious and more profitable.*"

The axioms from which he starts are these:

"The greatest act of justice the Prince can perform is to maintain himself."

"I term *justice* every thing that contributes to the maintenance of the State.

Machiavel relates that, on the return of a Venetian squadron, a conflict arose between the people and the crews. The interference of the magistrates had proved nugatory, when a retired officer, who was much respected by the sailors, succeeded in calming the tumult. The influence of which he had given so marked a proof became a subject of alarm: a short time afterwards he was arrested and carried to a prison, where he died. A Cornaro was sent to prison for distributing corn to the poor during a famine, his charity being attributed to ambitious views. What can be said of a government under which public or private virtue was a crime?

A foreigner of distinction, having had his pocket picked, indulged in some harsh expressions against the police. Some days afterwards he was quitting Venice, when his gondola was stopped, and he was requested to step into another. "Monsieur," said a grave personage, "are you not the Prince de Craon?"—"Yes." "Were you not robbed last Friday?"—"Yes." "Of what sum?"—"Five hundred ducats." "Where were they?"—"In a green purse." "And do you suspect any one of this robbery?"—"A valet de place." "Should you recognise him?"—"Without doubt." Then the interrogator pushes aside a dirty cloak, discovers a dead man holding a green purse in his hand, and adds, "You see, Sir, that justice has been done: there is your money; take it, and remember that a prudent man never sets foot again in a country where he has underrated the wisdom of the Government."

A Genevese painter, working in a Church at Venice, had a quarrel with two Frenchmen, who began abusing the Government. The next day he was summoned before the Inquisitors, and on being asked if he should recognize the persons with whom he had quarrelled, he replied in the affirmative, protesting that he had said nothing but what was in honour of the Signory. A curtain is drawn, and he sees the two Frenchmen with the marks of strangulation round their necks. He is sent away half dead with fright, with the injunction to speak neither good nor evil of the Government: "We have no need of your apologies, and to approve us is to judge." The religious orders were allowed no exemption. Some monks having been accused of irregularities towards their female penitents, their convent was first made acquainted with their crime, their trial, and their execution, when their bodies were brought to be interred.

In "Marino Faliero" and "The Two Foscari," Lord Byron has faithfully dramatised two episodes of Venetian history which strikingly illustrate the irresistible power and the stern unrelenting spirit of the tribunal. One chief magistrate, full of years and honours, is proclaimed a traitor and executed on the steps of his own palace: another dies degraded and broken-hearted, after being thrice compelled to gaze on a beloved son writhing on the rack. Yet the wheels of the State machinery revolve without a check, and no more account is made of a deposed or decapitated Doge than of a strangled mechanic or a missing gondolier. Another great poet, Manzoni, has portrayed with equal truth and force the manner in which the Republic managed to combine perfidy and ingratitude with cruelty, in their treatment of his hero, one of the most renowned soldiers of Italy, who had brought victory to their side.[1]

Bearing these things in mind, it is anything but reassuring to be told by M. Baschet that the average number of prisoners was small. " The examination of the *Informazioni*, which the secretary presented at the end of every year, enables us to establish the truth as to the number of prisoners of the Inquisitors. We see how restricted was the number if, with these authentic pieces before our eyes, we are willing to seek and accept the truth. It rarely happened that the prisons called *pozzi* (the wells), and those called *piombi* (the leads), were all occupied at the same time. In 1717 there is a single prisoner under the leads, two in the wells, and four in the *camerotti*. . . . The more we penetrate into the history of this extraordinary tribunal, the more are we convinced that it was still more appalling

---

[1] "*Il Comte di Carmagnola. Tragedia.*" Manzoni makes no allusion to the torture inflicted on Carmagnola, deeming it probably too revolting for dramatic treatment. He states in his preface that the death of Carmagnola proved the salvation of the Republic in the way the Venetians least anticipated. Their first suspicion of the secret League of Cambray was excited by the report of an agent at Milan, to the effect that a Piedmontese, known to be in communication with the French Government, was going about saying that the time had come when the death of his countryman Carmagnola would be amply avenged.

by the really impenetrable mystery with which it surrounded itself than terrible by its acts."

We arrive at a diametrically opposite conclusion. It was an inevitable result of this impenetrable mystery that the details of many current stories or traditions should be disproved by the Archives, when brought to light and carefully collated; but, on the other hand, these Archives teem with proofs of the guiding spirit and detestable character of the tribunal: nor can we place implicit faith in their secretaries as to the facts. When Howard visited the Venetian prisons in 1778, he found between three and four hundred persons confined in them, some of whom told him they would have preferred the galleys for life. When M. Cantu states that only one prisoner was found when the prisons were thrown or broken open in 1797, he proves too much. How many were found in the Bastille? But granted the occasional paucity of prisoners, may not the summary methods of gaol delivery pursued by the Inquisitors account for this supposed anomaly?

> "But let us to the roof,
> And when thou hast surveyed the sea, the land,
> Visit the narrow cells that cluster there
> As in a place of tombs. There burning suns,
> Day after day, beat unrelentingly,
> Turning all things to dust, and scorching up
> The brain, till reason fled—
> * * * * *
> Few houses of the size were better filled,
> Though many came and left it in an hour,
> Most nights—so said the good old Nicoli—
> For three and thirty years his uncle kept
> The water-gate below, but seldom spoke
> Though much was on his mind—most nights arrived
> The prison boat—that boat with many oars,
> And bore away as to the Lower World

Disburdening in the Canal Orfano,
That drowning place where never net was thrown,
Summer or winter, death the penalty."

Casanuova gives a minute description of the *piombi* (in which he was confined) and the *pozzi*: "The *piombi*, prisons destined to State-prisoners, are no other than the garrets of the Ducal palace; and it is from the large plates of lead with which this palace is roofed that they take their name." His cell, about ten feet square, was too low for him to stand upright: light and air were only admitted through a grating in the door, and the heat is described as stifling.[1]

In a subsequent chapter he says:

"Besides the *piombi* and the *camerotti*, the State Inquisitors possessed nineteen horrible prisons underground in the same Ducal palace. These resemble tombs; but they are called the *pozzi*, because there is always two feet of water which penetrates by the same grating through which they receive a little light. This grating is only a foot square. Unless the wretch condemned to live in these loathsome vaults prefers a foot-bath of salt water, he is obliged to remain all day long seated on a trestle which does duty for table and bed."

Describing his imprisonment in the *piombi*, Silvio Pillico says:

"Words cannot tell to what a degree the air of the den (*covile*) I occupied was inflamed. Looking due south, under a roof of lead and with a window looking on the roof of St. Mark, wholly lead, the reflection of which was terrible, I was suffocating. I had never conceived the idea of so oppressive a heat. To this suffering were added the mosquitoes, with which I was covered—the bed, the table, the chair, the walls, all were covered with them. . . . Then, suffering from such a scourge, and hopeless of obtaining a change of prison, some temptation to suicide came over me, and at times I feared I should go mad."[2]

[1] "Memoires," vol iii. ch. 4.   [2] "Le Mie Prigioni," p. 89.

In the teeth of tradition, general belief, and direct evidence Mr. Ruskin lays down: "The stories commonly told respecting the *piombi* of the Ducal palace are utterly false. Instead of being, as usually reported, small furnaces under the leads of the palace, they were comfortable rooms with good flat roofs of *larch* and carefully ventilated."[1] The accomplished writer of the article headed "Venice Defended" in the "Edinburgh Review" for July, 1877, quoting and improving upon Mr. Ruskin, says that the leads "are divided from the cells called the *piombi* by a solid ceiling of magnificent *oak* rafters." Considering the condition of Italian prisons within living memory, it is incredible that the so-called cells could ever have been comfortable, well-ventilated rooms, and it is for Mr. Ruskin to explain how, on his hypothesis, they acquired their bad reputation and their name. He is judiciously silent as to the *pozzi*, which, with equal truth and plausibility, might be represented as comfortable rooms for the summer occupation of the prisoners, kept cool by the admission of sea water. Recorded sentences of death by drowning abound, yet the writer of "Venice Defended" confidently refers to assurances by members of the Council of Ten "that the idea of drowning as a mode of judicial execution was too contemptible to deserve refutation."

The Ten and the Inquisitors uniformly acted on the maxim that dead men tell no tales. To demonstrate their cold-hearted calculated cruelty and utter recklessness of proof, we should be content to rely on the affair on which the "Venice Preserved" of Otway is based. On the 25th of May, 1618, Sir Henry Wotton, then English Ambassador at Venice, writes: "The whole town is

[1] "The Story of Venice," vol. ii. p. 93.

here at present in horror and confusion upon the discovery of a foul and fearful conspiracy of the French against this State; whereof no less than thirty have already suffered very condign punishment, between men strangled in prison, drowned in the silence of the night, and hanged in public; and yet the bottom is invisible." And so it remained, and remains still; nor is Muratori far wrong in asserting that nothing is clear except the fact that several hundreds of suspected persons were tortured and put to death. The supposed object of the alleged conspiracy—projected, it was said, by the Duke d'Ossuna, Spanish Viceroy of Naples, in concert with the Marquis of Bedemar, Spanish Ambassador at Venice—was neither more nor less than to seduce the foreign troops in the pay of the Republic, set fire to the arsenal, upset the government, and reduce the entire State under subjection to Spain. The first information was obtained from one Jacques Pierre, who had begun life as a pirate, and after being for some time in the service of the Duke d'Ossuna, had fled from Naples and obtained employment in some subordinate office in the arsenal. The notes or minutes of his disclosures, written by him in French, were translated at his request into Italian by a friend named Renault, with the view of their being laid before the Council. He declared himself the main agent in the plot, and represented his quitting the Duke's service as an overt act.

The first arrests were made on the unsupported evidence of this man, and we know of no direct or indirect proofs other than confessions and accusations extorted by the rack, or such as the Lion's Mouth was pretty sure to supply in such a contingency. Daru, who has devoted more than a hundred pages to the elucidation of the mystery, comes to the conclusion that the conspiracy was a myth, and that the executions were a blind to conceal from Spain a secret understanding between the Duke, the Court of France, and the Signory; nor does the terrible charge against the Venetian authorities, implied in this conclusion, startle him, although the arrests and executions extended over ten months, and he dwells on the paucity of information "collected from many hundred accused, who all underwent the question, and of whom one only was fortunate enough to make his judges pause on his condemnation." The atrocities committed to keep the whole transaction involved in darkness may be inferred from the so-called justificatory Report of the Ten, and the recorded Procedure:

"A long discussion took place whether they should spare the life of Captain Brushart, but for many considerations, *and in pursuance of the line they had taken to put to death all those who were implicated in this affair*, he was strangled on the night of St. Peter and St. Paul, which agrees with the 29th June; fifty of his co-accused were strangled, and a still greater number secretly buried.

"Two artificers, brothers, accused of having held communication with Pierre, were subjected to the torture during several hours; the one persisted in his denial, the other merely repeated his confessions; both were hanged the next day, and *twenty-nine prisoners were drowned the same night in the Canal Orfano, 'pour ne point ébruiter l'affaire.'*"

These are the very words of the Report. Besides those put to death in the city, two hundred and sixty officers and soldiers, arrested in the towns of the mainland, perished by the hands of the executioner. An artisan, who happened to be at Zara, was killed by shots from an arquebus, together with a soldier and a child who were attending on him. Pierre, who was with the fleet, was flung into the sea, the officer being especially enjoined not to give him time for confession, so that, according to the prevalent belief, his soul might perish with his body. Forty-five men, suspected of having had relations with him, "*were drowned without noise (sans bruit).*" Renault, a notorious gambler and drunkard, was seven times interrogated on the rack without uttering anything but imprecations against his judges, who, finding nothing more to be got from him, ordered him to be strangled in prison, and then exposed on the gibbet hanging by one leg. Antoine Jaffier was a French captain, who had vaguely deposed to a communication with Pierre. He received 4000 sequins as a reward, and was ordered to quit the Venetian territory within three days; but in passing through Brescia, he was arrested for having held communications with French officers, brought back to Venice, and drowned. Another witness, to whom a pension of 50 ducats per month and a gratification of 300 ducats had been assigned, was ordered to repair to Candia, where, immediately on his arrival, he was killed in a quarrel forced on him, *querelle d'Allemand* as it is termed.

"Thus, accused, accusers, all were judged equally guilty—those who had spontaneously given the first information, and those who later revealed a plot which the Government knew already, and those who owned themselves accomplices in a conspiracy in which they had been initiated without knowing the real object, and those who denied having had anything to do with it—all, without exception, perished, that no witness might remain who could depose to the circumstances. Five months afterwards the Doge, accompanied by all the nobles, might be seen going to the cathedral of Saint Mark to offer solemn thanksgivings to Providence."[1]

We need hardly add that there is little in Otway's play corresponding with the actual characters or occurrences besides the names, but he has partially followed the popular, though inaccurate, version of St. Real.

It not unfrequently happens that an individual case of cruelty or injustice makes more impression than an indiscriminate mass of cases, and it so happened that the Venetians, who had remained quiet during these wholesale tortures and executions, were suddenly aroused to a sense of the common danger by the untimely fate of one man. Antonio Foscarini had been four years ambassador to England, after filling the same dignity in France, when he was secretly accused by his secretary of having revealed the despatches of the Signory to foreign ambassadors. He arrived in Venice in March 1616; was arrested and interrogated, and remained in prison till July 1618, when he was declared innocent, and set at liberty. He lays the Relations of his two embassies before the Senate, of which he subsequently becomes a member. All of a sudden he is denounced in April 1622, as having had a mysterious understanding with the Nuncio and other Ministers in the house inhabited by Lady Arundel at Venice; he is arrested on the 8th, called before the Inquisitors, condemned on the 20th, and strangled in prison on the 21st. On the 20th of the following August, his accusers were re-examined, admitted the falsehood of the charge, and were executed. "These formidable judges," says M. Baschet, "who, however, might have relied on public policy and reasons of State as their justification, did not keep

[1] Daru, liv. xxxi.

silence, and by an admirable decree, that all magistrates, present and to come, should see written in letters of gold on the wall of the place where they sit, re-established in the face of the world the honour and reputation of the citizen whom, in their soul and conscience, under the weight of proofs that appeared overwhelming, they had condemned to the most infamous as well as most cruel of punishments."

A widely different account of their conduct is given by Sir Henry Wotton, who professes to have made "research of the whole proceeding, that his Majesty (James I.) may have a more due information of this rare and unfortunate example." The proofs that "appeared overwhelming," consisted of the depositions of three informers, to the effect that Foscarini had been in secret communication with the Spanish secretary, to whom no reference was made till after the execution. It was his positive denial and circumstantial disproof that led to the conviction of the informers; and the application of Foscarini's family for a revision of the sentence was actually refused on the ground that the false witnesses, being convicted of falsehood, were incompetent. But their confession preparatory to their final plunge into the canal being obtained through the priest, and published, the Council of Ten, after a delay of nearly five months, issued this hypocritical decree:—" Since the providence of our Lord God, by means truly miraculous and inscrutable to the human understanding, has brought to pass that the very authors and ministers of the falsehood and impostures fabricated against our late beloved noble, Antonio Foscarini, etc., it consorts with the justice and piety of this Council, on whom above all things it is incumbent to protect the honour and reputation of families," etc.

"Surely," adds Wotton, "in the three hundred years that the Decemviral Tribunal hath stood, there was never cast upon it a greater blemish, which is likely to breed no good consequences upon the whole."

The exposure having failed to correct the abuse, a proposal for abolishing the tribunal, or modifying its powers, was brought before the Great Council, and led to a series of animated debates, at one of which several of the members appeared, contrary to a standing regulation, in arms. Things came to such a pass, that at the annual election of the Ten the voting was partially suspended: there was no election, and consequently there was no longer any Council of Ten. At the next sitting, however, so complete a reaction was produced by the speech of a grave and dignified orator of advanced years, Baptist Nani, that not only was the tribunal confirmed, but Nani was named its chief, and the service he had just rendered to the republic was entered in the Minutes.

The most convincing argument advanced for the preservation of the Council of Ten was that it was the mainspring of the system, and that the whole machinery of government would be dislocated by its abolition. Its paramount authority embraced foreign as well as domestic affairs. Thus in 1538, the Ten, without communication with the Senate or Doge, gave private instructions to the Venetian ambassador at Constantinople to make peace with the Turks at any sacrifice, and were obeyed. They had spies in every Court; and annexed to an ambassadorial despatch, and addressed to their signories, is a billet, signed *Chiara, schiava della Gran Sultana* (Clara, the slave of the Grand Sultana). Their diplomatic servants were expected to be as unscrupulous as their masters. The ambassador, Daniel Dolfin, at Constantinople, having received orders to make away with the celebrated Comte de Bonneval as an enemy of Christianity and the Republic, replies that "the orders of the most illustrious and most excellent Signors are, and always will be, received with the highest consideration, and will be executed with the most rapid submission whenever there shall be means." In spite of their precautions, and the terrible fate that awaited an agent on the slightest symptom or suspicion of treachery, their own arts were successfully employed against them. In the Archives is a note, dated January 30, 1647, of a private interview between their ambassador at the French Court and Cardinal Mazarin, in the course of which Mazarin drew from his pocket and read a series of extracts from the recent despatches of the self-same ambassador relating to the Cardinal himself.

The eagerness of foreign Courts to become acquainted with the Venetian despatches was owing in no slight measure to the knowledge that they were not confined to formal matters of business, an ambassador of the Republic being especially instructed to keep the Signory minutely informed of all that was passing at the Court to which he was accredited; including the intrigues of courtiers and mistresses, the conflict of parties, and the secret influences at work. When he had fulfilled his mission, it was customary for him to present himself to the Senate within fifteen days after his return, and pronounce a discourse which, under the name of *Relazione*, was a comprehensive report upon the country which he had just quitted. On leaving the hall, he deposited in the hands of the Grand Chancellor the original text of his "Relazione," which was immediately placed in the drawers of the *Secreta* reserved for diplomatic documents.

"Transport yourself to that noble locality of the senatorial hall. See it illustrated throughout with the splendours of the Venetian school. The ceiling, the walls, covered by the works of the great masters, recall the glories of the country; on every side are the memorable images of illustrious ancestors. The Doge, clothed in the rich tunic of gold brocade which distinguished him: the sages and the councillors with their violet tunics: all the senators in purple robes: the Chiefs of the Ten, in tunics of a bright red, are there: a rumour had got abroad the evening before of a more than common interest for the morrow. The ambassador to France has returned: his reputation is great amongst the senators: he is a statesman, a fine speaker to boot."[1]

The scene, the audience, the occasion, were certainly well fitted to call out the full powers of the diplomatist, and the Venetian ambassadors

[1] "La Diplomatie Vénitienne. Les Princes de l'Europe au XVIme Siècle: François Ier, Phillippe II., Catherine de Médicis, les Papes, les Sultans, &c. D'après les Rapports des Ambassadeurs Vénitiens." Par M. Armand Baschet. Paris: Henri Plon. 1862. This work is distinguished by the same high merits as his "Archives." Several volumes of "Relazioni" have been published in France and Italy, and they have been turned to good account by many foreign writers. See "Le Relazioni degli Ambasciatori Veneti al Senato durante il Secolo XVI°. Edite dal Cav. Eug. Albèri. Firenze": in fifteen volumes, of which two are devoted to England. Lord Macaulay made a journey to Venice in 1856 for the purpose of consulting the archives. By the kindness of the Earl of Orford we have now before us a collection (in fourteen folio volumes, MS.) of the Despatches of the Venetian ambassadors at the Court of London from 1715 to 1739 (both inclusive) and, after an unexplained break, during 1744, 1745, and 1746. They were copied, by his direction, with a view to a meditated Life of his celebrated ancestor, the first Earl of Orford, which no one is better qualified to write. The "Relazioni" best known in England are those published by Mr. Rawdon Browne in 1854: "Four Years at the Court of Henry VIII.;" "Selection of Despatches written by the Venetian Ambassador, Sebastian Giustiniani, and addressed to the Signory of Venice. 1515-1519."

were carefully selected from amongst the ablest and most accomplished of the nobles. No wonder, therefore, that the "Relazioni" form an inestimable collection of materials for history. The only wonder is that they remained so long unappreciated except by a few men of letters; and that their real value is only just beginning to get recognized in this country.

M. Yriarte's "Patrician" is a perfect type of the Venetian ambassador, and his diplomatic career (clearly and spiritedly narrated) enables us to form a tolerably precise estimate of the man. He was nominated to the French Court on June 11, 1561, during the regency of Catherine de Medicis. His appointments are specified at the end of his instructions.

"You will receive for your expenses two hundred ducats of gold per month, without being obliged to render an account to any one. You are bound to keep eleven horses, including those of the secretary and his servant, and four couriers. We have ordered to be given you for your four months' subvention eight hundred ducats of gold; you will have a thousand ducats of gold for the present, according to the decree of the Senate of June 2nd; and to cover the expense of your purchases of horses' harness and trappings, three hundred ducats (at six livres four *gros* the ducat). We remit to your secretary, as gratification, one hundred ducats, and to the couriers who accompany you twenty ducats each."

In May 1568 he was named ambassador to Constantinople, the most important and lucrative of the embassies. The appointment is made by the Grand Council instead of the Senate, and twelve hundred members at least must be present at the nomination. It was a current opinion in Venice, says Daru, that when the Bailo (as this particular ambassador was called) departed for the embassy of Constantinople, he was presented with a casket of sequins, and a box of poisons. On this M. Yriarte remarks: "Certain historians, whom we cannot read without laughing now that we write with the original documents before our eyes, affirm that the Council of Ten, at the departure of the Bailo, solemnly presented him with a box full of sequins and another full of poisons. Even under these melodramatic exaggerations the truth appears, and the sentiment which has dictated them is even tolerably just. The sequins would symbolize the duty of not shrinking from expense in the service of the State, and of purchasing, if necessary, both the Seraglio and the Jews of the faubourgs of Stamboul. The poison would represent the duty of not recoiling from death, if it was necessary to serve the State and suppress a traitor or conspirator." But, the alleged solemnity apart, does not this admit that the historians were substantially correct? Was not the ambassador supplied with an unlimited amount of secret service money to be spent in bribery? Does it not appear from original documents that he was frequently directed to employ poison supplied by the Ten or their subordinates?

The legitimate or permitted profits in the shape of dues and privileges were such, that M. Yriarte compares the position to that of the Captains-General of Cuba, who were sent there to make their fortunes when they were illustrious and poor. It was computed that the Bailo could lay by a hundred thousand crowns in three years; and Marc Antonio remained Bailo for six. The whole of his despatches, four hundred in number, as well as his two "Relazioni," have been preserved, and abound in striking traits and incidents. The period was eventful. The main object of the mission was to conciliate the Sultan, Selim II., who was known to be hostilely disposed; and no means were left untried to reach him through the Grand Vizir, the Sultanas, and the favourite ladies of the hareem. Their common method of exaction, after receiving the usual presents in money and rich stuffs, was to commission the ambassador to procure for them European articles of ornament or use for which they never meant to pay. An entire page of a despatch is filled with the design of a large mosque lamp, of which nine hundred are to be made for the Grand Vizir. The vizir wants an organ: the Aga of the Janissaries, who is building a house at the Sweet Waters, some painted glass windows; and one of the sultanas a thousand basins of steel. This last order staggered the Senate, who, after grave deliberation, direct the Bailo to say that the metal was not a Venetian product or they should be most happy to oblige the lady.

The year after his arrival, December 13, 1569, a destructive fire broke out in the arsenal of Venice, and no sooner has the news, with an exaggerated estimate of the loss in ships and material, reached Constantinople, than the exactions are redoubled: the Grand Vizir demands another supply of lamps, and it becomes clear that the Turks are only watching for a pretence to declare war. This is found in the refusal of the Republic to concede Cyprus, which the Sultan sends a special envoy to demand. On the very day when the refusal is received by the Divan, Marc Antonio Barbaro is arrested and shut up in a fortress: an embargo is laid on all Venetian vessels in Turkish waters, and all Venetian subjects within reach are treated like their ambassador. The Republic retaliated by seizing an ambassador of the Porte returning from France, who, being also charged with a mission to the Doge, had stopped at Venice on his way. They thus secured a hostage for the safety of their representative; but the Turks had too little regard for life to be stopped by reprisals, and in the course of the following year they gave a terrible proof of their profound indifference to faith, honour, and humanity.

The defence of Famagosta, the principal city of Cyprus, was one of the most heroic exploits of the age: the combined conduct and valour of the Venetian governor, Bragadino, were the theme of universal praise: honourable terms were granted to the garrison; and when he notified his intention to be in person the bearer of the keys, the Turkish commander replied in the most courteous and complimentary terms that he should feel honoured and gratified by receiving him. Bragadino came attended by the officers of his staff, dressed in his purple robes, with a red umbrella, the sign of his rank, held over him. In the course of the ensuing interview the Pasha suddenly springing up, accused him of having put some Mussulman prisoners to death: the officers were dragged away and cut to pieces, whilst Bragadino was reserved for the worst outrages that vindictive cruelty could inflict. He was thrice made to bare his neck to the executioner, whose sword was thrice lifted as if about to strike: his ears were cut off: he was driven every morning for ten days, heavy laden with baskets of earth, to the batteries, and compelled to kiss the ground before the Pasha's pavilion as he passed. He was hoisted to the yard-arm of one of the ships and exposed to the derision of the sailors. Finally, he was carried to the square of Famagosta, stripped, chained to a stake on the public scaffold, and slowly flayed alive, whilst the Pasha looked on. His skin, stuffed with straw, was then mounted on a cow, paraded through the streets with the red umbrella over it, suspended at the bowsprit of the admiral's galley, and displayed as a trophy during the whole voyage to Constantinople. The skin was afterwards purchased of the Pasha by the family of Bragadino, and deposited, with a commemorative inscription, in an urn in the Church of Saints Giovanni and Paolo.

Marc Antonio was not ill-treated, nor could he have been subjected to a very rigorous confinement, for he managed to keep up a constant correspondence with the Republic; and when, after the battle of Lepanto, the Turks showed an inclination to negotiate, it was through him. "He was engaged five months in settling the terms, with such secrecy and such prudence, that this peace, so advantageous, was not known in Venice till the moment when the treaty was signed." It was so far from advantageous, that, as Montesquieu says, one would have thought it was the Turks who had gained the battle of Lepanto. The Grand Council, however, ratified it, and named Marc Antonio, in token of their approval, to the second dignity in the State. It was at his own pressing instance that he was recalled in March, 1574, and his principal "Relazione" was delivered in the May following. It contains a complete account of the Turkish empire, its resources, and its mode of government, with sketches of the Sultan and his ministers.

In 1543, the Patrician married the daughter of Marc Antonio Giustiniani, one of the family which, in the expedition of 1171 against the Greek emperor, furnished a hundred combatants all bearing the name. They perished (like the Fabii) to a man, and the race was only saved from extinction by taking the sole surviving member from a convent, and marrying him. M. Yriarte is obliged to own that he can learn nothing of the patrician's wife, or indeed of any of her fair contemporaries. He cannot even say whether she accompanied her husband on his embassies. "In France at this epoch, the woman is revealed by the part she plays, whilst at Venice she only appears in the fêtes—brilliant, dazzling, adorned to please the eyes of the princes or the illustrious travellers who passed through, and never revealed by her moral influence or civilising action." May it not have been owing to the part women had been playing in other countries that they were purposely kept in the background at Venice, where, moreover, manners had contracted somewhat of an Oriental tinge? "At Rome," says Sismondi, "the women whilst seeking to please, wished also to exercise power; they attempted to rule, through their lovers, the State, and with it the Church, which made part of the State; and they acquired more authority over the Romans in the tenth century than they were ever known to exercise in any other government. Two famous patricians, Theodora and her daughter Marozia, disposed, during the space of sixty years, of that tiara which the Henrys, at the head of German armies, a few years later, could not tear from their enemies."[1]

Venice differed widely from Rome, and indeed from every other Italian State, in this respect: we never find a woman playing a prominent part on the political arena there; and if Vidocq had been engaged to unravel any one of the complicated conspiracies which abound in Venetian annals, he would have derived little or no aid from his favourite maxim: *trouvez-moi la femme.*

[1] "Hist. des. Rép. Ital." vol. i. p. 95.

The story of Bianca Capello can hardly be considered an exception, for the scene of her principal adventures was Florence. The daughter of an illustrious family, beautiful, accomplished, and quick-witted, she had engaged in an intrigue with a good-looking young Florentine, named Pietro, the cashier of a bank. On her return from one of the nightly interviews with which she favoured him, she found the door of her father's house, which she had left open, closed against her—accidentally, it was supposed, by a baker's boy. Dreading discovery, she eloped with her lover to Florence, and threw herself under the protection of Francesco dei Medici, the son of Cosmo, the reigning Duke, and virtual sovereign as his representative. Francesco fell in love with her, assigned her a magnificent establishment as his avowed mistress, and handsomely provided for Pietro, who passed for her husband. He was found murdered : in the course of time Francesco's wife died, and the Prince, now Grand Duke, privately married Bianca. Getting more and more infatuated, he resolved to follow up the private by a public union, and sent an embassy to Venice to demand her in marriage, not as the daughter of Bartolomeo Capello but as the daughter of St. Marc. The laws of Venice forbade the marriage of any female scion of a noble house with a foreigner, but in the case of foreigners of distinguished position, the difficulty was got over by the adoption of the lady by the Republic. This was the formality observed when the Kings of Cyprus and Hungary accepted brides from Venice.

The conduct of the Venetian Government on this occasion is a striking example of their utter insensibility to elevated or honourable considerations of any kind when their interests were involved.

Bianca's character was notorious: she was more than suspected of having two or three times resorted to assassination to remove obstacles from her path: she had been repudiated by her family as a blot on their escutcheon, and the Council of Ten, at their request, had pronounced a sentence of perpetual banishment on Pietro and set a price of 2000 ducats on his head. Yet, in a full and brilliant assemblage of the authorities, Bianca was adopted as " the true and particular daughter of the Republic, on account and in consideration of the many eminent and distinguished qualities which rendered her worthy of every good fortune, and in order to meet with corresponding feelings the esteem which the Grand Duke had manifested towards Venice by this his most prudent resolution."

There was one person who watched these proceedings with very different feelings. Francesco's brother and heir-presumptive, the Cardinal dei Medici, was well acquainted with the character of his sister-in-law and hardly dissembled his hate. He accepted an invitation to a retired ducal residence, or hunting seat, where he was residing as the guest of the Duke and Duchess, when they both fell ill and expired within a few hours of each other. The Medici were as apt and unscrupulous in the use of poison as the Borgias; and opinion was divided between two theories of the catastrophe: one, that the illustrious pair were poisoned by the Cardinal; the other, that Francesco inadvertently partook of a dish seasoned by Bianca for his Eminence, and that, seeing the fatal effects on her lord, she swallowed the remainder. The popular belief was that the Cardinal had detected the poison by the change in the colour of his ring. On his accession to the dukedom, he not only denied the funeral honours due to the rank of his alleged victim, but caused her titles to be erased from all public documents, and *la pessima Bianca* to be substituted.[1]

Judging from old pictures and engravings, it would certainly appear that, excluded from intellectual pursuits, the Venetian ladies led a somewhat frivolous life. As M. Yriarte, referring to the works of Paulus Furlanas in 1572, observes: "We find nothing but attitudes, collations, displays of costumes: the little dogs are always reposing on the knees of their mistresses: we never see a woman occupied with a serious duty, or even an artistic pastime." It is to be feared that the little dogs on the knees or in the arms of their mistresses, may lead to equally unfavourable inferences in illustrations of the manners and customs of the English of our time.

One principal occupation of the Venetian ladies was giving their hair the golden or auburn tint which is so much admired in Venetian portraits and not long since was brought into temporary fashion in Paris and London by the *demi-monde*. The process required that the hair, after being wetted with the prescribed mixture, should be dried in the sun; and the Venetian beauties might be seen sitting for hours together in open balconies, wearing wide-brimmed hats, with the crown out, to protect the complexion.[2] One of their strangest fashions was the patten or stilt, which they used of such an extravagant height—eighteen inches or two feet—that a woman of rank could not go abroad without leaning on the shoulders of her maids.

---

[1] "Sketches," vol. ii. pp. 331-341. The story, glossed over by Daru, forms the basis of two of Malespini's novels, in which, of course, the most romantic colouring is thrown over it.

[2] "Les Femmes Blondes selon les Peintres de l'École de Venise." Paris, 1865. Edited by M. Feuilles des Conches. Various recipes are given, and the process is minutely described.

Acting on the true Chinese and Oriental principle, the Venetian husbands and fathers seem to have favoured this fashion. In a conversation which arose in a distinguished company before the Doge whose daughters were the first to discard the pattens, on some one saying that the ordinary shoes were incomparably more convenient, an elderly member of the Council exclaimed—"*Pur troppo commodi! pur troppo*"—(very much too convenient! very much).

The sumptuary laws, in restriction of female extravagance in dress, were severe, and particularly directed against pearls, for which enormous sums were given. But in anticipation of the public entry of the Duke of Savoy in 1608, it was resolved that, "notwithstanding any decree to the contrary, every lady who shall be invited to the said fête shall be permitted to wear all the vestments and jewels of whatever nature that may seem to her most favourable to the adornment of her person." The same permission was granted on the reception of Henry III.

"The middle of the hall of the Great Council was left empty, and two hundred noble ladies, chosen amongst the noblest and most beautiful, entered and took their seats on benches ranged against the walls under the large pictures representing the history of the feasts of the Republic. Clothed in white stuffs, adorned with diamonds and pearls, they presented an unequalled spectacle, at which the King was evidently surprised, despite his recollection of the magnificence and gallantry of the court of the Valois. A rich throne was raised at the bottom of the room, on which the King was seated, having on his right the Doge and the Dukes, on his left the Nuncio, the Grand Prior, and the lords of his suite. Gallantly remarking that he wished to breathe this parterre of flowers, he descended the steps of the throne followed by his suite, and advanced as if to pass in review all these noble ladies, who saluted gracefully in return. He allowed his gaze to rest for a moment on each, and from time to time let drop an exclamation whilst looking for a confidant at his side to whom he might express his admiration. Little by little the young nobles came to make their selections: then slowly, in cadence, the groups were formed to the sound of instruments, and passed successively before the throne, stopping to pay their homage."[1]

A French ambassador at Venice in 1735, pressed by his Court to obtain intelligence, writes thus:

"The access to nobles and secretaries is more difficult than formerly. The Abbé de Pomponne (ambassador in 1705) had at his command a courtesan, who was well paid, and kept him well informed. The principal nobles were in the habit of supping with her; they carried on their intrigues at her house, and spoke of public affairs. But we have no longer the same advantage: the nobles pay only passing visits to the courtesans. They now live familiarly with the ladies (*dames*). The young ladies who might be gained over are too ill-informed, seeing only young people and few good heads. The better-informed old ladies are difficult of approach."

It would be a mistake to suppose that this change in the habits of the nobles implied any improvement in morals. The women of condition could only obtain a divided empire with the courtesans by imitating them. "The parlours of the convents," says Daru, "in which the daughters of noble families were placed, and the houses of courtesans, although the police kept a watchful eye on them, were the sole points of union of the society of Venice, and in the two so contrasted places all were equally free. Music, collations, gallantry, were no more forbidden in the parlours than in the casinos. There were a great number of public casinos where play was the principal object."

[1] "La Vie d'un Patricien," p. 289.

At one of these, the Ridotto, as many as eighty gaming-tables have been counted, with a patrician presiding at each; the privilege of holding the bank being confined to the patrician order. In strange contrast to the regulation by which they evaded their promise to permit gambling between the columns, the Republic now openly encouraged it along with every sort of dissoluteness. "There was no doubt a moment," continues Daru, "when the destruction of fortunes, the ruin of families, domestic discords, determined the Government to depart from the maxims they had laid down as to the freedom of morals they allowed their subjects. They banished all the courtesans from Venice. But their absence was insufficient to reform a population brought up in the most shameful licentiousness. Disorder penetrated into the interior of families, into the cloisters; and they were obliged to recall, to indemnify, to coax back the women: *nostre bene merite meretrici* (as they are called in the decree), who sometimes surprised important secrets, *and could be usefully employed to ruin men who might otherwise become dangerous by their wealth.*"

The same detestable policy was continued to the end, and that end was fast approaching. "Be at ease," said Napoleon to Bourienne, "those rogues shall pay for it; their Republic *has* lived." Having recently called attention to the manner in which this ominous intimation was acted upon,[1] we shall merely add that their cowardice and meanness were on a par with his cynical contempt for international obligations and his bad faith. Cantu admits that they had ample resources, naval and

[1] The "Quarterly Review" for April, 1870: Art.: "Lanfrey's Napoleon."—Biographical and Critical Essays, Third Series.

military, for a stubborn and prolonged defence; but they were enervated to effeminacy: the Republic, rotten to the core, was ready to go down with a push; and when the question of resistance or non-resistance was put to the vote at the last sitting of the Great Council, the unqualified and instant surrender of their liberties, of their very existence as an independent people, was carried almost by acclamation, by 512 votes against 12.

The Venetian Republic, dating it from the closing of the Council in 1296, had lasted five hundred years; it was not merely the only European constitution that had successfully resisted revolutionary change during anything like that length of time, but it was the only modern aristocracy or oligarchy that ever held the supreme power long enough to constitute a settled government at all; for Lord Beaconsfield's favourite theory that, during a large part of the last century, the English constitution resembled that of Venice, is an amusing paradox at best. But the durability of an institution is only a merit or a good when the institution contributes to human happiness or intellectual progress—when it helps to make men wiser or better; not when it degrades and corrupts with a view to enslaving them, when it systematically undermines or stamps out every notion or sentiment of honour, generosity, virtue and patriotism, lest that very durability should be weakened or destroyed. The chief glories of Venice were won under her ancient Doges: her few illustrious men flourished in despite of her laws; and if she had lived only half her life, her reputation would stand better with posterity.

That, then, the Republic was a model of perverted ingenuity is undeniable, but to call it, as has been the fashion amongst historians, a masterpiece of political wisdom is tantamount to maintaining that the highest political wisdom consists in the successful application of the maxims laid down by Machiavel in "The Prince." Far from regretting the catastrophe, we feel irresistibly impelled to exclaim with the poet:

> "Mourn not for Venice—though her fall
> Be awful as if Ocean's wave
> Swept o'er her—she deserves it all,
> And Justice triumphs o'er her grave.
> Thus perish every King and State
> That run the guilty race she ran,
> Strong but in fear, and only great
> By outrage against God and man."

THE END.

LONDON: PRINTED BY WILLIAM CLOWES AND SONS, LIMITED,
STAMFORD STREET AND CHARING CROSS.

www.ingramcontent.com/pod-product-compliance
Lightning Source LLC
Chambersburg PA
CBHW022104290426
44112CB00008B/551